Business and Management Research

Business and Management Research

How to complete your research project successfully

Michael J. Baker

Westburn Publishers Ltd
Helensburgh, Scotland

Westburn Publishers Ltd
50 Campbell Street
Helensburgh
Argyll, G84 9NH
Scotland, UK

www.westburn.co.uk
Visit *www.businessandmanagementresearch.com* for online content

British Library Cataloguing in Publication Data
A catalogue record for this book is available from the British Library

ISBN 0-946433-02-X

Printed in Great Britain by Bell and Bain Ltd, Glasgow, Scotland

Contents

List of Figures

List of Tables

Preface

Like Ronseal, it is hoped that this book will do exactly what it says on the cover – help you complete a research project successfully.

In recent years, in the UK and elsewhere, there has been a large increase in the numbers of people entering Further and Higher Education. Many of these persons are studying business and management related subjects, and have to complete a research project as part of their formal qualification. This book has been specially written for them.

While there is no shortage of textbooks and monographs dealing with all aspects of research, and many are cited, experience in preparing students for project research work has highlighted that few offer a comprehensive overview of the issues and options facing the student embarking on such an exercise for the first time. Accordingly, this book seeks to give such an overview, starting with the reasons why we need to do research in the first place, and concluding with the writing up and presentation of one's findings. To do so three main sources have been drawn on.

First, several chapters are based on articles that appeared in *The Marketing Review*. These articles were commissioned by the Founding Editor, Caroline Tynan, and drew on a series of seminars given to postgraduate students in the Nottingham University Business School, and other universities where I have held visiting appointments. Second, several chapters have been developed from my book *Research for Marketing* (1991) which was primarily intended for persons wishing to commission and evaluate research into marketing topics. And, third, two chapters on doing research online have been contributed by Anne Foy, who has recently completed a major project using this relatively new research resource.

The perspective adopted is that, in business and management, research is undertaken to reduce areas of uncertainty surrounding decisions, and as an aid to decision making. In our view, research is concerned with the pursuit of knowledge as a source of competitive advantage, and this involves both understanding better what is already known (secondary research), as well as the creation of new knowledge through conceptualisation and theory building (primary research). In recent years there tends to have been something of a polarisation between different schools of thought as to the philosophical underpinnings of research, and to the differences between quantitative methods (scientific research) and qualitative methods (social research). In our view these approaches are complementary NOT competing, and both receive equal attention. While the coverage should be sufficient for the general needs of a person undertaking a research project, numerous references and recommended readings point the way for those looking for extended or more advanced discussion of particular topics.

Obviously, a book of this kind could not be written without the help and contributions of many others. I am particularly grateful to Glasgow Caledonian Business School, Monash University Department of Marketing, Nottingham University Business School and the University of Otago where I have been encouraged to work on the subject matter of this book while acting as a Visiting Professor. I am also grateful to Anne Foy for inciting me to write the book in the first place, for seeing it through to publication, and especially for contributing two chapters on the new opportunities offered by the Internet. Thank you all.

Michael J. Baker
Nottingham University Business School, June 2003

CHAPTER 1

The Role of Research Projects in Business and Management Studies

Synopsis

In this introductory chapter we review the nature of research and its role in decision making. When faced with a problem, one draws on experience and learning to see if this offers an acceptable solution. If it does not, it will be necessary to undertake research to throw more light on the issue. Such research will be most effective if undertaken in a formal and structured way, and comprises a series of linked activities that are the subject of succeeding chapters. The content of these and the best way to use the text are spelled out.

Keywords

research; scholarship; knowledge – tacit, explicit; decision-making.

Introduction

So, you want or need to do some research into a management topic and would like advice on how to set about the task? If so then, hopefully, this is the book for you. Based on almost 50 years experience of designing, implementing and advising on both commercial and academic research this book provides a concise and accessible overview and introduction to the process of management research.

So, what is "research"? If you were to ask the man on the Clapham omnibus[1] this question he would probably conjure up an image of someone in a white coat working in a laboratory. If old and asked to elaborate on this image then he would describe the person as a 'scientist', perceive them as male, either bald or with masses of unkempt hair and a beard and envisage the laboratory as being full of bubbling retorts, microscopes etc. If young then the image might be of an attractive, well groomed woman, of flashing lights, liquid crystal displays and electronic equipment. Both are concerned with using the 'scientific' method to solve research problems.

---

[1] This is a footnote, a device found in research reports and scholarly work. Its purpose is to amplify a point in the text, particularly when the writer is not sure that the reader is familiar with the reference. If you are not then you'll probably be reading this! The 'man on the Clapham omnibus' is a legal phrase used to describe the ordinary man in the street on whose views the interpretation of the English Common Law is widely based. You will not find many more footnotes in this book – my aim is to avoid jargon and obscure references as far as is possible.

Clearly, these are stereotypes and applicable to only one kind of research. Had you asked the man in the street to tell you what he understood by the words 'scholar' and 'scholarship' then the image of the person would be more likely to be of someone wearing a cardigan or kaftan working in a sepulchral library surrounded by piles of dusty tomes and laboriously transcribing longhand notes. Alternatively, a more modern image would be of someone working at a PC and surfing the Internet.

While these activities may seem quite different they share many common features. In fact, as we shall see, most if not all research will contain elements of both scholarship and the scientific method. Further, scholarship and the scientific method anchor the ends of a continuum within which there are many variants. If you are to understand and/or 'do' research it is vital that you are familiar with these philosophical issues as they will colour and influence the nature and substance of any research you may undertake, as well as the interpretation of prior research that has become codified as *knowledge*. Chapter 2 addresses these issues.

Knowledge is power

In the previous paragraph we asserted that the main outcome of research is information that may be codified as knowledge. The aphorism 'Knowledge is power' reflects a belief that has underpinned the development of civilisation. For much of recorded history the control or ownership of knowledge has been a source of power. It explains the influence of the Oracle at Delphi in Ancient Greece, the authority of organised religion, the Craft Gilds in medieval Europe and their successors the modern professions like Law and Medicine.

Today we are told we live in a knowledge based society, that knowledge is a source of competitive advantage and that tomorrow's winners in a global marketplace will be learning organisations.

But there are two kinds of knowledge – explicit knowledge and tacit knowledge. Explicit knowledge is information that has been defined, described and, usually, published. In other words it is in the public domain and available to all if they choose to make use of it. (This may involve payment of a licence fee or royalty to the owner of intellectual property rights but, in principle, you have access to it).

By contrast tacit knowledge is knowledge that has not been codified or published. It is the kind of knowledge that prompts us to inquire "How did you do that?" and for the performer being unable to explain precisely what it was they did. Often tacit knowledge is evident in superior performance and is a source of *sustainable* competitive advantage (SCA). Once your competitors are able to benchmark, capture and replicate tacit knowledge it becomes explicit, no longer exclusive and ceases to be a source of SCA.

The existence of these two kinds of knowledge makes it clear why 'research' is so important. Research as scholarship enables us to determine what is known about problems or issues of importance to us. Given that most knowledge is not in common circulation the re-discovery of extant knowledge through research can be a powerful source of advantage and performance improvement. At the other end of the spectrum blue sky, or basic research, may have no particular commercial or other purpose in mind. But it is this kind of research that leads to new insights and ideas, some of which will have a practical application and be converted into innovations. In turn, it is innovation that is the source of progress, and the primary source of economic growth and development. It follows that an ability to identify existing knowledge and create new knowledge are essential skills for persons filling, or hoping to fill leadership roles. Research is the key, and the undertaking of a research project has become an integral part of many formal business qualifications. Such projects are intended to show how learning and experience may be applied to the definition and solution of problems, either directly be the decision-maker or by others under their supervision.

Knowledge itself is not a homogeneous commodity – a proposition we return to in the next chapter. There is also a view that knowledge is 'luggage' – an encumbrance that slows progress and limits flexibility and movement. The more luggage you have the harder it becomes to move! In the *Times* on June 29th 2002 Professor Oswald of Warwick University argued that the British pre-occupation with home ownership and the acquisition of property (or luggage) was a significant factor inhibiting labour mobility, resulting in higher unemployment and lower economic growth.

Traditionally, rote learning and memorisation and the regurgitation of this knowledge were the defining features of what passed for education. Now the body of knowledge, even within narrowly defined subject areas, is growing so rapidly that learning by memorisation is a lost cause. What is needed today is knowledge of *where* knowledge is stored and *how* to access that part of it that may be relevant to your needs. We return to these issues in later chapters.

Old wine in new bottles

As we shall see in Chapter 2, there are significant philosophical differences concerning the nature and conduct of research, despite the fact that all schools of thought are ultimately engaged in the creation of new knowledge. At the outset, however, it is important to emphasise a significant difference between 'scientific' research and what we have loosely identified as 'scholarship'. The former is concerned with the *creation* of new knowledge, the latter with the *analysis and interpretation* of existing knowledge in an attempt to discover new knowledge. The domain of Business and Management Research lies somewhere in between. In the world of practice it will tend towards the collection of new information to solve specific problems; in the groves of academe it will tend towards theorisation based on extant knowledge supplemented by new data collection.

This difference in approach has important consequences as described in Richard Luecke's (1994) book *Scuttle your ships before advancing*. The theme of Luecke's book is that much is to be learned from the analysis of history and its objective is summarised succinctly in the opening paragraph of the introduction:

> Several years ago , Robert Hayes of the Harvard Business School wrote an article on *The Timeless Secrets of Industrial Success*. "Business pundits" he wrote, "seem to be forever rediscovering the truths known to those who lived two generations earlier . . . " He considered calling this Hayes's Law of Circular Progress until an erudite British businessman referred him to an 1843 edition of the *Edinburgh Review* that proposed a similar idea: "In the pure and the Physical Sciences, each generation inherits the conquests made by its predecessors . . . But in the moral sciences . . . particularly the arts of administration . . . the ground never seems to be incontestably won." That each generation receives the hard science intact but must ever *relearn* the moral sciences explains, perhaps, why we have succeeded in putting people on the moon while failing to resolve fundamental problems in education, in employment, and international peace. (Luecke 1994, p.3)

The title of Luecke's book is taken from an analysis of Cortés conquest of Mexico. At the beginning of the sixteenth century the Spanish began extensive exploration of the Caribbean in search of new lands and treasure. In 1518 Hernán Cortés was given command of an expedition to revisit the coast of the Yucatan peninsula from which a previous expedition led by Juan de Grijalva had brought back stories of gold and their meetings with the local inhabitants. Cortés sailed from Cuba in February 1519 with a fleet of 11 ships, 100 sailors and 508 soldiers.

Unbeknown to Cortés the interior of Mexico was inhabited by the Aztecs, ruled by the fabled Moctezuma, and a far more advanced race than the coastal natives encountered by Grijalva. Moctezuma lived in fear of a prophesy that the god Quetzalcoatl intended to take control of Mexico. The reports of the earlier Spanish landings convinced him that the Spanish were this invading force, and to be deterred at all costs. When Cortés landed on the coast he was met by emissaries of Moctezuma who presented him with gifts of gold, silver and jewellery, and an instruction that he was not to visit the capital inland. Unsurprisingly, the gifts only served to stimulate Cortés' curiosity and wish for more.

Having established a fortified camp on the shore, Cortés despatched

Moctezuma's gifts to his Emperor and then scuttled the remaining ships – there would be no going back! An account of Cortés' campaign, together with six other historical incidents which had a major impact on human affairs, is to be found in Luecke's book. Their analysis reinforces his view that:

> While science and medicine race forward, the people-related disciplines seem to go around in circles. The reason for this disappointing state of affairs may be the fact that the skills of leadership, of managing, of interpersonal relations are not easily taught in textbooks or in the classroom, but must be gained instead by individuals through their own experience. (Luecke 1994, p.4)

If Luecke genuinely believed that experience is the only sure method of learning important lessons it is difficult to understand why he bothered writing his book. In reality, his position reflects that of most professional activities which seek to combine formal learning with practical experience. Life is too short to acquire all the knowledge necessary for successful practice through experience alone. What is required is the transfer of what we know – explicit knowledge – through formal education combined with the acquisition of skills – tacit knowledge – through experience. It is for this reason that, in professional disciplines with an extensive knowledge base, students are required to demonstrate their ability to relate existing knowledge to the solution of current problems or, if necessary, create new knowledge where a solution is not to be found based on past experience. It is for this reason that most formal qualifications in business and management have a requirement that one undertake a project that involves an understanding of research methods and procedures and their application to the solution of a perceived problem.

The need for business decisions

The need to take a decision arises when one recognises the existence of a problem to which there are two or more alternative solutions. In other words we are faced with a choice and we need to decide which of several possible courses of action will lead to the most satisfactory outcome to the perceived problem. In general terms such decision-making may be classified as falling into one of three mutually exclusive states – certainty, risk and uncertainty. Under conditions of certainty the decision-maker will have no difficulty in selecting the preferred course of action in terms of their declared decision criteria as all the options will be known and capable of comparison in terms of these criteria. However, to be in this happy position one will need to collect and make explicit all the facts relevant to the problem which clearly requires one to have a formal means for gathering and analysing information.

However, the exhaustive collection of all information may be neither possible nor worthwhile – in which case the decision-maker will have to accept either risk or uncertainty as to the correctness of their decision. Estimating the value of information is itself a question of decision-making and gives rise to mixed feelings between academics and practitioners. One of the distinguished reviewers to the outline of this book (who is both academic and practitioner) questioned the inclusion of a discussion of EVPI (the expected value of perfect information) on the grounds that while it appears in many textbooks he has never come across it in practice. In my view this simply confirms the point that managers often exercise judgement to the neglect of techniques which could well improve the quality of that judgement by making explicit what factors need to be taken into account, and their relative importance one to another. Clearly, information will have a high value when there is a high degree of uncertainty and a substantial risk of making a bad i.e. 'expensive' decision. In these circumstances investing in research should be worthwhile, but one will still have to estimate how much information might be acquired and what it would cost to get it. However, questions such as these can only provide a crude guide as to the action to be taken and any problem with a 'high information value' would clearly merit some further clarification and investigation to determine precisely just what would be involved in collecting and analysing more data.

As to the difference between risk and uncertainty this largely depends upon whether or not one can make precise (quantitative/statistical) statements about the probability of given outcomes. If, for example, we know that 75 out of every 1000 eggs are likely to be infected with salmonella or listeria then we can state confidently that the likelihood of contracting one or the other of these diseases is 0.075, or approximately one in thirteen. What we cannot say, of course, without further information is which particular eggs are infected, or who is likely to contract the disease. However, the ability to quantify risk precisely is particularly helpful in areas such as assessing premiums for spreading the cost of a risk between all those likely to be exposed to it (insurance), or the degree of investment in further quality control measures upon a production line.

In risk situations one is able to make an objective estimate of the probability of an event; under uncertainty the best one can attempt is a subjective, qualitative assessment of the likelihood of any given occurrence. That said, theoreticians such as Raiffa and Schleiffer have shown clearly how one can use such decisions to develop rigorous analysis of uncertain decisions which also incorporate a sensitivity analysis to allow for one's intrinsic attitudes to risk and uncertainty. Such analyses make use of Bayes' theorem, and are collectively described as Bayesian analyses.

But, the question of the conditions under which a given decision can be made is only likely to become apparent after one has recognised that a problem exists, and given some thought to the relative importance and nature of the problem.

As we enter a new millennium, it is claimed that we are moving from an era of information scarcity to an era of information overload. In the course of the average day it has been estimated that we are exposed to at least 1500 advertising messages alone and it is obvious that if we were to give only 10 seconds to each we would waste over half a working day in the process. Fortunately, we are equipped with an inbuilt defence mechanism known as selective perception, which performs the chore of monitoring incoming information for us, and decides that the great majority is unimportant or of no immediate relevance, and prevents our conscious mind from considering the matter further. But if the cue or stimulus (bit of information) is particularly strong, or our subconscious has been 'programmed' to recognise it, then our subconscious will trigger conscious awareness of the cue to enable it to be given further consideration. On average about six advertisements a day survive this screening or filtering process. The success rate of more focused communications (direct mail or the telephone versus media advertising) is likely to be higher but, in every case, evaluation of the possible decision can only occur once we have been moved from unawareness to awareness.

Given recognition of the existence of a possible problem, even if it occurs in the positive guise of a better means if satisfying a need for which one already has a solution, then the decision-maker will seek to evaluate the implications of a possible change of behaviour in such detail as appears appropriate. For a low risk, low involvement decision – shall I buy a new snack product – probably the quickest and simplest way to gain the necessary information is to spend 40p and physically try the product – after all, it is your taste buds which will decide whether you like it or not. Conversely, with a high risk, high involvement decision, such as the purchase of a major durable good or a sub-assembly for inclusion in a piece of industrial equipment, one will seek to ascertain more about the essential properties of the new product (performance factors and cost-benefit) before even contemplating a trial, let alone a purchase.

As I have argued in proposing a composite model of buyer behaviour (Baker 2002) if the evaluation phase points clearly to a preferred solution, then the decision-maker has no problem. But, what happens if at the end of careful analysis one is unable to discriminate between two or more alternative solutions to a problem? Clearly one has a choice to make and the decision will require one to accept a degree of either risk or uncertainty in committing oneself to a course of action. This decision-making is the outcome of a process which may be characterised as 'successive focusing' and represented diagrammatically as a funnel (see figure 1.1). Of course, a decision may be made at any stage of the process to discontinue it, and it is possible to skip a stage, or give it only cursory attention in coming to a final decision, e.g.

secondary research accessed through a literature review (see Chapter 4) may produce a satisfactory answer and eliminate the need for further data collection through primary research.

Strictly speaking, business and management research is concerned with the formal search and analysis process and represents a deliberate and structured effort to provide answers to the problems faced by managers. Given recognition of a problem, the manager will then need answers to at least the following questions:

1   What information do I need?
2   Where is it available?
3   How can I collect it?
4   What is it worth?
5   Once I've got it how do I interpret it?
6   How can I combine the 'facts' with my own subjective judgement and experience in reaching a decision?

The answers to these questions are the subject of this book but, before attempting to answer them in detail, it will be helpful to provide an overview of the structure and content to assist you in deciding how best to make use of it.

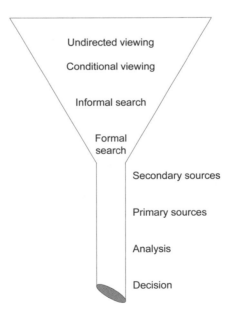

Figure 1.1 Successive focusing

Structure and content

A recent Editorial in the *Journal of Customer Behaviour* summarises well some of the problems of doing research in business and management where many of the issues relate to behaviour and human action, rather than inanimate objects like widgets on a production line:

> The process of undertaking research on 'behaviour' may not always develop according to some pre-formed plan: it may often be messy. The issues that are eventually identified as important may differ, sometimes significantly, from those which were originally defined; and the means by which the researcher's understanding develops may involve many unexpected twists and turns – there is often much 'tacking back and forth' between the data, the literature and the researcher's understanding. All this will seem very familiar to any moderately experienced researcher. Yet the way in which research is presented is often not as an exploratory journey in which serendipity is a fellow traveller, but rather as a well thought out, and carefully planned exercise which proceeded very neatly through a set of steps or stages. (Littler et al. 2003, p.2)

And so it is with this book – it follows a structure and sequence that is common to most texts concerned with the subject. If you are a novice researcher then you should work your way through the book, chapter by chapter, as the progression tracks the steps involved is initiating and completing a research project. It also reflects the way in which you will be expected to present a formal report of your research. But, don't be surprised if you have to 'tack back and forth' as you uncover new information and develop fresh insights. As for the more experienced researcher, it is hoped that the content of the individual chapters will provide a useful reminder of some of the main factors that need to be taken into account when tackling a new research project.

'Doing' research involves a sequential decision-making process. To begin with one must decide on a research *Strategy* and this will be largely determined by one's philosophical approach to the nature of knowledge. Basically there is a spectrum of alternatives anchored at one end by *Positivism* or quantitative analytical methods and at the other by *Phenomenology* or qualitative analytical methods. The origins and nature of these schools of thought, and hybrid or intermediate positions are discussed explicitly in Chapter 2 and re-occur throughout the text.

Next, one must decide on the research approach. This will depend heavily on one's philosophical standpoint and incline one to either *deduction* or *induction* – also discussed in Chapter 2. This decision will also be influenced strongly by the nature and extent of one's prior knowledge about the subject matter of one's problem. Where one has extensive knowledge of the situation giving rise to the problem one may already have clear hypotheses, on which information would enable one to solve the problem. In this case a deductive/quantitative study would usually be called for. Alternatively, when one encounters an entirely novel problem one can only speculate about it in an inductive way in an attempt to develop a theory as to its nature and possible solution. In this case a qualitative, exploratory approach is more likely to recommend itself. But, in both cases, once a problem has been recognised the very first step must be to establish what is known already about this 'kind' of problem. This is accomplished by a review of existing sources of cognate information – usually termed a *literature review* or *secondary research* (as distinct from *primary research* that involves the generation and collection of new information). This topic is the subject of Chapter 4.

You will observe that we have 'skipped' Chapter 3! Chapter 3 is concerned with the writing of a formal *research proposal* that sets out clearly what is to be attempted, why, how, when and where. But, before we can prepare such a proposal it is essential that we have a well-defined understanding of what is already known about the subject of inquiry. This has all the properties of Catch 22 – no research proposal without a literature review; no literature review without a research proposal. As with many things in life, for clarity of exposition we assume a linear sequence when the reality is iterative and circular. Thus, in Chapter 3, we explain that one needs to undertake a preliminary literature review to define the parameters of the research proposal which, in turn, will specify what exactly needs to be examined in our search of secondary sources. Much later, we will also see that, when analysing the new information generated by our research, we may need to return to the literature to enhance our understanding and interpretation of the new data.

Chapter 5, contributed by Anne Foy, discusses a relatively new and powerful resource for researchers – the Internet. In fact this the first of two chapters describing and explaining how to use the Internet in research with Chapter 5 looking at doing secondary research online and Chapter 12 dealing with primary data collection.

Once we have established what is already known about our research question, then we will need to select a suitable *methodology* for our investigation. (You will discover that there is an exception to this sequence in the case of an approach known as *grounded theory* where the researcher deliberately suppresses prior theory and speculation and collects data in an unstructured way for subsequent analysis). Basically, there are three broad options available – *observation, experimentation,* and *survey* and an overview of these is given in Chapter 6.

Chapters 7 to 11 each deal with particular research methods and techniques in more detail. Specifically, Qualitative Research Methods, Sampling and Surveys, Questionnaire Design and Interviewing. As noted, Chapter 12 is concerned with data collection using the Internet.

Chapter 13 provides a broadly based overview of data interpretation. Like most of the other chapters its purpose it to give you an indication of what methods are available, their distinguishing characteristics, and situations where you may wish or need to use them. Hopefully, this will help you decide on the choice of the most suitable method so that you may then consult one of the many specialised texts that deals with individual techniques in detail.

The final two chapters look at some of the matters involved in writing up your findings and presenting them both orally and in written form for peer review and judgement.

And so to work. In Chapter 2 you will be introduced to some of the factors that fundamentally affect our approach to doing research and to the interpretation of our 'findings'.

CHAPTER 2

Philosophical Issues and the Conduct of Research

Synopsis
The knowledge and experience that a person brings to problem solving and research will, inevitably, colour their approach, the research methods useD, and their interpretation of their findings. A brief history, of the origins and nature of the different schools of thought, or 'research, philosophies', provides a background for understanding their distinguishing features and relevance to the conduct of research. While interpretivism/positivism, induction/deduction, qualitative/quantitative are often seen as alternatives to each other, our review suggests that they are complementary rather than competing choices.

Keywords
research philosophy; positivism; interpretivism; social science; qualitative and quantitative methods; induction, deduction.

Introduction

In that research is a human activity it is inevitable that to some degree it will be influenced by the experience and behaviour of the researcher. As Littler et al. (2003) point out the researcher is rarely a neutral bystander, and so brings their own perspective, conceptual and ideological 'baggage' to the analysis of a problem The nature and extent of such influence, and the development of procedures and techniques to minimise its effect on research outcomes, are major issues. Indeed, the issues are a subject of study in their own right and have preoccupied scholars for hundreds of years since the Renaissance and Reformation of the 16th and 17th centuries prompted philosophers like Montaigne and Bacon to inquire into the nature of reason. For a book of this kind the question must be how much discussion to give to these issues?

To a large extent the answer depends upon the complexity and sophistication of the research question one wishes to answer. For undergraduate and postgraduate research 'projects' a basic appreciation of the major schools of thought will probably suffice. However, for persons embarking on a postgraduate research degree a fuller understanding is called for. Accordingly, in this and succeeding sections our aim is to cover adequately what is required for a basic appreciation, while providing sufficient information to enable readers to decide whether or not they wish to extend this and, if so, where to go next.

As noted in Chapter 1, the basic objective of all research is to understand better the world around as. Paradoxically, the greater the sum of human knowledge - what we believe we know –the more complex this task becomes and the greater the number of unresolved problems to which an inquiring mind may turn its attention. While the classical scholars of ancient Greece were polymath's, able to reflect on all aspects of the human condition, scholarship today has fragmented into numerous disciplines each of which is immediately concerned with only narrowly defined areas of inquiry. In part this fragmentation has come about as a result of theoretical developments and, in part, as a result of methodological developments.

Today, as Robson (1993) has observed there are two basic approaches to doing research. The first "- is variously labelled as positivistic , natural science based, hypothetico-deductive, quantitative or even simply "scientific"; the other as interpretive, ethnographic or qualitative - among several other labels"(p.18). In the great majority of student textbooks these different research approaches are distinguished as quantitative or qualitative and frequently presented as if they are either/or alternatives. As we shall see this is far from the case, and many research designs incorporate elements of both schools of thought.

In this chapter, to understand how and why this perceived polarisation has occurred, we review briefly how the schools of thought have developed over time. Based on this brief historical review we then seek to identify the defining characteristics of the two schools so that the student may develop a clear view of their own and decide when, and under what circumstances one approach may be preferred to another.

For some this chapter may appear unnecessarily abstract and academic, and somewhat removed from their perception of research as an activity whereby one gathers, analyses and interprets new information in order to solve problems. While we have tried to reduce this impression we cannot stress strongly enough that some awareness and understanding of the major issues discussed here is vital to the design and execution of useful and meaningful research. Indeed, in the absence of an explanation of one's own research philosophy and the assumptions underpinning it is possible that your work may be dismissed as flawed and lacking in foundation. As Easton and Araujo (1997) advise, you must make explicit why you have adopted your own preferred approach and demonstrate why you consider it to be superior to other possible approaches. The content of this chapter is intended to help you identify the options available to you and then justify the course of action taken.

A brief history of research philosophy

(The content and structure of this section has been strongly influenced by Murphy, E., Dingwall, R., Greatbatch, D., Parker S., and Watson, P. (1998),

'Qualitative research methods in health technology assessment: a review of the literature', *Health Technology Assessment*, Vol. 2: No.16, pp.1-272).

Observation and experimentation are the foundations upon which civilisation and human progress are based. Through observation of the world in which we live, and by a process of trial and error, we develop insight and understanding through which we can then communicate to others. While learning by doing may have much to recommend it, and may be vital to the acquisition and development of skills, it is an inefficient and time consuming activity. On the other hand, if this hard won experience, or 'tacit' knowledge', can be made explicit it can then be communicated and transferred to many – initially by means of an oral tradition and then by permanent records and accounts.

For many, the origins of modern thought are to be found in the period of Classical Greek civilisation, and the writings of philosophers like Aristotle and historians like Herodotus. However, while direct linkages exist between the ancient civilisations and society today, the immediate sources of contemporary thinking about issues in the social sciences are to be found in the Renaissance of the 16th century through to the Enlightenment of the 18th century. As Murphy et al. comment:

> It is in this period, for example, that we first find debates about whether we know the world around us as the creation of our perceptions or as an objective, observer-independent reality which anticipate the current arguments about social constructionism. These scholars also began to explore the respective merits of inductive and deductive reasoning and to consider the nature of causal explanation in social matters. (Murphy et al. 1998, p.16)

These debates are still current today, albeit that they have become embedded in the evolution of the social sciences and a range of distinctive disciplines with their own traditions and methodological preferences. Nonetheless, some knowledge of the nature and sources of the original ideas is important if we are to understand how we have arrived at the present position.

Prior to the Reformation it was the Catholic Church that determined what was acceptable as 'knowledge'. In turn, this meant that any alternative explanation was heretical and to be suppressed. It was this position that was attacked by philosophers such as Montaigne and Bacon who rejected dogma and posed the question 'How can we be sure about what we know?' (*scepticism*). Essentially, the answer was through a process of systematic inquiry and the testing of evidence acquired through observation.

But, this begged the question as to the reliability and validity of observation and the process of induction whereby generalisations may be derived and developed out of particular instances. Succeeding generations of philosophers were to address these questions.

To begin with Hobbes (1588-1679) adopted a radical view, now identified as 'hyperbolic doubt', that asked "how do we know our observations are an accurate reflection of the external world we are observing" (op.cit. p.18). (For an explanation of terms such as op.cit and ibid see the appendix of Chapter 4. For a fuller listing of other abbreviations you may come across visit *http://www.lib.unimel.edu.au/catalogues/libresearch/abbreviations/Intro.html*).   In extremis, this question inquires how can we know that the world or its observers exist at all? According to Descartes "Cogito, ergo sum" – "I think, therefore I am" – so I must exist and so must my immediate perception. This conclusion resulted in a change in emphasis from attempting to understand the world by inferring the rules that governed it, to a concern for our perceptions, and the means of interpreting and understanding them. In turn, this called for a clear distinction between induction and deduction as modes of thinking.

Murphy et al. cite Dilman (1973) as a modern definition of these two constructs: "[Induction] is where we reason from a piece of information, however complex or elaborate this may be, to a conclusion that is logically independent of it". By contrast, deduction is where "the relation between premise and conclusion, by virtue of which I am justified in inferring the latter from the former, is internal and can be gathered from the premises and conclusions alone... what the conclusion states is already contained in the premise or premises". (p.19)

The resolution of "hyperbolic doubt" was the focus of attention for several decades culminating in the notion of *immaterialism* as conceived by Bishop Berkeley (1685-1753). According to Berkeley the existence of a 'real' world was immaterial; what mattered are human perceptions and their interpretation. In other words, the object of interest and inquiry is what we now identify as the *social construction* of the world, which is the basis of much modern qualitative research.

The view that we live in a world of ideas (*idealism/immaterialism*) was challenged by other thinkers who believed in an objective reality (*realism*) that is governed by regularities and laws amenable to description and analysis through the use of what we now call the *scientific method*. Where the two schools of thought appear to part company is that while idealists are willing to accept the identification of relationships arising from the application of scientific methods, and the mathematical models and laws on which they are based, this did not amount to an irrefutable proof as it is always possible that there is an alternative explanation. In truth, scientists believe this too, for otherwise they would have discontinued research in many fields of inquiry long ago.

If the object of scientific inquiry is to develop more powerful explanations with predictive capabilities then it is necessary to inquire into the nature of causation. While Berkeley touched on this it was central to the thinking of David Hume (1711-1776) who was to have a major influence on the Scottish Enlightenment, whose members are credited by Murphy et al. as laying "the foundations for most of the modern social sciences". According to Murphy et al.:

> *Causation* describes a relationship that has three elements:
>
> - Contiguity in time and space
> - Priority in time in the cause before the effect
> - A necessary connection between cause and effect. (Murphy et al. 1998, p.23)

In other words, if we think A causes B then we believe and expect that A will always cause B. However, it is important to qualify this assertion by recognising that in coming to such a conclusion one would wish to validate one's personal observations of this association of events by testing it through replication, and/or against the experience and conclusions of others.

Given acceptance of causal relationships then it becomes possible to develop analytical models in which we can deduce conclusions from established premises.

In social science research, the debate about the interpretation of observation and experience (*interpretivism*) is frequently seen as being in opposition to an alternative school of thought, identified as *positivism*. Positivism is a concept attributed to August Comte (1798-1857) which he developed in detail in his *Positive Philosophy*. Basically, positivism is a refutation of the notion of immaterialism developed by Berkeley, Hume and Kant discussed earlier. As conceived by Comte, all sciences exist in a hierarchy with the most remote from human control (physics) representing the foundation and ascending through a hierarchy of phenomena each based on the level below it, viz: chemistry, biology and sociology (a word coined by Comte). According to this conceptualisation, "The possible laws of social organisation, then, were limited by the laws of biological organisation, which were limited by the laws of chemistry, which were limited by the laws of physics". (op.cit. p.32). Thus, if we could derive laws of social organisation we would be able to design better societies, in the same way that the laws of physics enable us to design better machines.

While modern notions of positivism have departed somewhat from Comte's original statement, its essential proposition remains that "Our observations have not been passed through any filters before they reach us so we know it directly. This world contains no inherent judgements of value. Truth is a matter of correct description and ideas like justice or beauty have no referent in it". (ibid. p.31). So, according to Giddens (1974) positivism in the social sciences has three specific methodological implications:

1. The methodological procedures of natural science may be directly adopted to social science.
2. The outcomes of social scientific inquiry will look like those of natural scientific inquiry.
3. Social science is a technical enterprise with no necessary value implications. (Ibid p.32)

While all three implications are not observed by individual social scientists the overall impact of positivism has been substantial, especially in economics and psychology.

Fundamentally, however, the distinction between deductive reasoning, based on laws (*determinism*), and inductive reasoning, that admits human behaviour is influenced by beliefs and values, remains. Murphy et al. cite John Stuart Mill as a philosopher who initially endorsed Comte's positivist approach but who became distinctly less supportive on closer inspection and analysis concluding that "..the social sciences cannot expect to produce conclusive predictions or determinist laws. Social life is much too complicated". (ibid. p.33). However, Mill's suggestion that the social sciences be modelled on Physics was not intended literally and was subject to numerous variations leading Murphy et al to comment "Indeed, it is arguable that what he [Mill] intended might be better represented as a metaphor than a model and that a great deal of wasted effort resulted from an effort to follow it slavishly. (p.34)

In summarising the relevance of Mill's contribution to the philosophy of science debate, Murphy et al. state succinctly why the social and natural sciences both have much to contribute but why, in the final analysis, induction rather than deduction is likely to dominate in business and management research. We make no apologies for citing this observation in full:

> The social sciences are founded on inductions from observation just as much as those of the natural sciences. While a strictly experimental approach may not be feasible, Mill's sequence – observe – induce – formulate – deduce – hypothesise – test – observe – is consistent throughout. The problem of achieving exactness in the social sciences is the complexity of the phenomena, their tendency to interact and to feed back. It is for these reasons that the social sciences cannot expect to achieve the degree of predictive power available in the natural sciences: the regularities simply do not exist to make this possible. Once we move away from a certain macro-level, society is a succession of unique

occurrences. As far as the task of government or management is concerned, however, summaries and low-level laws are still better than reacting to every situation *de novo*. The manager who has some understanding of the principles in generating some particular state of affairs, and the ways in which they might interact with each other to create a situation that has not occurred in this precise form again, is better placed to judge what lines of action are likely to be more or less effective and what information will be needed to assess and modify these if necessary. The successful manager, then, is unlikely to be a cook following a recipe book but a chef using a general understanding of the nature of ingredients and the available technologies of preparation, cooking and service to create and innovate. (Murphy et al. 1998, p.36)

The chapter from which the above quotation is taken is 40 pages in length and provides an excellent overview of the history and diversity of qualitative methods. The quotation itself occurs approximately in the middle of the chapter with the remainder dealing with developments in British social science from the 1920s onwards. Much of this material is to be found in modern texts and it is for this reason that we have concentrated on an overview of the historical and philosophical antecedents of current preferences and practices. In our view, some knowledge of these antecedents – where we have come from – is essential to an appreciation of the choices facing the researcher today but is less often covered in modern textbooks.

One source that we believe will be of particular value to both established researchers and students new to the subject is *The A – Z of Social Research*. Edited by Robert Miller and John Brewer, and published by Sage Publications in 2003, this encyclopaedic reference work contains 122 entries ranging from 800 to 3000 words in length, and contributed by nearly 50 different scholars. This book was found to be particularly useful in checking out the basic accuracy of the definitions and explanations used in this text. However, the 'A – Z's' especial value is that, in addition to elaborating on many of the topics introduced in this book, it also provides definitions and explanations of concepts, ideas, methods and techniques beyond the scope of an introductory text of this kind, as well as references to other authoritative sources. Consult it!

The evolution of professional social science

During the nineteenth century the rapid growth in population and urbanisation resulting from the Industrial Revolution prompted research into a number of social issues including disease, public health, education etc.. Much of this research was based on the analysis of official statistics and surveys of disadvantaged populations with a view to improving the quality of life, especially of the working classes or 'proletariat'. The Victorian era also stimulated public interest in the exotic lands of an expanding Empire and particularly the behaviour and institutions of their inhabitants. This led to what Murphy et al. identify as the first research-led social science to be created in Britain – social anthropology.

Social anthropology was based primarily on what we now call *participant observation* (see Chapter 7) which, according to Malinowski (1921), must observe three cardinal principles:

1. Scientific values.
2. Immersion or involvement e.g. living among the people under study.
3. Application of special techniques for collecting, ordering and presenting evidence.

In the 1930s these principles were implicit in the establishment of Mass Observation as an organisation for documenting and promoting aspects of everyday life through the use of diaries and focused surveys of particular topics. While the data resulting from such research might be quantified and analysed statistically the emphasis was unequivocally on observation of social behaviour, problems and institutions in an effort to understand better underlying processes, regularities and relations.

It was immediately following the Second World War that changes in society precipitated an emphasis upon the statement of formal theories, and the use of quantitative methods in economics, psychology and sociology. While qualitative methods still enjoyed some popularity in community studies, the newly emerging fields of business and management studies were strongly attracted to quantitative methods, building upon the traditions of Taylor's 'scientific management', work study, and the success of operational research in solving real world problems during the war and post-war period.

Qualitative and quantitative methods

From the brief review of the evolution of philosophical and methodological issues involved in social science research, it has become clear that this currently centres on the perceived differences between qualitative and quantitative methods. In this section we seek to identify the sources and nature of these differences with a view to suggesting when one or the other might be more appropriate, as well as situations where a combination of methods may be called for. To begin with we examine the arguments that quantitative and qualitative research are fundamentally different, and then turn to a consideration of the relationship between the two.

At the outset it is important to recognise that many researchers regard quantitative and qualitative research as antithetical, and so polarise discussion into an either/or debate. Basically, quantitative methods are usually regarded as more robust, leading to actionable results and recommendations whereas qualitative methods are seen as lacking in rigour, resulting in indecisive outcomes. The polarisation is particularly acute in business and management, where behavioural researchers argue the importance of understanding the underlying beliefs, values and attitudes that motivate human activities, while shareholders and managers are preoccupied with quantifying the outcomes from different courses of action so that they may invest in those that promise the best long-term return on investment. At the time of writing (2003) the latter concern is in the ascendancy, and reflected in the American Marketing Science Institute's Research Priorities for 2002-2004, which puts Marketing Metrics as its number one concern.

Increasingly, however, this tendency to polarise the two approaches has been challenged. To begin with it is pointed out that the differences are nowhere as near clear cut as they are claimed to be. Thus, inspection of the approaches and methods followed by researchers regarded as 'qualitative' reveals that it is based on assumptions and practices usually identified as being 'quantitative'. Similarly, 'quantitative' researchers frequently adopt what might be classified as qualitative methods. Proponents of this school of thought argue that the choice between the two is a matter of 'horses for courses' and that one should select the approach most suited to the research question and issues under consideration. But, to make this choice, one must first establish what the main differences between quantitative and qualitative methods are seen to be.

As we saw, when tracing the evolution of the philosophical assumptions underpinning research, these tend to have polarised and it is this that has underpinned much of the quantitative OR qualitative debate. Murphy et al. highlight three main dimensions of this debate that they classify as:

Idealism versus realism
Induction versus deduction
Naturalism versus artificiality

Some of the distinguishing features of these constructs have been touched on earlier and extended discussion and analysis is to be found in our primary source which, itself, is based on a very comprehensive review of the literature, and in Miller and Brewer. Only a brief discussion is possible here.

In simple terms *Realism* subscribes to the view that there is a reality that exists independent of the observer while *Idealism* regards reality as existing in the mind of the observer. The implication is that there are as many 'realities' as there are observers. Clearly, realism is suited to quantitative methods, as there are objects that can be measured, while idealism deals with subjective perceptions that are better captured by qualitative methods. Unfortunately, this simplification does not capture the existence of different schools of thought concerning the precise definition of either idealism or realism and variants of them. However, unless such details are central to your research the simple distinction will suffice to enable you to decide which point of view you incline to.

With regard to *Induction* and *Deduction* Murphy et al. cite Williams and May (1996) who state: "Research that is purely deductive begins with a theoretical system, operationalises the concepts of that system and then sets out to gather empirical data to test that system. Research that is purely inductive, on the other hand, starts with the collection of data and moves from there to a general conclusion. It involves the derivation of a general principle from a set of specific observations.

Note the qualification 'pure'. In the same sense that 'pure competition' is essentially an abstraction that permits analysis of various kinds of imperfect competition , so pure induction/deduction are useful notions in helping to understand how people solve problems (research), usually through a combination of both kinds of reasoning.

One of the strongest advocates of pure deductive research is Karl Popper (1902 – 1994) who regarded the source of an idea or theory as irrelevant. What matters is that such ideas should be subjected to detailed evaluation using deductive reasoning (*critical rationalism*) to see if the idea can be falsified. If it cannot then the idea will be accepted as true, and depended on as a basis for future research until such time as it may be falsified, and rejected in favour of a new, more powerful explanation.

At the opposite end of the spectrum, a purely inductive approach is recommended by Glaser and Strauss (1967) in what they term '*grounded theory*' (see Chapter 7). According to this theory, the researcher should derive theory from data (induction) uncontaminated by pre-selection or pre-conceived ideas as to its nature and import.

While some researchers may attempt a 'purist' approach, most research incorporates elements of both induction and deduction with induction being facilitated by qualitative methods, and deduction by quantitative methods. In the real world the interplay between induction and deduction has a major impact on the way in which managers/decision-makers both commission and interpret research. This topic is addressed by Hamlin (2003) in an amusing paper in which he highlights the distinction between induction and deduction, and the effect that an ingrained preference for one or the other may have on both the selection of a research methodology, and the interpretation of the findings. Hamlin summarises the essential differences between induction and deduction in figure 2.1.

These differences are then illustrated with an example from everyday life that is familiar to us all and highlight the difference between the 'pure' and practical application of the concepts. The example given is illustrated in Figure 2.2 and involves crossing the road. As Hamlin comments:

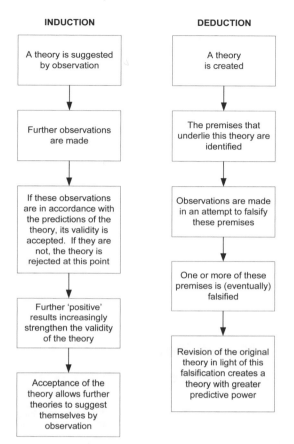

Figure 2.1 A simplified representation of the process of inductive and deductive theory testing
(Source: Rob Hamlin, 'Induction, deduction and the pig headed decision maker: why we should learn to love them all', *The Marketing Review*, forthcoming, 2003)

Every day billions of people are confronted with this situation, and with the associated theory 'I will not die if I step onto this crossing when the green man is showing'. It's a theory. And an associated action, whose outcomes are life and death, so they couldn't be more important to the individual. . . . There is no doubt that adopting the deductive approach would decrease your chance of dying – but at what cost in time? The huge majority of individuals are prepared to trade-off the chance of dying against the saving in time that adopting the inductive approach offers. Take a look next time you approach a pedestrian crossing. You may see a few who may acknowledge the deductive route by glancing at oncoming cars. However, most shamble into the path of death without even a glance

- so confident are they of the validity of their extensively inductively tested theory.

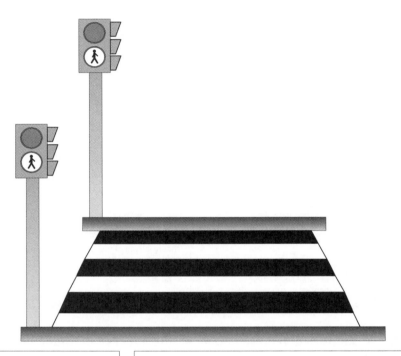

THEORY: I will not die if I step onto this crossing when the green man is showing.

'INDUCTIVE' APPROACH
"I have done this 15,000 times before and not died, so there's no chance that I'll die if I do it this time"

'DEDUCTIVE' APPROACH
"This theory relies on several falsifiable premises/assumptions, including, but not restricted to:
1 - the lights facing the traffic are red
2 - the oncoming driver (if any) can see the red light
3 - the driver interprets this signal as a command to stop
4 - the driver is able to react to this signal by applying the brake
5 - the driver is willing to react to this signal by applying the brake
6 - the brakes of the car work
Only if all these premises are supported will I risk my life by stepping onto the crossing."

Figure 2.2 'Everyday' induction and deduction at a pedestrian crossing
(Source: Rob Hamlin, 'Induction, deduction and the pig headed decision maker: why we should learn to love them all', *The Marketing Review*, forthcoming, 2003)

The point made so effectively by Hamlin (and further illustrated in his paper) is that in the real world we do take into account the value of perfect information and select the course of action that we think will yield a satisfactory outcome. In doing so we are likely to combine both inductive/qualitative and deductive/quantitative methods.

The distinction between naturalism (qualitative) and artificiality (quantitative) is that "the former investigates naturally occurring settings, while the latter is restricted to phenomena that are artificially created by the researcher". (Murphy et al. p.72). Researchers following a naturalistic approach should use non-intrusive methods, and avoid superimposing pre-conceived ideas or structures over the phenomena under investigation. By contrast, artificiality exists where the researcher imposes structure on the research issue in terms of its conceptualisation (experimentation) and/or choice of methods – structured interviews/surveys etc.. Superficially, 'natural' research is seen as qualitative, and 'artificial' research as quantitative.

While the three dichotomies outlined above indicate that different philosophical standpoints and assumptions may predicate a preference for either a qualitative or quantitative approach, Murphy et al. distinguish a number of other considerations that will influence the decision.

To begin with it is proposed that the choice of method should be made "entirely on instrumental and pragmatic grounds" (p.58). According to this point of view the distinction between methods is of fairly recent origin (post 1940) and resulted from the rise of logical positivism. Prior to 1940 the two methods tended to be used in combination and so-called 'combinationists' would now distinguish three scenarios according to an implied hierarchy of preferences distinguished as:

Qualitative research as the senior partner
Qualitative research as the junior partner
Horses for courses

The second perspective regarding choice of method sees quantitative and qualitative as "deriving from fundamentally different paradigms" (op.cit. p.61). Following Guba and Lincoln's (1994) definition of a paradigm as " the basic belief system or world view that guides the investigator, not only in choices of method but ontologically and epistemologically fundamental ways" the earlier distinctions between Idealism and Realism etc. may be seen as paradigms. However, as we have seen, while some would argue that adoption of one paradigm necessarily requires one to choose one methodology over the other, most researchers would see the methods as complementary.

The third perspective promoted by researchers designated as *'critical theorists'* sees the choice between quantitative and qualitative as depending upon ideological and/or political grounds. Researchers of this persuasion, which includes post-modernists and post-structuralists, reject traditional science and with it quantitative methods, leaving them firmly in the qualitative camp.

From this summary it is abundantly clear that a myriad of factors will influence the choice of methods, either alone or in various combinations. Murphy et al devote 11 pages to a discussion of research practice that pre-dispose one to the use of qualitative methods. Their discussion is organised around six features identified by Bryman (1988) as characteristic of qualitative research. Murphy et al. stress that this is an organisational device and that many of the items on the list have been contested by others. Nonetheless, the list does cover the points most frequently referred to by advocates of qualitative methods and so is reproduced here:

- commitment to viewing events, actions, norms, values etc. from the perspective of those being studied
- emphasis upon the description of the setting being investigated
- emphasis upon context and holism
- emphasis on process flexibility of research design
- reluctance to impose *a priori* theoretical frameworks at the outset. (Murphy et al. 1998)

Choice of qualitative method

While the choice of particular qualitative method will be dealt with in more detail later it will be useful to complete this chapter with a preliminary identification of what Cresswell (1998) has designated the 'Five Traditions'.

The starting point for Cresswell's book is an attempt to answer the question "How does the type or tradition of qualitative inquiry shape the design of a study?"(p.2). To do so he identifies five different *traditions* of qualitative inquiry by which he means "...an approach to qualitative research that has a distinguished history in one of the social science disciplines...", and then explores their application in research design.

Six phases of research design are identified, namely: "philosophical or theoretical perspectives; the introduction to a study, including the formation of the purpose and research questions; data collection; data analysis; report writing; and standards of quality and verification". Each of these is dealt with in some detail in later chapters as are the five research traditions Creswell lists:

1. Biography
2. Phenomenology
3. Grounded theory

4. Ethnography
5. Case studies

While these are discussed in more detail in Chapter 7 at this juncture it will be helpful to identify their key features before examining the broader issue of research design in Chapter 3. Our reason for doing so is based on the belief that the preceding discussion of philosophical issues, points clearly to the fact that these colour and condition our personal preferences and practices when solving problems or research issues. It follows that one must be sensitive to the influence this will have on our research behaviour.

While there are several kinds of *biographical* research they share the common feature that they are concerned with an *individual* and their experiences. These may be in the form of a self-report or *autobiography* or a *biography* prepared by another person based on oral reports and or written materials. Alfred Sloane's *My Years with General Motors* is an example of the former and *The Unknown Iacocca* of the latter.

By contrast *phenomenological* studies are concerned with the experiences of more than one person in relation to a concept or phenomenon which is the focus of study. Here the objective is determine the "essence" of the shared experience.

Grounded theory is an approach promoted as recently as 1967 by Glaser and Strauss in which the researcher is required to generate or 'ground' theory in their observations rather than apply or use an extant theory to explain and understand observation of an activity or phenomenon.

Ethnography evolved from the study of comparative cultures by anthropologists in the early twentieth century. Today it embraces a wide variety of different schools of thought including structural functionalism, feminism, critical theory and postmodernism among others. The common thread that links these schools of thought is an emphasis on the first-hand collection of data based on the observation of people in everyday situations and activities.

Finally, *case studies* involve a detailed and in-depth description and analysis of a 'case' or 'bounded system' using multiple sources of information. One or multiple cases may be studied leading to the statement of 'assertions' or generalisations derived from the analysis.

(*The A – Z of Social Research* gives explanations of all these traditions and sub-fields).

Summary

Even if one believes that there are real objects to be observed (*realism*) it is clear that observation of them is subject to a phenomenon known as *selective perception* and so liable to error.

In simple terms, selective perception means that we see what we expect to see and that we interpret such stimuli in terms of our expectations. In turn, our expectations are based on our beliefs, values and the assumptions we have formed as a result of formal learning and experience. Hans Christian Anderson's fairy tale of "The Emperor's New Clothes" is a classic case of selective perception. According to the story, confidence tricksters posing as tailors convince the emperor that they have made him a magnificent suit of new clothes. The emperor and his courtiers' initial perception is that he is naked but, on being told that the clothes are only visible to discerning and gifted people, they agree that the clothes are truly magnificent and the Emperor should display them in public. A parade is organised and the populace informed of what they are meant to see. All agree that the new clothes are truly magnificent with the exception of one small boy who trusts the evidence of his own observation and announces "The Emperor has no clothes".

In science, a major change of perception of this kind is referred to as a *paradigm shift*. As Dooley (1990) explains ". . . scientists working on a given problem share certain basic assumptions and research tools that shape their observations of a reality. This shared framework has been called a **paradigm**. Paradigms are like lenses through which we see the world."

According to Kuhn (1970), scientific research looks for solutions to problems within the existing paradigm, until such time that conflicting evidence requires a paradigm *shift*. Underpinning this approach is what Bertrand Russell (1948) called "the faith of science". As Dooley (op.cit.) explains "By this phrase he meant that we assume that there are regularities in the connection of events and that these regularities (or "laws") have a continuity over time and space". (p.7) Many of the scientific breakthroughs since the mid eighteenth century lend support to this assumption, demonstrating the worth of establishing a baseline of what is 'known' and believed at a given point in time, on which new research may be based and advances made.

By contrast, social scientists lack the same shared base and so go off at tangents to one another. This tendency is a consequence of the lack of agreement as to the philosophical foundation of social science implicit in our earlier review of positivism versus interpretivism, quantitative versus qualitative and so on. Thus, as Luecke argues, because social scientists lack a firm baseline they frequently re-discover and re-invent themselves. In short, we fail to learn the lessons of history.

According to Dooley "Social research is devoted to explaining social events, that is, to determining the causation of our social reality". In other words, to real world problem solving. Basically, a problem is a phenomenon or event for which we lack an immediate explanation. Obviously, if we can explain a situation we don't have a problem! But, faced with a problem or unexplained event , our natural reaction is to decide whether it matters or not. Only if it does matter will we speculate on the possible causes and look for a solution. Such speculation or search for an explanation is *theorising*.

Given a theory or theories, research is required to determine whether or not they offer an acceptable explanation. To establish this we will have to observe the phenomenon carefully and then decide if the observations confirm or disconfirm the theoretical explanation. Further, to establish this beyond reasonable doubt we need to replicate the research, often many times, and show that a causal relationship actually exists.

As we have seen, for causation to be proved we must satisfy certain rules of evidence. To begin with A must precede B. Some years ago Baker and Hart (1989) undertook a rigorous study of the sources of competitive success using a series of measures that earlier studies suggested were 'critical success factors'. In the event our results showed only a limited association, or correlation, between the critical success factors and the independent variable "success". In fact the analysis only yielded 9 relationships that we thought worthy of comment. One of these was a strong positive association between investment in market research and overall success. Given that a frequent reason for 'failure' (lack of success) is that an organisation lacked sufficient knowledge of its proposed market, this would seem to be an important finding. Unfortunately, we could not claim that doing market research increases the likelihood of success because we had no information on whether the firms involved invested in market research and then became successful or, that because they were successful they could afford to spend money on market research – a sort of insurance policy. The latter is an alternative hypothesis and its existence means that we could not claim causation.

The point we are seeking to make in this chapter is that, while we undertake business and management research to illuminate and possibly 'solve' real problems in an 'objective' way our efforts will inevitably be prone to subjective influences. It is important that we appreciate how these subjective influences, or our 'research philosophy', impact on both our choice of research methodology, and our interpretation of the new information generated by our research. Of necessity, the coverage has been limited given that most research projects are of limited scope, and unlikely to dwell on the issues introduced here. But, as should have become clear, these are very important issues and you need to be aware of them.

For doctoral candidates, or others undertaking a major piece of research, then wider reading is essential. Further, an informed discussion of the questions raised here is likely to be expected as an important element in any report explaining the reasons for undertaking research and reporting its outcomes. Whichever description applies to you, an awareness of these matters, and reference to them, will be expected in the development of a proposal to do research, which is the subject of the next chapter.

Recommended reading

Hughes, John and Sharrock, Wes (1997), *The Philosophy of Social Research*, 3rd.edition, Harlow: Adison Wesley Longman Limited
A clear, comprehensive and accessible introduction to a notoriously difficult topic.

Miller, Robert L., and Brewer, John D. (Eds.) (2003), *The A – Z of Social Research*, London: Sage Publications
Excellent definitions and discussions of the major issues and topics involved in social research.

Murphy, E., Dingwall, R., Greatbatch, D., Parker S., and Watson, P. (1998), 'Qualitative research methods in health technology assessment: a review of the literature', *Health Technology Assessment*, Vol. 2: No.16, pp.1-272
Although focused on health technology assessment the coverage of qualitative research is excellent.

CHAPTER 3

Writing a Research Proposal

Synopsis
While a great deal has been written about the conduct and execution of research comparatively little attention has been given to the essential first step – writing a research proposal. This chapter seeks to address this omission by providing practical advice on the identification and selection of a suitable topic. Idea generation, screening, choice of research approach, drafting a proposal and finding a supervisor are all covered.

Keywords
research proposal, idea generation, screening, research approach, supervision

Introduction

Many formal qualifications contain a requirement that one should complete some form of Research Project, Thesis or Dissertation. This requirement is often viewed by candidates as a 'threatening experience' for at least two reasons. First, 'research' implies a scholarly task for which only the most gifted are suited, and then only after some kind of arduous training. Second, the project represents a significant proportion of the total assessment often accounting for between 15 and 25 per cent or more of the overall grade. Performance on the project can make or break the student! Fortunately, there are numerous excellent sources of advice on the execution of research projects but, almost without exception, they have remarkably little to say about the crucial first steps – identifying a suitable topic and writing a research proposal. In this chapter we offer some practical advice on how to get started.

The first thing to establish is precisely what is required and expected of the student. Once the nature of the task has been determined it is important to draw up a framework for managing the project efficiently and effectively, and some guidelines will be proposed. Next, we look at what many consider to be the most difficult task of all – the identification and selection of a suitable subject or topic. Having selected a topic one must choose an appropriate methodology for researching it, and prepare a first draft proposal for discussion with potential supervisors. Advice on both these stages and the criteria on which they will be assessed is given. Once the proposal has been accepted it only remains to execute it, but that is the subject for a later chapter.

What is a 'research project'?

As hinted in the introduction 'research projects' masquerade under different identities with some referring to them as a Thesis and others as a Dissertation. In the United States the distinction between these terms is clearly understood with 'Thesis 'referring to an undergraduate research project and 'Dissertation' applying to a postgraduate research study, usually at the doctoral level. In the United Kingdom, and many Commonwealth countries with similar Higher Education systems, the distinction is not clear-cut and the terms are frequently used interchangeably as if they were synonyms of one another. Despite this potential for confusion most degree awarding and professional bodies publish detailed specifications of what is required together with formal regulations. It follows that the Golden Rule must be *get a copy of the requirements and regulations.* Some examples of these are given below.

Strathclyde University Graduate School of Business publishes the following guidance for MBA Projects:

The project purpose

Your MBA project is intended to provide you with an opportunity to explore at length some aspect of theory or methods, knowledge or skills, introduced in the earlier stages of the MBA. Your exploration might, for example, take the form of:

- A trial of theory or methods in a real situation – perhaps in your own organization;
- Development or customising of methods for use in a real situation;
- Testing or extending theory through survey, interview, observation of a real situation, or investigating sources of secondary data;
- Extending your knowledge base in a particular area through extended literature search and interviews;

And so on.

The primary aim of this exploration is to enhance your own learning in an area of your own choice. The only stipulation is that the area of learning must in some way relate to the material – or at least the spirit of it – covered by the MBA.

The 'Guide to Writing Masters Dissertations' published by the Department of Marketing has the following to say:

The dissertation is the final stage of the Masters degree and provides the opportunity to show that you have gained the necessary skills and knowledge to organise and conduct a research project. It should demonstrate that you are skilled in delineating an area, or areas, suitable for research; setting research objectives; locating, organising and critically analysing the relevant secondary data; devising an appropriate research methodology; drawing conclusions; and making relevant and practical recommendations.

A dissertation is a "formal" document and there are "rules" that govern the way in which it is presented. It must have chapters that provide an introduction, a literature review, a research methodology, results and analysis and, finally, conclusions and recommendations. Business reports or marketing plans on their own, are not acceptable as Masters dissertations; the structure and framework of the dissertation should be the same regardless of type. If the dissertation is part of the MSc International Marketing degree course, then it must have a substantive international aspect.

Masters level dissertations are distinguished from other forms of market research by their attempt to analyse situations in terms of the 'bigger picture'; they seek answers, explanations, make comparisons and arrive at generalisations which can be used to extend theory – as well as *what*, it addresses *why*? The most successful dissertations are those which are specific and narrowly focused.

These extracts are taken from Guidelines, extending to over 30 pages in length, that are given to every student. They cover every aspect of the task including topics such as undertaking a literature survey, referencing and formal presentation of the completed work. Obviously the content of such a document spelling out the specific requirements of an examining body take precedence to the generalized advice given here and in the sources cited for further reading.

Once the scope and nature of the task have been established one needs to draw up an action plan for managing the task effectively Davis and Parker (1997) propose three ways for enhancing task management:

1. *Planning* – the more clearly a task is defined the more efficient and effective the execution.
2. *Scheduling* - this requires a realistic apportionment of the time available to the various tasks, the development of a critical path and the identification of opportunities for parallel working e.g. the writing up of a literature review while waiting for data to be processed.
3. *Stopping rules* – unlike physical tasks most knowledge based work cannot be completed unless you can decide when a satisfactory

outcome has been achieved. It is up to you to spell out what this is and get the supervisor's agreement – hence the earlier comment that "The most successful dissertations are those that are specific and narrowly focused. (Davis and Parker 1997)

Despite the variations which exist between different kinds of project and between institutions and examining bodies, the task and process remains much the same and may be summarised as follows:

- Formative Thinking
- Developing a Pool of Topics
- Reflection and Screening
- First Draft Proposal
- Find a Supervisor
- Agree the Proposal
- Implement

While it is suggested that one should develop the first Draft Proposal before finding a supervisor, in some cases prospective supervisors may publish lists of topics of interest to them. If this is so, and there is a topic of interest to you, this could significantly shorten the process described below. Otherwise, it is important that you have some preliminary ideas of your own a) to identify possible supervisors and, b) to promote an effective discussion with the potential supervisor.

Formative thinking

As a broad generalisation two scenarios may be envisaged. The first is that the 'researcher' has been given a specific problem to solve. This scenario is most likely where a supervisor has suggested a theme to you or, if you are a part-time student in full-time employment, you can see a problem needing to be solved related to your own job. The second scenario is where you are faced with the proverbial blank sheet of paper and have to come up with a topic of your own.

While both scenarios will require many of the same steps in developing a viable proposal, the latter is more complicated in that one has the additional challenge of selecting a topic which meets the course requirements and is 'do-able' with the resources available. Either way the first step is to define the issue or problem to be addressed in clear and precise terms so that there can be no ambiguity about what is to be attempted. Even when the problem or topic has been specified the researcher must be careful to spell out precisely how the words used are to be interpreted, what are the scope and boundaries of the project and what is deemed to be inside and outside these boundaries.

This is especially important when working with another or others on a group project as, once agreed, the problem definition becomes the benchmark against which all subsequent actions and outcomes will be measured.

So where do new ideas come from? The guidelines cited earlier gave some advice but, for students of business, perhaps the best advice is to think of the New Product Development Process. You will recall that the first step in the process is idea generation and it is this that formative thinking is all about.

In *Product Strategy and Management* (1998), Susan Hart and I devote the whole of Chapter 9 to Idea Management and offer a comprehensive review of techniques and approaches for generating ideas. Most authors of books concerned with research projects offer similar advice but the scope is usually narrower than suggestions for idea generation contained in books on innovation. For example in their excellent book *The Management of a Student Research Project* Sharp and Howard (1996) only offer four pages of advice on generating ideas compared with thirty in Baker and Hart. While Sharp and Howard assume the appointment of a supervisor prior to the formative thinking stage, who may be proactive in suggesting topics, they also recognise that many supervisors will expect the student to put forward ideas to which they will react. As possible sources of ideas they suggest the following:

1. Theses and dissertations.
2. Articles in academic and professional journals.
3. Conference proceedings and reports generally.
4. Books and book reviews.
5. Reviews of the field of study.
6. Communications with experts in the field.
7. Conversations with potential users of the research findings.
8. Discussions with colleagues.
9. The media.

To these Davis and Parker (1997) would add:

1. Current events.
2. Generally accepted but unproved suppositions.
3. Unproved or weakly proved assertions by an authority in the field.
4. Theories and concepts without supporting research.
5. Different approaches to testing important results.

Obviously, these are not mutually exclusive alternatives and one may wish to consult several sources to confirm that a possible topic has real potential. Given a pool of topics then, as with new product development, the next step is to subject them to rigorous screening.

To facilitate screening it will be helpful to prepare what Davis and Parker call 'Topic Analyses' which they describe as follows:

> The topic analysis is essentially a simplified proposal form providing a rough outline of factors relating to a dissertation. The parts are as follows:
>
>   1.   Problem, hypothesis or question.
>   2.   Importance of research.
>   3.   Theory base for research.
>   4.   Significant prior research.
>   5.   Possible research approach or methodology.
>   6.   Potential outcomes of research and importance of each. (Davis and Parker 1997)

In other words it may be considered as a mini proposal or 'concept test'.

Clearly, the amount of detail will vary according to the scope of the research with much more detail being required for a doctoral dissertation than a three month research project. Sharp and Howard (1996) (from whom Davis and Parker may well have derived the notion of the Topic Analysis) offer a useful table comparing the content and scope of a Topic Analysis with a fully developed Research Proposal. In doing so they state;

> Whereas a topic analysis should contain just sufficient information for a decision to be reached on the line of research to be pursued, the research proposal should be seen as the document which finally establishes both the need for the study and that the researcher has or can acquire the skills and other resources required. (Sharp and Howard 1996)

Thus, while a Topic Analysis will normally be from 2 to 5 pages in length, a Research Proposal for a Doctoral degree may extend to fifty pages or more, and for a Master's Project to ten or more pages. The main difference between the Topic Analysis and a Research Proposal is that the latter will be introduced by an Abstract or Executive Summary, and will provide an outline of how the completed work might appear in terms of chapters and their content.

Jankowicz (2000) suggests that one should develop a "Provenance Table" to help flesh out ideas into possible topics. The purpose of the Provenance Table is to clarify how a "topic fits into the whole body of ideas and knowledge, how it relates to other topics you might have chosen, but didn't." As described (p.45ff.) a Provenance Table will help you:

- decide how unacceptably vague, or appropriately specific, your initial idea might be, thereby guiding the process by which you change your initial, vague ideas into a developed form;

- specify research objectives for your empirical work;
- identify the taught courses which are relevant to your topic, offering subject matter which your literature review will need to describe, and concepts which are relevant to the argument you will be building;
- identify lecturers who would make an appropriate tutor for your topic once you've worked it up into a final form;
- suggest the types of reading you'll need to do in preparing your dissertation – and even provide a pointer to its location in the library.

Clear guidance is given on the construction of a Provenance Table together with examples.

In recent years there has been an increased emphasis on completion rates for all kinds of graduating courses and, particularly, for research degrees. As a result of this emphasis doctoral degrees in the social sciences have tended to become more structured and seen more as a professional qualification than an opportunity to undertake a piece of original research under limited guidance and supervision. In turn this has led to much greater importance being attached to the formal Research Proposal, and many institutions now require that a candidate makes a formal presentation and defence of their Research Proposal to a Thesis Committee. Such Committees may approve the proposal, suggest modifications or even reject it. Normally, submission and defence of a doctoral research proposal would occur in the first 12 to 15 months of a 33 month programme and represents a much bigger hurdle than it did in the past. The benefits are that acceptance of a proposal is endorsement of the proposed research, and implies that it satisfies the criterion of symmetry described below. It follows that if the candidate executes the proposal according to plan they should succeed!

For Research Proposals associated with Honours and Masters degrees tutors will usually require the student to start thinking about a suitable topic and possible supervisor well before they are expected to start on the project itself. For Honours degrees it is usually recommended that the student start work on their dissertation during the vacation preceding the Honours year, and then work on it in parallel with their formal courses. For Masters' students formal courses are normally completed in the first 9 months of the course with the final 3 months being set aside for the project. However, Masters' students would be expected to have agreed their project well before the start of the full time work period.

Screening ideas

Davis and Parker (1997) suggest eight important characteristics for a good dissertation topic:

1. Research needed and interesting.
2. Theory base for research
3. Amenable to research methods.
4. Achievable in a reasonable time.
5. Symmetry of potential outcomes.
6. Matches student capabilities and interests.
7. Attractive for funding.
8. Area for professional development.

With the exception of '5' these are self-explanatory. By symmetry of outcomes is meant that a research project will typically have more than one potential outcome and that any one of these would be acceptable, i.e. confirming or rejecting theory/hypothesis will constitute a contribution to knowledge which, in turn, may consist of:

1. New or improved evidence.
2. New or improved methodology.
3. New or improved analysis.
4. New or improved concepts or theories.

In deciding whether an idea meets these criteria it is often helpful to apply what I call the 'Kipling Test' following the advice given in a verse by Rudyard Kipling:

I keep six honest serving-men
(They taught me all I knew)
Their names are What and Where and When
And How and Why and Who

Rudyard Kipling (1902) 'The Elephant's Child', *The Just So Stories for Little Children*

Accordingly you should ask yourself:

- What do I want to do? i.e. Who is it for?
- Why is it important?
- What issues/other subjects does the topic relate to?
- Where and How will the research be undertaken?
- When i.e within what constraints will the research be implemented?

Two critical questions that need to be addressed in screening ideas for research are:

1. Who is the intended audience?, and
2. What basic approach is to be taken?

Mauch and Birch (1993) distinguish between "academic" and "professional" disciplines. Academic disciplines consist of a unified body of knowledge and are primarily concerned with adding to that body of knowledge. By contrast professional disciplines comprise "…. Diversified information and concepts that focus on the efficient and effective conduct of some operation…" (p.10). While both kinds of discipline emphasise the same requirements of originality, individuality and rigour there are several conceptual and administrative differences between them. These are summarised by them as set out in Table 3.1. Business related research projects are most likely to fall into the 'professional' category.

Research approach

With regard to the basic approach to be taken the major distinction is between *positivistic* and *interpretivistic*. Robson (1993) comments [There are two basic approaches to doing research. The first] "is variously labelled as positivistic, natural science based, hypothetico-deductive, quantitative or even simply 'scientific'; the other as interpretive, ethnographic or qualitative – among several other labels." (p.18) As discussed in some detail in Chapter 2, these different approaches rest on different philosophical assumptions about *ontology* (theory concerning the nature of social entities (Bryman 2001)) and *epistemology* (what is regarded as acceptable knowledge in a discipline (Bryman 2001)). In turn these differing perspectives will have a significant influence on one's choice of methodology and research methods.

Frequently, these approaches are seen as opposed to one another and distinct alternatives. This distinction is implicit in Table 3.2. In our view, the approaches are complementary and many research projects will employ a combination of both methods. However, it is necessary to issue a 'health warning' here. Not all academics share this view, and many will not even regard them as alternatives. One approach will be acceptable, the other not. It follows that you need to establish the supervisor's preferences before committing yourself to any given approach. Alternatively, you will need to find a supervisor sympathetic to your own preferred position.

Traditionally, within the business and management disciplines, the scientific method has been seen as more rigorous and more likely to yield valid results. However, much will depend on your core discipline. If it is Econometrics or Management Science then it is likely that you will already be inclined to a positivistic/quantitative stance. Conversely, in Human Resource Management and Marketing an interpretivistic/qualitative emphasis prevails. The foundation of scientific research is the existence of a *theory* that Robson defines as "A general statement that summarises and organises knowledge by proposing a general relationship between events – if it is a good one, it will cover a large number of events and predict events that have not yet occurred or been observed." (p.18)

Table 3.1.   Distinctions between research in academic disciplines and professional disciplines

	Academic Discipline Research	Professional Discipline Research
Purpose	To increase knowledge in a particular disciplinary field.	To increase knowledge about a matter relevant to the practice of the profession and to reinforce the attitude of using objective and systematic approaches to problem solving.
Scope	Topics studied clearly related to other problems within the same Discipline	Unrestricted so long as the research has demonstrated implications for society's professional enterprises.
Worth	Worth is assessed in terms of the amount it advances knowledge, clarifies or adds to a theory. Stimulates further investigation.	Potential application of the findings to professional practice and knowledge.
Justification	Knowledge is accrued for its own sake.	To question or validate aspects of professional practice and to contribute to their improvement.
Position on the relevance of values	Matters of value are deliberately eschewed, except as primary data.. The objectivity of the academic scholar is most closely tied to dealing with concepts, ideas, animate or inanimate objects, materials, documents and events	Both matters of substance and value can be legitimate and necessary topics of inquiry; sometimes values are the essential data subjected to study.
Methodology of Research Acceptable	Each discipline recognises particular methods that have been shown to uncover or prove matters of importance to the discipline.	Methods are invented or adapted to suit the problem.
Approval/ Acceptance	Judges from within the discipline.	Judges from the profession expert in the field and specialists from other disciplines (Academic and Professional) whose competencies bear especially on the topic.

(Adapted from Mauch, James E. and Birch, Jack W. (1993), *Guide to the Successful Thesis and Dissertation*, 3rd. Edition, New York: Marcel Dekker Inc.)

Given the existence of a theory, scientific research involves five sequential steps:

1. Formulating a hypothesis about the relationship between two or more events or concepts derived from the theory which may be tested.
2. Operationalising the hypothesis by defining how to test/measure the

proposed relationship.

3. Testing the hypothesis using the prescribed methods.
4. Analysis that will either confirm the theory or lead to its modification or rejection.
5. Replication to ensure that the observed outcome has not occurred by chance.

Table 3.2.   Qualitative versus quantitative research

Qualitative	Quantitative
Soft	Hard
Dry	Wet
Flexible/fluid	Fixed
Grounded	Abstract
Descriptive/exploratory	Explanatory
Pre-scientific	Scientific
Subjective	Objective
Inductive	Deductive
Speculative/illustrative	Hypothesis testing
Political	Value free
Non-rigorous	Rigorous
Idiographic	Nomothetic
Holistic	Atomistic
Interpretivist	Positivist
Exposes actors meanings	Imposes sociological theory
Phenomenological	Empiricist/behaviourist
Relativistic case study	Universalistic survey
Good	Bad
Bad	Good

(Source: Halfpenny, P. (1979), "The Analysis of Qualitative Data', *Sociological Review*, Vol 27. No. 4, pp.799-825)

Clearly, the scientific approach depends upon the existence of a theory which begs the question 'where do theories come from?' The answer is that theory arises from observation, speculation and conceptualisation and it is these processes that characterise the interpretivist approach. Thus research, and the creation of new knowledge, combines speculation about the existence of relationships and inquiry to establish whether a theory already exists that offers a satisfactory explanation of the relationship. If so, one may wish to test whether the theoretical generalisation explains the particular case using the scientific method outlined earlier. On the other hand, one may find that there is not an extant or established theory that provides a satisfactory explanation for the perceived relationship. If this is so then one would proceed in exactly the same way by formulating a working hypothesis and testing it. If the results confirm the hypothesis then we have a new theory, and may subject it to further testing by applying the findings to future occurrences involving the events or concepts that prompted the speculation in the first place. It follows that the two research traditions are inextricably linked, one to the other, in a cycle that involves a combination of both primary and secondary research – a somewhat confusing nomenclature in that secondary research (is there an existing explanation/theory of a phenomenon) should always precede the collection of new data to test hypotheses (primary research).

Having established that the two traditions or approaches are not mutually exclusive, either/or options, it should be recognised that the need for and purpose of a research proposal will influence the degree of emphasis placed upon a positivistic or interpretivisitic perspective. In the world of business, problem solving and decision making rarely call for the degree of precision and certainty that one would expect in science, medicine or engineering where error could lead to fatal consequences. Further, because the subject of business research is largely about human behaviour which, in turn, may be influenced or changed by the actions of the problem solver/researcher, it is unlikely that the degree of precision looked for in true 'scientific' research could be achieved. In consequence, much business research tends to make greater use of interpretivist methods, and be directed towards the solution of specific rather than generalised problems. This is certainly the case with the kind of project work that is required when studying for formal qualifications up to the Master's level. (Doctoral research extending over three years or more will usually involve both interpretivistic and positivistic methodologies.)

Where the choice is left to the researcher probably the most important consideration is that the topic should be intrinsically interesting to them. Further, where the time available for the completion of the project is limited, it will be helpful to choose a topic from a domain or field of which one already has some background knowledge and understanding. Thus, in the course of one's studies, it is likely that one will have come across a number of contentious and/or unresolved issues that might form the basis of a useful and interesting project. Similarly, given that most topics contained in a curriculum are highly focused one may see an opportunity to test the applicability of findings or theory in one subject to another context. For example, the notion of opinion leadership is widely used in many social sciences (see Everett Rogers' *Diffusion of Innovations*) but may not have been applied to a particular context in which you are interested e.g. Launching a new high technology product.

Once one has a generalised idea about a research topic or problem the first thing to do is establish that it really exists, and has not already been solved by someone else. This is not a trivial task, but should not be confused with the kind of detailed secondary research that frequently comprises the first step in implementing a research proposal. What we have in mind is an attempt to classify the nature of the problem to be solved so that we can check with informed others (your subject tutor, the business librarian etc.) whether or not they regard it as an unresolved issue. Clearly, if someone has posed a problem for you it is reasonable to assume this is the case. If, however, it materialises that this is not the case then this finding should itself satisfy the symmetry of outcomes issue identified earlier and so result in a satisfactory outcome. But, if you have chosen the subject yourself, you should seek the advice of someone knowledgeable about the general field from which it is taken. An obvious choice here would be a potential supervisor.

Assuming one has defined the problem or issue precisely, as recommended earlier, it is likely that some "keywords" will have emerged. If so then a quick check of the index of a leading and up-to-date textbook should confirm what current thinking is about the topic. Similarly, the same keywords may be used to conduct a preliminary search of likely sources to establish what if anything has appeared since the authoritative textbook appeared. At this stage there is no need to access such sources, but a listing of them will help persuade your supervisor that you have identified a real issue of current interest. (The detailed evaluation of secondary sources is generally referred to as a *literature review* and is the subject of Chapter 4).

If the tentative research question passes this initial screening then we should firm it up and state it explicitly in a formal way.

Drafting the proposal

As noted earlier the Research Proposal is a critical element in the research process. Essentially, it may be regarded as a contract between the researcher and the 'client' for whom the research is being performed and, once accepted, becomes a blueprint for the implementation of the project. That said it has to be recognised that the execution of research is often an uncertain business. After all if we knew the answer to a problem there would be no need for research in the first place. It follows that, as we implement our research proposal, we may find that there is a need to modify our original approach. In this sense we may modify the blueprint, but it will still remain as a benchmark against which the final outcome may be assessed.

Irrespective of whether the Proposal is for a shorter Honours or Masters dissertation or full blown Doctoral thesis the content will remain much the same and will contain the following:

Title
Outline
Overview
Objectives
Research Methods
Research Plan
Bibliography

Title

A good Title should summarise, succinctly, precisely what the research is about. While a 'snappy' title is good for catching the attention and stimulating interest, it should be remembered that the primary audience for most projects is a client who is more concerned that the title describes the nature and scope of the project that they have approved. The requirements are not mutually exclusive and a sub-title may be used to elaborate an eye-catching title. e.g. Scotland the Brand: An investigation into the impact of the 'Made in Scotland' label on consumer buying behaviour for food products in French retail outlets.

Outline

The Outline should provide an indication of how the finished work might appear as listed in a Table of Contents i.e. chapter headings and sub-headings.

Overview

The Overview sets out what the research proposal is all about and provides the background to the Abstract. To begin with it should spell out what the research *issue* is and why it is important. For example, 'Does a product's country of origin affect its sales?'. Given that many countries require that products carry a label that specifies the country in which they were made, the answer might work to the advantage (or disadvantage) of a producer seeking to develop a new export market. A preliminary literature review would quickly reveal that there is an extensive body of work that addresses this issue, but that there is no clear or unequivocal answer to the question. Specifically, a great deal depends upon the nature of the product, the country of origin, the country of sale and the customer's prior knowledge and experience of the product category and the country of origin. In order to answer the question we need to specify a product and a market, and then design a test instrument to collect primary data from prospective customers to establish if and in what ways the 'Made in ...' label might influence their buyer behaviour. Accordingly, our Overview should persuade the reader that there is an Issue and that we are sufficiently familiar with the current state of knowledge to be able to research the Issue in a meaningful way.

Objectives

The Objective or Objectives spell out what exactly the research is intended to achieve; e.g.

1. To clarify how, and in what ways, a product's country of origin might influence buyer behaviour. (To answer this question we will have to undertake a critical review of the relevant literature.)

2. To establish what values French consumers have towards Scotland as a Country of Origin. (The purpose here is to establish a generalised response or stereotype of French consumers attitudes towards the 'Made in Scotland' label.)
3. To determine whether 'Made in ..' labels modify French consumers attitudes and buying behaviour for the particular product category under investigation. (The specific research Issue.)

Research methods

Most authorities confine the content of this section to the research approach to be followed (positivist/interpretivist/hybrid), the research techniques to be used and the data analysis methods. In addition, we believe that explicit recognition should be given to the critical literature review as suggested by the first objective set out above. Given the size and complexity of most research issues it is unrealistic to expect that students will have undertaken an exhaustive review of the relevant literature before selecting their research issue. The preliminary "Topic Analysis", described earlier, is to define a *prima facie* research issue so that prospective supervisors or other experts can confirm that it is worth following up. Possible exceptions are the Doctoral proposal, and grant applications to funding bodies where a broader knowledge of the field might be expected.

Research plan

This is the place to set out the 'housekeeping' arrangements. This includes matters such as the proposed timetable and the resource requirements covering both access and finance. Here one has to convince whoever is assessing the proposal that it is indeed 'do-able'. For example, if you propose to collect data from French consumers do you speak the language? How do you propose to test and validate the test instrument? How long will it take to collect the data, and have you sufficient cash to cover the costs? Etc. etc.

Bibliography

A short listing of the key sources you have consulted in developing your proposal.

Finding a supervisor

If you have read this far you will have gathered that the role of the Supervisor is critical. It should also have become apparent that, while we have left this until last, in many cases the first thing to do is find a supervisor. Blaxter et al. (1996) cite Phillips and Pugh in spelling out students' and supervisors expectations of each other, viz:

Students expect their supervisors:

- To supervise them;
- To read their work well in advance;
- To be available when needed;
- To be friendly, open and supportive;
- To be constructively critical;
- To have a good knowledge of their research area;
- To structure tutorials so that it is relatively easy to exchange ideas;
- To have sufficient interest in their research to put more information in the path of researchers;
- To be sufficiently involved in their success to help them get a good job at the end of it all!

If you can find someone who meets all these criteria you are indeed lucky! If you can, then they will expect their students:

- To be independent;
- To produce written work that is not just a first draft;
- To have regular meetings;
- To be honest when reporting on their progress;
- To follow the advice that they give, when it has been given at the student's request;
- To be excited about their work, able to surprise them and fun to be with.

Some institutions spell out the supervisor/student relationship in considerable detail in their formal publications. Among the best that I know of are those published by the University of Otago in New Zealand (*http://www.otago.ac.nz*). Different advice is contained in the *Handbook for Research Masters' Degrees* and the *Handbook for PhD Study*. In addition various Departments issue their own extended advice, particularly for Honours students. With permission we reproduce the section from the Masters' handbook covering the kinds of issue that a student might wish to discuss with a supervisor. (You are encouraged to visit the web site and review the other detailed advice available there *http://www.otago.ac.nz/research/ research_student_resources.html*).

Supervisor/Student Understandings

1.Expectations regarding a Master's thesis

Issues to discuss might include:

- Are the student's background and performance adequate for the proposed topic and level of investigation?

- Is the topic or area of investigation appropriate to the proposed supervisor? If it is well outside the supervisor's own areas of research, the work involved in adequate supervision may tend to be neglected or lead to considerable frustration.
- Are available financial and physical resources likely to be adequate for the proposed research?
- Does the proposed supervisor have adequate time to take on this research student?
- What form should the thesis proposal take?
- What is the appropriate structure of the thesis?
- What is the appropriate length?
- What referencing conventions should be followed?
- What are the general expectations for successful theses?
- What are good examples in this field?
- Examiners of Masters' theses are given the following information. Do any of these statements require discussion or clarification?: "For your information, a thesis submitted for a Master's degree should contain the results of independent research which might reasonably be expected of a diligent and competent student after not less than twelve months of full-time study. The thesis should demonstrate that the student has the ability to carry out research and/or the ability to carry out constructive criticism, and to report the results of such work clearly, accurately and succinctly. It is not a requirement that the results should necessarily represent a substantial contribution to knowledge in the field".
- If publication arises from the research, what are the expectations regarding who will be listed as author(s) and in what order?

2. Meetings
Issues to discuss might include
- What is the intended frequency of meetings?
- Will the student have access to the supervisor outside the scheduled meeting times?
- Who has the responsibility to initiate meetings if they are not scheduled regularly?
- What should happen when one person can't make it to a meeting?

3. Absence of supervisor
Is it likely that the supervisor will be absent on leave during the project? If so, who will be the alternative supervisor?

4. Advice and support
Issues to discuss might include:

- Development of the research proposal: how much input will there be from the supervisor?
- How often, how detailed and how rapid should feedback from the supervisor on the general progress of the project be?
- Is the student likely to need special assistance with specific aspects of the project or during the writing up stage?
- Are there relevant personal circumstances that might make the completion of the thesis difficult?

5. Time-frame
What is the time-frame for the project, i.e. what is expected to be completed at the end of each 3 month (or as agreed) period?

6. Any other supervisor/student issues

As we have pointed out, all institutions will normally have guidelines setting out what a student is required to do to satisfy the requirements for a formal academic award and it is these that have to be followed precisely. Our reason for quoting the above set of questions in full is because you will not always receive such useful advice about establishing a relationship with a supervisor, and the issues listed are very important ones, especially for the student. Accordingly, they should be considered a benchmark with which to compare the guidelines published by your own institution, and you should not be afraid to raise any of these points if they are not referred to explicitly.

We would also reiterate that this is only an extract from a document dealing with a particular category of research project. You will find a lot more detail on the web site given regarding supervisor/student relationships and expectations.

Summary

In this chapter we have concentrated on the preliminary stages of the research process – the writing of a Research Proposal. Often this part of the process receives only limited coverage by comparison with the other stages such as conducting a literature review, selecting a research method, data collection and analysis. Certainly this is true of many of the books written on the subject of writing theses and dissertations, including several of those that we have cited. This neglect is surprising in that virtually all writers agree that the ultimate success of a research project is largely determined by the quality of the original proposal. As in other fields of endeavour, careful reflection, conceptualisation and planning pay dividends. In the words of the military maxim "Time spent in reconnaissance is seldom wasted" or, put another way "Look before you leap". We can do no better than recommend the advice given by Irving and Smith:

1. Examine your guidelines.
2. Identify a general subject area.
3. Conduct an initial literature review.
4. Narrow the subject down.
5. Select the most appropriate research methods.
6. Put together a proposal.

(Irving and Smith 1998)

Assuming your proposal is accepted then all that remains is to execute it! This is the subject of the rest of the book, starting with *Writing a Literature Review* in the next chapter. In conclusion, however, we cannot over-emphasise that the more time and thought put into the *planning* of a research project, and the development of a research proposal, the more likely one is to achieve a satisfactory outcome.

Recommendations for further reading

Barzun, Jacques and Graff, Henry F. (1977), *The Modern Researcher*, 3rd. Edition, New York: Harcourt Brace Jovanovich Inc.
Takes the view that all research leads to a report whatever it may be called. Written from the perspective of a historian.

Blaxter, Loraine, Hughes, Christina and Tight, Malcolm (1996), *How to Research*, Buckingham: Open University press
A widely used textbook on research methods courses. Better than average coverage of the preliminary stages. Good checklists and summaries, exercises etc.

Davis, Gordon B. and Parker, Clyde A. (1997), *Writing the Doctoral Dissertation*, Hauppauge, NY: Barron's Educational Series Inc.
As the title indicates the main emphasis is on doctoral dissertations. However, contains much practical advice for anyone developing a research project.

Gill, John and Johnson, Phil (1997), *Research Methods for Managers*, 2nd. Edition. London: P. Chapman
Good general coverage.

Irving, Ray and Smith, Cathy (1998), *No Sweat: The Indispensable Guide to Reports and Dissertations*, Corby: Institute of Management Foundation
Short, easy to read with lots of practical tips. 182 pages plus 5 useful Appendices

Mauch, James E. and Birch., Jack W. (1993), *Guide to the Successful Thesis and Dissertation*, 3rd. Edition, New York: Marcel Dekker Inc.
Good chapter on developing a research proposal.

Cont'd...

Phillips, E.M. and Pugh, D.S. (1994), *How to Get a PhD: A Handbook for Students and their Supervisors*, 2nd edition, Buckingham: Open University Press
A 'classic' but concerned primarily with doctoral dissertations.

Robson, C. (1993), *Real-world Research: A Resource for Social Scientists and Practitioner Researchers*, Oxford: Blackwell
Exactly that!

Saunders, Mark, Lewis, Philip and Thornhill, Adrian (1997), *Research Methods for Business Students*, London: Pitman Publishing (3rd edition 2002, London: FT Prentice Hall)
Good overall coverage of the whole process. Chapter 2 deals specifically with 'Formulating and Clarifying the Research Topic' and contains 8 pages on Research Ideas and 5 pages on Writing a Proposal.

Appendix : Forms of dissertation

This Appendix is taken from the Dissertation Guidelines given to students taking the Honours programme in Marketing at the University of Otago. It is reproduced with the permission of the Head of Department, Professor Rob Lawson. It can also be found online at *http://marketing.otago.ac.nz/ marketing/ study/mart480guidelines.html#11*

Appendix A: Forms of Dissertation

A dissertation can take different forms. Unfortunately it is not possible to formulate rigid guidelines for each and every possible variation. Besides the general guidelines for scholarly work stipulated above, the following are applicable to individual types and studies:

Using an existing data set

- thoroughly review the literature, paying particular attention to the most recent work. Are there any "gaps" (aspects that need to be clarified that have not been researched or that need to be replicated to assess their validity for NZ circumstances)?
- generate hypotheses based on the gaps or on the findings of earlier studies (in the case of a replication study)
- test the hypotheses against the data
- evaluate the findings. Do they differ from previous findings? If so, can you offer an explanation?
- what are the implications for marketing?

An experimental/pilot/exploratory study

- thoroughly review the literature, paying particular attention to the most recent work. Are there any 'gaps" (aspects that need to be clarified that have not been researched or that need to be replicated to assess their validity for NZ circumstances)?
- generate hypotheses based on the gaps or on the findings of earlier studies (in the case of a replication study)
- decide on an appropriate methodology.
- how will the sample be drawn? Will you use a convenience sample?
- how will the data be gathered? Structured interviews? A mail survey?
- how will the data be analysed?
- test the hypotheses against the empirical findings.
- evaluate the findings. Do they differ from previous findings? If so, can you offer an explanation?
- what are the implications for marketing?
- a general criticism of all experimental studies is questionable external validity. Explain what you have done to overcome this potential problem.

Developing a validated measuring instrument

- thoroughly review the literature, paying particular attention to the most recent work. Has anyone called for the development of an instrument that could measure a particular construct?
- specify the domain of the construct, conceptualise the construct based on the literature review.
- generate questionnaire items which could measure the construct. This ought to be based on the literature review, informal discussions, focus groups, etc. Depending on the nature of the study, you could have between 50 and 100 items after this phase.
- generate data via mailed questionnaire, shopping mall interviews, etc.
- purify the measure by means of reliability analyses and validity analyses. Depending on the number of items you started with, you could have between 25 and 40 items left after this phase.
- **(Your supervisor may want you to stop here)**
- generate new data
- generate data via mailed questionnaire, shopping mall interviews etc.
- purify the measure by means of reliability analyses and validity analyses. Depending on the number of items you started with, you could have between 15 and 25 items left after this phase.
- evaluate the convergent validity of the instrument.

The steps that should be used to develop a measuring instrument are set out in the following article:

Churchill, G.A. 1979. A Paradigm for Developing Better Measures of Marketing Constructs. Journal of Marketing Research, XVI (February): 64-73.

For a practical execution of these steps, see:

Kohli, A.K., Jaworski, B.J. and Kumar, A. 1993. MARKOR: A Measure of Market Orientation. Journal of Marketing Research, XXX (November): 467-477.
Deng, S. and Dart, J. 1994. Measuring Market Orientation: A Multi-Factor, Multi-Item Approach. Journal of Marketing Management, 10(8): 725-742.

A replication study

A good example of a New Zealand replication study is:
Sunde, L. and Brodie, R. 1991. Consumer Evaluations of Brand Extensions: A Replication of a North American Study. New Zealand Journal of Business, 13: 1-11.

Developing a theoretical model

- thoroughly review the literature, paying particular attention to the most recent work. Has anyone called for the development of a model to improve our understanding of some marketing concepts?
- if necessary, conduct exploratory research: focus groups, business executives, industry experts, etc.
- collate and refine the unstructured results by identifying common ideas, consistent patterns or trends and add your own observations and insights
- repeat the process of the exploratory research (eg., another round of focus groups) to test more formal and structured propositions
- define concepts (what is an intrinsic attribute? what is quality? what is a reputation?)
- specify relationships in the form of, for instance, propositions, with supporting evidence, e.g.: The literature on hedonic quality measurement (Court 1939; Griliches 1971) maintains that price is the best measure of product quality. Others have shown that brands, appearance and retail outlet are more important indicators of quality for most products. Because services are often largely of an intangible nature precluding the use of physical attributes such as brands, it is proposed that service customers use intrinsic attributes such as reputation to deduce quality in the services. Thus:
  Proposition 1: most consumers use intrinsic attributes to deduce quality in services.
- illustrate your theoretical model graphically, showing all hypothesised relationships
- provide guidelines on how the model can be empirically tested/validated
- discuss research implications
- discuss managerial/marketing implications

An excellent article on this topic/method is:

Zeithaml, V.A. 1988. Consumer Perceptions of Price, Quality and Value: A Means-end Model and Synthesis of Evidence. Journal of Marketing, 52(3): 2-22.

A meta-analysis

A meta-analysis is a quantitative approach to synthesising the results of multiple related studies.

- a meta-analysis involves the integration of the quantitative summaries of previous studies. In other words, it is a statistical analysis of the results of earlier studies in order to facilitate generalisations.

- thoroughly review the literature, paying particular attention to the most recent work. Are there any "gaps"? A "gap" in this instance is often a concept/relationship etc that has been researched before but the results are somewhat inconsistent. An example could be: does job satisfaction lead to better job performance? A meta-analysis is thus a re-analysis of existing data to answer the original research question. Normally, improved statistical techniques are used.

- it is important to note the weaknesses of earlier studies and to record the possible influence of these deficiencies on the previously reported results.

- it is important to realise that different studies can be compared. Meta-analysis experts point out that there is no need to synthesise and integrate studies that are exactly the same. They ought to produce the same results. Generalisations will necessarily entail ignoring some distinction that can be made among some studies. Some studies may, however, be so different that they need to be ignored.

- generate hypotheses, based on the gaps or on the findings of earlier studies (a replication).

- test the hypotheses against the results of the data analysis.

- evaluate the findings. Do they differ from previous findings? If so, can you offer an explanation?

- what are the implications for marketing?

If you want to read more on this method, see:

Glass, G.R., McGaw, B. and Smith, M.L. 1981. Meta-analysis in Social Research. London: Sage Publications.

For a New Zealand example, see the following discussion paper held in the Commerce library:

Skoko, H. and Williams, L. 1996. A Content Analysis of Educational Advertising in Canterbury, Lincoln University.

A case study

A case study analyses actual "real world" occurrences and has three primary requirements:

- a cause and effect relationship should be established, e.g., because company XYZ was poorly positioned, it was unprofitable; improving its positioning led to an increased market share.

- it ought to be studied using a specific time frame, e.g., marketing strategies used or changed during a specific time period should be analysed.

- a comparison between marketing theory and the events described in the case should be made. In other words, the validity and relevance of what is taught in marketing need to be assessed. Issues that should be addressed include: how was the marketing mix manipulated? Which strategies were used (penetration, skimming, innovation etc)? Why were they successful/ unsuccessful? What were the outcomes (market share, profitability etc.).

From this should follow some normative guidelines.

A content analysis

A content analysis is a research technique used to objectively and systematically make inferences about the intentions, attitudes and values of individuals by identifying specified characteristics in textual messages. Material that has been studied in content analyses previously include different types of advertisements. CEO letters to shareholders in company reports, executive interviews, consumer interviews, mission statements, financial reports and job advertisements.

The basic steps include:

- a literature review
- the variables/constructs/trends etc that will be studied must be identified
- objectives/hypotheses must be formulated
- typically, a time frame is specified (e.g. print adverts during the last 10 years)
- a decision is made on how the sample will be drawn. Normally it is a convenience sample e.g. selected magazines
- the method of coding must be decided (human coding used to be the norm but computer coding is increasingly being used)
- a decision needs to be made how inter-rater reliability will be measured
- test the hypotheses against the results of the data analysis
- evaluate the findings. Do they differ from previous findings? If so, can you offer an explanation?
- what are the implications for marketing?

Kassarjian, H.H. 1977. Content Analysis in Consumer Research. Journal Consumer Research, vol. 4 (June): 7-18.

Holbrook, M.B. 1977. More on Content Analysis. Journal of Consumer Research, vol. 4 (December): 176-177.

Kolbe, R.H. and Burnett, M.S. 1991. Content-analysis Research: An Examination of Applications with Directives for Improving Research Reliability and Objectivity. Journal of Consumer Research, vol. 18 (September): 243-250.

Resnik, A. and Stern, B.L. 1977. An Analysis of Information Content in Television Advertising. Journal of Marketing, January: 50-53.

CHAPTER 4

Writing a Literature Review

Synopsis
The reviewing of existing literature relating to a topic is an essential first step and foundation when undertaking a research project. In this chapter we examine the purposes and scope of a literature review; the selection of sources; citation and referencing; taking notes, organizing material and writing up.

Keywords
Literature review; citation and references; research

Introduction

In the previous chapter we discussed some of the issues encountered in selecting a suitable topic for a research project and the development of this into a formal research proposal. In this chapter we consider a task which bridges both topic selection and the first step in implementing a research project - the conduct of a literature review. It should be noted that the term 'literature review' encompasses the evaluation of *all* sources of information or data that relate to a topic and is not confined solely to academic publications

The evolution and creation of new knowledge proceeds generally by a process of accumulation. Thus, in presenting his new theories, Isaac Newton observed, "If I can see further it is because I am standing on the shoulders of giants". In other words his insights and novel proposals were only possible by building on the discoveries of those who had gone before him.

However, accumulation has its drawbacks too. Often the process is unselective and libraries are full of dusty tomes, some of which may contain nuggets of gold but most of which are dross. The dilemma that faces a person encountering a new problem for the first time is " Has this problem occurred before and, if so, was a satisfactory solution found?" Theoretically the answer to this question is to be found in the concept of the expected value of perfect information (EVPI).

While the concept of the EVPI is well-known in theory it would seem that it is seldom used in practice - at least in a formal way. In essence the concept proposes that one should invest in acquiring a new information relevant to the solution of a problem to the point where the marginal cost of another "bit" of information is equal to the marginal value of the enhanced knowledge and understanding acquired. Experience suggests most of us do this in a qualitative and informal way, even if we are unaware of the formal calculation of EVPI. Researching the literature, what is already known about a topic, is an intrinsic element of problem-solving. The dilemma is how much time and effort (cost) one should invest in this task compared with the time and effort one might invest in primary or original research designed specifically to solve the problem in hand.

This is a very important issue, which may lead to severe differences of opinion between theoreticians and practitioners. For the theoretician, reinvention of something that is already known is wasteful and indicative of flawed research methods. For the practitioner, the issue is whether reinvention is more cost-effective than exhausting the existing sources of information that may be relevant before undertaking the new research into the issues presented by the problem to be solved. As with a most things, a compromise may be the only way forward. If we can define and agree what is involved in conducting a "perfect" literature review when no constraints apply then it should be possible to agree what would be adequate and satisfactory when constraints do apply. In other words, " fitness for purpose" is our goal.

In light of these comments we have adopted the following approach. First, we summarise the purposes of a literature review and then look at its scope and the selection of sources. Next we examine the important issue of citations and references, which is of central importance to the process. We then conclude with some advice on taking notes, organizing your material and writing it up.

The purposes of a literature review

In the Introduction we noted that knowledge grows through a process of accumulation. Occasionally, a scholar or researcher will make a major breakthrough that will change the world's understanding of the subject, and open up completely new ways of thinking about it, like a new volcanic island emerging from the ocean floor. Newton's articulation of the Laws of Gravity or Einstein's Theory of Relativity would fall into this category. However, such seminal contributions are rare indeed and most subjects grow and develop like a coral reef through the slow and gradual accretion of myriad microscopic pieces. In undertaking a piece of research it is vital that we steer a careful course if we are to avoid the dangers of shipwreck. Indeed while colliding with an island through lack of observation would constitute extreme negligence, running aground on a poorly charted Reef can be just as fateful! The purpose of a literature review is to avoid the calamities of ignorance and the reinvention of what is already known.

> [a literature review is] a critical Search for an analytical framework, or frameworks, which you can put to work to test a hypothesis (if you're

adopting a positivist approach) or to systematically investigate a set of issues. (Jancovicz 2000, p.178)

By contrast with the amount of advice available on the subject of writing a research proposal, much more has been written about the task of writing a literature review. In addition to the book's recommended in Chapter 3 "Writing a research proposal" there is a number of other specialist texts which deal specifically with the subject in hand. Among these one of the best known is *Doing a Literature Review* by Chris Hart. This book, published by Sage Publications, is an Open University set book, positioned as a practical and comprehensive guide to researching, preparing and writing a literature review. The text deals clearly with a number of important issues.

According to Hart the literature review has at least the following purposes in research:

1. Distinguishing what has been done from what needs to be done;
2. discovering important variables relevant to the topic;
3. synthesising and gaining a new perspective;
4. identifying relationships between ideas and practice;
5. establishing the context of the topic or problem;
6. rationalising the significance of the problem;
7. enhancing and acquiring the subject vocabulary;
8. understanding the structure of the subject;
9. relating ideas and theory to applications;
10. identifying of the main methodologies and research techniques that have been used;
11. placing the research in a historical context to show familiarity with state-of-the-art developments. (Hart 1998, p.27)

Gabbott (2002) proposed a very similar list when addressing the Doctoral Colloquium of the Academy of Marketing, viz:

1. To identify gaps in what has been published.
2. To avoid re-inventing the wheel.
3. To indicate where others have stopped so you can carry on.
4. To identify other people working in the same field.
5. To increase your breadth of knowledge.
6. To identify seminal work.
7. To identify opposing views.
8. To demonstrate that you can access previous work in your area.
9. To identify methods or approaches relevant to your thesis.

Or, more simply, to describe and evaluate the work already done in the area in which you are interested.

A little later Hart offers advice on the planning of a literature research. He suggests that this involves six basic steps, namely:

- Define the topic
- Think about the scope of the topic
- Think about outcomes
- Think about the housekeeping
- Plan the sources to be searched
- Search the sources listed (Hart 1998, p.32)

In Chapter 3 we alluded to the circularity that exists when defining a topic and undertaking a literature review. In order to define a topic it would seem necessary to consult the literature that relates to that topic. However, once one has defined the topic it then becomes possible to identify which literature may relate to it. Indeed, in developing a research proposal it may be necessary to scan the literature relating to several topics in order to decide which topic one wishes to develop further. It follows that there are different levels of a literature review. In developing a topic description the scope will be limited, whereas once one has defined the topic the scope of the review will be determined by the extent of the literature itself, the scope and nature of the assignment to be attempted, and the resources available to the researcher.

Ideally, the scope of a piece of research will be defined by the title given to the chosen topic. When it is crafted carefully the title of the piece of research will consist largely of keywords. It is the combination of these keywords that set the parameters of the research itself. Nowadays most students embarking on a literature review will have access to online databases. If one were to input a single key word such as "Marketing" most search engines would come up with millions of possible information sources. If we were to add the phrase "of blood transfusion services" the number would likely be reduced to a handful. If we were to further qualify the scope of the project by adding "in Transylvania" we might well discover a single entry under the name of Count Dracula.

In Chapter 3 we observed that one of the problems you will experience is the need to review some literature to establish whether or not there is a research issue that deserves further investigation. Usually, this review will have been limited to major texts and the abstracts of the most frequently cited sources. Now is the time to return to this preliminary shortlist and dig deeper. Bear in mind also that acceptance of a research proposal implies agreement with the information and arguments contained within it. The issue now is the degree and extent to which the existing literature reinforces or challenges the basic issue your research proposal addresses.

The purpose of a literature review is to demonstrate that one is familiar with what is already known about a subject. This should include a domain theory or theories that have evolved together with any criticisms of them. To begin with one should consult those sources most likely to contain a summary or overview of the key issues relevant to a subject. Major textbooks, particularly those that have stood the test of time and appeared in several editions, are a good place to start. Inevitably a textbook is never completely up-to-date but, at least, the better ones will contain a discussion of the main ideas and concepts together with a review of comment and criticism of these, and citation of the work of those who have made major contributions to the field. Thus textbooks provide a start point from which to begin, and reflect what is the accepted knowledge base.

Another good place to start is with encyclopaedias or reference books. While major reference works like the *Encyclopaedia Britannica* or *Encarta* may contain entries on some business and management related topics, one is more likely to find dedicated entries to such issues in specially commissioned reference works such as the *International Encyclopedia of Business and Management*. Over the years I have been involved with several such ventures in the marketing discipline including *Marketing: theory and practice* (third edition 1996); *The Marketing Book* (5th edition 2003) and the *Encyclopaedia of Marketing* (second edition, 1999). All these anthologies share a number of common features:

- The individual entries are contributed by acknowledged experts on the topic, many of whom have authored leading textbooks on the subject.
- Each entry provides a concise overview of the current state of thinking, identifies major schools of thought and their proponents;
- Entries are authoritative and suggest references for further reading for those wishing to explore the topic in more detail.

Overviews of the kind described above are undoubtedly a good introduction to the literature relating to a topic. However, they are also likely to suffer from a number of deficiencies. Few meet adequately the criteria suggested by Hart (1998) for a "quality" literature review when he observes:

> Many reviews, in fact, are only thinly disguised annotated bibliographies. Quality means appropriate breadth and depth, rigour and consistency, clarity and brevity, and effective analysis and synthesis; (Hart 1998, p.1)

While textbook authors, and contributors to anthologies and encyclopaedias, will usually satisfy the first six criteria to some degree, their remit often precludes them from drawing conclusions of their own leading to the statement of working hypotheses to be tested by further research. In the context of designing and implementing a research proposal the literature review is but one element in the process, and not an end in itself in the way that a textbook entry is.

Although a literature review may be an end in itself, in the context of designing and implementing a research proposal it is but one element in the process. Either way it is essential that it meet the criteria identified by Hart. To do so requires one to learn recognised skills and techniques and to observe conventions that have evolved which define scholarly research. Among these skills Hart suggests:

- time management
- organisation of materials
- computer use
- information handling
- online searching
- writing (Hart 1998, p.3)

The need to manage one's time effectively was discussed earlier, particularly the need to establish clear stopping rules i.e. to accept that a piece of research has been completed in terms of its declared objectives despite the fact that many issues may not have been resolved. As noted earlier "fitness for purpose" must be our watchword.

The organisation of materials is essential if one is to obtain the maximum return from the scrutiny of existing sources of information. In the absence of a structured approach it is likely one will overlook relevant materials and/or mislay or misplace important references. Few things are more frustrating than locating ideas or insights critical to one's argument only to find one cannot trace the origin through a correct citation. We return to this issue later.

Computer use, information handling and online searching are skills that most students will have acquired some time before they are required to undertake a substantial research project. Indeed many will have learnt the skills in school or in their first year in higher-education. Successful online searching depends upon both familiarity with computers and information handling skills. Given the importance of the electronic media further advice on online citation is offered later, as are some suggestions on writing up. First, however, we must look at a topic central to any literature review – the correct identification and acknowledgement of the work of others.

Citation

The correct identification of published materials is a vital element of all scholarly research. In 1950 the British Standards Institution (BSI) published a set of 'Recommendations' (BSI 1629) which are based on a scheme prepared by the International Federation of the National Standardising Associations (ISA), which was the forerunner of the International Organisation for Standardisation (ISO). The current version of BS 1629 is dated 1989 and is complemented by BS 5605: 1990 "Recommendations for Citing and Referencing published material". BS 5605 was developed to provide a concise guide "... sufficient only to identify a source unambiguously and to indicate its nature,..." as such it does not cover special cases nor the degree of detail which is described in BS 1629. Citations to unpublished documents are the subject of a separate publication BS 6371: 1983. However, for all practical purposes BS 5605: 1990 should be your source of first choice if it is necessary to look this far for a reliable authority.

The latter statement introduces an important issue for the researcher. As we have noted on several occasions, knowledge generally grows by a process of accumulation rather than a cataclysmic insight. The issue for the researcher is: "Can I depend on the authority of earlier researchers or do I need to consult the original sources myself?" For the purposes of this chapter I felt it necessary to review the British Standards myself, as this is the recognised authority on the subject. Accordingly, you should be able to depend on the advice given here as being both authoritative and correct. This also applies to recognised texts such as Hart or Jankowicz or the guidelines published by libraries or academic departments for the information of students. For example, students at Nottingham Trent University have access to an excellent pamphlet "Citing References: a guide for users", compiled by David Fisher and Terry Hanstock for Library and Information Services. This guide is also based on the BSI recommendations and follows them precisely and accurately but, to convince myself of this, I referred back to the original source. Satisfied by the authority of Fisher and Hanstock as a reliable source much of the following material is based directly on their excellent pamphlet. In addition, the appendix attached to this chapter is taken directly from their pamphlet and you'll find a website reference which will allow you to access the full text of the pamphlet as well as a number of other useful guidelines prepared for student use.

The point I am making is that it would be futile to keep reinventing the wheel by checking out every reference cited by an earlier researcher whose work you are using yourself. On the other hand you shouldn't assume that publication means a source is correct - it does not! As the Founding Editor of the *Journal of Marketing Management,* and a reviewer for a number of other leading academic journals, I am conscious that many articles are padded out with numerous references, which it is highly unlikely the author has actually consulted themselves. For example, Fisher and Hanstock acknowledge their indebtedness to several sources for their advice on citing electronic publications - the International Organisation for Standardisation (1997), Cross and Towle (1996), and Li and Crane (1993 and 1997). You will not find these sources cited at the end of the book because I have not accessed them. Further, the interpretation of these original sources is that of Fisher and Hanstock and it is them I am citing as my authority. If you revert to Li and Crane and find them to have been misreported then I will have compounded the error by depending on an interpretation of their work.

So what is a poor researcher to do?

1. Select your own authorities with care - remember the authors of established texts will have had their work scrutinised by many other experts.
2. Identify one or two of the key references cited by your authority and check them out for yourself. (Nearly every major Marketing book will refer to Ted Levitt or Michael Porter somewhere-you should read these anyway!)
3. Don't pad out your own literature review or bibliography with second-hand references. However, as I did, it is quite acceptable to indicate your source drew on another's work. If the reader of your work wants to check them out they will have to go back to your source to find them.

If your interpretation differs from that of your chosen authority then you will have to decide whether you can depend on it or not for the interpretation of other sources cited. Perhaps the first thing to do is analyse what is the basis for the difference of opinion, and whether two or more interpretations are acceptable, and on what grounds. If you decide they are, you should advise your reader of the fact as they, too, may wish to check out the original source and the authority's interpretation of it before deciding for or against your analysis. Secondly, you should look at another major source cited by your authority and see if you agree or disagree with their interpretation. If you don't agree then you must decide whether to drop your authority in favour of another whose views match more closely with your own i.e. you believe that your interpretation would coincide with the authority if you were to consult all the sources which they depend upon, as I have with Fisher and Hanstock; or decide there is room for more than one interpretation, and make this clear in your own write up.

Fisher and Hanstock give three reasons why we cite references:

1. to acknowledge debts to other writers.
2. to demonstrate the body of knowledge upon which your research is based.
3. to enable all those who read your work to locate your sources easily.
   (Fisher and Hanstock 2002)

They also distinguish between Citing and Referencing when they define *citing* as "the way a writer refers from the text to the source used (i.e. the References)", and *referencing* as "the process of creating a bibliographic description of each source". For all practical purposes the two are inextricably inter-related.

On the assumption that you have heeded the advice offered, and conducted an adequate review of the literature along the lines suggested, it is important that you report accurately what you have done and give appropriate recognition to the work of others. Hart identifies several reasons why failure to cite sources properly may result in your work been thrown into question, namely:

> *falsification* misrepresenting the work of others
> *fabrication* presenting speculations as if they were facts
> *sloppiness* not providing correct citations
> *nepotism* citing references of colleagues that are not directly related to your work.
> *plagiarism* the act of knowingly using another person's work and passing it off as your own. (Hart 1998, p.181)

While all these faults are to be avoided, and can be through accurate record-keeping, acts of plagiarism are most likely to have serious consequences. While carefully reporting the work of others will be seen as true scholarship, copying or lightly rewriting another's work without attribution can lead to legal action for infringement of intellectual property rights. Academic bodies apply severe penalties, including expulsion, to persons found guilty of plagiarism and are taking increasingly stringent measures to detect it. (Given the case of downloading information from online sources and cutting and pasting this into what purports to be an original work, software has been developed to detect such infringements.) The full and correct citation of references is the best way of keeping out of trouble.

There are two basic approaches to citing references:

1. By numbering them sequentially.
2. By citing the author and date of publication - known as the Harvard system.

Both systems have their advantages (and disadvantages) and are widely used. As there are no clear cut rules for their use it is important to check out the preferences of the person or organisation for whom the literature review is been written. Course handbooks, publishers' guidelines and academic journals invariably contain detailed guidelines on how to cite references.

Of the two main approaches to citing references - the Harvard, or author/date, and Numeric systems, the Harvard system is the more popular of the two and is most widely used in business and management studies. Personally, I prefer this because experience shows that if you omit a reference or wish to insert an additional one it is far easier to add another Harvard reference to an alphabetically organised bibliography than it is to re- number all references in your work that follow a change. Fortunately, auto footnoting has largely eliminated this problem. However, the choice may not be up to you as most institutions and publishers have a preferred house style, and you will have to use it. It follows that you need to be familiar with both systems.

Both the Harvard and Numeric systems satisfy the three criteria given by Fisher and Hanstock (2002) cited earlier. The fact that both continue to be used confirms that both have advantages and disadvantages. The main distinction between them lies in the method of citation: the references are identical apart from the position of the date. In this book I am using the Harvard system so that every time I refer to a source I specify the name of the author(s) and the date of the publication I am referring to. If I were using the Numeric system then every reference of whatever kind would be numbered sequentially - hence the editing problem if you leave one out! An advantage of the Harvard system is that you know immediately whose work has been referred to and when it appeared; following the Numeric system you have to look at the footnote and/or the bibliography at the end of the paper, chapter, book or whatever. On the other hand when writing a literature review you may well come across different schools of thought or multiple authorities in which case the flow of your argument would be broken if you have to list, say, 15 different authors and dates as opposed to stating " numerous authors 2-17 have agreed that...."

At several places in this and Chapter 3 we have argued against reinvention. In this spirit that we could see little merit in writing our own set of guidelines for Citing References and, with the permission of David Fisher at Nottingham Trent University, an Appendix is attached to this article which a reproduces the relevant pages in the article to which we have made frequent reference.

Getting started

We have already touched on some issues regarding the scope of a literature review and advise that this should be proportionate to the task in hand. That required for a term essay will be significantly less than that required for an honours or masters dissertation. In the case of a research degree such as an M Phil, equivalent to one year's full-time study, then up to 50 per cent of the thesis could be appropriate. For a PhD depending on whether primary research is to be undertaken, then anything from 30 to maybe 80 per cent might be expected. Irrespective of the time available, the quality of the final outcome will depend greatly on how efficient and effective you are in selecting and synthesising the material considered in your review.

At several places we have cited Hart (1998) as an authoritative source. His book *Doing a Literature Review* comprises 230 pages of analysis and advice covering all aspects of the process. It is obvious that here we can only cover the basics and cannot deal in depth with some of the more philosophical issues involved in doing research. That said, in this section we offer some advice on several topics which are the subject of separate chapters in Hart's book, namely:

selecting sources
analysing arguments
organising at your material

Selecting sources

As suggested earlier, perhaps the best place to start a review of a topic is with a recent and authoritative textbook from a well-known publishing house. While publishers are not infallible and can publish flawed work, they generally use expert reviewers to appraise proposals and manuscripts. In consequence, books carrying the imprint of a major publisher such as Butterworth Heinemann, Sage or Thomson Learning are likely to be of high quality, and the authors are likely to have identified the main strands of research and their proponents. For the reasons given earlier, you should check out at least some of the major sources yourself.

In doing so you will find that earlier researchers built upon the work of others too, and it can be worthwhile and rewarding to check out the authorities cited by the current authorities. For example, in the mid-1990s I attended a meeting of the newly formed Technology and Innovation Special Interest Group (SIG) of the American Marketing Association as I had written my own doctoral dissertation on the adoption of new industrial products at the Harvard Business School in the late 1960s. At this meeting my younger colleagues expressed great enthusiasm for what they considered the most pressing research issues of the time, while I experienced a strong feeling of deja vu. Eventually, I ventured to suggest that Ray Corey had described, investigated and explained the phenomenon under discussion. This contribution was greeted with a blank looks and a chorus of "whose Ray Corey?". Ray Corey was a distinguished professor at Harvard Business School for many years in the field of what was then called industrial marketing, and is now referred to as business-to-business marketing. During the early 1950s Ray undertook research into the problems experienced by firms introducing radically new materials, like aluminium and plastics, to the market for the first time. His findings were published by the Harvard Business School Press in 1956 in a book called *New markets for new materials*. In my view the insights provided by the in-depth case studies he reports are as relevant today as they were then. The great pity is that few if any are aware of them. Indeed many researchers would not bother to consider any reference more than 10 years old as a matter of principle. In a subject like physics this may be an acceptable strategy. In the social sciences it can be disastrous and lead at best to much unnecessary rediscovery and reinvention and, at worst, to incorrect deductions.

A popular subject, Relationship Marketing is a case in point. Many leading American academics believe this to have been "discovered" by Professor Fred Webster in a seminal article entitled "The changing role of marketing in the corporation" published in the *Journal of Marketing* (1992). This is indeed a very important reference and one which anyone doing a literature review on relationship marketing should read for themselves. But, the Scandinavian school has been researching the issue for more than 50 years prior to this and also deserves recognition, although Webster appears to have been unaware of their existence.

Put simply, if you stick to the most recent and frequently cited sources it is unlikely you will attract adverse comment from those appraising your work. On the other hand it is quite likely you will overlook the earlier important contributions, and so be guilty of reinvention. Less likely, but much worse, you may perpetuate a mistaken interpretation of earlier research. It is for this reason you must check out landmark studies yourself, and not depend on second hand interpretations of them. It is a well-known fact that repetition can lead to distortions - start a rumour among your friends and see what happens once it has been in circulation for a while!

Finally, there's always the possibility that you might discover something overlooked or misinterpreted by those who have researched the topic before you. On such discoveries are academic reputations built!

When referring to Ray Corey's work earlier we used terms that described the content of research - description, investigation and explanation. Most research studies will cover all three but some may consist solely of description, and some of description and explanation. When citing references it is important to identify clearly what aspect of the source you are reporting. Usually a researchers' description or definition of a phenomenon or topic will predetermine the working hypothesis, which prompts an explanation and/or the need for new research leading to an explanation. As noted in Chapter 1 the selection and definition of a research issue or problem, the choice of research methodology, and selection of analytical techniques may all affect the outcome of a research project. It follows that you need to select approaches that are congruent with one another if you are to avoid mistaken outcomes.

At several places we have made the point that undertaking a preliminary literature review is an integral part of developing a research proposal. It follows that if our proposal has been accepted we will already have:

1. come up with a tentative title.
2. developed a list of key words.
3. identified some key sources.

This will be of considerable help when we set about the literature review proper. However, we still need to decide where to start. Different authors have different preferences. Our own is to follow the sequence:

1. Textbooks.
2. Specialist encyclopaedias and handbooks.
3. Journals.
4. Databases.

This sequence differs somewhat from that suggested by Sharp and Howard (1996) who propose that you start with relevant theses or dissertations in the library of your institution. In my view, this may lead to confusion as Theses and Dissertations tend to be highly focused and specific, and so may not give a broad enough overview of the topic in which you are interested i.e. other authors will have selected that literature that is directly relevant to their specific topic, which is unlikely to be the same as your own unless you are replicating their study.

My own preference is for what I term "successive focusing" (se p.8) where you start with a broad view and narrow this down by applying increasingly selective criteria and definitions so as to include or exclude material.

However, Sharp and Howard include a number of very useful flow charts for researching particular categories of material such as books, articles, recent references etc and you should refer to their pages 88-96 for advice on this.

It is a well-known fact that knowledge and publication have been growing exponentially in recent years. In the UK the introduction of the Research Assessment Exercise (RAE) as an input into the formula for allocating public funds to Higher Education institutions has resulted in increased pressure on academics to publish scholarly research. The result has been an enormous increase in the number of specialist publications, such as journals and Proceedings of conferences, not to mention posting work in progress on the Internet. Inevitably, this welter of publications has led to a decline in the incremental value of many marginal contributions (know among academics as "slicing the salami"!).

One of our reasons for recommending that you start with text books and encyclopaedias is that the experts that have written them should have identified the most relevant sources when compiling their work. If this is so your task should be to see if anything has emerged since the primary authorities were published, and update them accordingly. As well as restricting the volume of material to consider, you should also be much better-informed and able to discriminate between the relevant and less or irrelevant sources.

For journal articles an important criterion is the frequency with which earlier research is quoted by other researchers. This is best determined by consulting a citation index, which provides just this kind of information. (Sharp and Howard (1996) discuss citation relevance trees and using citation indexes at pages 79-83.) However, frequency is not the sole criterion, and we have already warned that some authors merely cite sources without having consulted them on the grounds that they appear in other people's research. Accordingly, you should pay particular attention to those citations which contain some detail of the source being reviewed.

Surfing the Internet and using online databases is a topic in its own right and cannot be gone into here. However advice on citing electronic references is given in the Appendix and there is an extended discussion of research using electronic methods in Chapter 5.

Having identified potential sources, the first thing to do is read the abstract to decide how closely the source matches the research question that interests you. Taking those that appear to bear directly on your subject matter you must now analyse the key arguments contained in them. Equally important, you must keep a careful record of everything you may wish to include in your final write up.

Taking notes

Traditionally, the recommended way to take and keep notes has been to use note cards three by five or four by six inches in size. Nowadays, with the widespread availability of online sources, from which you can cut and paste, hand held scanners which can hold 1000 or more pages of A4 text, and hand-held computers with usable keyboards, you may decide that writing notes and then transcribing them is an unnecessary extra step in data entry. While trained in research methods long before the availability of such modern aids to note-taking I do make use of them, but I still prefer to use the traditional note card for the majority of my preliminary research. Be warned, this may just be a function of my advanced years and familiarity with the traditional methods. On the other hand I can still usually find information about my engagements from my hard copy Diary much more quickly than most of my colleagues with the latest model of upmarket PDA. I have also mastered a voice-recognition program and so can dictate my notes direct onto my PC as I'm doing at this moment.

Among the reasons I, personally, prefer to take handwritten notes is that I find it makes me think much more carefully about what I want to record, and how to record it, than simply highlighting the passage then downloading it to my computer's memory. When I do this I invariably find that I have to re-review the verbatim transcript to decide what idea prompted me to save it in the first place. Remember, a literature review is not a list of quotations from identified authorities, but your interpretation of their work. Verbatim quotations are important but you will still need to justify your selection and use of them.

Despite the author's preference for handwritten notes, it is accepted that many people will have much superior word processing skills. If you have, then direct data entry may well save you time and duplication of effort. Indeed, software has been developed specifically for the purpose of classifying and synthesizing notes into a logical and coherent structure. If you do keep your notes in an electronic format then remember to back up your files frequently, and keep a duplicate copy quite separate from your normal work place.

However you decide to keep your records, the first thing to do every time you access a source is to make an accurate record using the guidelines for citations given in the appendix. At first sight this may seem a potential waste of time as what appeared to be highly relevant turns out to be useless and to be discarded. This is what research is all about. Negative outcomes are just as valuable and relevant as positive ones. Just think of the time you can save later researchers following your foot steps (or footnotes!) if you report that you are aware of P. Guff (2000) in their "A load of drivel", *Journal of Obscurity*, Volume 1, Number 1, and found it useless.

By the time you embark on your first serious research project it is likely you will have had several years' experience of taking notes and developed a system that suits you. If it does, and is both efficient and effective from your point of view, then it probably conforms to the advice to be found elsewhere, and you shouldn't think of changing it if it suits you. However, if you feel your note-taking is not as good as it might be then the following tips may be useful.

1. Develop a search plan. In the course of writing a research proposal you will have identified what appear to be the major themes and key issues related to your topic. Most, if not all of these, will have been reduced to keywords and it is these that you should guide your search.

2. Don't economise on note cards. When it comes to organise and structure your literature review it will be much simpler to do this if you prepared a separate card for each key word for each source. The first card in each set is the source card itself so you will have prepared one for P. Guff as soon as you set out to read his article. If nothing of use is found then record this on the source card. Otherwise, prepare additional cards each identified as P. Guff (2000) and the key word, which the note addresses. Like a paragraph, a source card should only deal with one major idea.

3. Summarise in your own words. Only quote verbatim when you wish to communicate the precise viewpoint of your source to act as a peg on which to hang similar arguments, as an endorsement or reinforcement for a particular line of argument, or as a counterpoint to an alternative school of thought. (Remember to cite the precise page location of verbatim quotes so you, and others, can verify them if necessary).

4. Keep to the point. In the course of any research you're bound to turn up all kinds of interesting information which is new to you. If it does not relate directly to the topic in hand, ignore it.

At several points we have indicated that research or inquiry involves three main elements - description, investigation and explanation. *Description* is the essential first step in any piece of research for it defines and delineates precisely what the object or phenomenon to be researched is, and is not. Once something has been described it becomes possible to classify it, and assign it to a category with similar attributes or properties so that we can establish whether, and to what degree, it conforms with or departs from what is already known about that category. This process of comparison and classification is *investigation* as a result of which our understanding is enhanced so that we may *explain* better the original research question and possibly extend and improve our understanding of the larger issues to which it is related. Much of this process involves what Hart (1998) terms "argumentation analysis" - the subject of Chapter 4 in his book.

As Hart explains, the purpose of argument is to persuade others to accept a particular point of view by a "providing sufficient reason (or evidence) for the point to be accepted by others " (p.80). The nature of the argument, and the principles relevant to it, is far too large and complex a subject for a chapter of this kind. Perhaps the main point to emphasise here is that the social sciences deal with much more soft or qualitative data "based on supposition, inference and assertion" (Ibid, p.80) than do the physical sciences. Such data, much of it based on perception rather than objective measurement, calls for particular care and techniques in its interpretation. Hart's chapter provides an excellent overview of some of the major issues and you should refer to this for detailed explanation and advice.

Organising your material

You will have gathered by now that while the product of research - an assignment, term paper, dissertation, article, book etc - appears to be linear in nature, with a clear beginning, middle and end, in fact it is the outcome of a largely circular process. Thus, one has to undertake a preliminary literature review to establish the existence of research issue, and then one has to undertake a more extensive literature review to illuminate the issue in greater detail. Similarly, in order to research a literature we need a framework and structure to guide our selection and analysis. Then, having gathered data we need to arrange, analyse and synthesise the material so as to present a clear and structured account of our findings, and the conclusions we have drawn from them. It is largely about analysis and synthesis.

According to Hart (p.110) "analysis is the job of systematically breaking down something into its constituent parts and describing how they relate to each other - it is not random dissection but a methodological examination". Clearly, the purpose of analysis is to enhance our understanding of the factors or variables, which make up an object or phenomenon and the ways in which they relate to and/or interact with one another.

By contrast, synthesis involves "rearranging the elements derived from analysis to identify relationships or show main organising principles or show how these principles can be used to make a different phenomenon" (Hart p.111).

Analysis is essentially objective in character and follows defined procedures using well-known and extensively validated techniques such as content analysis. By contrast, synthesis is often creative and requires one to look beyond the known and accepted relationships to see if one can come up with new and more powerful explanations of the phenomenon in which one is interested.

For many years I have argued that Marketing, like most other professions such as architecture, engineering, medicine etc. is a synthetic discipline in that it seeks to combine and integrate insights, ideas and knowledge from other social sciences into a comprehensive explanation of behaviour in the real world, in order that one may intervene in, and influence the behaviour or activity in which one is interested.

Synthetic explanations are invariably more powerful and those provided by the elements integrated by the synthesis. For example, Philip Kotler (2000) in his now a standard text on *Marketing Management*, points out that different social sciences have quite different explanations of Buyer Behaviour and distinguishes at least four:

1. The Marshallian economic model.
2. The Pavlovian learning model.
3. The Freudian psychoanalytic model.
4. The Veblenian social-psychological model.

The key features of these four models are as follows:

The Marshallian economic model postulates that buying decisions are the result of "rational" and conscious economic calculations designed to maximise the buyer's utility or satisfaction. Industrial or Organisational Buyer Behaviour is usually believed to be of this type.

Pavlov's learning model contains four central concepts: drive, cue, response and reinforcement. Drives may be inherited or learnt - hunger is a basic physiological drive, ambition is learnt - but they are usually latent or passive until stimulated by a cue. In the case of hunger, this may be internal (being physiologically hungry) or external (the sight or smell of food), but either way response is called for. Only if the outcome is satisfactory will reinforcement occur and the new learned behaviour become habitual. Or, as Pavlov would have termed it, a conditioned response.

The **Freudian psychoanalytic model** is concerned with the subconscious motivations which direct and condition Behaviour.

Finally, the **Veblenian model** proposes that man's attitudes and behaviour are conditioned by the norms of the social groupings to which he belongs: culture, sub culture, his social class, his reference groups and his family affiliations.

Each of these models, however, provides only a partial explanation and the real world buying decision would seem to be a composite of conscious and subconscious reactions to a variety of stimuli - some objective, measurable and "rational"; others subjective, difficult to quantify and often dismissed as "irrational". In turn, the reactions or responses will be the product of a host of social and cultural influences reflecting the decision makers' background, upbringing and current affiliations.

The relative importance of all these influences will vary considerably, depending upon the novelty of the situation to the buyer, and the degree of risk associated with the decision.

From the foregoing very abbreviated summary, it should be clear that a working model of Buyer Behaviour will have to contain far more variables than any of the single disciplinary explanations, which suppress or assume away the complications of real life.

While this example is based on a marketing issue, very similar cases are to be found in other areas of business and management research. Business and management problems are often complex and 'messy' involving multiple 'players', influences and inputs with the result that single disciplinary explanations are unlikely to be adequate. It follows that, to avoid the sin of re-invention touched on earlier, one must cast one's net widely in seeking to establish what is already known about the research questions implicit in the research issue.

So, now you have consulted a large number of sources and assembled a copious collection of notes. In the process it is quite likely that you will experience at least two emotions. First: " Is there no end to the information that has some bearing on the subject? " And, second, a feeling of deja vu -

while the ideas presented in most research papers are treated as if they were new they seem to be only marginally different from other work which you have already reviewed.

To deal with the first problem you must constantly and consistently apply your definition of the perceived boundaries of your research topic, and ruthlessly exclude or discard anything that falls outside the boundaries.

As you defined these boundaries before you started your detailed search, it may well be that you have to revisit and refine your definitions and boundaries. In doing so you need to explain and justify your decisions. But, in doing so, you will anticipate and address the question every researcher dreads "Why didn't you...?" While those sitting in judgment of your work may not agree with your reasons or arguments, they should assess it against the criteria and definitions you have proposed. Provided these are not fundamentally flawed, or fly in the face of reason, then you should be able to achieve a satisfactory grade even though your examiner holds an opposing view.

The obverse of too much information is too little. However, it is not uncommon to find that having assembled an impressive list of sources the more one reads them the less and less the value added. The problem now is when to discontinue a search for the mother lode. As a qualified Prospector- you have been told how to identify the most likely sources - you should be able to decide when to stop digging. Of course, there is a risk that you will miss the discovery of a lifetime, but the laws of probability should tell you that such discoveries in research occur about as often as winning the jackpot on the lottery.

In field research, the rule of thumb is that beyond 15 exploratory interviews you are unlikely to identify any radically new issues. So, perhaps the same rule applies to the vast majority of literature reviews, and you should break off the search and not go beyond 15 citations on a major research theme, unless you are continuing to uncover worthwhile additional information.

An excellent summary of the steps involved in searching existing sources of information or *secondary research* is provided by Stewart in Table 4.1.

Writing Up

Once we have reached the point of diminishing marginal returns the time has come to impose structure on our raw materials and write them up. Anyone who has had to write anything knows that the most difficult thing is to get started. In the case of our literature review, however, we have a head start as we began by defining its scope, and the themes or issues we expected to encounter. Inevitably, some may not have materialised or seem unimportant, while others will have emerged that demand attention. That said, we should have a fairly good idea of what the finished article should look like.

Table   4.1. How to get started when searching published sources of secondary data

Step 1	Identify what you wish to know and what you already know about your topic. This may include relevant facts, names of researchers or organisations associated with the topic, key papers and other publications with which you are already familiar, and any other information you may have.
Step 2	Develop a list of key terms and names. These terms and names will provide access to secondary sources. Unless you already have a very specific topic of interest, keep this initial list long and quite general.
Step 3	Now you re ready to use the library. Begin your research with several of the directories and guides listed in Appendix 5A. If you know of a particular relevant paper or author, start with *the Social Science Citation index (or Science Citation Index)* and try to identify papers by the same author, or papers citing the author or work. At this stage it is probably not worth while to attempt an exhaustive search. Only look at the previous two or three years of work in the area, using three or four general guides. Some directories and indices use a specialised list of key terms or descriptors. Such indices often have thesauri that identify these terms. A search of these directories requires that your list of terms and descriptors be consistent with the thesauri.
Step 4	Compile the literature you have found; is it relevant to your needs? Perhaps you are overwhelmed by information. Perhaps you have found little that is relevant. Rework your list of key words and authors.
Step 5	Continue your search in the library. Expand your search to include a few more years and one or two more sources. Evaluate your findings.
Step 6	At this point you should have a clear idea of the nature of the information you are seeking and sufficient background to use more specialised resources.
Step 7	Consult the reference librarian. You may wish to consider a computer-assisted information search. The reference librarian can help with such a search but will need your help in the form of a carefully constructed list of key words. Some librarians will prefer to

produce their own list of key words but it is a good idea to verify that such a list is reasonably complete. The librarian may be able to suggest specialised sources related to the topic. Remember, the reference librarian cannot be of much help until you can provide some rather specific information about what you want to know.

Step 8 If you have had little success or your topic is highly specialised, consult the *Directories, Directory Information Guide, Guide to American Directories, Statistics Sources, Statistical Reference Index, American Statistics Index. Encyclopaedia of Geographic Information Sources*, or one of the other guides to information listed in Appendix 5A. These are really directories of directories, which means that this level of search will be very general. You will first need to identify potentially useful primary directories, which will then lead you to other sources.

Step 9 If you are unhappy with what you have found or are otherwise having trouble, and the reference librarian has not been able to identify sources, use an authority. Identify some individual or organisation that might know something about the topic. The various *Who's Who* publications, *Consultants and Consulting Organisation Directory. Encyclopaedia of Associations, Industrial Research Laboratories in the United States* or *Research Centres Directory* may help you identify sources. Don't forget faculty at universities, government officials, or business executives. Such individuals are often delighted to be of help.

Step 10 Once you have identified sources you wish to consult, you can determine whether they are readily available in your library. If they are not, ask for them through interlibrary loan. Interlibrary loan is a procedure whereby one library obtains materials from another. This is accomplished through a network of libraries that have agreed to provide access to their collections in return for the opportunity to obtain materials from other libraries in the network. Most libraries have an interlibrary loan form on which relevant information about requested material is written. Interlibrary loans are generally made for some specific period usually one to two weeks. Very specialised, or rare, publications may take some time to locate, but most materials requested are obtained within a couple of weeks. If you would like to purchase a particular work, consult *Ulrich's International Periodicals Directory, Irregular Serials and Annuals: An International Directory,* or *Books in Print* to determine whether a work is in print and where it may be obtained. Local bookstores often have computerised or microform inventories of book wholesalers and can provide rapid access to books and monographic items.

Step 11 Even after an exhaustive search of a library's resources, it is possible that little information will be found. In such cases it may be necessary to identify experts or other authorities who might suggest sources you have not yet identified or consulted. Identifying authorities is often a trial-and-error process. One might begin by calling a university department, government agency, or other organisation that employs persons in the field of interest. Reference librarians often can suggest individuals who might be helpful. However, a large number of such calls may be necessary before an appropriate expert is identified.

Source: David W. Stewart (1984), *Secondary Research, Information Sources and Methods* (Beverly Hills. Calif: Sage Publications) pp. 20-22. © 1984 Sage Publications Inc. Reprinted by permission of Sage Publications, Inc. For reference to the appendix in the table, please consult original source.

In Chapter 7 Hart (op.cit.) discusses "writing the review" in considerable detail, and proposes that a review may be structured in one of at least three ways which he defines as:

1. Summative evaluation.
2. Analytical evaluation.
3. Formative evaluation

All three approaches (and combinations/permutations of them) contain three basic elements but the emphasis on these will vary according to the chosen structure. In essence these three basic elements are those discussed earlier, namely:

> **description** of what is known;
> **investigation** or analysis of this work;
> **explanation** of what you believe this means.

Where the emphasis is largely on description (summative evaluation) the thrust is on defining and establishing the existence of an issue or problem with suggestions for addressing it. Where the emphasis is on investigation (analytical evaluation) then one is concentrating on the nature of a problem, its cause and effect as a basis for action to solve it. Finally, an emphasis on explanation (formative evaluation) compares and contrasts the various points of view that exist on a problem as a basis for determining which is to be preferred and what might be to be done to confirm this.

To a considerable degree your choice of emphasis will be determined by that of the earlier work that you are reviewing. In turn, your own conclusions and recommendations may well propose a shift of emphasis in order to address the issues underlying your research problem. For example, earlier studies may be long on description but short on analysis, or vice-versa.

Irrespective of the structure you adopt, effective writing depends upon satisfying a number of criteria. While the topic of writing up is the subject of Chapter 14, at this juncture you should not be surprised that the first and most important criterion is to address "the needs of the intended audience." In other words, "Whom are you writing for?"

If it is a tutor or supervisor, to satisfy the requirements of formal qualification, then this is the primary audience, and your presentation should be tailored to their needs. If you are writing for publication, then the nature and positioning of the publication will have a major influence on the profile of its readership, and so upon the preferred style and structure. For example, an academic journal such as the *Journal of Marketing Research* emphasises substance over style and may be inaccessible to the vast majority of business people with an interest in marketing research. By contrast the *Harvard Business Review* emphasises style and presentation over substance with the result that the readers of JMR may see its approach and content as lacking rigour. As with any other product or service, the perceived value of your literature review will be determined by the needs and expectations of the reader. Hart (1998, 198) suggests the reader will be looking for evidence that:

1. you have a clear understanding of the topic;
2. you have identified all major studies related to your topic and discussed most of them;
3. you have developed, on the basis of your review, a clearly stated research problem;
4. you have drawn clear and appropriate conclusions from prior research;
5. you have established and described the various points of view related to your research topic;
6. you are proposing valid Recommendations based upon analysis of the information contained in your sources;
7. you have demonstrated that there is a genuine research issue that has to be addressed. (Adapted from Hart 1998, p.198)

In satisfying these criteria it will help greatly if:

1. You seek to gain and sustain the interest of your reader. Try to communicate why you feel your topic is important and why you are enthusiastic about it.
2. You have a clear beginning, middle and end. You should tell the reader what you're going to tell them, why, and in what manner. Tell them,

following the logic and structure you have laid out, and then tell them what you have told them by summarising the key arguments and conclusions/Recommendations drawn from your analysis.

3. Write clearly and coherently - there is a world of difference between scholarship and obfuscation. It is your task to make the complex clear, not to confuse the reader with obscure and obtuse references in the mistaken belief that the more difficult it is to understand the more erudite it must be.

4. Finally, try it out on an intelligent layperson with no pretensions to expertise on the topic to see if it passes the acid tests of being both understandable and interesting.

Summary

Remember, when writing you need to tell the reader what it is you intend to tell them (and how), then tell them in such detail as is necessary to get across your message, and then, to make sure, tell them what you've told them.

In this Chapter we began with a short discussion of the purposes of a literature review and argued that 'fitness for purpose' must be our watchword; i.e. we need to demonstrate a sufficient familiarity with prior work on the same topic to convince the reader that we are fully aware of its strengths and shortcomings, and that the research issue we are seeking to address is a real one. The scope of this review will depend significantly on the nature of the project, and the needs of the intended audience.

Given that a literature review is an account of previously published work of all kinds (including electronic), it is vital that we identify correctly the sources of the material referred to in our survey. To do so we must be familiar with the conventions for citing correctly such earlier work, and we discussed this topic in some detail. In addition, the Appendix attached to this article contains detailed advice on the use of the two main systems – the Harvard and Numeric systems – as well as the citation of electronic references.

Next, we looked at the selection of sources and offered some advice on an approach that we identified as 'successive focusing', beginning with established textbooks and progressing through specialist encyclopaedias and handbooks to journals and databases. Some advice on note taking and organizing the material collected was then given.

Finally, we looked briefly at how to set about writing up the fruits of our labour into a coherent and convincing statement on which to found our proposals for our own original research.

Given the completion of a literature review, and refinement of the research issue and the questions relating to it, the next step is to select the appropriate methodology – the subject of the next chapter. However, before turning to this it is important to stress that in some kinds of study, and especially grounded theory, one may collect data before reviewing the literature to see how the findings relate to prior work. Further, in that we do research to enhance our understanding of a problem, it may well be that in the course of collecting new information we become aware of work that was not included in the original literature review. If this is the case then it may be necessary to return to the literature in order to help position and interpret your new findings.

Recommendations for further reading

Barzun, Jacques and Graff, Henry F. (1977) *The Modern Researcher*, 3rd. Edition, New York: Harcourt Brace Jovanovich Inc
Takes the view that all research leads to a report whatever it may be called. Written from the perspective of a historian.

Blaxter, Loraine, Hughes, Christina and Tight, Malcolm (1996) *How to Research*, Buckingham: Open University Press
A widely used textbook on research methods courses. Better than average coverage of the preliminary stages. Good checklists and summaries, exercises etc.

Davis, Gordon B. and Parker, Clyde A. (1997) *Writing the Doctoral Dissertation*, Hauppauge, NY: Barron's Educational Series Inc.
As the title indicates the main emphasis is on doctoral dissertations. However, contains much practical advice for anyone developing a research project.

Gill, John and Johnson, Phil (1997) *Research Methods for Managers*, 2nd. Edition, London: Paul Chapman
Good general coverage.

Hart, Chris, (1998) *Doing a Literature* Review, London: Sage Publications Ltd.
A practical and comprehensive guide to researching, preparing and writing a literature review. Essential reading.

http://www.wisc.edu/writing/Handbook/ReviewofLiterature.html
Visit this site for useful advice

Irving, Ray and Smith, Cathy (1998) *No Sweat: The Indispensable Guide to Reports and Dissertations*, Corby: Institute of Management Foundation
Short, easy to read with lots of practical tips. 182 pages plus 5 useful Appendices

Jankowicz, A.D., (2000) *Business Research Projects*, 3rd Edition, London: Thomson Learning
The book deals with every stage of project work: from inception, reading-up, gathering and analyzing data, to presenting and writing your report. A first class guide to the subject.

Cont'd…

Robson, C. (1993) *Real-world Research: A Resource for Social Scientists and Practitioner Researchers,* (Oxford: Blackwell)
Exactly that!

Sharp, John A. and Howard, Keith, (1996) *The Management of a Student Research Project,* 2nd. Edition, (Aldershot: Gower)
An Open University book that offers much practical advice recognizing the limited resources available to most students.

Appendix

The following material is taken from David Fisher and Terry Hanstock, *Citing References,* 4th. Edition(rev) (2002) ©LIS Nottingham: Library and Information Services, Nottingham Trent University and is reproduced with the permission of David Fisher. The full text may be found at: *http://www.ntu.ac.uk/lis/library/citingrefs.htm* together with a number of other very useful guides specially prepared for the use of students. *http://www.ntu.ac.uk/lis/library/lisguides.htm*

Contents
Introduction
Methods of Citation - Harvard & Numeric
Quotations
Book references (Harvard)
Journal article references (Harvard)
Electronic publications (Harvard)
Other materials that can cause problems (Harvard)
Official publications
Legal references
References using the Numeric system
Citing references for items you have not actually read
Problems with dates
References

Introduction

This guide is based on the British Standards BS 1629 and BS 5605 (see British Standards Institution 1989 & 1990). However, the Standards do not cover all materials equally thoroughly and so, where necessary, we have developed our own guidelines based on what we consider to be best practice. This is particularly true in the case of the Internet and other electronic publications, as there is currently little consensus regarding how they should be referenced.

Why bother to cite references?
☐ To acknowledge debts to other writers
☐ To demonstrate the body of knowledge upon which your research is based
☐ To enable all those who read your work to locate your sources easily

The process of citing references consists of two interrelated parts:

a) **Citing** - the way a writer refers from the text to the sources used (i.e. the references)
b) **Referencing** - the process of creating a bibliographic description of each source. Put simply, this means the provision of a consistent description of the elements needed to identify a source: author, date, title, publisher, etc.

There are two main citation/reference systems - the **Harvard** (also known as the Name & Date) and the **Numeric**. You will see that this guide gives more space to the Harvard than the Numeric system. The reason for this is that a majority of departments at The Nottingham Trent University recommend the **Harvard** approach. However, if you need to use the **Numeric** system, the guide will also be of help because many of the **Harvard** referencing examples can be adapted to comply with the **Numeric** system by merely altering the place of the date in the reference. Don't worry about this now, it should all become clear when you start using the guide.

Don't panic! Reference citing is not that difficult. The main thing is to be consistent and don't mix the Harvard and Numeric approaches. If you work through the examples in this booklet you should be able to tackle most types of publication.

Good luck!

Methods of Citation

Let us look first at how you refer from your text to the description of the documents you are using. You need a way of identifying each source you use in your text.

You will see that the **Harvard** and **Numeric** styles of citation are very different from one another.

Harvard System

This is by far the most straightforward way of citing references, because all you need to do is mention the author and date of publication:

The work of Dow (1964), Musgrave (1968) and Hansen (1969) concluded...
It has been argued (Foster 1972) that the essential...
...the results of the survey were inconclusive (see Kramer 1989).

The person reading your work can then locate the full description of the item you have cited by going to the alphabetical list of references you have provided at the end of your report, essay or dissertation.

You may need to cite more than one work by the same author published in the same year. You can do so by adding letters after the dates, e.g.,

Dow (1964a) and Dow (1964b).

If you are giving exact quotations from other works you should identify the page numbers, e.g.,

Dow (1964, p. 28).

Insertion of extra citations is no problem as the references are listed in one alphabetical sequence.

Numeric System

Numbers are inserted into the text which refer to a numerical sequence of references at the end of your document, e.g.,

Dow[7] and Jenkins[9] , or Dow (7) and Jenkins (9).

You can also use numbers on their own, e.g.,

it can be argued[10]...it can be argued (10).

Page numbers can either be given in your list of references, or after the numbers in your text, e.g.,

Dow[7] p. 27 or Dow (7 p. 27).

Quotations

As indicated in the above examples, whether you are using the Harvard or Numeric system, you should provide page numbers if quoting from a document in your text. There are certain other generally accepted conventions which you might like to observe, these are described below. If you are only quoting a few words, it is usual to do the following:

Jones (1989, p. 114) has challenged, what he calls, the 'peculiar assertion' by Howard that the moon is populated by librarians.
Smith (1986, p. 4) has argued '...it is simply not possible to know everything...[but] it can be stated that some knowledge is attainable.'

The quotation forms part of your text and is indicated by enclosing it thus "or". The ... indicate omissions. Square brackets [ ] tell your reader you have added your own words to the quotation.

If you are quoting a longer passage, it is common practice for the whole quotation to be indented:

> Heresy requires the presence of at least a semblance of orthodoxy, a remaining vestige of an established paradigm, a doctrine or truth open to contradiction or challenge. Likewise transgression needs a limit, indeed each term evokes the other...(Smart 1993, p. 121).

The above conventions are not prescribed by national or international standards, but have been included because they are usually adhered to by the academic community.

Book References (Harvard System)

A reference is the description of the source you have used. In addition to the conventions for referencing a book by a single author, we include a variety of more complex examples of works that you might need to reference.

You should use the title-page rather than the cover of the book as the source of your reference. The order of the elements (including upper and lower case and punctuation) of the reference is:

AUTHOR, Date. Title. Edition. Place: Publisher. Numeration within item (if only a part is cited.)

Single Authors

DOW, D., 1964. *A history of the world*. 3rd ed. London: Greenfield.

If neither a place nor a publisher appears anywhere on the document then use:

(s.l.) to indicate place unknown (sine loco)
e.g., (s.l.): Greenfield

and

(s.n.) to indicate name unknown (sine nomine)

If you do not know the publisher, you are not going to know the place either, so you will have to do the following:

(s.l.): (s.n.) But try to find publisher if at all possible!

Multiple Authors

3 or less

CUTLER, T., WILLIAMS, K., and WILLIAMS, J., 1986.
Keynes, Beveridge and beyond. London: Routledge & Kegan Paul. (N.B. The order in which authors are given is that of the title page.)

4 or more

PEARCE, I.F., et al., 1976. *A model of output, employment, wages and prices in the UK* .Cambridge: Cambridge University Press.
Editors

CHESTER, D.N., ed., 1951. *Lessons of the British war economy*.
Westport: Greenwood Press.

Style Tips

You must highlight titles of books using: bold type, underlining, italics etc. You can enclose date in brackets if you wish e.g.,

DOW, D. ed. (1964)
ed. is a suitable abbreviation for editor.

Corporate authors

ASSOCIATION OF DIRECTORS OF SOCIAL SERVICES & COMMISSION FOR RACIAL EQUALITY, 1978. *Multi-racial Britain: the social services response.* London: Commission for Racial Equality.

Conferences

The first element of the reference should be the individual(s) or organisation responsible for editing the proceedings. If these cannot be traced, begin your reference with the name of the conference. If possible, you should include the place and date of the conference.

PAEPCKE, A., ed., 1992. *OOPSLA ' 92 conference on object-oriented programming systems, languages, and applications, Vancouver, 18-22 October, 1992.* New York: The Association for Computing Machinery.

CUNNINGHAM, S., ed., 1993. *Computer graphics: SIGGRAPH 93 conference proceedings, Anaheim, California, 1-6 August, 1993.* New York: The Association for Computing Machinery.

If you need to cite an individual paper within published conference proceedings, the author of the paper becomes the first element of your reference. You should also include the page numbers of the contributed paper. eg,

COOK, W. R., 1992. Interfaces and specifications for the smalltalk-80 collection classes. **In**: A. PAEPCKE, ed. *OOPSLA '92 conference on object-oriented programming systems, languages, and applications, Vancouver, 18-22 October, 1992.* New York: The Association for Computing Machinery, pp. 1-15.

"*In*" references

These are used when citing, for example, a chapter from an edited work. The format is similar to the conference paper reference above.

ROBINSON, E.A.G., 1951. The overall allocation of resources. *In*: D. N. CHESTER, ed., *Lessons of the British war economy.* Westport: Greenwood Press, 1951, pp. 34-57.

Theses and dissertations

McCARTHY, D.F., 1981. *Group representation in the plural society: the case of the poverty lobby.* Ph.D. thesis, Cambridge University.

Anonymous works

If the book does not appear to have an author use 'Anon'

ANON., 1964. *A history of radio.* London: Beacon Press.

Collaborative Works

Encyclopedias, dictionaries and other similar publications can be referenced by the title

The Europa World Yearbook, 1996. London: Europa Publications Ltd.

Journal Article References (Harvard)

The order of the elements (including upper and lower case and punctuation) of the reference is:

AUTHOR, Date. Article title. Journal title, volume (part), pages.

GREENFIELD, J., 1990. The Sevso Treasure: the legal case. *Apollo*, 132 (341), 14-16.

GOTT, R., 1989. Crumbs and the capitalists. *The Guardian*, 20th Jan, 21-22.

Multiple Authors - same rules apply as in **Book References (The Harvard System)**.

Do not worry if no author is mentioned in the source of your reference. All you need to do is as follows: eg,

ANON., 1989 . Obscenity or censorship. *The Economist*, 312 (5 August), 33-34.

Points to note

You should always indicate both volume and issue/part. In the above examples the numbers before the brackets refer to the volume and those inside the brackets to the part. eg,

e.g.   *Apollo*, 132 (341)

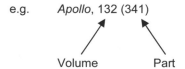

Volume   Part

Style Tips

You must **highlight the journal title** not the article title. Months can be abbreviated as in the above example, Jan for January.

You can add pp. before page numbers in journal references if you wish, but it is not necessary to do so.

Apollo,132 (341), pp.14-15.

Electronic Publications (Harvard)

An increasing amount of information is becoming available in a variety of electronic formats. At the time of writing, there is little agreement as to how such works should be referenced. This section is very much our own interpretation of what we consider to be best practice. Our ideas are based upon elements drawn from a variety of sources including: the International Organization for Standardization (1997), Cross and Towle (1996) and Li and Crane (1993).

Our own view is that electronic references are not so very different from the hardcopy formats discussed elsewhere in this booklet. The aim, as usual, is to provide sufficient information to enable others to trace the works you have consulted. As with all referencing, consistency is the key. The examples below, which are consistent with the Harvard style, are merely suggestions and are not intended to be prescriptive.

Internet Sources

Individual Works

The order of the elements (including upper and lower case and punctuation) of the reference is:

AUTHOR or EDITOR, year. Title [online]. Place of publication: Publisher. Available at: <URL> [Accessed Date].

The term publisher may seem a little odd when talking of Internet resources. It seems usual to regard the organisation responsible for hosting the pages as the publisher. However, we view the place of publication/publisher sections as optional. As long as you supply the URL then the site can be traced. The 'accessed date' means the date you visited the site. It is important to give this as pages and their locations change with great frequency, and you are informing your readers that the information was accurate at the date stated.

LIBRARY & INFORMATION SERVICES, 1997. *Electronic Resources: a subject guide to selected resources on the Internet* [online]. Nottingham: The Nottingham Trent University. Available at: http://www.ntu.ac.uk/lis/ eresources.htm[Accessed 22 November 2002].

DEFOE, D., 1995. *The fortunes and the misfortunes of the famous Moll Flanders* [online]. Champaign, Illinois: Project Gutenberg. Available at: http://promo.net/cgipromo/pg/t9.cgi?entry=370&full=yes&ftpsite=http://www.ibiblio.org/ gutenberg [Accessed 18 November 2002].

If a Web page does not appear to have an author, we would recommend referencing it by title.

ii Electronic Journal Articles

AUTHOR, year. Title. Journal Title [online], volume (issue). Available at: <URL>[Accessed Date]

If you cannot discern volume/issue details simply omit them. Indicating pages can be a problem as they are often not given in electronic journals, so we suggest omitting them, eg,

COYLE, M., 1996. Attacking the cult-historicists. *Renaissance Forum* [online], 1(1).

Available at: http://www.hull.ac.uk/english/ renforum/v1no1/coyle.htm [Accessed 18 November 2002].

HAMMERSLEY, M., and GOMM, R., 1997. Bias in social research. *Sociological Research Online* [online], 2(1). Available at: http://www.socresonline.org.uk/socresonline/2/1/2.html [Accessed 18 November 2002].

If you are quoting from an article in an electronic journal in the body of your text, you should provide as exact a location as possible. For instance, you could give the paragraph number (if available).

Electronic Mail

Discussion lists

AUTHOR, year. Title of message. Discussion list [online], day and month. Available at: email address or web address [Accessed Date].

SMITH, D., 1997. UK unemployment definitions/figures. *European-Sociologist* [online], 13 June. Available at: http://www.jiscmail.ac.uk/lists/European-sociologist.html [Accessed 18 November 2002].

THOMAS, R. 2002. Employment policy. *European-Sociologist* [online], 27 October. Available at mailto:angela.donaldson@ntu.ac.uk [Accessed 18 November 2002]

Both of the above approaches are acceptable ways of referencing emails from discussion lists.

Personal email

AUTHOR, (email address) year. Title of email, day and month. Email to: recipient's name (email address).

Referencing personal emails, like any personal correspondence, is probably not something you are likely to need to do very often. But, as most sources we have consulted cover them, we thought it would be remiss of us not to include them.

HIGGINS, J., (Jeff.Higgins@univ.ac.uk) 1996. *Email is fun*. 20 June. Email to: Peter Smith (Pete.Smith@amb.ac.uk).

CD-ROM and Online Databases

These formats cover a range of resources from bibliographic databases to full-text books and articles.

Bibliographic databases

DATABASE [type of medium, eg, online or CD-ROM]. (Inclusive dates). Place: Publisher.

ABI/INFORM [CD-ROM]. (1986 - April 1997). Louisville: UMI.

ECONLIT [CD-ROM]. (1969 - March 1997). (s.l.): Silverplatter.

or
ECONLIT [CD-ROM]. (1969 - March 1997). [London] : Silverplatter.

Both ECONLIT examples are correct. The first example indicates that no place of publication is listed on the CD ROM. The second example indicates that the place of publication is known but not listed on the CD ROM.

Electronic Journal Articles

Our recommendations are similar to those given for citing journal articles from the Internet. However, for sake of clarity, we thought it useful to create this separate section.

AUTHOR, year. Title. Journal title [type of medium], volume(issue), pages if given. Available from: database title [Accessed Date].

In the following examples I have used the same article from different databases to illustrate minor changes in your referencing:

EZARD, J., 1995. Lottery comes up to scratch in an instant. *The Guardian* [CD-ROM], 29 December, 4. Available from: The Guardian and The Observer on CD-ROM [Accessed 19 June 1997].

EZARD, J., 1995. Lottery comes up to scratch in an instant. *The Guardian* [online], 29 December. Available from: Reuter Textline [Accessed 19 June 1997].

As you can see, the main differences are changes in [type of medium] field and no page numbers on second reference (because Textline does not provide them).

Individual works

These could comprise works by individual authors, conference proceedings, encyclopedias, dictionaries and myriad other types of publications. Our general advice would be to follow the examples given for printed materials and add a [type of medium] field after the title.

ALBERS, J., 1994. *Interaction of color* [CD-ROM]. New Haven: Yale University Press.

ANDERSON, L., 1995. *Puppet motel* [CD-ROM]. New York: Canal Street Communications, Inc.
COOK, R.L., ed., 1995. *Computer graphics: SIGGRAPH 95 conference proceedings, Los Angeles, California, 6-11 August, 1995* [CD-ROM]. New York: The Association for Computing Machinery.

RANKY, P.G., [no date]. *An introduction to flexible automation, manufacturing and assembly* [CD-ROM]. Guildford: CIMware Ltd.

We have omitted [accessed date] as the content of such individual works is not going to change. However, if you think there is any possibility that the content of the electronic work you are citing may be subject to change, then it would be as well to include the accessed date.

Other Materials that can cause Problems!

British Standards Publications

BRITISH STANDARDS INSTITUTION, 1981. BS 5930: 1981. *Code of practice for site investigations.*

Patents

AZIZ, A., 1997. *Method and apparatus for a key management scheme for Internet protocols.* United States Patent Application 68-438. 27 May.

Published Music

Stravinsky, I., 1920. *Three pieces for clarinet solo.* London: Chester, Ltd.
Sound Recording

ELY, J., 1990. Drivin' to the poorhouse in a limousine. *In: Live at Liberty Lunch.* Stereo sound disk. New York: MCA, MCG 6113, side B, track 2.

Illustration

GOSSE, S., 1912. *The Garden, Rowlandson House.* Etching and aquatint. At: London: British Museum Department of Prints and Drawings. Register number 1915-27-41.

Films, Videos and Broadcasts

As a general rule, they should be cited by title, as they are usually collaborative ventures with no one person being the 'author' as such.

Father Ted, 1995. Episode 1, Good Luck Father Ted. TV, Channel 4. App.21.
Now Voyager, 1942. Film. Directed by Irving RAPPER. USA: Warner.
Crimewatch UK, 1993. TV, BBC1. Jan 21.

Official Publications

This section is divided into two parts: **UK Official Publications** and **European Union Publications**.

UK Official Publications

1. Government Publications

These can be treated in the same way as corporate authors, but should be prefixed with GREAT BRITAIN.
GREAT BRITAIN. School Curriculum and Assessment Authority, 1997. *The Parents guide to national tests...* London: The Stationery Office.

GREAT BRITAIN. Department for Education and Employment, 1996. *Setting targets to raise standards: a survey of good practice.* London: Department for Education and Employment

2. Official Reports of Parliamentary Debates (Hansard)

References to Hansard should include the following -

- abbreviation of House of Commons or House of Lords - HC or HL
- the abbreviation 'Deb'
- Parliamentary Session in round brackets
- volume number • the abbreviation 'col.'
- column number

HC Deb (1990-91) 195 col. 311
HC Deb (1990-91) 195, written answers col. 41
HL Deb (1990-91) 529 col. 111

3. Official reports of Parliamentary Debates in Standing Committees

References to Standing Committee proceedings should include the following
- the abbreviation 'Stg Co Deb'
- Parliamentary Session in round brackets
- Standing Committee identifying letter
- title of legislation under discussion
- the abbreviation 'col.'
- column number

Stg Co Deb (1980-81) Co E Finance Bill col. 46

4. Parliamentary Papers

Parliamentary Papers cover a variety of subjects and include Select Committee proceedings. Each House of Commons Paper has a serial number printed at the bottom left of the title page. House of Lords Papers are identified by a serial number in the same place but enclosed within round brackets.
References should include the following -
- abbreviation of the House - HC or HL
- Paper number
- Parliamentary Session

Repair and Maintenance of School Buildings HC 648 (1990-91)

1st Report of the Select Committee of The House of Lords on Televising the Proceedings of the House HL (213) (1984-85)

References to reports issued by Joint Committees of the House of Lords and the House of Commons should include both serial numbers followed by the Parliamentary Session

Joint committee on Statutory Instruments - Minutes of Evidence... HL 32, HC 15-vi (1981-82)

Command Papers

Command Papers are presented to Parliament 'by command of Her Majesty'. There are a number of different types, including –

- statements of government policy - often referred to as 'White Papers'
- discussion or consultation documents - often referred to as 'Green Papers', but note that not all Green Papers are published as Command Papers
- reports of Royal Commissions
- reports of Departmental Committees
- reports of tribunals or commissions of inquiry
- reports of permanent investigatory bodies such as the Law Commission and the Monopolies and Mergers Commission
- treaties and agreements with other countries or international organisations
- annual accounts

Command Papers are numbered sequentially regardless of Parliamentary session. The running number and prefix can be found at the bottom left-hand corner of the cover and title page. The prefix has changed over the years and care should be taken in citing this abbreviation correctly. The series of Command Papers published so far have been numbered as follows -

1st series [1]-[4222] 1833-1869
2nd series [C. 1] - [C. 9550] 1870-1899
3rd series [Cd. 1] - [Cd. 9239] 1900-1918
4th series [Cmd. 1] - Cmd. 9889 1919-1956
5th series Cmnd. 1 - Cmnd. 9927 1956-1986
6th series Cm. 1 - 1986-

References to Command Papers should include the following -

- title
- Command Paper number
- year of publication

Royal Commission on Local Government, 1966-1969
        (Cmnd. 4040, 1969)

European Union Publications

COM documents

COM documents are proposals for new legislation put forward by the European Union. The final versions are only published after much discussion with interested parties - earlier drafts are not generally publicly available.

References to COM documents should include the following –

- the title
- the last two digits of the year in round brackets
- the serial number
- the word 'final' to indicate that it is, in fact, the final version and not one of the earlier drafts.

Proposal for a Council directive on uniform procedures for checks on the transport of dangerous goods by road, COM (93) 965, final.

Secondary legislation

All references to secondary legislation should include the following –

- its institutional origin - Commission or Council
- its form - Regulation, Directive, Decision
- its unique number
- its year of enactment
- the institutional treaty under which it was made - EEC/EC, ECSC, Euratom.
- the date it was passed

Optional information can include the title of the legislation and a reference to the issue of the Official Journal of the European Communities in which it was published.

Regulations are normally cited with the name of institutional treaty, followed by the legislation number and the year of enactment.

Council Regulation (EC) No. 40/94 of 20 December 1993 on the Community trade mark

A shorter version would be cited as follows –

Council Regulation 40/94/EC

Directives and Decisions are cited by the year of enactment, the legislation number and then the institutional treaty.

Council Directive 90/365/EEC of 28 June 1990 on the right of residence for employees and self-employed persons who have ceased their occupational activity

Commission Decision 94/10/EC of 21 December 1993 on a standard summary form for the notification of a decision to award the Community eco-label

Shorter versions would be cited as follows –

Council Directive 90/365/EEC

Commission Decision 94/10/EC
An example of a comprehensive citation for an EEC regulation follows –

Council Regulation (EEC) No 2015/92 of 20 July 1992 amending Regulation (EEC) No 1432/92 prohibiting trade between the European Economic Community and the Republics of Serbia and Montenegro (OJ No L205, 22.7.1992, p 2)

Official Journal references

References to the Official Journal should include the following –

- OJ series -
  - L (Legislation)
  - C (Communicatons and Information)
  - S (Supplement)

- issue number
- date of issue
- page number eg,

    OJ No. C311, 17.11.93, p.6

Legal References

1. Acts of Parliament

Within the legal profession the generally accepted method of citing an Act of Parliament is by its short title:

Education Reform Act 1988

This should be sufficient when the Act is simply being mentioned in the text of an article or essay. However if featured in a bibliography or list of references, the Act's chapter number should be added for completeness.

Further and Higher Education Act 1992 (c.13)

Acts are numbered in sequence throughout the calendar year. Public General Acts are given arabic numerals. Local and Personal Acts are given lower-case roman numerals. N.B. Before 1 January 1963 a more complex system was in operation based on regnal years - the year beginning with the date of the Sovereign's accession to the throne - and the dates of the Parliamentary session, the period from the state opening of Parliament until the end of the session.
Education Act 1944 (7&8 Geo 6 c.31)

2. Parliamentary Bills

Each Parliamentary Bill has a serial number in the lower left hand corner of the title page. Formerly the number was enclosed in square brackets for Bills originating in the House of Commons and in round brackets for Bills originating in the House of Lords. House of Commons Bills are still numbered in this manner, but House of Lords Bills are now designated 'HL Bill' followed by a number without brackets.
References to Parliamentary Bills should include the following:-

- short title
- Parliamentary Session in round brackets
- its serial number. Note that a Bill is renumbered whenever it is reprinted during its passage through Parliament

    Education (Student Loans) Bill HC Bill (1989 - 90) [66]
    Further and Higher Education Bill HL Bill (1991 - 92) 27

3. Statutory Instruments
References to Statutory Instruments should include the following –
- short title
- the abbreviation 'SI'
- year of publication
- number

National Assistance (Assessment of Resources) Regulations 1992 SI 1992/2977

4. Law Reports
Every law report series has its own mode of citation. Citations for specific cases usually contain:-

- the abbreviation of the law report series
- the year the case was reported
- the volume number (where appropriate)
- the number of the page where the report starts
  [1989] 1 WLR 675

This refers to the case *Rayware Ltd v Transport & General Workers Union* which can be found in **volume 1** of the **Weekly Law Reports** for **1989** starting at **p 675**.

There are a number of guides to legal citations and abbreviations and these can be found in the Law Reports Citators sequence at the beginning of the Law Reports Collection.

References Using the Numeric System

An alternative method of creating references.

The only major difference between **Numeric** and **Harvard** references is the position of the date.

In the numeric system the date goes at the end of the monograph reference.
The order of the elements (including upper and lower case and punctuation) of the reference is:

Author. Title. Edition. Place: Publisher, Date. Numeration within item (if only a part is cited)

7. LAYDER, D. *Understanding social theory. London:* Sage, 1994.

The entries are numbered and run in numeric order. For the creation of particular types of reference e.g., for official publications, conferences, journals etc. follow the examples given for the **Harvard** system but alter the place of the date.

Journal article references are sometimes confusing so here is an example of a numeric one:

12. GREENFIELD, J. The Sevso Treasure: the legal case. *Apollo*, 1990, 132(341), 14-16.

Points to note

All references are numbered (e.g., 7 and 12 above) and are matched with the numbers used in the text.

Sometimes the author's name is not inverted as there is no need because the order is numerical and not alphabetical.

You will often see the terms **Ibid.** and **op. cit**. used in the references.

Ibid. means - in the same book or passage and is used when references are consecutive. eg,

1. DAWSON, J. *How to cite references*. London: Fictional Publications, 1922.
2. Ibid. p.24

Op. cit. means - in the work previously referred to **and** is used when other references intervene. e.g.,

1. DAWSON, J. *How to cite references*. London: Fictional Publications, 1922
2. JONES, K. *All your questions answered*. London: Fisher Publications, 1972
3. DAWSON, J. *Op. cit.* p. 26

The page references above refer to the books cited. If you think it is necessary you could also include the title of the book in the **Op. cit.** reference, eg,

DAWSON, *How to cite references*, Op. cit.

Citing References for Items you have not Actually Read

How to cite works referred to in textbooks etc.

Let's suppose you mention an article by Colin Smith which has been referred to by Gibbs and Carroll in their book *One hundred interesting things to do with a cited reference*, written in 1978. You have **not read** the actual article by Smith **only** what Gibbs and Carroll have written **about it**.

Using the **Harvard System**, you could do the following within your text:

The work of Colin Smith (see Gibbs and Carroll 1978, p.28) is very interesting...

In the references at the end of your work, you would give the full details of Gibbs and Carroll **(see main guide for examples)** but not Colin Smith because you have not read the article and your readers can find reference to it in Gibbs and Carroll.

Using the **Numeric System** you could do the following within your text:

The work of Colin Smith (see Gibbs and Carroll[1]) is very interesting...

In the numbered references at the end of your work give full details of Gibbs and Carroll at 1 (or whatever the number happens to be). See main guide for examples.

Problems with Dates

When looking in a book for a date to cite, chances are you will find more than one! You will always find a copyright date, but you may also have printing and different edition dates. Which one do you choose?

One of the reasons for giving references is so that others can locate works you have referred to, so you need to supply the date that most accurately reflects the particular version of the book you are using.

Editions - if you are using a 2nd or later edition of a book, always give the date of that edition, not the original publication date. The reason is quite simple - a new edition of a book indicates the text has been substantially revised (often with totally different page numbers from previous editions) and so you need to make it clear which edition you are referring to.

Reprints - as the name suggests, do not usually involve any change to the text, so it is normal practice to give the copyright (or originally published) date. However, if you believe that page numbers have changed during reprints and you have quoted pages in your work, then give printing date of version you are using to avoid any confusion.
If you cannot trace a date of publication you will have to put [no date] within your reference.

References

ANON., *Guide to Citing Internet Sources* [online]. Bournemouth: University of Bournemouth. Available at http://www.bournemouth.ac.uk/library/ using/guide_to_citing_internet_sourc.html [Accessed 25 November 2002]

BRITISH STANDARDS INSTITUTION, 1989. BS 1629: 1989. *Recommendations for references to published material.*

BRITISH STANDARDS INSTITUTION, 1990. BS 5605: 1990. *Recommendations for citing and referencing published material.*

INTERNATIONAL ORGANIZATION FOR STANDARDIZATION, 1997. *Excerpts from International Standard ISO 690-2* [online]. Ottawa, Canada: National Library of Canada. Available at: http://www.nlc-bnc.ca/iso/tc46sc9/standard/690-2e.htm [Accessed 25 November 2002].

SMART, B., 1993. *Postmodernity*. London: Routledge.

CHAPTER 5

Using the Internet to Find Information
Anne Foy

Synopsis
In recent years the Internet has become a useful repository of knowledge, enabling users to search for information on any topic at the click of a mouse button. However, the sheer size and nature of the Internet mean that researchers must be wary, and the following of a few simple guidelines can ensure that you utilise the Internet to its maximum potential, and to your maximum benefit.

Keywords
Internet; browser; search engines; metasearching; catalogues; databases; privacy; copyright

---

Introduction

A new medium has emerged over recent years which presents fresh research opportunities for researchers. The Internet has the potential to revolutionise the accessibility of information worldwide, but it also provides a potential survey population on an unprecedented scale. This chapter focuses on using the Internet for secondary research, with Chapter 12 looking at using the technology of the Internet to conduct primary research.

There is a difference between the Internet and the World Wide Web (WWW or Web). The Internet, or "Net" is the physical network of computers and cables which allow the Web to exist. The Web is the abstract information and media which are housed on the computers of the Internet. Thus, we talk of Internet connections and Internet Service Providers, because they are physical entities, i.e. the telephone line and the servers (host computers) of the company that is our Internet Service Provider (ISP, for example, AOL or Compuserve), as opposed to 'websites' made up of 'webpages' which are the information held upon these servers.

A brief history of the Internet

The Internet, that is the physical network of computers necessary to host the web, really became possible with two major breakthroughs in 1961 – the commencement of commercial production of the silicon chip, allowing computers to dramatically reduce in size and increase in speed, and the introduction by IBM of the 'Compatible Time Sharing System' into some of its computers, which allowed computers to be networked for the first time. (That is, more than one 'remote' terminal could access the same information on a central 'host' computer, effectively linking two computers together).

At the same time as these technical breakthroughs, the whole approach to computers and technology was undergoing a revolution. After the launch of Sputnik I in 1957 by the USSR, the Americans created ARPA, the Advanced Research Projects Agency. This agency was designed to make sure that America became sufficiently technologically advanced to keep ahead of the Russians, and in 1962 appointed John Licklider to head its Computer Research Programme. Licklider was a visionary who had already published his 'Galactic Network' theory, which foresaw a global network of computers accessible to all. Although still limited by technology – in 1965 Berkeley and MIT were linked via a telephone line, which revealed the telephone system was unable to cope with the data demands of programming of that era - by December 1969 ARPANET came into existence, with 4 computers at different sites, growing to 23 host computers in December 1971. By 1972, the origins of e-mail appeared, and during the early '70s a common language for the different networks to communicate was developed, TCP/IP (transmission control protocol/Internet protocol). Government departments and academic institutions were quick to see the potential of the emerging technologies and by the early 1980s networks from the UK and the rest of Europe were joining the original ARPANET. With the influx of new connections, in 1982 ARPANET took on the TCP/IP standard.

At this stage, it is considered that the Internet was born – that is, the physical network. The incredible growth of the medium saw several more milestones – in 1984 the number of host computers reached 1000, and Domain Name Servers were introduced. Domain names are the addresses used to navigate the web – for example Strathclyde University's domain name is strath.ac.uk. Really, these names are the front end of a numeric code assigned to each host computer, but names are a lot easier to remember than large number strings – also known as IP addresses. National Governments decided to back the growth of the new media, with the British government endorsing JANET (the Joint Academic Network) which linked British Universities, and the US creation of NSFNet (National Science Foundation Network). NSFNet in particular, boosted the growth of the Internet by not only supplying supercomputers, allowing a massive increase in the amount of traffic able to use the Internet, but also by making this use exclusive to research and education users. This had the added (and intended) effect of encouraging private Internet Service Providers to join the Net, which again massively increased the amount of traffic which could be supported. By 1989, the number of hosts had risen to 100,000, and to 300,000 a year later.

At this stage the Internet still carried very plain, text based information, with the first search engine, Archie, not being developed until 1990. The Internet was mainly a messenger service rather than the multimedia experience we know today. The creation of the Web itself began in 1989 with

Tim Berners–Lee and colleagues at CERN in Geneva, who not only invented the phrase World Wide Web, they also pioneered the use of HTML. HTML (Hypertext Markup Language) is the computer language which allows users to click on a word or picture and be transported to another web page or site, allowing the multiple layering of information which is now such a common aspect of multimedia. The introduction of HTML, and the new browser technology which utilised it (pioneered by Mark Andreesen's MosaicX in 1993, which he later commercially developed into Netscape), allowed a graphical interface which was infinitely more appealing than the previous text based model. By 1994 there were 3.2 million hosts and 3,000 web sites, and in a year the number of hosts doubled and the number of web sites increased by 22,000. By 1998, the number of hosts was 36.8 million, and the number of websites 4.2 million. (All of the preceding information was summarised from two main sources; R. T. Griffiths, 'History of the Internet' (accessed 2003) and Angus J. Kennedy *Rough Guide to the Internet* (2002)).

The new media of the Internet is still growing at an amazing rate. In December 1997, *Science* Magazine reported the size of the web as approximately 320 million pages, and in February 1999, *Nature* reported it as being about 800 million publicly available web pages (Lawrence and Giles 1998 and 1999). In 2000 the Censorware Project estimated that in a 24 hour period as many as 4,020,000 new pages were added, and 44,900,000 pages were changed on the web (19 May 2000) – and consider also that the size of a web page is not finite like a sheet of A4. (You can find current statistics for web size estimates at *http://wcp.oclc.org/*). Remember that more than one website can sit on a server, giving rise to the phenomenon of 'virtual hosting'. This makes it likely that traditional methods of web counting using IP addresses are underestimating the number of sites on the web.

Constant advances in technology are making the web more and more available to people – for example through GPRS and WAP mobile 'phones, and the growth of digital broadcasters offering Internet and e-mail services through our television screens. On top of this is the increasing speed of access available to the Internet. Consider that dial-up modems levelled out with the 56k modem, which meant at maximum speed it could transfer 56 kilobits of information per second up and down an ordinary phone line. Double ISDN lines upped this to 128k, and now the advent of permanent 'broadband' connections (also known as ADSL - asymmetric digital subscriber line) are allowing connection speeds of up to 512k, enough to provide streaming video. Consider also that not only can telephone lines and cable provide these services, but that satellites can also allow users remote access from a telecommunications hub to transmit and receive data.

The web then is a massive potential resource for researchers – it can be both a repository for knowledge, and it can also be a source for potential subjects.

A little background knowledge

Before we discuss the process of researching online, there are a few basic pieces of information which can aid the researcher. Websites are built in a similar structure to the folders on a computer which store documents. Each website is a big folder which has other smaller folders within it, and within each folder can be web pages or the components that make up web pages, such as graphics. The web page address is made up by the order of the folders, with the domain name at the front and the name of the webpage at the end, and each section of the address has a purpose. So, a typical web page address might be:

http://www.strath.ac.uk/business/research/index.html

which breaks down as follows:

http://	Protocol	Hyper Text Transfer Protocol – this signifies the kind of website – for example, FTP stands for File Transfer Protocol and indicates sites which can have files uploaded onto them.
www. strath	Server name	Stands for World Wide Web. Most websites use this denomination. Strath represents the name of the institution, in this case Strathclyde
ac.uk	Top level domain	This extension indicates what kind of site this is. .ac.uk are UK academic institutions. American institutions are .edu and except in the case of the US the last two letters generally indicate the country of origin, e.g. .de is Germany, .au is Australia. We will look at domain extensions as a determinant of reliability later in this chapter.
/business	Folder	This is the name of a folder within the site
/research	Sub-folder	This is a sub folder of the /business folder
/index.html	Web page file name	This is the name of the web page itself

It is important to understand this structure. If, for example, you have been given a specific web address, yet you get an error message when you try to go to the page online, you can use the address to try and find a page that works. Each folder on a website usually contains a default page, also known as the home or index page. If you couldn't find the above page, you could try entering *http://www.strath.ac.uk/business/research* or you could go even further back to *http://www.strath.ac.uk/business* until you found a page that worked, and from there you can try and use the links on the working page to find what you are looking for.

Another useful tool is Refresh. If a page does not load properly this is the first thing you should try, which effectively reloads the page. All web pages which you visit are temporarily stored on your computer hard drive and you can set your browser and PC to clear these periodically. If you use a shared PC in a computer lab these are normally set to delete these temporary files when you log out at the end of a session. If you are concerned about this you can learn to do this manually, and you should read the section on privacy below. MAC and PC users also need to make sure they are aware of the basic commands of their chosen operating system, and also the specific attributes of the Internet Browser they use. Each has their own merits.

Other things the web user should be aware of are privacy, viruses and hackers, particularly if they use email as well as just browsing on the web. Whilst the Internet has been hailed as making information more freely available, it has also been compared to 'Big Brother'. Anyone's movements on the net can be traced, and emails are not a secure method of communications. There are ways around this - *http://www.anonymizer.com* can give users access to software which claims to allow anonymous surfing and emailing (the ethics of this kind of software will be discussed in Chapter 12). Most websites record information about visitors to the site, called log files. These files can be analysed for useful information about visiting surfers. In Chapter 12 we will look at the uses of this information for those engaged in using the Internet for primary research.

Cookies are something that most net users come across. These are small pieces of code that allow websites to identify users – for example, many sites use cookies to identify returning visitors so they can be greeted by name, and indeed some sites require users to have cookies enabled to allow them to login and use the site. You can set the security settings in your browser to stop websites placing cookies on your hard drive, and you can also delete them at any time from your Temporary Internet Files folder. The disadvantage of cookies is particularly relevant if you share a PC – anyone using that PC is considered to be 'you' when they visit the same site. If you come across terminology and acronyms you do not understand a useful site is NetLingo (*http://www.netlingo.com*) which is a dictionary of online terminology. Netlingo can also help you identify abbreviations and Internet 'slang' you may encounter in emails and forums, such as emoticons (small graphics designed to add emphasis and expression to plain text, such as ;-) for a wink, or a mini-graphic such as ☺) and terms such as IMHO (In My Humble/Honest Opinion). Remember that the Internet is still a text based medium, so be careful with the language you use. Sarcasm and humour can be difficult to detect, particularly when you are communicating with someone whose primary language is not the same as your own, and this is why people use these emoticons to help convey meaning.

As the Internet grows so do the problems of spam. Spam are unsolicited emails, and they are increasing all the time. NUA showed that levels of unsolicited emails in the workplace have climbed in some cases to more than 39 per day (NUA Internet Surveys 2000a), and in May 2003, for the first time there are reports that spam accounts for over 50% of workplace email traffic (*http://www.silicon.com*). There are a few basic rules which any Internet user can adhere to to restrict this. Always be wary of giving out your email address, and indeed any personal details, online. If you are visiting sites where you are required to give an address so that you can log in and use the site, it is worth investing in a web based email service account, for example Hotmail or Yahoo Mail. Most browsers and accounts like Hotmail also allow you to change your email receiving settings so that you only receive email from sources you specify. Unidentified emails are automatically sent to the junk folder for you to review, and dispose of as you please.

However, it is best if you do not give out your details too readily to begin with. Always look for the data protection statement on sites. Although these are not required by all countries, most reputable sites will carry a statement and allow you to opt out of receiving promotional materials. In July 2002 a new EC directive on Privacy and Electronic Communications moved to change this so that users must 'opt-in' to receive marketing information, and UK law will change in October 2003 in relation to this directive. (See *http://www.parliament.uk/* for more information).

Always be wary of opening email attachments. It is worth investing in a good antivirus programme and most such as Norton (*http://www.norton.com/*) or McAfee (*http://www.mcafee.com/*) offer online updating of virus definitions to keep the software up to date. If you are exchanging work with people by disk, always virus scan both before giving a disk to anyone else, and on receipt of other people's disks. It is also worth thinking about a software firewall for protection when you are browsing on the Net. A popular current version is ZoneAlarm (*http://www.zonelabs.com*) which not only stops software on your PC from connecting to the Internet without your approval, but also stops people from trying to gain access to your PC when you are online.

Every server has an IP (Internet Protocol) address – a numeric code, which identifies it to software and sits underneath the non-numeric domain names now used. Furthermore, every computer when it logs online has an IP address. If you use an ISP such as CompuServe or AOL this tends to be one randomly allocated to you as you go online. You can request to have a 'static' IP address which means your computer is always identified by the same numeric code, and this allows sites to restrict access to visitors with approved IP addresses. For example, university libraries can subscribe to online publications using this system. They provide the publisher with a range of IP addresses which cover their campus access computers, and the publisher codes their website to allow users who come in using one of these approved

IP addresses to download material or access secured areas of their site without having to use a password.

The initial stages of the research

Whilst the web is massive, it is also chaotic. Tempting as it may be at the beginning of a research project to simply go to a search engine and dive in to the information available, in many cases this is in fact a complete waste of time. This is because whilst there is a huge amount of information on the Net, it is not all reliable. Previous channels of communication such as books, film and television have been compiled with an element of choice in what stories were told, leaving control over information as it was presented with the providers. However, the web is open to all to air their views. As we shall see, this of course creates problems of quality control. From a post-modern perspective, this multiplicity of opinions online may seem a good thing, and indeed provides various interpretations to study, particularly for observational researchers, but in the initial stages of a specific research project this can be more confusing than helpful. Ó Dochartaigh describes the main areas and groups for which the Internet is an outlet:

1. The news (post 1993)
2. Pre-copyright restriction publications (normally pre-1920s)
3. Information about academics and academia
4. Global coverage
5. Activists
6. Not-for-profit groups
7. Marginal groups
8. Government and officialdom
9. Media and business
10. Archives
11. Statistics
12. "The lonely, the deluded, the obsessive" (Ó Dochartaigh 2002, pp.15-18)

A key point in perceptions of online culture is described by the famous cartoon from *The New Yorker* by Peter Steiner. In it, a dog is sitting in front of a computer at the keyboard, and telling another dog next to him "On the Internet, nobody knows you're a dog". (You can find a copy of this at *http://www.cartoonbank.com*). And to continue Steiner's metaphor, of course, you don't know if anyone else is a dog. So, finding trustworthy information on the Internet requires caution.

This is not to entirely denigrate the web. If you know where to look, and what to look for you can find the right material, but you need to have some experience of research to get this far – an inherent catch-22. Unfortunately, the majority of users of the Internet will not be as discriminating as academics when using information they have gathered. This is not only reflected in the use of this information offline, but in the use of information in other websites online. So, for example, if the overwhelming presentation of Scottish history and identity on the Internet is a stereotypical *Braveheart* tartan extravaganza, it follows that this is what is being presented to the world as the true history and identity of Scotland, and if one person sees a tartan styled website and thinks 'I like that' then they may create their own tartan website, and so the myth is perpetuated. The question of the legitimacy of information found online is paramount, and guidelines on how to detect the reliability of online information will be offered later in this chapter.

I would suggest that the net is used in the following stages in completing the initial research for any project.

1. Use local library catalogues online to find books that are to hand in the research field
2. Use online book e-tailers and new book lists to give you ideas about recent books
3. Use article databases to find more in-depth coverage
4. Use author homepages to find out the latest ideas in the research field
5. Use selective searching for relevant sites and email lists
6. Use raw data online

Use local library catalogues

If you are new to the research area you will need to cover basic reading to give you a start – see Chapter 4 on **writing a literature review.** An ideal place to begin is to use online library catalogues to see what is readily available in your field. Most University, and many major public libraries allow their catalogues to be searched online, and these not only show you what is available, but if it is actually in the library, and if you can reserve the item. You can also use metasearch capabilities (running a search on multiple sources simultaneously) to search different library catalogues . For example, at *http://www.copac.ac.uk/* you can search multiple UK university libraries (22 at the time of writing) as well as the British Library, so if a particular book you are interested in is not available at your own institution you can request an inter-library loan. However, I would advise caution at this early stage in using any of the worldwide search engines, for example WorldCat (an institutional subscription is needed to access this but you can find out more at *http://www.oclc.org/worldcat/*). Not only will you pull up a huge number of results, but finding a resource in New Zealand is not much use if you are based in the UK.

A further important function of libraries is that they can be the gateway for access to academic resources online. Increasingly on the web you need to pay for academic content. However, many institutions have e-subscriptions to the major journals and online resources you would need to use at this stage of the research. Normally, an institution will ask you to register to get a username and login to use these services, but once this has been activated, you can use these passwords off-campus to get access these materials. However, at this early stage in the research process I would recommend resisting the urge to get stuck in to these resources. Until you know exactly what you are looking for, you can waste a great amount of valuable research time swimming around in the sea of information available. The purpose of initial reading is to help you focus your research. The more focused you can be about what is you are trying to research, the easier and quicker it will be to utilise the Internet to its maximum potential, and to your maximum benefit.

Use online book e-tailers and new book lists

Of course, your local library is not always guaranteed to have what you want, or it may be that your initial searches are not focusing on the area you want, or only finding out of date resources. This is when it is useful to visit online book sellers such as Amazon *http://www.Amazon.com*, Books on Line *http://www.BOL.com* or Barnes and Noble *http://www.BN.com* to give you ideas about what is currently available. For example, your library may have a copy of a book which is some years old, but searches on these e-tailers will alert you to any more up to date versions. They can also give you useful information on publishers and ISBN numbers which can help you track down a local copy of the books you are after.

You may find that there is a particular publisher which specialises in your field of research, so it can be worth tracking down publishers online to see if they have any other relevant or upcoming books of interest – most publisher websites carry information on forthcoming publications. The best way to find out the newest book releases in the main English language markets is to use Whitaker BookBank (visit *http://www.whitaker.co.uk* for more information). This is a regularly updated CD available from most good reference libraries which will tell you all of the current books and upcoming book releases in your field. You can also use Bookfind at *http://www.bookdata.co.uk/ bookfind_online.html* Again this is a subscription service but you can register for a free trial subscription at the time of writing.

Once you have completed your primary reading and have begun to narrow down the research field, you can start looking for academic journal articles. You will often find the same articles referenced in different books, and these are the best place to start the next stage of your online search.

Article databases

Increasingly journal articles are becoming available online. Make sure that you check which products your institution has a subscription to. There are a number of providers of electronic full text journal articles, and some of the major resources for business and management researchers can be found at the following sites:

Ingenta (*http://www.ingenta.com*)
Ingenta carries over 5,400 full text publications and 26,000 publications from over 230 publishers. It is full searchable and, depending on the participating publisher's agreement, can offer both personal subscriptions and pay per view download of articles as well as institutional electronic access. It also offers email alerting.

ScienceDirect (*http://www.sciencedirect.com*)
ScienceDirect, run by Elsevier, carries over 1,800 journals online, and offers institutional subscriptions, pay per view and email alerting.

Emerald (*http://www.emeraldinsight.com*)
Emerald (formerly known as MCB University Press) has its own website, and has several databases - Emerald Fulltext carries "40,000+ searchable articles from over 100 Emerald journals". Institutional subscription and pay per view are available, as well as other services such as email alerting.

ABI/INFORM (and other Proquest products *http://www.il.proquest.com/*)
There are various versions of this database: "ABI/INFORM Global is the complete database, covering more than 1,600 leading business and management publications, including over 350 English-language titles from outside the U.S" (*http://www.il.proquest.com/products/pd-product-ABI.shtml*) This offers an institutional subscription.

Academic Search Premier (and other EBSCO databases *http://www.epnet.com/academic/default.asp*)
Again there are various versions of this database product: "*Academic Search™ Premier* offers critical information from many sources found in no other database. This resource contains full text for 3,990 scholarly publications with more than 100 going back to 1975 or further" (*http://www.epnet.com/academic/acasearchprem.asp*) Again this offers an institutional subscription.

Other useful online resources for researchers in this field include:

LEXIS NEXIS *(http://www.lexis-nexis.com)*
This database is actually in two parts, with Lexis covering mainly legal information, and Nexis covering the full text of over 2,300 newspapers and other media resources such as broadcast transcripts. Within these there are a range of services such as 'Academic Universe', or 'Congressional Universe' which covers US government documents. There is also statistical information available, again mainly US sourced.

Northernlight *(http://www.northernlight.com)* and
Elibrary *(http://www.elibrary.com)*
Northernlight works on a pay per view basis, with a charge per article depending on the length of the article, whilst Elibrary is a subscription based service. You can save searches and subscribe to email alerting of new information which matches your criteria. These are services for which you sign up for personal use rather than using your institution for access. Generally they do not cover the full text of high quality academic journals, however, they do cover the major magazines and newspapers.

Infotrieve *(http://www.infotrieve.com)*
Infotrieve is a service to access journal articles and other resources which are either available electronically or offline. They can photocopy any article and send it to you by post or fax . This service is especially good for articles which have not been digitised for online use.

Factiva *(http://www.factiva.com)*
As of January 2003, this large database has encompassed Dow Jones Interactive, as well as newswires, media transcripts and company reports provided by institutions such as Reuters and Associated Press.

SSCI *(http://www.isinet.com)*
This is part of the larger ISI Web of Science, but is different from most other databases in that it is a citation index, which allows you to see which articles are frequently referred to and by whom. For example, if there is a specific author in your particular field that you are interested in, you can search for all the articles in the database which have referenced that particular author, or even a specific paper.

BIDS *(http://www.bids.ac.uk)*
Bath Information and Data Services acts as a gateway to several academic databases of particular relevance to UK researchers. For example this service provides users at UK institutions access to the ISI Social Science Citation Index.

SOSIG (*http://www.sosig.ac.uk*)
In the UK SOSIG, the Social Science Information Gateway professionally catalogues sites, which can help ensure reliability.

HERO (*http://www.hero.ac.uk/*)
HERO (Higher Education and Research Opportunities in the UK) acts as a gateway or portal site to the UK's academic and research institutions, and has information on aspects such as funding and good practice. This incorporates the old NISS information.

JISCMail (*http://www.jiscmail.ac.uk/*)
JISCMail is a mailing list service for the UK academic community, and currently has 74 business / management categorised lists.

Regard (*http://www.regard.ac.uk*)
Carries information on ESRC funded projects dating from the mid 1980s

UKDA (UK Data Archive) (*http://www.data-archive.ac.uk*)
An archive of digital data in the social sciences and humanities.

Useful webpages for business and management researchers are also those of the main journal publishers in the field, and these include:

Cambridge (*http://www.journals.cup.org*)
Carfax (*www.carfax.co.uk*) this includes SARA the Scholarly Articles Research Alerting service.
Routledge (*www.journals.routledge.com*)
Sage (*www.sagepub.co.uk*)
Taylor and Francis (*http://www.tandf.co.uk/*)
Westburn (*http://www.westburn.co.uk*) this website also offers access to Westburn's free online resource The Marketing Dictionary, a dictionary with over 2700 marketing terms, defined by academics, cross-referenced and hyperlinked to each other.

(For more information on these and other sites see Hewson et al. 2003 ; Mann and Stewart 2000; Menabney 2003; Ngai 2003 and Ó Dochartaigh 2002)

Academic publishers are moving towards the immediate delivery format of SGML (Standard Generalised Markup Language) and PDFs or other types of documents can be generated on request. PDFs are the most widely used format on the web. This stands for Portable Document Format and you will need Adobe Reader (available from *http://www.adobe.com*) to open these files. The advantage of them is that they can preserve the exact look of a published article, including diagrams, in an electronic format.

Another important feature of the digitisation of articles is the adoption of CrossRef (see *http://www.crossref.org*) whereby publishers can register their journals with a centralised system which automatically creates hyperlinks between articles as they become available online. The beauty of this system is that the SGML is updated every 24 hours from the central CrossRef information and, as PDFs or other file formats are generated on demand, they are created with the most up-to-date information available .

Be aware there are online databases which only cover the abstracts of journal articles, but do not have the full text available. This is particularly the case with older journals' content. If there is an article you are desperate for but cannot find online, it is worth contacting the publisher directly to see if they can provide the article. The other option is to use a service such as Infotrieve or indeed the British Library (*http://www.bl.uk/*). These can photocopy the article and post or fax it to you.

There is also the phenomenon of online only journals. Although the advent of the online journal can make articles available to a wider audience, again there is no quality control in that there is nothing to stop anyone from starting an online journal. Furthermore, the danger here is that so many people will start online journals, with more and more specialised remits, that research presented on-line could become fragmented. It is more difficult to establish an online journal than it is to transfer an existing journal to the web, in terms of advertising the site and gaining peer recognition. Thus you should be careful to check both the editorial board and editorial policy of online-only journals, and also to see if the institution which the journal is based at is reputable in the field. Double-blind peer review is the preferred standard for proper academic papers.

A further online development is the digitisation of entire books. *http://www.questia.com* requires a subscription but then gives access to thousands of books online in full text. Because the whole text is digitised, entire books can be easily searched for specified terms. From an academic viewpoint this is quite worrying, as users can search for and read specific passages without reading the contextual surrounding information – however, one could argue that this is already the case with indexing in normal books. Taylor and Francis is one of the publishers developing the use of e-books to include flexibility in being able to download individual chapters of different books for specified periods of time to enable researchers to build up their own project-specific electronic library. Visit *http://www.ebookstore.tandf.co.uk* for more information. As yet no one leader has emerged in standardised reader software, but this is a field which is developing rapidly. A factor to be careful of when using digitised books is the date of original publication. Due to commercial copyright laws, which differ from country to country, some content may only be digitised once it is a certain number of years from publication, and ÓDochartaigh notes that there is very little restriction on anyone digitising books published prior to the 1920s.

Another good source of information for researchers embarking on a project is dissertations online, and the leading provider is ProQuest (*http://www.proquest.com*), although this is US based in coverage. Some databases only offer abstracts, others allow the full text download of these, usually at a price. Other sources include Aslib (*http://www.theses.com*) and the British Library (*http://www.bl.uk/services/document/theses.html*).

You should also try to find out the current dissertations being undertaken in your field of research, particularly important if you are required to do original research for a higher degree. It would be incredibly frustrating starting a three year research programme only to be 'beaten to the punch' by someone else in another institution. Of course, this can also open up networking and collaborative opportunities. Good places to start are departmental home pages, which often list graduate research projects in progress (link to any UK institution from *http://www.scit.wlv.ac.uk/ukinfo/*), and also research council pages (a listing is at *http://www.rcuk.ac.uk/*) which often detail research currently being funded.

Another resource you will find online in the field of business and management are case studies. The biggest single global bibliography of management case studies and materials is COLIS, operated by the European Case Clearing House (ECCH). You can access their site by visiting *http://www.ecch.cranfield.ac*.uk and clicking on the COLIS logo. Other useful case studies sites include *http://www.businesscases.org/* and *http://harvardbusinessonline.hbsp.harvard.edu*

Author homepages

Once you have become more comfortable with the research area, you will begin to know who the major voices in the field are. It can be a good idea to track down their homepage on the Internet, which are usually hosted by their affiliated institution if they have one. On this you can usually find a bibliography of all their research, and also information on work in progress. This can also be a good time to look for other useful links. An author you are interested in may be a member of an academic body devoted to their research field, for example the British Academy of Management or the American Marketing Association. Often these academic bodies hold regular conferences which are a good resource for work in progress and the latest ideas, as well as being ideal networking opportunities for the ambitious researcher.

One note of caution though. Do not at an early stage in your research directly email other researchers with vague questions. Just because email has made people more accessible does not mean that this kind of approach is welcomed. Only email another researcher when you have a specific question to ask, and only once you have exhausted other possible resources.

Selective searching

Once you have followed these initial steps you should be ready to begin using search engines to find more information. By this stage you should have considerably narrowed down the research field, and a good strategy is to make a list of keywords which describe your research interest. These should be ordered with the most general words first and the most specific ones last. Remember to account for different possible spellings of words (for example, color and colour, specialize and specialise). This is extremely important because the more specific you can be with your search terms, the easier it will be to find what you want. If your most specific search does not pull up the required results, simply drop the last word from the list and search again. You must also keep records of search terms. The net is a constantly evolving resource, and will change over the course of your research. Whilst some sites can offer to email you to keep you up to date every time certain pages are changed, this can lead to a welter of unwanted emails. Instead, record your searches and then every few months during the research process, run them again. This will help you keep track of new online information.

Different search engines use different methods of searching. Many online search engines use Boolean logic. There are three main Boolean 'operators':

AND	sometimes symbolised as +
OR	this is particularly useful in 'nested' queries and when using ( ) – see below
NOT	sometimes symbolised as - this also sometimes needs to be termed AND NOT

Other operators used include:

NEAR	documents are searched for both words, but only if they appear near each other within the document
" "	documents must include the *exact* phrase contained in the quotation marks
*	allows searching for different extensions from the * for example, Scot* could search for Scotland, Scottish, Scots etc.

So, you can combine these terms to specify a search – for example:

Business AND management
"Customer relationship management"
Marketing AND (advertising OR promotion)

Search engines

If you are using multiple search engines you must familiarise yourself with the specific rules of each one, otherwise you cannot accurately compare results. For example, Google sees quotation marks as indicating the order of words to be searched for, rather than meaning that the words must appear together as some other search engines do. You should also investigate how the search engine ranks the results it comes up with. As Google is at the time of writing one of the web's most popular search engines, we will use it as an illustration for some of the features available on modern search engines – remember to check the features of the one you are using.

A high ranking on Google would seem to indicate some kind of popularity and reliability, and Google's PageRank™ system (for an explanation of how PageRank works visit *http://www.google.com/technology/index.html*) is more complex than a simple popularity contest. Google's caching service and translation abilities also make it a useful research tool and *http://www.google.com/technology/whyuse.html* does a good job at explaining these main features.

Another useful tool for users is the Google toolbar, (*http://toolbar.google.com/*) which can be downloaded from their website and which adds an extra toolbar to your browser window from where you can immediately search Google and find out other information, such as the rank of the page you are visiting, and also the ability to highlight the search term wherever it appears on the page you are at. This is useful for a researcher in that you do not have to waste time visiting the Google main page to search, you simply type your search terms into the box on your toolbar and hit return, and you are automatically sent straight to Google's results pages for your search terms. It should be noted that currently this toolbar only works with Internet Explorer browsers, and that the full version of the toolbar tracks browsing habits to help in its own research. You can choose not to enable this tracking function when you download the software. Other alternatives are available, for example Teoma *http://www.teoma.com/* or Yahoo *http://companion.yahoo.com/*. A development of this is Ultrabar, from which you can search a number of different search engines and even add your favoured search engines to the list. (*http://www.ultrabar.com*). Some of these will work on different browsers.

Google is currently an extremely popular search engine due to its uncluttered design and good ranking system. It actually powers the searches run from many other sites, including the BBC. However, things can change online very quickly, and it is the researcher's responsibility to ensure they are using the most up to date technology available. For more information on search engines visit *http://www.searchenginewatch.com/*

Of course there are other search engines, mainly AltaVista

(*http://www.altavista.com*), All the Web (*http://www.alltheweb.com/*) and Yahoo (*http://www.yahoo.com*). Some of these operate a 'directory 'structure by which you can narrow your search down to specific categories, and in some cases sites are assigned to categories by hand rather than by an automated system. There are also 'natural language' search engines such as AskJeeves (*http://www.askjeeves.com*), and then there are metasearches, the best known being MetaCrawler (*http://www.metacrawler.com*), and also Profusion (*http://www.profusion.com*) and Dogpile (*http://www.dogpile.com*).

Be aware though that many search engines use robots or crawlers to search for webpages. On some sites these cannot penetrate the underlying databases, so they cannot give full coverage of the content on the site. Some reports estimate that only a small percentage of online content is indexed by the major search engines.

Saving what you have found

If you find a very good site on your subject, make sure to 'bookmark' it (Add to Favourites in Internet Explorer), You may find that this site carries links to other useful sites not found by search engine, and the site may also be a member of a 'webring' a linked group of sites on a similar topic. For more on webrings see page 116.

One very important aspect of researching on the Internet is what to do when you find something useful. There are two main ways of keeping track of information found on the Internet. The first is to print out the pages you have found. This has the advantage that modern browsers print the address of the page and the date on each page of the printout, although you should check that long addresses are all on the printout. A disadvantage of this is that not all webpages are built with printing in mind, and text may run off the page, and there may also be excessive graphics and extra printouts which are not required. You can highlight portions of the text and choose to print this 'selection' only; however, check in case the printer does not print out the accompanying webpage and date information. Also be careful when using webpages with frames (multiple sections compiled of individual web pages for example a side bar which is static, with the central display page only changing). It is easy to note down the wrong page address because your browser is seeing the static 'frame' page as the address, which of course does not change. Make sure to have the 'status' bar switched on in your browser. As you move your mouse over a link the address of the link will appear in the status bar, and this way you can check that you have the correct page address when linking from frames.

An alternative is to save the webpage to a folder on your PC. If you choose this option, remember that the page saves as the filename you assign to it, *not* its web page address, and that you will actually create two things –

the web page itself, and a sub-folder of the same name which will hold all the components of the web page, for example the accompanying graphics files. When you wish to reopen a page make sure you click on the page itself rather than looking in the matching folder. The date you save the page should be in the document properties information.   It is vital when citing a web page reference to give the full address of the page, and the date the page was accessed. Some pages may give their date of origination, or their most recent update date, which is also useful information if it is available. The dynamic nature of the web means information changes quickly, and you should not reply on being able to revisit pages you have found at a later date. If you do need to find a page which seems to have disappeared, a good idea is to make use of search engine caching. See page 86 for advice on referencing Internet sources.

It is also vital to keep track of where you have been online. Even if you visit a web page which sounds like it would be useful but in fact is not, keep a note of it. Otherwise, in 6 months time you may find yourself needlessly revisiting irrelevant pages. As with any research notes, make sure you have a structured approach to archiving the online information you gather.

Online access to raw data

The Internet is of prime importance when it comes to the quick dissemination of information – for example, the estimated number of people who downloaded the Starr Report from CNN interactive in the first two days it was available was 1.7 million. (Wall Street Journal 1998) Statistics on the use of Google in the aftermath of 11 September 2001 showed that on the day itself, news related searches on Google increased by a factor of 60. In the immediate aftermath of the attack over 6000 users a minute were looking for the link to CNN (Wiggins 2002). Now, consider that *http://www.cnn.com* would be an obvious place to start for most web users and you see how important Google has become, with over 150 million searches daily. Remember that one of the services Google uses is its 'cache' facility, at which a 'snapshot' of each webpage is stored by their webcrawler.   Google also acknowledged to its users that broadcast medium was still the quickest way to get information. This is due to the lack of capacity online for so many simultaneous users and the need for streaming video links to be as quick to disseminate information as television. However, these improvements to the net, the so called 'digital convergence', is coming in which all computing, telecommunications and broadcasting will be handled by a single network, namely the Internet (Odlyzko 2002).

Newspapers are readily available from a number of sources. Not only is it possible to go to the archives of many papers from their home pages, it is also possible to use search engines such as *http://www.northernlight.com, http://www.elibrary.com* and *http://www.paperboy.com* to track down articles from many papers simultaneously. For an up-to-date listing of potential resources a good guide is the annually updated *Rough Guide to the Internet* by Angus J. Kennedy.

There are also numerous databases of information online. Good places to start searching for this kind of information are government pages, normally designated by the .gov domain extension, and these can lead you to information such as census statistics. Remember to use your common sense in using what appear to be official documents - Ó Dochartaigh (2002, p.71, p.204) warns that often advocacy groups try to make their sites appear official, and different countries may have state-run news agencies, or differing agendas for their official site, for example tourism. Your research funding council will also probably be able to direct you to raw data online in your field – see *http://www.rcuk.ac.uk/* for links to the major UK funding councils.

Psychology of the Internet

Once you have formulated your research plan and have a clear idea of your objectives, this can be a good time to begin to make use of the Internet Community through forums, email lists and the like. Before you begin to use these kinds of resources it is wise to remember that the Internet is in many ways a society, and as such has its own unofficial rules on behaviour.

Although early commentators on the Internet argued that the lack of social cues, and the transitory nature of the Internet were barriers to any real sense of community, this has proven to be unfounded. Wallace (1999) highlights the words of Eric Hochman (1995), who described his online community, ECHO, as 'our own separate little world, one with its own mythology, jargon and social order; in other words, it has its own culture … rather than being an external thing that we adapt to, or have imposed upon us, we're collectively creating it, here and how, as we post.' The Internet is being used more and more as a tool for creating and maintaining identity.

Whilst some authors have proposed that such virtual communities could eventually lead to a 'hive mind' mentality, with humans as unthinking drones (for example, Rosenberg 1997), this is unlikely. However, the basic concept that members of a community can act in unison in their presentations and perceptions is a useful one. A lot of this community feeling is engendered through email lists, forums and newsgroups.

An interesting aspect of this group identity is conformity – an aspect all too ably shown in the web context by the presence of *flamers*. Conformity, whilst not being as prevalent as in 'real-world' communities, is still present to a degree on the Internet (Smilowitz, Compton and Kent 1998), and this is important because members of an online group can therefore be influenced to conform to norms of the group. On the Internet in general there has been a proposal that there should be some sort of Hobbesian Leviathan, a sort of online "god" to moderate the Internet. In a small way these already exist, often as moderators in forums (Wallace 1999). On the level we are talking about, this can be characterised as the moderator (sometimes self-appointed) of discussion threads online. Therefore, their perception of the topic is given weight by their perception as Leviathan (moderator) rather than by any formal qualification.

This is further backed up by an effect on group perception which is magnified by the web, polarisation. Studies have shown that computer-mediated communication (CMC) brings out more extreme opinions in people. Whilst this means that, within a like minded group, there is a tendency for the group to move to a more extreme position, individuals also find it easier to break off, and perhaps even start their own groups (Spears, Russell and Lee 1990). Furthermore, individuals who do dissent are found to be ineffectual in online situations in comparison with real world groups. (Mcleod, Baron, Marti and Yoon 1997). Consequently, like-minded individuals tend to stick together, creating a strong, self-perpetuating group. We could hypothesise that stereotypical views of such aspects are perpetuated and strengthened through such groups as they grow. Individuals who dissent drop off the edges of such groups, leaving a homogenous image being put forth. Essentially, this means that whilst researchers should be as specific as possible when choosing online communities to join, they must also be wary that they experience a balanced presentation of the topic. As with any resource, researchers must always be vigilant to the potential bias in a social grouping.

A good example of the potentially homogenising effect of the Internet terms is the creation of Webrings whereby individual websites join other sites to form a ring, often with a central hub which lists all the sites in the ring. All sites display the same Webring logo to identify their affiliation, and sites may belong to more than one ring. Sites tend to have the same outlook and aims, and anyone can apply to have their site join the ring. In this case, the person who 'owns' the ring has approval over what sites may join. However, we have no idea of what criteria ring owners are using to allow sites to join – some owners of very large Webrings may not even check new sites. So, if someone finds one site in the ring, they are automatically encouraged to visit other sites in the ring though hyperlinks.

Interestingly, the web at the same time as bringing information to the masses, can be seen as acting as an exclusive, ivory tower, device. The immediacy of the electronic world allows joint research projects to take place in real-time and specialists in diverse areas to concentrate even further on these by virtue of having a virtual academic community, distancing them physically from their own immediate academic community and leading to increasing tiny areas of specialisation, as discussed in *Electronic Communities:*

Global Village or Cyberbalkans? (Van Alstyne and Brynjolffson 1997).

This specialisation is in a sense creating a "two-tier" online community. However, this academic / non-academic divergence is not unusual in the offline world. As with most aspects of the sociology of the Internet, the best practice is to be aware of important factors in your offline reading and research and then apply this awareness to the online world. Thus again, it is vital that researchers are aware of the issues of their project before diving in to the online world. This may save them from making some Internet social faux-pas.

Netiquette

There are a couple of basic rules of Netiquette which web surfers should familiarise themselves with.

- Always read the FAQ (Frequently asked questions) section of a site or list before asking questions yourself.
- Never type in CAPITALS. THIS IS THE ONLINE EQUIVALENT OF SHOUTING.

Other rules are common sense - remember that not all net users have English as their first language. Also remember that it is easy for people to forge their online identity, so think before you address remarks to other posters. Mind your language, and remember that what you post is there in written form for all to see. Failure to pay attention to these simple rules can attract unwanted attention.

Flamers are those who send sharp emails to new group members who fail to observe netiquette or ask annoying questions which are covered in the FAQ (Frequently asked questions) section. They also can engage in 'flame wars' with other members of the group over any disagreement. *Trollers* are even worse in that they deliberately set traps to catch *newbies* for the amusement of the rest of the list. They post statements which are obviously incorrect and let new users of the list point out the mistake, whilst of course, everyone else on the list knows this is a trap. Consequently, even in newsgroups there is a hierarchy of membership, and this inner circle effect means the Internet is not as egalitarian as it likes to think it is. This kind of group mentality demonstrates that online communities can display the same insecurities and internal politics as any real community.

Using email lists and forums

There are a number of routes to interacting online. Email lists tend to be newsletters despatched on a regular basis and to which users sign up. No interactivity is required from them, beyond joining or leaving the list.

Groups are more interactive. These Newsgroups, sometimes called Usenet (User's network, Usenet being the original incarnation of these kinds of online lists, which has now been subsumed by Google Groups), are a slightly different proposition. Instead of people subscribing to the list and being emailed all the messages on the list, these messages are held on a central repository, and tend to be part of a totally automated system. This means that they are often unmoderated and consequently 'things have become so bad that many newsgroups have been abandoned by anyone but the spammers and flamers and are utterly worthless as research resources.' (Ó Dochartaigh 2002). Because of this problem, Usenet II has been set up at *http://www.usenet2.org*, which is limited to subscribed universities or colleges. However, these bear in mind that newsgroups may also genuinely reflect the people who use the web.

Other main hosts of these kinds of groups include Yahoo (*http://groups.yahoo.com/*) and Topica (*http://www.topica.com*). Statistics on groups are available, for example those hosted by Yahoo show a summary statistic of the list detailing the date the list was created, how many users there are, whether the list is moderated, private, and a month by month breakdown of the number of messages posted to the list.

Although the origins of the web envisioned an academic utopia where experts could be consulted by anyone, the practicalities of life soon took over. Discussion lists and newsgroups which had started with a core group of experts found themselves deluged with newbies (new users) who did not know or observe the netiquette of these groups (Ó Dochartaigh 2002). The thing that drove the academics underground into closed lists was the immense number of repetitive and often inane questions which flooded the lists. However, some academic gems still survive if you know where to look. H-net has developed into a wider, although US biased, resource. These lists have an editor and an editorial board and have many of the same editorial policies as academic journals. There are other academic lists to be found, and in the UK these are usually based at the JISCmail service.

It is always worth joining a list and lurking (receiving the list emails but not participating in the discussion) for a couple of weeks to get the feeling of the group before posting. New users should always read the groups FAQ's and always introduce themselves to the list before they post for the first time. Again, though, the researcher must exercise restraint in joining lists. The more specific the list, the more likely it is to be useful. Posting the same message on several different lists (cross-posting) instead of targeting it to the most appropriate list is frowned upon. Also be aware that lists operate on a principle of reciprocity. For users to get something out of the list, they also should contribute. Researchers should be wary of spending too much time getting sucked into the arguments and discussions of the list at the expense of their project. Lists can easily lead the unwary researcher far off topic. If you intend conducting primary research on the web, lists also have other potential dangers, and there are particular ethical concerns which need to be addressed, and we shall return to this topic in Chapter 12.

Forums are on-line discussion boards, often devoted to a particular topic, called a 'thread'. Users may take part in the discussions, ask questions of fellow members and read content posted. You can also often go back and edit posts you have previously made, unlike 'real time' conversations. Forums are sometimes also called Bulletin Boards, and are to be found at many web sites. They usually have a guru or on-line moderator who tends to be a specialist in the topic and can get involved in regulating the site, as well as policing it for inappropriate content. The advantage of these sites for the uninitiated researcher is that they are a quick way of getting an answer to a question – however, there will be a myriad of answers given from different users and again, there is no quality control. Even the controller of the forum may only be someone who is interested in the field, not necessarily someone who knows a lot about it.

Real time discussions are found as a feature of Chat Rooms where users can view the topic of discussion and choose to join in. When they enter the chat room, other users are alerted to their presence, and they can see the other people currently in the room by their username. Although people may select any username, this must be backed up by an active email address. Therefore, if anyone wants to make direct contact, the software will forward relevant emails to users, who can then decide to reply directly to the contactor and make their email address known to them. Of course, using passport accounts like Hotmail and Yahoo can help users concoct a web identity which would take a lot of work to be traced to their real identity. The ethical implications of using chat rooms in research are discussed in Chapter 12.

Reliability of information

The Internet is increasingly being used for educational purposes, and this is a particularly important point. Because the Internet is being used in a formal education setting as an instructional tool from a young age, a new generation is growing up who have been taught to use the Internet as a resource for authoritative information on any subject. Thus the Internet is becoming the research method of choice for a new generation. However, there are problems.

Ebersole (2000) surveyed students in ten public schools in America and found that although students reported that 52% of their time on the web was spent in research and learning, only 27% of the sites sampled in the survey were found to be 'suitable' for that purpose, and students were found to be visiting commercial sites at a much higher proportion that other domains.

As a source of information, students rated the web as excellent 44% of the time and good 46% of the time. Whilst the .gov and the .org sites visited in the Ebersole study were the most highly rated for educational purposes, only 4% of the sites visited were .org and 1% .gov, whilst 77% were .com, which received the lowest rating for educational value. (It should be noted, however, that .com domain names can be reliable sources of information – for example, all the major newspaper resources in the world use .com domain names as they are commercially based. Using a domain name extension as a qualifier for example, .com usually referring to commercial sites, .edu or .ac.uk usually referring to academic sites, is really a heuristic device rather than an accurate reflection of content.)

Researchers should also try to authenticate information found online by finding out if it is replicated in authoritative sources. For example, there is a well known story that the first Space Shuttle, originally supposed to be named *Constitution*, was actually named *Enterprise* after fans of the television sci-fi series *Star Trek* wrote over 400,000 letters to the White House demanding the name change. Now, this information can be found online in several places, for example at the website *http://www.enterprisemission.com/tran4.html* (personal site of Richard C. Hoagland) However, it is also replicated on the official NASA website which adds legitimacy to the claim. (*http://science.ksc.nasa.gov/shuttle/resources/orbiters/enterprise.html*   and *http://www-pao.ksc.nasa.gov/kscpao/shuttle/resources/orbiters/enterprise.html*
Ironically *Enterprise* was a pilot craft and never actually flew in space.

Based on Alexander and Tate's (1999) analysis, Ó Dochartaigh identifies the following questions which should help clarify the authority of the source material:

1.   Is it clear who is responsible for the document?
2.   Is there any information about the person or organisation responsible for the pages?
3.   Is there a copyright statement?
4.   Does it have a print counterpart which reinforces its authority? If there is a print counterpart does it have a date of publication?
5.   Are sources clearly listed so they can be verified?
6.   Is there an editorial input?
7.   Is spelling and grammar correct?
8.   Are any biases and affiliations clearly stated?
9.   Is advertising clearly differentiated from information?
10. Are 'opinion' elements clearly labelled as such?
11. Are their dates for when the document was first produced or first put on the web?
12. Are there dates for when the document was last updated or revised?

However, these rules are not hard and fast. The net is still an evolving technology and its rapid growth has meant that a standardised template for documents did not evolve naturally. Recently there has been a drive to amend this by the creation of a standardised template for webpages with certain information encoded. The growing use of XML (Extensible Markup Language) will allow for standardisation and will also allow the quicker integration of databases of information. Essentially this means that multiple databases from different organisations can be searched from the same single search engine if they share the same basic standardised structure and language. Dublin CORE is a further extension of this which lists 15 items of information which every document should carry, including copyright, date and publisher information, and it is hoped that the meta information (the coding which search engines initially seek out to categorise web pages) on each web page will hold these 15 items. (more information on Dublin Core can be found at *http://www.purl.oclc.org/dc*)

Copyright and the Internet

Not all web pages carry a copyright symbol or statement, but this does not mean that they are not covered by copyright. Due to the myriad of differing copyright laws across the world the golden rule is, if in any doubt, **always ask permission**. Your institution's guidelines should cover their rules about this. Copyright is part of the wider group of protective principles covered by the term IPR (Intellectual Property Rights), and this includes copyright, confidential information, patents, trade marks and design rights. (Graham 2003). Useful sites to find out more include *http://www.booktrust.org.uk/ copyright.htm* the Copyright Licensing Agency *http://www.cla.co.uk/*, the British Copyright Council *http://www.britishcopyright.org.uk/* and BUBL *http://link.bubl.ac.uk/copyright/* The UK Government's web site which will have the most up to date legal is at *http://www.patent.gov.uk/* and also see *http://www.intellectual-property.gov.uk/std/resources/copyright/index.htm*

You may hear the term 'fair use' or 'fair dealing' used to describe using a limited amount of someone else's work. There are no hard rules in the UK about this, and different publishers have different limits for use, for example Blackwells' Publishers webpage on permissions to reproduce text in other publications states:

Please do not contact us for permission if you wish to reprint:

- a single extract from a book totalling a maximum of 400 words
- a series of extracts from a single book totalling a maximum of 800 words (provided that no one extract exceeds 300 words)

You may reprint the material described above free of charge subject to an appropriate acknowledgement to author, title and Blackwell Publishing. (*http://www.blackwellpublishing.com/Rights/text1.asp* accessed 5 June 2003)

Generally these rules apply when work is being republished for commercial gain, for example, in another book. However, remember that your completed dissertation will probably be going into your University Library. You must check how your University deals with submitted dissertations – some may digitise them for storage which requires extra permission than just producing a hard copy. Once you know how your dissertation will be stored, and how many copies will be made, you should seek any permissions required. Always leave plenty of time for this as some publishers may take a while to respond, or you might find it difficult to track down a copyright holder. The best route is to ask permission, and to clearly explain what the permission is for, the exact reference of the original material, how many copies will be made and where they will be available, and how you intend to reference the item (see the appendix of Chapter 4). For use in research projects which are not being made commercially available most publishers will not charge a permission fee.

Researchers should also note that there is debate over whether all forms of communication should fall under the terms of intellectual property, including for example, email communications. See Chapter 12 for a discussion of the ethics and impact of the data protection act on using such materials in your research project.

Researchers should also be very wary of plagiarism. Whilst the Net has made it easier to find information to plagiarise and a plethora of sites offer pre-written work, the same technology means that it is easier than ever for plagiarism to be spotted with a simple search using software, e.g. from *http://www.canexus.com/eve/index.shtml* or *http://www.turnitin.com/* Even a search on Google for a suspect turn of phrase can catch out a student.

Summary

The Internet can yield a high number of resources for secondary research, and defining the scope of the project in advance will enable the researcher to focus their searching. Researchers should be aware of issues of privacy, intellectual property rights and reliability when using materials sourced from the Internet, and the issues involved in using the Net for primary research are explored in Chapter 12.

Recommendations for further reading

Ó Dochartaigh, N. (2002), *The Internet Research Handbook: a practical guide for students and researchers in the social sciences*, (London: Sage Publications)
This is an excellent guide to using the Internet to find information

Kennedy, Angus J. (2002), *The Rough Guide to the Internet* (London: Rough Guides Ltd)
This is a handy guide to getting started on the Internet, with information on how to connect to the Net, using email, netiquette and a directory of web sites.

CHAPTER 6

Selecting a Research Methodology

Synopsis
Having identified a research issue or question one must select a research strategy and appropriate methodology for collecting information that will illuminate the problem. In this chapter we look first at the research strategy and the scientific approach to problem solving. The primary research methods of Observation, Experimentation and Survey are discussed in some detail. The chapter concludes with a look at qualitative methodologies and the differences between cross-sectional and longitudinal research.

Keywords
research strategy, scientific methods, observation, experimentation, survey, qualitative methods, cross-sectional and longitudinal research designs.

Introduction

In Chapter 4 we developed the theme that knowledge accumulates over time and that the purpose of research is to extend and improve both our knowledge and understanding. It follows that the first step in any research project must be to establish what is already known about the topic or problem in which we are interested and secondary research, or a review of the existing literature, is the place to begin.

In the course of conducting a literature review it is possible that we will discover the answer to our research question and so have no need to undertake any new research as a solution to our problem already exists. Usually, however, we will find that while earlier work throws light on our problem it does not provide a precise solution to it. A gap exists between what is known and what we need to know to solve our problem. However, the literature review will enable us to define more clearly what the nature of this gap is and what additional information is required to eliminate it. Once we have defined our information needs then it becomes possible to determine the most appropriate method or methods for collecting this information. In this chapter we review these methods in some detail.

First, however, we need to consider the more basic issues raised in Chapter 2 concerning approaches to the conduct of research and research strategy. Next, we explore the three primary research methods – Observation, Experimentation and Survey Research – with a short discussion of qualitative methods. Finally, we review the difference between cross-sectional and longitudinal procedures.

Research strategy

In Chapter 2 we suggested that there are two broad approaches to research – positivistic and interpretivistic. This distinction rests basically on one's personal philosophy concerning the conduct of research with positivists emphasising an inductive or hypothetico-deductive procedure to establish and explain patterns of behaviour while interpretivists seek to establish the motivations and actions that lead to these patterns of behaviour. The selection of a research strategy will be strongly influenced by one's preferred approach.

An excellent book that provides extensive advice on preparing research proposals is *Designing Social Research* by Norman Blaikie (Cambridge: Polity Press 2000). This book is based on many years' experience of teaching courses on social science research and contains a wealth of advice for persons wishing to develop a research design. In it Blaikie discusses research strategy and methodology in detail.

To begin with Blaikie makes a clear distinction between 'methodology' and other aspects of the research process that are often subsumed under this umbrella term. Thus Blaikie uses the term *"research design"* for the planning aspect of a research project, *"research strategy"* for the logic of enquiry and *"methods"* for the execution of the project. *"Methodology,"* on the other hand, includes a critical evaluation of alternative research strategies and methods. (p.9) He continues: "Research strategies provide a logic, or set of procedures, for answering research questions..." (p.24) and identifies four distinct alternatives – *Inductive, deductive, retroductive* and *abductive.* These are defined as follows:

> The inductive research strategy is the commonsense view of how scientists go about their work. According to this view, meticulous and objective observation and measurement, and the careful and accurate analysis of data, are required to produce scientific discoveries. (Blaikie 2000, p.102)

Deductive research, also known as "the hypothetico-deductive method, or falsificationism" was developed by Popper "to overcome the deficiencies of Positivism and the *inductive* strategy."(p.104). Deductive research involves the statement of a hypothesis and the conclusion drawn from it, the collection of appropriate data to test the conclusion and the rejection or corroboration of the conclusion.

"The *retroductive* strategy is the logic of enquiry associated with the philosophical approach of Scientific Realism..."(p.108). Like deductive research it "... also starts with an observed regularity but seeks a different type of explanation. In this strategy, *explanation* is achieved by locating the real underlying structure or mechanism that is responsible for producing the observed regularity...*Retroduction* uses creative imagination and analogy to work back from data to an explanation." (p.25)

The fourth research strategy, identified by Blaikie as *abduction*, is associated with a range of interpretivistic approaches. These are particular to the social sciences whereas the three preceding strategies are common to both the natural and social sciences.

Blaikie identifies himself as only one of three social scientists who have used the concept of abduction. In his words "The idea of *abduction* refers to the process used to generate social scientific accounts from social actors' accounts for deriving technical concepts and theories from lay concepts and interpretations of social life." (p.114)

The basic distinction between the different schools of thought are spelled out clearly by Blaikie:

> Positivists are concerned with establishing the fundamental patterns or relationships in social life and Critical Rationalists are concerned with using such patterns to form explanation arguments. However, Interpretivists argue that statistical patterns or correlations are not understandable on their own. It is necessary to find out what meaning (motives) people give to the actions that lead to such patterns. (Blaikie 2000, p.115)

Clearly, seeking to understand behaviour is at the very heart of the business and management disciplines and it is for this reason that interpretivism has attracted an increasing following among those undertaking research in the field. However, many researchers feel uncomfortable with what they perceive as a subjective and relativist view of the world by comparison with the objective and absolutist perspective of the physical scientist that underpins the scientific approach to problem solving. Thus the emphasis in both research and publication in business and management tends to positivist if for no other reason than that it yields results that can be readily tested and validated. By contrast the relativist view is that there is no single social reality but a multiplicity each of which is 'real' to the persons sharing a given point of view and basing their actions upon it. Both procedures are discussed in this and later chapters.

The scientific approach to problem solving

In the opening paragraph of the first chapter of what is widely considered to be one of the definitive texts for research students in the social sciences Selltiz et al. (2nd Ed 1959) state unequivocally: "The purpose of research is to discover answers to questions through the application of scientific procedures. These procedures have been developed in order to increase the likelihood that the information gathered will be relevant to the question asked and will be reliable and unbiased.   To be sure, there is no guarantee that any given research undertaking actually will produce relevant, reliable, and unbiased information. But scientific procedures are more likely to do so than any other method known to man."

To begin with then it will be helpful to define the nature of the scientific method itself.

At the outset it is necessary to recognise that while social science research in general, and marketing research in the particular, follows the same basic process as pure scientific research, and is based upon the same procedures of observation and experimentation, it differs significantly in that, as well as information, social science research is concerned with subjective, human values. The point about any research is that it is triggered by a desire to know more about a phenomenon and it appears possible that more information on this may be obtained through observation and experimentation. In the pure sciences where one is dealing with objective data then the cycle of scientific research would follow the sequence illustrated in Figure 6.1 which is derived from Popper (1968).

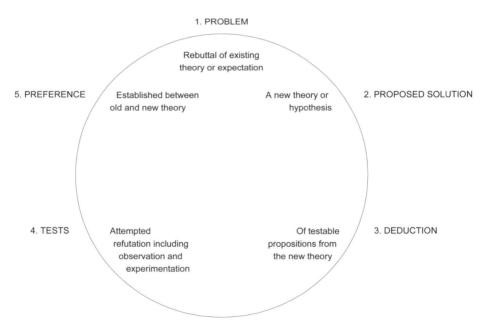

Figure 6.1 The cycle of scientific research (derived from Popper 1968)

In the pure sciences the process of research is predominantly intellectual and prompted by the desire to improve and increase knowledge and understanding of the world in which we live. Intellectual curiosity also underlies applied and social science research but here the dominant motivation is usually practical - the desire to improve on something or even create something new with a specific end use or purpose in mind. That said, the process is largely the same, albeit that the objects of social science research are often less amenable to research than other natural phenomena. In part this intractability may be due to the relative youth of modern social science compared with the modern natural sciences (in the Golden Age of the Greek Philosophers, and for many centuries thereafter, there was no distinction between them!)

In the natural sciences research has uncovered the existence of natural laws such that it has been possible to develop theoretical explanations not just of how things are but also how, given observance of the qualifying conditions, they will be in the future. While some progress has been made in the social sciences the theoretical foundations are less secure. The ability to replicate exactly tests of one's theory and hypotheses make it difficult, if not impossible, for the social scientist to predict outcomes with the same accuracy and reliability as the pure scientist.

Of course, pure science doesn't stand still either, which is why the research cycle is common to them both. At the outset one recognises the existence of a problem because one's existing knowledge and/or experience is insufficient to guide or inform one exactly how to proceed. Faced with a problem one is most likely to speculate or hypothesise as to the answer by drawing on past knowledge or experience, and extrapolating from it. In cases where one has strong feelings about the likely outcome then one may formulate positive hypotheses while, where one is uncertain and can anticipate several possible outcomes then one would formulate a null hypothesis. Selltiz et al. (1959) cite Cohen and Nagel who stated:

> We cannot take a single step forward in any inquiry unless we begin with a suggested explanation or solution of the difficulty which originated it. Such tentative explanations are suggested to us by something in the subject matter and by our previous knowledge. When they are formulated as propositions, they are called hypotheses.
>
> The function of a hypothesis is to direct our search for the order among facts. The suggestions formulated in the hypothesis may be solutions to the problem. Whether they are, is the task of the inquiry. No one of the suggestions need necessarily lead to our goal. And frequently some of the suggestions are incompatible with one another, so that they cannot all be solutions to the same problem. (Cohen and Nagel 1934)

Given the research hypothesis (or 'theory') then one will proceed to deduce a series of further working hypotheses (testable propositions) as the basis for determining precisely what information is required to enable one to test them. It is these Propositions which will largely govern the approach taken to data collection and the precise questions asked, and of whom if the data cannot be obtained by observation alone. Data collection, and the question of how we analyse and interpret data in order to decide whether we can draw acceptable conclusions and come to a decision on our original problem, are the subject of later chapters. First, one must develop a research design and to do so will have to decide between observation, experimentation or a sample survey (or some combination of them) as the most appropriate means of securing the data necessary to test our hypotheses and, hopefully, solve the problem, which initiated the cycle. It is to this we turn in the succeeding sections.

Observation

It is generally accepted that while business research is not a sufficient condition for competitive success, in the medium to long term it is certainly a necessary condition for continued survival. This conclusion may be reached by considering, for example, the explanations offered for marketing failures where a lack or absence of marketing research is most frequently cited as the primary cause. Alternatively, the reasons advanced for marketing success often cite the identification of a marketing opportunity unrecognised by competitors. Either way, keeping one's finger on the pulse of the marketplace is seen as an essential and continuing concern of the firm's management.

Observation may be both informal and formal. When undertaken as part of one's normal daily routine it is usually informal and loosely structured – often referred to as 'scanning' e.g. reading the *Financial Times*. Observation has a critical role to play in this activity. By contrast, observation within research is a scientific technique - indeed it is the basis of the scientific method - which is characterised by a much more structured and systematic approach than that called for in a scanning mode.

Fundamentally, the distinction between scanning and observation as a scientific technique is that scanning is only partly structured and is intended to maintain an awareness of information, actions and events which may have a bearing upon the decision makers' judgement and/or action. On the other hand, observation consists of the systematic gathering, recording and analysis of data in situations where this method is more appropriate - usually in terms of objectivity and reliability - and able to yield concrete results (e.g. the flow of persons in a shopping centre) or provide formal hypotheses about relationships which can then be tested by experimentation or survey analysis. Hence, scanning is often a precursor of observation and may result in the formulation of tentative hypotheses leading to formal observation and the development of conclusions or formal hypotheses for further testing.

Although observation may be regarded as a technique in its own right it is probably used most often as an element of one or other of the other two methods. In experimentation, observing and recording behaviour may well be the single most important technique while in survey analysis interviewers will frequently record factual information both to reduce the burden on the respondent (e.g. type of property, make of consumer durable) and to ensure accuracy where the respondent may be unsure about the correct answer (make of tyres on your car). A simple inspection will immediately provide an accurate factual answer. Similarly, a meter can record precisely what channel your TV is tuned to, while questions asking you to recall this at some later date could result in considerable response error.

A major advantage and disadvantage of observation as a research method is that it is very largely a 'real-time' activity. With the advent of low cost video cameras it is true that one can record events for later analysis but this is certainly not possible for participant observation where the direct involvement of the observer is an essential part of the methodology. Participant observation is particularly suited to the gathering of qualitative data where one is seeking to establish the behaviour of the subjects in a particular context (family decision making, board meeting, etc.). However, unless the observer is unknown to those they are observing, which is often difficult to achieve, there is always a danger of influencing the very behaviour one is seeking to monitor due to the control or Hawthorne effect. Similarly, another danger is that by becoming a participant the observer will change their own attitudes and/or behaviour and so introduce bias into their observation. (For an extended review of the uses and problems which relate to participant observation the reader should consult Moser and Kalton (1971, 2nd edition 1985). Stephen Brown provides an example of the value of an observation study in his article "Information seeking, external search and 'Shopping' behaviour" (*Journal of Marketing Management*, 1988, 4, No.1, pp.33-49). As the author notes in his introduction "Few topics in consumer research have generated as much discussion as pre-purchase information seeking;" but, that said, there is a clear difference between the research findings which show that consumers do not 'shop around' and the retailers belief that they do. Brown suggests that both interpretations may be correct but reflect a different perspective. Thus, retailers observe how consumers behave, while the great majority of academic researchers survey consumers and invite them to recall and reconstruct their actual behaviour. But, in doing so, most respondents focus solely upon the purchase decision and ignore or forget their antecedent behaviour when they were acquiring information and evaluating it prior to making a shopping expedition. To overcome this deficiency Brown undertook a weeklong observation study in a shopping centre and observed the behaviour of 70 groups of shoppers from their time of entry to their time of departure. While only regarded as an exploratory study Brown identified three main types of shopping behaviour, leisure shopping (17%), chore or purposeful shopping (41%), and mixed activity (42%) from which it was inferred that consumers use the occasion of shopping trips to gather information on products which they are not purchasing, presumably for future reference should it be required, i.e. 'shopping around' in the retailer's sense is incidental to the main purpose of the trip. To test this hypothesis Brown proposes a much more rigorous design incorporating both observation and face-to-face interviewing underlining the importance of using observation to help formulate hypotheses and then combining it with other approaches to test those hypotheses.

In sum, observation is usually the first step in the scientific method. Having identified a problem observation (successive focusing) allows one to define those areas or issues whose detailed examination may provide a solution to the problem. (A longer discussion of observational techniques is contained in the next chapter).

Experimentation

Because of the dynamic and complex nature of most business problems few are readily amenable to the experimental approach used so widely in the physical sciences. However, some specific problems are suited to an experimental design which, if properly controlled, will yield better and often less expensive data than can be obtained from a survey.

In an experiment the researcher usually seeks to control all the variables so that by varying one while holding the others constant they can determine the effect of the input or independent variable upon the output or dependent variable. It follows that a basic requirement for the conduct of an experiment is that one must be able to specify all the relevant variables. It is also implied that one has a theory, which can be stated as a hypothesis or hypotheses about the nature of the relationship between the variables, e.g. if two identical objects carry different prices then prospective buyers will perceive the higher priced object to be of higher quality. Alternatively, one may hypothesise that the colour of a product's packaging will influence the consumer's perception of it without any specific hypothesis about what colour will have what effect.

In a nutshell, experiments are usually undertaken to determine if there is a causal relationship between the variables under investigation. Moser and Kalton (1971) avoid a detailed philosophic discussion of the nature of causality but provide a useful guide to its determination. If A is a cause of the effect B then normally there would be an association between A and B. Thus, if smoking causes lung cancer one would expect that more smokers than non-smokers would contract the condition. All the statistical evidence points to this conclusion but some will seek to dismiss or ignore it on the grounds that smoking is neither a necessary nor sufficient condition for contracting lung cancer. A sufficient condition would mean that all smokers would invariably get lung cancer while a necessary condition would exist if people only got lung cancer after smoking. Clearly, neither of these conditions obtain, as there are many non-smokers who catch lung cancer. That said, the degree of association between smoking and lung cancer is so high, i.e. we can measure how many smokers and non-smokers get lung cancer and will discover that the likelihood of a smoker getting the disease is many times greater than a non-smoker, that the Government now insists that tobacco products should carry a formal health warning – 'Smoking Kills'.

Evidence of causality is also to be found in the sequence in which events occur, it being obvious that a subsequent event cannot be the cause of an antecedent event. That said, while an antecedent event may be the cause of a subsequent event we will have to apply other tests of causality to determine whether in fact this is the case. In addition to tests of association we will also have to determine if there are any intervening variables, which may influence the apparent relationship (or even disguise it by masking the relationship or making it disappear). Moser and Kalton (1971) exemplify the problem in terms of the observed association between the income of the heads of households (I) and their conservatism (C) as measured by some suitable index. While C may increase or decrease in parallel with I (or vice versa!), and we may measure the degree of association through the calculation of the coefficient of correlation we cannot impute any causality to the relationship without also determining the time sequence - did I precede C or vice versa - and whether or not there are any intervening variables such as education, occupation, age or whatever, that might explain the relationship better. The more the possible number of intervening variables, the more complex the task of determining whether or not they have any bearing upon the relationship. It follows that in designing experiments one must have a particular concern to determine the degree of association, the sequence of events and the possible effect of intervening variables.

To address these problems 3 broad kinds of experiment are available, all of which require the establishment of a control group against which to compare the experimental group, namely:

1. After-only design
2. Before-after design.
3. Before-after design with control group.

In an after-only design the experimental group is exposed to the independent variable which it is hypothesised will cause a particular effect and their subsequent behaviour or condition is compared with that of the control group which has not been so exposed. For example, a new 'cold' remedy is administered to 100 volunteers and the progress of their cold compared with that of the 100 members of the control group who must be as closely matched as possible with the experimental group in terms of age, sex, physique, general state of health, etc. If the experimental group show a dramatic improvement then, assuming no intervening factors, we may assume there is a causal relationship between remedy and cure and express this in quantitative terms of the degree of association established.

Before-after designs are commonplace in marketing where the experimenter is seeking to determine the effect of a specific factor on people's attitudes and/or behaviour. In these cases the same people are used as both the control and experimental group. Suppose one wishes to assess the effect of a change in a marketing mix variable - price, packaging, product performance, advertising, etc. etc. - upon a group of consumers, the first step must be to establish a benchmark of their current attitudes/ behaviour. Given the benchmark the group is then exposed to the modified marketing mix (always bearing in mind you can only vary one factor at a time) and their attitudes/behaviour measured again. Because of the experimental effect (see below) it would be dangerous to assume that all change detected is a direct consequence of the variation in the mix variable. That said, if change occurs it is reasonable to assume that, in part, this is due to the change in the independent variable.

The third design - before-after with control group - is generally recognised as the best of the three options in that it combines elements of both the preceding types and, most importantly, has established a benchmark for the control group before exposing the experimental group, i.e. one can quantify the similarities between control and experimental groups and not merely assume their similarity as is the case with the after-only design.

In all experiments the primary concern must be for *validity* and Moser and Kalton (1971) cite Campbell and Stanley's checklist of the 12 most frequent threats to validity.   The first 8 of these refer to internal validity and are:

1.   History.
Here the problem is to ensure that some extraneous factor, including prior experience, is not the cause of an observed outcome. The establishment of a control group and clear definition of the antecedent beliefs and status is the major defence against this source of invalidity. Even so, the fact that many experiments are not instantaneous but involve the passage of time may allow some external event to influence the experiment.

2.   Maturation.
Independent of any specific environmental event the passage of time is likely to influence respondent performance, e.g. fatigue, boredom or, in the case of experiments designed to measure long-term effects, ageing itself.   Before-after designs with control groups offer the best protection against this source of invalidity.

3.   Testing.

Given that we learn from experience it is unsurprising that the mere act of participating is likely to result in modification of our attitudes/behaviour if for no other reason than that it gives salience to something, which previously had been of little or no importance. Once again the before-after with control design enables us to assess the effect of this factor.

4.   Instrumentation.

The conduct of experiments frequently involves the use of more than one test instrument, e.g. questionnaire, or the interpretation of test scores, which involves judgement. The potential for bias is obvious and can only be guarded against by careful testing of instruments and the establishment of objective measures wherever possible.

5.   Statistical Regression.

For a variety of reasons discussed in some detail by Campbell and Stanley (1966) there is a natural tendency for test subjects to gravitate towards the mean score on a given test when tested more than once. Whether this is because poor performers try harder and high performers become complacent or, as in the case of say the Delphi forecasting technique, 'deviants' gravitate towards the security of the average is a matter of speculation - the existence of the phenomenon is not!

6.   Selection.

Experimental design demands that experimental and control groups should be as near identical as possible. Patently, to claim that the inhabitants of Slough (a favoured location for test markets) are the same as the inhabitants of, say, Aberdeen because the demographic structure of the towns' populations are similar (an after-only design) is a travesty of reality as anyone familiar with the two towns will appreciate. Before-after designs help overcome some of the problems of bias due to selection as the same persons are being studied throughout. That said, many of the other threats to validity - maturation, testing, etc. - will be more acute. Specialist texts, such as Moser and Kalton (1971) provide extensive advice on how to minimise these problems, which are beyond the scope of this chapter.

7.   Experimental mortality

Quite simply means that some of the subjects will 'die' or drop out during the course of the experiment and so may threaten its validity.

8.   Selection maturation

This is a problem that occurs when persons volunteering for an experiment may possess a quality absent in non-volunteers and it is this which leads to the observed effect or outcome. (Campbell and Stanley 1966)

In addition to the 8 sources of internal invalidity cited Campbell and Stanley also give examples of 4 sources of external invalidity, i.e. the extent to which the findings can be generalised and applied to other persons. One example of this is Reactivity. *Reactivity* describes the interaction effect of testing as a result of which the 'subjects' behave differently than they would otherwise have done. A classic example of this is the so-called – 'Hawthorne Effect' in which the performance of both experimental and control groups improved largely because of the awareness of the groups that they were being monitored. According to Moser and Kalton (1971) "Often in designing studies the demands of internal and external validity compete; the stronger the design is made in internal validity, the weaker it becomes in external validity. In general, surveys are strong on external validity but weak on internal, while for experiments it is the other way round." The authors provide extensive advice for controlling the effects of extraneous variables (pp.220-224) but these are of primary interest to the specialist and will not be considered further here.

Survey research

While observation and experimentation both have an important role to play in business and management research it is the survey which is the best known source of primary data collection, not only in marketing but the social sciences in general.   Undoubtedly this owes a great deal to their widespread use in polling opinion on political issues or other matters of current interest and concern such as health and food, or the effects of environmental pollution.

What then is a survey?

Moser and Kalton (1971) devote over 500 pages to the subject of Survey Methods in Social Investigation but decline to offer a definition on the grounds that any "such a definition would have to be so general as to defeat its purpose, since the terms and the methods associated with it are applied to an extraordinarily wide variety of investigations, ranging from the classical poverty surveys of 100 years ago to Gallup Polls, town planning surveys, market research, as well as the innumerable investigations sponsored by research institutes, universities and government." In the Westburn Dictionary of Marketing, Baker is less restrained and asserts that a survey is "The evaluation, analysis and description of a population based upon a sample drawn from it." In the Marketing Handbook (1965) Mayer adds to this attempt at a definition when he states "The essential element in the survey method is that the data are furnished by an individual in a conscious effort to answer a question." Thus Mayer sees the essence of surveys as posing questions ('the questionnaire technique') and goes on to add:

> The survey method is the most widely used technique in marketing research. Some people go so far as to regard the questionnaire technique as being synonymous with marketing research. Unfortunately, the method is so universally employed in this field that many researchers use the survey technique when one of the other methods, the observational or experimental, is more appropriate. (Mayer 1965)

Tull and Albaum (1973) support all three of the preceding views when they write, "Survey research is a term that is susceptible to a variety of interpretations. As most often used, it connotes a project to get information from a sample of people by use of a questionnaire. The question may be designed to obtain information that is retrospective, concurrent, or projective with regard to time. They may be asked in a personal interview, by telephone, or sent to the respondent by mail." Tull and Albaum stress that surveys are concerned with understanding or predicting behaviour and offer as their definition: "Survey research is the systematic gathering of information from (a sample of) respondents for the purpose of understanding and/or predicting some aspect of the behaviour of the population of interest."

Consideration of these definitions indicates that surveys are concerned with

- Fact finding
- By asking questions
- Of persons representative of the population of interest
- To determine attitudes and opinions; and
- To help understand and predict behaviour.

The design and execution of surveys, and the methodology and techniques available is the subject of Chapters 8 - 11. Here we must be content with a broad overview of the survey method covering:

- The Purposes for which surveys are used
- The Advantages and Disadvantages of Survey Research
- Issues and Topics suited to surveys.

The purposes of survey research

Mayer identifies 3 kinds of survey, which he classifies as factual, opinion and interpretive, each of which is seen as having a distinctive purpose.

As the name implies factual surveys are concerned with securing hard, quantitative data on issues such as usage, preference and habits, e.g.

> How much beer to you drink?
> What is your preferred brand?
> Where do you normally drink beer? etc. etc.

In other words, such surveys are concerned with actual behaviour while in opinion surveys the objective is to get respondents' views upon the topic under consideration. Such opinions are almost always qualitative and may or may not be based upon actual experience. For example, a teetotaller may have quite strong perceptions about brands of beer without ever having consumed them. However, consumers' attitudes and beliefs based upon past knowledge and experience are of particular value in helping to plan future strategy, e.g. in designing a new product, developing a copy platform or selecting a distribution channel. As with factual surveys, a major purpose is to try and quantify the strength and direction of opinion as a basis for future decision-making.

Table 6.1   Taxonomy of surveys

1. Classical Poverty Surveys (Booth, Rowntree, Bowley, Ford)
2. Regional Planning Surveys
3. Government Social Surveys
4. Market, audience and opinion research
5. Miscellaneous:
- Population (Census)
- Housing
- Community studies
- Family life
- Sexual behaviour (Kinsey)
- Family expenditure
- Nutrition
- Health
- Education
- Social mobility
- Occupations and special groups
- Leisure
- Travel
- Political behaviour
- Race relations and minority groups
- Old age
- Crime and deviant behaviour

Source: Adapted from Moser and Kalton (1971)

By contrast interpretive surveys are used in circumstances where the respondent is asked to explain why they hold particular beliefs or behave in a particular way rather than simply state what they do, how, when and where, etc. Interpretive surveys are often the first step in primary data collection when the researcher is trying to get a feel for the topic under investigation, and will often involve the use of projective techniques such as picture and cartoon tests, word and object association tests, sentence completion tests, and role playing. Depth interviewing and focussed group interviews are also widely used, often to define questions to be used in a formal questionnaire for use in the factual or opinion survey.

Most market research surveys have a practical objective - to provide information on which to base decisions - while surveys of other populations are usually undertaken for theoretical reasons to enhance understanding. While such information may well be used as an input to decision making this is not its primary purpose. Table 6.1 summarises the multiplicity of surveys identified by Moser and Kalton (1971), the great majority of which are undertaken from a background of intellectual curiosity rather than to provide inputs to the solution of particular problems.

Advantages and disadvantages of survey research

In an article "The use of the survey in industrial market research" (*Journal of Marketing Management*, 1987, 3, No. 1, pp.25-38) Susan Hart confirms that the survey is the most usual form of primary research undertaken and attributes its popularity to the following factors:

(i)   The objectives of most research require factual, attitudinal and/or behavioural data. Survey research provides the researcher with the means of gathering both qualitative and quantitative data required to meet such objectives.

(ii) One of the greatest advantages of survey research is its scope: a great deal of information can be collected from a large population, economically.

(iii) Survey research conforms to the specifications of scientific research: it is logical, deterministic, general, parsimonious and specific (Hart 1987)

Alreck and Settle (1985) consider that the main advantages of surveys are that they are:

Comprehensive
Customised
Versatile
Flexible
Efficient

By 'comprehensive' Alreck and Settle mean that the method is appropriate to almost all types of research (cf. Mayer's factual, opinion and interpretive categories of survey). The other four advantages are closely interrelated and boil down to the fact that one can design surveys to suit all kinds of problems and budgets. Naturally, 'dipstick' or 'quick and dirty' research where a limited budget and time pressures dictate only limited sampling using judgemental methods will lack the credibility (and validity) of the properly designed survey in which carefully designed and tested questionnaires are administered professionally to a statistically representative sample of the population. That said, virtually any research is better than none, and there is considerable evidence to show that diminishing returns set in early in terms of the insights gained from research, and also in terms of the confidence one can attribute to one's findings. Given then that the essence of marketing is that one should seek to determine the precise needs of prospective customers, a pragmatic approach which seeks to acquire additional information consistent with available resources is to be preferred to no research on the grounds that it lacks the rigour called for in the experimental sciences. While such rigour is attainable, the question is whether it is possible, necessary and/or worthwhile. In most student and practical projects it is not!

Of course surveys also have their disadvantages and Hart cites the following:

(i)   The unwillingness of respondents to provide the desired data. The overriding concern here is of the non-response error, which can invalidate research findings.

(ii) The ability of respondents to provide data. In studying managerial decisions, it is important to target individuals in the organisation with the knowledge and experience of the subject under examination.

(iii) The influence of the questioning process on the respondents. Respondents may give the answers they think the researcher will want to hear, thus distorting the accuracy of the data. (Hart 1987)

Response errors, accidental or deliberate, may be reduced significantly through careful design and execution of the test instrument and are discussed by Webb (2000).

Issues and topics suited to surveys

From the above discussion, and particularly Table 6.1, it is clear that surveys can be used to gather data on virtually any problem which involves the attitudes and behaviour of people in either their individual capacities or as members of various kinds of social and organisational groupings. Within the domain of marketing research Alreck and Settle (1985) distinguish eight basic topic categories, namely:

Attitudes
Images
Decisions
Needs
Behaviour
Lifestyle
Affiliations
Demographics

Of course, these categories are neither mutually exclusive nor independent but, to the extent that they often require different treatment and measures, the classification provides a useful guide to survey planning.

Alreck and Settle subscribe to the cognitive-affective-conative (CAC) model of attitudes and see attitudes as a predisposition to act. They also assert that attitudes precede behaviour. In other words if you can define and measure attitudes you should be in a good position to predict behaviour. However, many researchers prefer the expectancy-value (EV) model developed from the work of Heider, Rosenberg and Fishbein which does not seek to establish a link between attitude and behaviour and so can accommodate problems of the kind touched on earlier when examining the purposes of survey research - namely, the teetotaller who may have strong positive attitudes towards brands of beer but with no intention of translating their attitude into behaviour. The point we are seeking to make is that one must be careful not to assume a causal relationship between attitude and behaviour, albeit that the notion of consistency in both CAC and EV models indicates that if behaviour does occur it is most likely to be consistent with the pre-existing attitude - if one exists! Either way an understanding of underlying attitudes will clearly be of great value to the business planner.

Image is defined in the *Westburn Dictionary* as "Consumer perception of a brand, company, retail outlet, etc. Made up of two separable but interacting components, one consisting of the attributes of the object, the other consisting of the characteristics of the user." The most important word in this definition is *perception*. Objectively it is possible to list all the attributes of a product or service, but the importance assigned to these attributes is likely to vary from individual to individual. It is for this reason that in personal selling the seller will invite the potential buyer to list and rank order the specific attributes they are looking for in the intended purchase so that, in turn, the seller can focus on those elements of importance to the particular buyer. But in mass markets, or when composing copy in support of personal selling, one must seek to determine the image of the object under consideration and then define clusters of attributes which correspond to worthwhile segments in the market place. Surveys offer this potential, particularly through the use of scaling devices as discussed in Chapter 9.

Given knowledge of people's attitudes, and some insight into their image of different products or services, the next thing the marketing planner would like to know is how they actually choose between alternative courses of action. Elsewhere (*Journal of Customer Behaviour*, Spring 2002) I have proposed a simple, composite model of buyer behaviour, which incorporates elements of the economic, psychological and sociological models and argues that, when faced with a need, the consumer will consult their store of past experience (learned behaviour) to see if they have an acceptable solution. If not, the decision maker will seek to acquire relevant information on performance attributes, and cost- benefit data on possible solutions to their need. This information will then be evaluated in terms of the decision maker's own perceptions and preferences, and a choice made of the item, which best satisfies these. If marketers are to influence this process then they require knowledge of the information used by consumers and the evaluative criteria applied in order to arrive at a preferred solution. Survey research offers a means to acquire this information.

Needs is a word often used loosely by the marketer and as if it were synonymous with wants, *desires*, preferences, *motives* and goods. *The Westburn Dictionary* makes it clear that only if there is no choice will needs and wants become synonymous otherwise needs represent basic requirements such as food, shelter, clothing, transportation, entertainment, etc. (c.f. *Marketing Myopia* by Ted Levitt) while wants comprise highly specific means of satisfying these basic needs. Desires are largely synonymous with wants but the term implies rather more commitment to a given solution than preference. *Motives* have a connotation of action in that people are seen as being motivated to do something, usually to achieve a *goal*, which is satisfaction of the need through behaviour. Scaling provides a means to documenting all of these dimensions through survey research.

According to Alreck and Settle (1985) "The measurement of *behaviour* usually involves four related concepts: what the respondent did or did not do; where the action takes place; the timing, including past, present, and future; and the frequency or persistence of behaviour." Such data is factual and readily acquired by standardised questionnaires using what, when, where and how often questions, usually with multiple-choice answers provided to speed up completion. Of course such questions are frequently combined with others designed to measure the other categories of topics, and may be regarded as a benchmark against which to assess them.

While it is convenient for purposes of data collection and analysis to identify clear-cut factors or variables such as Attitudes, Images, etc., actual behaviour is the outcome of the interaction of all these factors. In order to capture this complexity many researchers prefer to use composite measures, which describe behaviour in the round. Lifestyle is such a construct - and is concerned with "Distinctive or characteristic ways of living adopted by communities or sections of communities, relating to general attitudes and behaviour towards the allocation of time, money and effort in the pursuit of objectives considered desirable" (*Westburn Dictionary*). Validated batteries of items for inclusion in lifestyle research are widely available and usually cover four main dimensions - activities, interests, opinions (hence AIO research) and possessions. The identification of subgroups or segments with similar lifestyles has been greatly improved with the development of multivariate analysis techniques utilising the full capabilities of modern computers.

Behaviour is strongly mediated by the social context in which it occurs. It follows that an understanding of the nature of social interaction is central to an understanding of actual behaviour. In this context *affiliation* in terms of the membership of both formal and informal groups is a rich source of data of particular value in predicting likely behaviour. For example, membership of a referent group may exercise a significant influence on what is considered an acceptable dress code (IBM and blue suits, students and jeans), place in which to live, type of holiday, car, etc. Similarly, an understanding of the composition of a group and relationships within it may provide useful guidance when introducing a new product to the market place by helping to identify the opinion leaders (those to whom other group members turn for information and advice), and concentrating one's selling-in effort on these individuals. Survey methods are very appropriate to research of this kind.

Alreck and Settle's final category demographics is perhaps the most obvious and easily measured dimension associated with consumer behaviour. In addition most governments collect copious data on the structure and composition of the population, which provides a reliable and inexpensive base line for other survey research.

Qualitative research techniques

Earlier, when considering the issues involved in defining problems and selecting possible approaches to solve them, we touched on the distinction between quantitative and qualitative research. While these two approaches are often presented as if they are opposing and mutually exclusive research methodologies, it was pointed out that they are in fact complementary and supportive approaches to the conduct of research. Our discussion of the research cycle, and the main techniques of observation, experimentation and sample survey in the preceding pages, should have confirmed this view. However, some further elaboration will be useful here before turning to a more detailed examination of sampling and data collection techniques in succeeding chapters.

In the marketing discipline, experience has shown that qualitative research is particularly useful in a number of specific situations, which may be summarised as:

1. Traditional preliminary exploration
2. Sorting and screening ideas
3. Exploring 'complex' behaviour
4. Developing explanatory models of behaviour
5. Enabling the decision maker to experience the world as consumers see it
6. To define unfilled needs and means of satisfying them.

Most of these uses are self-explanatory and address the issue raised earlier, namely, that social science research is concerned not only with facts but also with values. Through using qualitative research it becomes possible to discover what some of these underlying values are for, while one may seek to infer them from observing actual behaviour, the only real way one can establish 'why?' people behave as they do is to ask them. Even then it is not easy to get respondents to give you the real reason, for we all have a tendency to rationalise behaviour (hence the emphasis upon price as an acceptable reason for not making a purchase rather than by giving offence and saying the article in question was useless, ugly or what have you). There is also the well-known human tendency to want to please, and so give the researcher the answer you think they are looking for.

To overcome these difficulties, qualitative researchers have developed a whole battery of projective techniques so that the respondent is invited to speculate how someone else would behave in a given situation, e.g. by completing a sentence, by filling in the dialogue in a cartoon, etc. Of course, the only real basis we have for such speculation is our own knowledge and experience, attitudes and opinions, so it is hardly surprising if the projected behaviour is similar to how we would behave in the given situation. Gordon and Langmaid (1988) devote a whole chapter to Projective and Enabling Techniques, which they classify into 5 categories:

Association
Completion
Construction
Expressive
Choice-ordering

Within the Association procedures are to be found traditional word association tests such as "Tell me the first thing that comes to mind when I say detergent", through the classic Rorschach ink-blot test, to the construction of brand personalities, e.g. could you imagine Foster's Lager as a person and describe them to me. A further refinement is to provide the respondent with a pile of words and pictures and ask the respondent to choose those they associate with a brand name or product.

Completion procedures invite respondents to complete a sentence such as "People who drive Porsche motor cars are..." or the missing dialogue in a conversation between two persons. Brand mapping, in which respondents are invited to group like brands/products according to various criteria, is also regarded as a completion technique, and enables the researcher to determine how consumers see the products competing with each other in the market place.

Construction procedures also invite respondents to construct a story from a picture (Thematic Apperception Tests), or in response to projective questions, through bubble procedures (you write in what you think the character in the drawing/cartoon is thinking) to the classification of stereotypes, e.g. you define a category of consumer and ask respondents to specify their consumption behaviour.

Expressive procedures also involve the use of drawings and the invitation to the respondent to describe their perceptions of the person and/or context. They may also include role-playing in which the respondent is asked to act out a particular activity, e.g. purchasing a product or playing the part of a named brand.

Finally, choice ordering is just that and asks respondents to rank order objects in terms of specific criteria - a technique which is very useful in determining what alternatives will be provided in multiple choice questions, or for coding the answers to open-ended questions.

However, projective techniques are only one approach to qualitative research, relevant mainly to marketing studies. Other qualitative methods widely used in other disciplines such as group discussions and depth interviews are dealt with in Chapter 10.

Cross-sectional and longitudinal studies

There can be little doubt that when people speak of marketing research they are concerned primarily with a specific, one-off or *cross-sectional* study designed to address a particular problem, which is facing them. However, given that most business and management problems are dynamic and evolve over time, it would seem sensible that a significant part of the firm's research effort should be devoted to longitudinal studies - a view which is considerably reinforced when it is recognised that it costs approximately 5 times as much to create a new customer as it does to retain an existing one, or that staff turnover can significantly affect costs and productivity. In this section we shall examine the nature of longitudinal research by comparison with ad hoc or cross-sectional studies, and then review its use in both the business and consumer setting.

What is it?

According to Wancevich and Matteson (1978) "Longitudinal organisational research consists of using techniques and methodologies that permit the study, analysis and interpretation of changes that occur over a time period sufficiently long to assess meaningful change in the variables of interest, as well as to facilitate researcher and managerial understanding about causality." In other words, longitudinal analysis is concerned with the collection of data by means of observation, experimentation or over time with the primary purpose of describing and explaining change in these objects or respondents over the period of the research.

In the social sciences generally there are numerous examples of the use of longitudinal methods, particularly in the case of cohort or *tracking* studies in which the researchers have traced the development and behaviour of the subjects over extended periods of time. Clearly, the benefit of such studies is that they provide insight and understanding of the process by which change occurs, which is quite different from the large scale cross- sectional study of a population as a consequence of which one subdivides it into a set of major segments, e.g. psychographic, life style or benefit segmentation. In the latter case one can define distinct sub-groups in terms of their present behaviour, but can say little about how this developed or about what would be required to change it. Similar weaknesses may also exist in the case of data collected by continuous methods, e.g. Neilsen Audit, Attwood, where the primary emphasis is upon *what* rather than why.

In brief, cross-sectional studies involve the investigation of one or more variables as they are at a particular point in time, while longitudinal studies require the measurement of the same variables or factors on a number of successive occasions over a defined period of time. Because of the sequential nature of longitudinal research it is possible to avoid the greatest weakness of the snapshot approach of the cross-sectional study, namely that any explanation of the data collected is *retrospective*. As an SSRC Working Party reported (1975) "The hazards incurred when any survey shifts from description of the contemporary situation of a population sample to an overt or implicit attempt to identify causal influences retrospectively are heightened by the time-span of recall and by the salience of the subject matter."

Small wonder then that 'helpful' respondents may well provide misleading explanations of why they behave in a particular way when faced with requests to recall past decisions of comparatively minor importance in their lives as a whole such as the difference between Brand A and Brand B.

Inevitably, cross-sectional or ad hoc studies are unable to deal adequately with dynamic behavioural changes and properly designed longitudinal surveys are necessary to monitor such change. By 'properly designed' is meant, research, which consists of measurement of the same objects/

respondents at a series of different points in time as opposed to what often passes for a longitudinal study, which is a series of cross-sectional studies at specified points in time. While this may appear to be a counsel of perfection, it is one which is felt to be justified, particularly where one is seeking to establish causality, and when concerned with organisational as opposed to individual behaviour where the consequences of misunderstanding are likely to be larger and longer lived. A good example of the problems and importance of establishing causality is to be found in Gordon et al.'s (1975) study of the adoption of innovations by hospitals. It was hypothesised that increased centralisation of authority in a hospital would result in a reduction in its willingness to innovate in the purchase of new equipment. But, in order to test this hypothesis, it is clear that one must discriminate between two quite distinct possibilities. First, where authority is decentralised it may be that innovative individuals will purchase new equipment and introduce it to the system. On the other hand, an equally plausible causal priority is that where a hospital (as a system) has acquired new equipment then it will be more dependent upon individual physicians and their expertise and so involve them. A cross-sectional study to determine the relationship between centralisation and responsiveness to change would have failed to discriminate causal priority between the two variables.

Similarly, the longitudinal study helps to reduce the possibility of making incorrect causal inferences, which, as Likert (1967) has demonstrated, may occur due to the time lag between certain classes of causal and end-result variables. Longitudinal research also helps overcome what Seiler (1965) has termed the single cause habit in which, based on a single data set from a cross- sectional study, one imputes all the observed effects to single causes. In reality, behaviour is invariably the outcome of a time-related process, and one should seek to monitor the causal chain which results in given outcomes, and so avoid unduly simplistic interpretations of events recorded by the snapshot of a cross-sectional study.

In summary, and as Kennedy (1982) has pointed out, "(the) literature would appear to advocate the use of longitudinal methods on the basis of the facts that this particular research methodology addresses the issue of causality; identifies time lags between cause and effect; permits analysis of dynamic processes; minimises the probability of hidden third-factor error and enables the researcher to monitor the actual occurrence of changes in dependent and independent variables. Longitudinal research would appear to afford the potential to eradicate problems of causality, produce more exact conceptualisation of process, develop better predictive models of growth and change and facilitate the identification of contextual constraints."

Unfortunately, few academic research projects, and particularly student projects, are sufficiently well resourced to permit the adoption of a longitudinal approach.

Summary

In this chapter we have taken a broad look at the issues involved in selecting a research design, i.e. the method and approach by which we seek to secure the additional information necessary to solve our problem. From this review certain broad principles emerge.

The first principle is that research is usually initiated because our current knowledge and experience appear insufficient or unsatisfactory to explain an issue of importance to us. Irrespective of whether this perception is prompted merely by intellectual curiosity or is the response to a practical problem which needs to be resolved, the most usual approach is to follow the so-called scientific method. In essence the scientific method requires us to formulate hypotheses as to the causes and possible solution to our problem, and develop these into testable propositions.

The second principle is that, in formulating hypotheses and developing these into testable propositions, we would be well advised first to use observation to see if we can discover an acceptable explanation, and then see if experimentation will help clarify the relationship between the phenomenon under scrutiny and the factors which appear to be associated with it. In the natural sciences where it is possible to control many of the variables, which may be influencing the interaction(s) in which we are particularly interested, experimentation will often provide an acceptable solution. However, in the social sciences, where the main focus of interest is usually human behaviour, it is rare that one is able to apply sufficient controls to make experimentation successful. Further, one is usually concerned to know 'why' people behave in a particular way, and inference from observed or experimental data is notoriously weak in doing this satisfactorily. Accordingly, having exhausted the possibilities of observation and experimentation, most researchers will wish to undertake some form of sample survey of the population in which they are interested.

The third principle is that just as one proceeds from observation, to experimentation to sample survey, so one should first undertake qualitative research before attempting to quantify the direction and extent of any hypothesised relationships. We return to this issue in greater detail in Chapter 13.

Finally, it is clear that while one-off, or cross-sectional studies may provide brief illumination of a problem it is much preferable if decision-makers and researchers keep track of issues of interest to them through longitudinal studies.

Recommendations for further reading

While some of the references given may appear 'dated' they are original sources that underpin many of the current textbooks. Whether you wish to revert to the original sources or depend on current explanations of them is a matter of choice.

Alreck, Pamela L. and Settle, Robert B. (1985) *The Survey Research Handbook*, Homewood, Ill.: Richard D. Irwin (2nd edition 1995 Irwin Press)

Blaikie, Norman, (2000) *Designing Social Research*, Cambridge: Polity Press

Cresswell, John W. (2002), *Research Design*, 2nd edition, London: Sage Publications
Covers quantitative, qualitative and hybrid/mixed methods approach

De Vaus, David (Ed.) (2002), *Social Surveys* 4 volume set, London: Sage Publications
An-up to-date reference work covering all aspects of survey methods

Moser, C.A. and Kalton, G. (1971) *Survey Methods in Social Investigation*, 2nd Edn London: Heinemann (2nd edition 1985)

Tull, D. S. and Albaum, G. S. (1973) *Survey Research* (Aylesbury: International Textbook Co. Ltd)

CHAPTER 7

Qualitative Research Methods

Synopsis
'Research Methods' looks at observation, including ethnography, grounded theory,and case studies, in more detail.

Keywords
Observation; unstructured; structured; ethnography; grounded theory; case studies

Introduction

In the preceding chapter we looked briefly at the three primary research methods – observation, experimentation and survey. In this chapter we examine these techniques in greater detail with an emphasis on a number of qualitative techniques – ethnography, grounded theory and case studies.

It will be recalled that the first thing to do when faced with a question is to see if an answer to it already exists. While 'asking the audience' or 'phoning a friend' are options, addicts of 'Millionaire' realise that these alternatives are useful, but neither exhaustive nor infallible. What we would really like to do is consult a comprehensive and authoritative source such as Encyclopedia Britannica or, possibly, initiate an online search through the Internet. Such secondary or desk research is an essential first step in defining an issue or problem and establishing what is already known about it. Only when we have searched all the possible sources of recorded information without finding an answer should we consider undertaking new or primary research to collect new facts or intelligence. When we do, invariably we will start with some form of observation.

Observation

Observation is one of the three principal research methods – the other two being experimentation and survey. In some shape or form observation is the starting point for all research – it is an observed event or stimulus that prompts mental inquiry into its meaning and possible relevance. In the absence of understanding, and/or a satisfactory explanation, we look for additional information to help us understand and interpret the phenomenon that has come to our attention. In other words we do some research, and this usually starts with further observation. However, as Bryman (2001) notes the notion of 'observation' as a research technique has been largely displaced by the more fashionable concept of 'ethnography'.

Ethnography – literally 'nation writing' – is defined as 'The scientific description of races and cultures of mankind' (Concise Oxford Dictionary). Under this definition the writings of Herodotus and other historians of the Classical Era would qualify as 'ethnography', as would the accounts of explorers, missionaries and colonists in more recent times.

Ethnography developed as the principle research methodology of the social anthropologist, epitomised by Margaret Meade's famous studies in the 1930s of Pacific Islanders. In the Introduction to Growing Up in New Guinea she wrote: "I made this study of Manus education to prove no thesis, to support no preconceived theories. Many of the results came as a surprise to me. This description of the way a simple people, dwelling in the shallow lagoons of a distant South Sea island, prepare their children for life, is presented to the reader as a picture of human education in miniature." No doubt Glaser and Strauss (1967) would regard this as an example of grounded theory which we discuss later.

Perhaps the main difference between simple 'observation' and ethnography is the extent to which the researcher becomes involved in the object of their research. While observers may be thought of as external to the events they are observing, and so detached and objective, ethnographers are closely involved in the subject matter they are studying and, as a result, may acquire more information and greater understanding at the risk of losing some of their objectivity. The similarities and differences between observation and ethnography will be explored in greater detail in the following pages. Both are widely used in social and business and management research.

To begin with, it is clear that observation is an integral part of all research. However, to qualify as a scientific technique Selltiz et al. state that observation must satisfy four criteria:

> Serve a formulated research purpose
> Be planned systematically
> Be recorded systematically and related to more general propositions
> Be subjected to checks and controls on validity and reliability (Selltiz et al. 1959, p. 200)

In some cases observation may be the primary research method; in others it may be combined with other methods of data collection, such as interviews or questionnaire based surveys, while in the case of secondary research the researcher is dependent on the observations of others.

As a primary research method, observation is particularly useful when seeking to establish how people actually behave. Through direct observation one avoids the possibility of distortion that may arise when people are asked to report their own behaviour. One may also detect actions that have become so habitual or integrated into other behavioural patterns that the individual is unaware of them, and so does not report them when asked what they did or how they would do something. Observation can also overcome the problems of ability or willingness to report behaviour.

The downside of observation is that the observer has to be present when behaviour occurs, which can be a laborious and time consuming process. Often it will be simpler to ask members of the population under investigation what they did, or might do under given circumstances, than wait for those circumstances to arise naturally. There are also many situations when the observer would not normally be able to gain access, although the popularity of TV shows like 'Big Brother' suggests that people today are less inhibited about displaying personal and intimate behaviour than they used to be.

Applications in business and management research

Observational and ethnographic techniques have widespread application in business and managerial research - indeed 'scientific management' is extensively based on the findings from such research. Behaviour in the workplace prompted the interest in time and motion study (later work study) which underpinned the emergence of mass production and mass distribution. In turn this led to mass consumption and the emergence of market research to throw light on consumption behaviour, both in the home and in the market place. It would not be an exagerration to claim that management as a professional practice arose out of interdisciplinary attempts to synthesise the psychologists interest in individual behaviour, with the anthropologists and sociologists interest in group behaviour, into a holistic explanation of production and consumption.

Specific examples of the application of research to managerial issues is to be found in:

Frederick W. Taylor's The Principles of Scientific Management, (1911) in which he spelled out the benefits from analysing in the minutest detail all the actions involved in a given task and then determining the optimum sequence and time to be spent on each action. (Work study).

Elton Mayo's The Human Problems of an Industrial Civilization (1933) describing the Hawthorne Studies into the motivation of workers in the Relay Assembling Test Room at Western Electric's Hawthorne works in Chicago. The study was experimental in that it involved the selection of five women workers and observation of their work in a test facility. The observed increase in productivity was attributed to the workers improved morale from having been chosen and becoming part of a special group.

Henry Mintzberg's *The Nature of Managerial Work* (1973), a classic observational study in which the author analysed what managers actually did in their daily work. His principal finding that most managerial work is involved in short-term fire fighting was diametrically opposed to the widely held perception of managers as long-term strategic thinkers.

In the field of Qualitative Market Research Philly Desai gives an extensive listing of marketing issues that lend themselves to observational methods. These he divides into two broad categories:

> Going wider: looking at the physical and social contexts within which behaviour is embedded.
> Going deeper: looking in detail at the micro level of human behaviour, the routines and habitual actions to which we pay little or no attention. (Desai 2002, p.19)

As examples of going wider he cites how people behave in different kinds of retail outlet, the interactions between customers and sales persons, and between persons shopping in company, lifestyle issues and the different social identities that individuals may adopt in different social settings.

In the case of going deeper the emphasis is on low involvement processing i.e. the multitude of everyday decisions we make without much attention e.g. selection of a brand off a supermarket shelf, and habitual behaviour which rarely rises to the level of conscious thought such as driving to work.

From these example it is clear that observational studies offer considerable opportunity to the student required to undertake a small piece of project based research, as well as to those pursuing the more ambitious requirements of a dissertation or thesis for a research degree.

Depending on the nature of the study, observational techniques can range from relatively unstructured through to highly structured. In the case of exploratory research, when one is seeking to 'get a feel' for a situation, it is often best to follow an unstructured approach rather than impose a pre-conceived structure on it – a cardinal principle of grounded theory. However, if one is seeking to clarify or amplify the tentative conclusions based on reported data then a more structured approach is called for as one has specific issues to be addressed. Finally, if one is implementing an experimental design to establish causality, then the nature of the observation will be rigorously prescribed in advance and form an integral part of the experiment.

Irrespective of the degree of structure the investigator must address four key issues:

What specifically is to be observed?

How and in what form are observations to be recorded?
How to maintain accuracy and consistency in recording observations?
What is the relationship between the observer and the observed and how is this to be established and controlled?
(Adapted from Selltiz et al.)

In order to satisfy these criteria it is clear that one must both develop a precise protocol, and develop skills in observation so as to ensure comparability between observations, and enhance both the reliability and validity of the observations themselves. There is an extensive literature that highlights how people see what they expect to see, or overlook particular activities, even when they have been asked to look closely and report exactly what they have seen, that points to the need for both the training of observers, and strict control over observational studies.

A classic example of distortion was given by Hastorf and Cantril (1954) in They Saw a Game in which they reported the perceptions of rival supporters of two Ivy League football teams. Following an incident on the field the two teams became involved in a brawl which resulted in the referee cancelling the game. Hastorf and Cantril interviewed supporters as they left the stadium and found that, while everyone had seen the same incident, the description and interpretation of it was almost diametrically opposed according to which team you supported.

The nature and extent of both training and control procedures to identify and limit such variability will be governed according to whether the observation is to stuctured or unstructured.

Unstructured observation

Unstructured or participant observation is a technique developed mainly by social anthropologists in their studies of human groups and societies, especially in cultures different from those of the observer and where language differences made direct questioning and communication difficult. Given such a novel situation the obvious question is "What should I observe?"

While there is a particular aspect of relationships and/or behaviour in which one is especially interested, until one has formed a generalised picture of everyday life it is impossible to know how relevant or important this is to the group under study. So, to begin with, there will be no distinct focus and everthing will be observed in an attempt to distinguish patterns of activities and behaviour. This was the approach taken by Margaret Meade reported earlier.

Two of the disadvantages of observational studies are immediately apparent. First, everyday life tends to follow patterns based on seasonal changes and the rituals that have developed around them. If this is so then we will require at least a year to establish if this is the case, and maybe another or more years to confirm our observations, and, if eclipses play an important role in beliefs and behaviour, possibly a good deal longer still! Second, even if we have learned the language, the object of study may be unaware of behaviour that is novel to us because it is so embedded that they no longer can explain 'how we do things around here'.

A third problem, that grounded theory may help us resolve, is that of seeing what we expect to see. Ideally, grounded theory requires us to dismiss any pre-conceived ideas we may have about a phenomenon under investigation. In a perfect world, we would approach a new problem with a completely open mind and record accurately exactly what we saw until we had gathered enough information to begin to distinguish patterns and relationships in the data. These patterns and relationships would then form the basis of speculation and hypotheses that we could seek to verify by repeating the data gathering exercise. Obviously, this is a counsel of perfection. Perception becomes reality, and our perception is the outcome of a lifetime's learning and experience. It is hardly surprising that the social and behavioural sciences lack the rigour and objectivity of the physical sciences with their standardised measurements, procedures and controls. On the other hand, if we are aware of these dangers we can take steps to reduce and minimise them and, in our view, the main benefit of the grounded theory approach is that it sensitises us to the problem and encourages us to address it.

In the beginning, it will be useful to identify just what the observer should be looking for. Selltiz et al. propose that there are five significant elements of any social situation that are deserving of attention:

The participants.
The setting
The purpose.
The social behaviour i.e. what actually occurs.
Frequency and duration

Information on these five factors will help answer five of the six basic questions with which all research is concerned – Who, What, Where, When and How – it cannot, of course, tell us Why? Given sufficient observations, as in an experiment for example, we may be able to infer this. Otherwise it will be necessary to complement our observations with direct questioning of the person(s) whose behaviour we wish to understand and explain.

Of course, this assumes that the data we have gathered is accurate, reliable and valid in the first place. A number of devices/procedures will help achieve this.

Perhaps the most obvious contribution to accurate observation is to make a permanent record of the event. With modern technology it is now commonplace to make both audio and visual records of an incident so that they may may be reviewed one or more times and by one or more interpreters. This facility increases enormously the ability to check out precisely what occurred and secure other more detached and perhaps more objective interpretations of it than may be expected from someone directly involved in the original data gathering.

Naturally, recording, transcribing and re-reviewing data takes time and attracts additional costs, and this will undoubtedly constrain the researcher depending upon how much reliance is to be placed on the final analysis. Similarly, where observational data are used to construct questionnaires then matters of accuracy etc. may be deferred to the analysis of the information yielded by them.

While audio and video recording are widely accepted and comparatively inexpensive to apply, there will be occasions when it is not possible to use them. In these circumstances it will be necessary to take notes and write these up as complete description after the observation has taken place. Attention to a few ground rules will help ensure the validity and reliability of one's records:

> Record the 'facts' not your interpretation of them. This comes later.
> Record as much detail as you can, i.e. try to remain detached and uninvolved and don't try to sort out your material while you are gathering it.
> Don't take anything for granted.
> Consider everyone involved – don't assume that only a few key individuals matter.
> If you have prepared a check list then review it to see you have covered all the issues involved and have a complete record.
> Write up your notes as soon after the event as you can. You might find it easier to dictate these and then make a transcript or, as voice recognition software improves, have your computer make one for you.
> If possible use more than one observer so you can compare notes and clarify any differences or omissions.
> If possible get the person(s) observed to read through your notes for accuracy and completeness.

The last point presumes that the subject of your observation is aware that you are observing them. This raises the important question of whether observation is overt or covert. Ever since Elton Mayo reported his famous Hawthorne study (as discussed at p.151) it has been apparent that when people know you are watching them they are likely to modify their normal behaviour in some way. This is true of subjects in experimental settings and respondents in surveys who wish to help the researcher with their inquiries. It follows that to secure more objective data it would be better to collect it without the knowledge of the subject. In many cases this will raise serious ethical concerns and the researcher will have to give careful consideration to Codes of Practice and get clearance from the appropriate Ethics Committee before undertaking a covert study.

That said, there are many situations where direct covert observation can be very instructive and constitute no threat to individual privacy. For example, as a newly appointed Director of a carpet manufacturing company I thought it would be useful to spend some time in retail outlets observing how prospective buyers approached the merchandise on display, and interacted with sales staff. It soon became apparent that most single people were browsing, and gathering background information on what was available, while most couples were more committed to making a purchase. This observation was validated by approaching the individual/couples who confirmed this pattern of shopping behaviour; i.e. one person did the identification and screening; the second person endorsed/confirmed the final selection.

A less obvious finding was that when choosing a carpet people first looked at the design but then looked at the back of the carpet. When asked 'Why?' two expanations were offered. The first was that you could tell the quality of a carpet by the backing material, and that jute backed carpets were superior to others. It was generally older persons or those who had been told this by their mother who gave this explanation. The second explanation was far more prosaic – the label describing the properties of the carpet is on the back! However, this 'finding' led to much more effort being given to label design and content reflecting the attention and importance attached to it by the prospective buyer.

Structured observation

As noted earlier, observation can range from largely unstructured to highly structured. In exploratory research observation is usually unstructured or lightly structured. However, as exponents of grounded theory and other forms of exploratory research would stress, the rigour in such studies is achieved through systematic analysis. But, for descriptive inquiries, case studies, and experimentation to test causal relationships the researcher should have developed a conceptual framework and, possibly, a series of hypotheses that will predetermine the nature of the data to be observed and recorded.

To begin with, it is likely that one will attempt to record every aspect of behaviour (as recommended earlier). With familiarity and experience it becomes possible to classify specific actions or incidents into a lesser number of categories making the recording more accurate and reliable especially when using multiple observers. If recording in 'real time' then the fewer the categories to be recorded and the more explicit the definition of what actions fall into a given category the better the result. With an audio-visual record then even more complex and detailed analysis may be attempted.

In recording observations one is concerned with both the frequency and sequence in which acts or events occur. Frequency can be measured by keeping a simple tally, and checking the appropriate box on a pre-prepared record sheet or rating scale, but reporting the sequence or pattern of incidents or happenings will require a more elaborate procedure. Often this will call for the use of more than one observer, and a clear division of responsibility as to precisely what each is to record. Once again an audio visual record will greatly facilitate analysis and make it possible for a single researcher to examine several different dimensions of the observed behaviour without additional assistance.

Ethnography

As is apparent when one compares more recent texts on research methods with older ones the discussion of Observational methods and techniques now tends to be dominated by entries on ethnography or participant observation. We noted earlier that ethnography is a particular form of observation in which the researcher immerses themselves in the activities of a social group whose behaviour is the subject of their study. Such close and often intimate involvement presents a number of problems and issues, some of which have been identified in our more general discussion of observation. These may be summarised as:

Overt or covert?
Access.
Role to be played by the observer.
Data collection and recording.
Analysis of data.

Most of these issues have already been discussed. However, some elaboration may be helpful.

Bryman (2001) following Bell (1969) suggests issues of overt and covert observation should be combined with the setting in which the research occurs. The latter may be classified as 'open' or 'public' and 'closed' yielding a fourfold classification (p.293). A number of examples of specific studies are cited from which it is concluded that overt observation is much more common than covert, mainly for the ethical reasons touched on earlier. Further, ethnographic studies usually involve more than simple observation in that the researcher will often interact with the subjects under observation by becoming involved in their behaviour as a member of a group and/or through asking direct questions, interviewing etc. Gathering such information covertly may be an activity practised by government intelligence services but is likely to be frowned upon by academic researchers.

Access is a problem with all social science research. The longer and more detailed the proposed inquiry, and the more it involves interaction with people, the more problematic it becomes. It follows that as most ethnographic studies involve extensive interaction over prolonged time frames then access issues may be paramount. However, virtually all groups have a leader and this person will act as both gatekeeper, giving or denying access, and champion/opinion leader. If you can get their endorsement you're in!

In the case of formal groups or organisations, leaders are usually easy to identify by a title or the position they fill. But, in the case of large or complex organisations the person with the ultimate authority to grant or deny access may be quite distant from the context or setting in which the researcher is interested e.g. the buying group in a division of the company. In these cases you may have to enlist the aid of a member of the group in which you are interested to act as advocate and champion of the particular piece of research you wish to pursue, to get top management approval.

Gaining support for a project is much more likely when you can demonstrate that the research will be of direct benefit to the collaborating organisation. A particular issue here is the question of confidentiality. As a researcher your objective is to identify solutions to problems of general interest, leaving narrow, specific and context limited problems to operational management and consultants, with the intention of publicising your findings to as wide an audience as you can command. That the problem is not insuperable is evident in the very large number of detailed case studies of named organisations that are to be found in the Case Clearing House or reported in articles and books. Alternatively, when exploring a phenomenon or matter of widespread concern to a number of similar organisations or groups, it may be possible to anonymise the identity of the research subjects. However, the latter is more usual when undertaking survey research than the kind of in-depth investigation that qualifies as an ethnographic study.

While getting approval to research a group or activity is essential, it is still necessary to gain the support of the members of the group you wish to study, and this may be quite another matter. Inevitably, someone 'injected' into a group with the approval of senior management is liable to be seen as a spy, and will have to work hard to dispel such a view. To do so you will have to show how the work may benefit the group members, and reassure them that specific incidents and actions will not be attributed to identified individuals. You will also need to persuade them of your own qualifications for conducting the study, and explain fully and precisely what it is you are interested in and how you intend to gather information.

These same conditions also apply when seeking to study informal groups although the fact that the nominal and actual leader are normally the same person means that their approval will be crucial. These persons may also fill the role of 'Key informant' (Bryman 2001) - persons who have special knowledge or insights, can introduce the researcher to other persons in a network and facilitate entry to events or rituals that play an important role in group behaviour. Obviously, such key informants can be of great assistance with the caveat that one should not become over-dependent on them for fear of losing one's own objectivity.

The role of the observer is generally determined by their degree of involvement from totally detached – a covert observer watching what people do in a retail outlet – to totally involved – Margaret Meade and Pacific Islanders. Each level of involvement has its advantages and drawbacks and these are discussed by Bryman following Gold (1958) and Gans (1968). For the researcher the key issue is to explain and justify the level of involvement adopted, while acknowledging what the strengths and weaknesses of their approach are – obviously concluding that the 'ends justify the means'!

Matters of data recording were outlined in the earlier section on observation in general but more explicit advice is to be found in Bryman op.cit. pp.304- 306.

In summary Desai (2002) lists the characteristics of ethnographic research when used in a business and management context as:

A focus on the cultural and social content of people's actions and beliefs – looking at people as whole individuals, rather than compartmentalised consumers.
Seeing the world from the point of view of the participants, and avoiding imposing the researchers' cultural frameworks.
Allowing people to use their own language to describe their world.
Looking at behaviour in the place and time at which it actually occurs – in the home, the office, the car, the supermarket.
A long-term invovement with individuals or groups.
The use of a range of data collection methods, including interviews, group discussions, informal conversations and observations of behavioiur, and also the inclusion of cultural artefacts as part of the data – e.g. photographs, films, drawings.

A recent issue of Marketing Business (November/December 2002) contained a feature article entitled 'Big brother is watching you' that described the use of ethnographic techniques in marketing research. While there is obviously disagreement between practitioners as to how rigorous such studies are, with some maintaining that only trained anthropologists (You need to have sat in a mud hut and gathered material.') are adequately qualified, others take a more pragmatic view. One practitioner asserts "Ethnography is not research per se; it's looking at what we don't know we don't know... You can only find that out by living with people and going shopping with them." This 'deep hanging around' is seen as a major source of insight from which working hypotheses and more formalised data collection can be developed.

Grounded theory

Passing reference to grounded theory has been made in several places already. When discussing the basic difference between a positivistic or interpretivistic (Phenomenological) approach to research, grounded theory was identified as an example of the latter with theory evolving from observation of a phenomenon. Such theorising might be limited to a specific relationship – a substantive theory – or be generalised to embrace a class of relationships through the statement of a general theory.

Further reference was also made, when reviewing observation as one of the three principal research methods, when it was suggested that in its purest application grounded theory consisted of an attempt at completely unstructured observation in which the observer started with no preconceived ideas about the object of their study, but simply recorded information as it emerged. The theory then emerged from the systematic analysis of the data secured from the observations. It is with this analysis that we are now concerned.

To begin with it is important to identify the important philosophical distinction between the grounded and other approaches to the analysis of qualitative data of the kind collected in observational studies. In essence, the grounded theory approach to analysis seeks to tease out and define underlying relationships through an inductive and intuitive interpretation of the data. In contrast the alternative approach adopts a deductive interpretation by seeking to convert qualitative data into quantified data by means of content analysis which may be regarded as an attempt to introduce objectivity into subjective data by examining the frequency with which events or facts occur and then developing and testing hypotheses about these associations.

In other words, grounded theory seeks to derive structure through the analysis of non-standardised data, while surveys define a stucture and then collect standardised data to enable the testing of hypotheses on which the structure is founded.

While the grounded theory approach is relatively new in the social sciences, having first been described in Glaser and Stauss' seminal book *The Discovery of Grounded Theory: Strategies for Qualitative Research* (1967), it has become a widely used technique in business and management research.

However, it is probably true to say that few persons claiming to use grounded theory do so in the highly structured and systematic way prescribed by the founders; nor do many researchers address a database without some preconceived issue or problem in which they are interested. This would certainly be a high risk strategy for a research student with only a limited period of time in which to demonstrate their understanding of research philosophy and procedures, and an ability to implement that understanding through the execution of a research project.

In my own direct experience of supervising over 50 doctoral candidates in marketing, only two followed a rigorous grounded theory approach – an incidence of less than 5 per cent – and the same statistic applies to those theses on which I have acted as external examiner. However, many more had elements of the method in their early, exploratory phases, as have numerous Masters and Honours dissertations.

By now it should be more than clear that there is no single preferred method of doing research. What is important is that one should be familiar with the options available and the situations when one might be preferable to another, while remaining sensitive to the advantages and disadvantages of taking any given course of action. It follows that if one is to claim that they are using a grounded theory method then one must be familiar with the characteristics and features of the method so as to be able to demonstrate that they have abided by these conventions or, alternatively, why they have departed from them with a justification for doing so. Given Pascale's famous aphorism, "It is not certain that everything is uncertain", provided you explain what you have done and substantiate your reasons for doing it, others will not be able to dismiss your work on procedural grounds, and will be forced to consider the implications of your findings. In this spirit it will be helpful to summarise the key features of grounded theory analysis. In doing so we follow closely the advice given by Easterby-Smith et al in the belief that the relevant section was probably written by Dr Andy Lowe, a long-time colleague at Strathclyde and avid exponent of the technique on which his own doctorate was based.

Starting from the assumption that one is working with transcripts of in-depth interviews, seven major steps in anaysis are identified:

> Familiarisation
> Reflection.
> Conceptualisation.
> Cataloguing concepts.
> Recoding.
> Linking.
> Re-evaluation.

Many of these steps are self-explanatory and full descriptions of them all are to be found in the original source. Superficially, at least, the nature and sequence of events would seem to follow common sense.

To begin with we read through the data we have collected to remind ourselves of its scope and content, and see if any preliminary questions or ideas emerge. Next we consider whether any of our preliminary thoughts may be related to any other bodies of knowledge with which we are familiar, leading to the formulation of some preliminary working hypotheses. We may discuss these with others who might have a view on them, and be able to offer comments or suggest potentially useful lines of inquiry.

Given some tentative ideas/hypotheses, the third step is to begin and formalise these as concepts, and then return to the original data to validate their existence and the context in which they occur. In the process yet other hypotheses/concepts may appear and be documented.

The fourth stage is where the researcher begins to impose some structure on the raw data by organising it into related groups or categories. Inevitably, by beginning to reduce the data it will lose its original richness, and care must be taken to document the processes whereby one classifies individual observations into a lesser and more manageable set of categories. It is acknowledged that the coding of information in this way runs counter to the spirit of intuition that drives the adoption of a grounded approach. Easterby-Smith et al imply that beginners may need to catalogue information on cards or a computer database, with the inference that experienced researchers do not. Personally, I have difficulty with this point of view. While the dyed-in-the-wool qualitative researcher may claim that one is abandoning the philosophical foundations of the interpretivist position by organisning and recording data in this way, I find it difficult to see how one could possibly remember all the information without classifying it in some way.

Irrespective of whether or not one records the concepts coming out of stage four, the next step is to compare these once again with the places where they occurred in the raw data to check out their validity, and how they relate to other concepts. In doing so it may be necessary to create new categories or collapse others which deal with the same basic idea.This exercise leads naturally into step 6 where patterns and frameworks begin to appear, enabling one to generalise from the particular and develop a theoretical statement which links the data into a holisitc explanation of the phenomena. Easterby-Smith et al suggest that it is at this point that one develops a first draft for discussion and comment with others and get feedback.

Finally, depending on the feed back, one re-evaluates one's preliminary conclusions and makes appropriate amendments. These may or may not require further field research. But, as we have seen, it is rare for any piece of research to resolve all the questions that prompted it in the first place; added to which new questions almost always arise from the new research itself.

Also, for those researchers who regard qualitative reserch as an essential precursor to the collection of more objective data, findings from the grounded theory study will provide the principal foundation for this.

Case studies

An increasingly popular method in Business and Management research is the writing of case studies,despite the fact that it has been criticised for its "mindless empiricism" in that no attempt is made to link the description with theory, and its tendency simply to record information without any attempt to strucure or analyse that information. The latter is often true of the material recorded in descriptive case studies used as learning tools in business and management education following the 'case method' made famous by the Harvard Business School. However, in many situations case studies may be the most useful and appropriate method to answer research problems of what Perry (2001) terms the "how and why" kind as contrasted with the research problem concerned with "what" or "how should?".

Perry (2001) draws on an extensive body of literature when he distinguishes between descriptive case studies and case research when he states that "...case research is:

> an investigation of a contemporary, dynamic phenomenon and its emerging (rather than pardigmatic) body of knowledge;
> within the phenomenon's real-life context where the boundaries between the phenomenon and context under investigation are unclear;
> when explanation of causal links are too complex for survey or experimental methods so that single clear outcomes are not possible;
> using interviews, observation and other multiple sources of data."
> (References omitted).

As someone who has studied at Harvard Business School I would not exclude the descriptive case study from consideration as a research method. Such case studies usually contain a great deal of detail, and so may be regarded as a particularly comprehensive collection of linked observations. The fact that much of the detail may be extraneous or even irrelevant to the identification and solution of a problem (or research issue!) is also true of much data gathered using other research methods. The challenge for the student using case studies is to separate the relevant from the irrelevant, and then organise and structure what is left so that it is suitable for meaningful analysis.

At HBS the objective was to derive 'currently useful generalisations' which could be used to help solve new problems with similar characteristics to those from which the CUG had been derived. This 'clinical' approach to learning takes more time and is less comprehensive in scope than courses based on textbooks and lectures; but the lessons learned are likely to remembered long after other studies if for no other reason than that one has developed the CUGs or working hypotheses oneself. In a book written to celebrate the use of the case method at Harvard (McNair 1954) one of the contibutor's acknowledged using case studies "… has none of the conspicuous advantages of teaching accepted truths. As a method it is crude and clumsy in execution; it is inefficient in that no scale of accomplishment can be established and empirically applied; it lacks the technical excellence ordinarily associated with good teaching and the finished art of the pedagogues. Nevertheless, … if the fullest opportunities of case insrtuction are realised, the *whole method becomes nothing but practical application of the theory that the power of thinking and not the acquisition of facts is the ultimate of our educational ideals.*" [Emphasis added]

As such, as a supervisor, I would not preclude the analysis of descriptive case studies as a suitable basis for a dissertation or thesis. Indeed a great deal of scholarship in the Humanities, especially History, consists of re-reviewing recorded accounts with a view to confirming or challenging earlier interpretations.

The distinction made by Perry is essentially based on whether or not the researcher is actively involved in the gathering of the information to be used in answering a research question. In our view this is a secondary issue, and much of the advice offered by Perry is equally applicable to the analysis of pre-existing case studies.

A similar view applies to the distinction made by Stake (1994) between intrinsic and instrumental case studies. According to this classification intrinsic case case studies are those like the Hawthorne studies where the researcher is interested in a particular case and explores it in great detail. By contrast, instrumental case studies are seen as examples of a phenomenon or issue and are used as being representative of a class of similar cases for the purposes of theorising and drawing conclusions.

As Schiavulli found when researching the formation of clusters, the categorisation is stronger on paper than in practice. In her study the cases were both intrinsic and instrumental in that her sponsors (Scottish Enterprise) were primarily interested in the particular (intrinsic) question of whether it would be possible to promote/create/acclerate an optoelectronics cluster in Scotland, while the wider academic issue was instrumental in that it was interested in the process of cluster formation per se. This observation led Schiavulli to an important conclusion for researchers in general: "Researchers should mind more about the logic of inquiry underpinning their personal research as a particular and unique issue, rather than pay too much attention to the orthodox modes of doing research".

As Schiavulli's supervisor I endorsed this view but, be warned, some supervisors/examiners/reviewers would not, which makes this a risky strategy to follow. It is for this reason that at several places we have emphasised the importance of making it clear that you are familiar with the orthodox and conventional research methods and methodologies and have justified your selection of the specific choice made. It is also the reason that when you come to publish your findings you need to identify an outlet that is sympathetic to the approach you have chosen.

From these comments it should be clear that case research is, or can be, a mixture of both methodologies and methods. When evaluating prior research as part of one's literature review we are dependent on existing records or descriptions, some of which may well be case studies. Having identified a research issue we will usually want to do some exploratory research which will involve observation of a case or cases of the phenomenon in which we are interested, and may involve interviewing. Based on our findings we develop a theory, supported by a number of hypotheses, which we can then test through more focused observation, including case studies, or by experimentation and/or survey. And so the cycle continues.

Case research: history and evolution

Case methods are among the oldest means employed by humankind in describing, exploring, and explaining various phenomena. The earliest usage of the case study technique is attributed to Hippocrates who presented 14 classic case studies of disease some 2300 years ago (Bonoma, 1985 p.1). In the field of sociology the case research approach is closely associated with the members of Frederick lePlay School of France and the Chicago School (George Mead, Herbert Blumer, Robert Redfield are among some prominent members of the time). Malinowski employed the method extensively in founding the modern anthropological tradition. About 1935, the case study proponents of the Chicago School faced serious challenges from the advocates of statistical survey techniques, and the restoration of the method had to wait to the formation of a second Chicago School represented by Strauss, Glaser and Becker. In particular, it was the seminal contribution of Glaser and Strauss (1967) that revived interest in theory building research rather than efforts aimed at theory verification (cf. Glaser 1998).

Case research is an appropriate strategy that is "well suited to aspects of marketing where there is relatively thin theoretical base or complex observation task" and when the context of the object of study cannot easily be separated from the focal object (Bonoma 1985, p.203). Gummesson argues that the case study method allows in-depth and holistic understanding of multiple aspects of a phenomenon, and the interrelationships between different aspects.

Holism may be viewed as the opposite of reductionism. The latter consists of breaking down the object of study into small, well-defined parts. This approach goes all the way back to the 17th-century and the view of Descartes and Newton that the whole is the sum of its parts. This leads to a large number of fragmented, well-defined studies of parts in the belief that they can be fitted together, like a jigsaw puzzle, to form a whole picture. According to the holistic view, however, the whole is not identical with the sum of its parts. Consequently the whole can be understood only by treating it as the central object of the study." (Gummesson 1988, p.76-77).

There has been in the recent past a great acceleration in formalising case research strategy. Yin advocated a quasi-experimental version of case research. Indeed, his book remains the most influential one for case researchers. Yin argued that there is a "frequent confusion regarding types of evidence (e.g. qualitative data), types of data collection methods (e.g. ethnography), and research strategies (e.g. case studies)" (Yin 1981, p.13). Indeed, case research is a versatile strategy that has many distinguishing characteristics. Yin (1994, p.13) offers a technical definition of case study: case study is an empirical inquiry that investigates a contemporary phenomenon within its real-life context, especially when the boundaries between phenomenon and context are not clearly evident.

Yin further states some of the data collection and analysis strategies that the case study inquiry deals with:

> Copes with the technically distinctive situation in which there will be many more variables of interest and data points, and as a result
> Relies on multiple sources of evidence, with data needed to converge in a triangulated fashion, and as another result
> Benefits from the prior development of theoretical propositions to guide data collection and analysis.

An experiment, for instance, deliberately divorces a phenomenon from its context, so that attention can be focused on only a few variables (typically, the context is "controlled" by the laboratory environment). A history, by comparison, does deal with the entangled situation between phenomenon and context, but usually with non-contemporary events. Finally, surveys can try to deal with phenomenon and context, but their ability to investigate the context is extremely limited. The survey designer, for instance, constantly struggles to limit the number of variables to be analysed (and hence the number of questions that can be asked) to fall safely within the number of respondents that can be surveyed. (Yin 1994, p.13).

Case studies are best equipped to deal with situations when a holistic perspective of both the context and object of study is required. Because of its rather unique ability to address complex phenomena, case research always has "too many variables (V)" compared to the number of observations (O) to be made (Yin 1981). This V>>O inequality (number of variables far exceeds number of data points) is precisely what makes the case study method singularly appropriate, and most other methods, including standard experimental and mail survey designs, totally unsuitable. Mail surveys are suitable if the number of variables of interest is low in relation to the number of data points. In fact, unless the number of variables is matched by several multiples of number of respondents cases, some techniques of analysis such as factor analysis simply cannot be applied with any degree of external validity (Hair et al. 1995). On the other hand experiments require laboratory like conditions that divorce a phenomenon from its context and control variables that are not of interest.

In the last two decades, they have been some significant methodological developments in the area of case research. The case research processes are by now rather well-established (Glaser and Strauss 1967; Bonoma 1985; Gummesson 1988; Eisenhardt 1989; Yin 1994) and recent papers (for example Perry 1998) draw together different strands of writings and provide detailed guidance on why, how, when and where to implement the research strategy. Indeed the case of methodological rigour has been made very clear in the new genre of writings (Eisenhardt 1991; Dyer and Wilkins 1991).

In general the acceptance of alternative research methodologies has been in ascendancy in recent times owing to the greater methodological rigour displayed in both the adoption and implementation of these research strategies. In case research, scholars agree that the versatile nature of the tool allows both theory building and theory testing, although it is generally the former that it is known for. Yin (1994, p.13) was the first to make the distinction between the traditional "statistical generalisation" and "analytic generalisation". Yin argues that the sampling logic is not appropriate with case studies and likens cases to experiments or surveys, and suggests that in analytic generalisation one draws theoretical inferences, thereby obviating the intermediate step of drawing inferences to populations. Both Yin (1994) and Eisenhardt (1989) suggest that multiple cases can be compared to one another with a view to establish either "literal replication" or "theoretical replication" leading respectively to confirmation and disconfirmation of results. In effect, the process of multiple cases could be useful for both building and testing theories through the application of comparative logic

Easton's analysis of some of the strategies used in case research throws light on the underlying methodological and philosophical perspectives.

Bonoma, for example, suggests a stage model that has echoes of logical empiricism/falsificationism...Yin's preferred strategy is more deductive style [testing of hypothesis derived from theory developed beforehand]...

Mitchell's position, for example, is essentially   realist and logical empiricism... Yin and Bonoma adopt similar positions when they use the empiricists criteria of validity and reliability to guide the way in that research is conducted. *If case research is represented as the creation and testing of theory in miniature, it cannot be immune from the epistemological problems that such activities attract in other forms of research"* (1995 pp.478-479 references deleted), [emphasis added].

It is generally agreed, however, that case studies are useful and important when seeking to develop theory inductively through description and analysis of new and emerging phenomena such as relationship marketing. However, case studies differ from 'pure' grounded theory in that one does not start from the position that one has no prior assumptions about the phenomena to be studied. Rather, case study research admits that the researcher brings prior knowledge and understanding to their observations and so combine induction and deduction in selecting and interpreting information. Initially, case studies will be exploratory in nature but, as one gathers and analyses more information, so a tentative theory will begin to form. In turn, this will shape the inquiry and data collection and become 'confirmatory' research with the benefit that inconsistent findings will require one to modify the emergent theory as one proceeds.

For purposes of research training, students are invariably required to demonstrate familiarity with prior research cognate to their research issue through the completion of an appropriate literature review. Such familiarity is also expected when seeking funding and/or support for research projects. In other words, issues deserving of research are prompted by some stimulus and this is usually associated with a context that calls for examination in order to establish if the issue is a real one needing further research. However, while it is difficult, if not impossible, to articulate a research issue without some prior expectation or working hypotheses, it is important that these do not directly influence the line of inquiry taken in the exploratory interviews. Perry (1998) recommends that one start with a question that is content free and invites the interviewee to relate their experience.

At the same time it is important for the interviewer to have prepared a list of topics or issues they wish to explore with the interviewee. While it is hoped that these will emerge spontaneously, in which case the interviewer can cross them off their check list, in many cases it will be necessary to 'steer' the exchange throught the use of probes. [These are discussed in Chapter 11, p.255ff on interviewing]. Ideally, probes should develop naturally from comments made by the interviewee, be couched in the language they are using, and call for a discursive rather than "yes/no" answers.

While many studies have been based on a single case study, e.g. the Hawthorne experiments. Or two, e.g. Burns and Stalker's analysis of organic and mechanistic organisational structures, most researchers will use a multiple case approach in order to enable cross-case analysis. In selecting cases, similar guidelines apply as to in-depth interviewing in other forms of qualitative research. First, the choice of respondents should be governed by replication rather than sampling logic. By this is meant that one is not seeking representativeness as in a survey,but the choice of cases that will provide either literal or theoretical replication, i.e. cases that will yield either similar or contrary results respectively for predictable reasons.

With regard to the number of cases one should study opinion varies between 4 and 10 (Eisenhardt 1989) up to 15 (Miles and Huberman 1994). On the other hand, one of the most influential case study analyses of all time – Peters and Waterman's "In Search of Excellence" – was based on 42 cases. In short, there is no fixed number, and the best advice is to continue collecting data until diminishing returns set in. Thus with 'rich' and detailed case studies a few may suffice but, where access is difficult and/or the field of interest is broad, one may need considerably more individual cases to generate sufficient data for analysis.

One must also take into account the number of interviewees in each case or unit of inquiry. In some circumstances, for example functional management in SMEs, there may be only one person representative of the function in a firm. By contrast, if one is researching into new product development then several different functions may be involved, calling for multiple interviews within a single firm. Much the same would apply if investigating issues such as organisational culture when the views of people at different levels within a firm would be desirable. Once again the guiding principle should be to continue collecting data until redundancy sets in.

When it comes to the analysis of case data the same rules apply as to any other data base. In short, data needs to be classified into meaningful categories which may then be compared to establish the nature and degree of asociation between them (see Chapter 13). Similarly, the writing up of the findings from case based research should follow the same protocols and procedures as apply to studies using other forms of data collection (see Chapter 14). However, you may wish to consult Perry (1998) for more specific advice.

Summary

In this chapter we have been concerned primarily with a selection of qualitative methods most frequently used in business and management research – structured and unstructured observation, grounded theory, ethnography and case studies. (Biography, referred to in the preliminary discussion of qualitative methods in Chapter 2, has not been considered here as it is rarely a suitable topic for project research). All these methods are widely used, especially in the exploratory phases of research when one is seeking to gain a better understanding of a problem or phenomenon as a basis for conceptualisation and theorising.

In many cases, exploratory research of this kind will be sufficient for the purposes of the kind of project required of Honours or Masters students and, depending on its scope and depth, for Doctoral dissertations too. According to the level of the qualification, and the proportion of it attributable to the thesis or dissertation, there will be an expectation that at the conclusion of a piece of exploratory research one will be able to identify what else needs to be done to answer fully the research question that prompted it in the first place. Usually, this will consist of a statement of further issues needing examination and/or confirmation/falsification, i.e. to test the propositions or working hypotheses derived from the research. Such testing is the province of quantitative research through experimentation and survey of the kind introduced in the previous chapter.

Both quantitative and qualitative research make use of a number of techniques – the selection of respondents to study, the construction of test instruments for eliciting information from the selected respondents and the administratioin of the test instrument. These are the topics of the next three chapters that deal respectively with sampling, questionnaire design and interviewing.

Recommendations for further reading

Bryman, Alan (2001), *Social Research Methods*, Oxford: Oxford University Press

Bryman, Alan (Ed.) (2001), *Ethnography*, 4 volume set, London: Sage Publications
An important reference work combining a guide to methods and their application with landmark studies using this approach

Desai, Philly (2002), "Methods Beyond Interviewing", In: *Qualitative Market Research, Volume 3, Qualitative Market Research: Principle and Practice*, London: Sage Publications

Mason, Jennifer (2002), *Qualitative Researching*, 2nd edition, London: Sage Publications
An established and well regarded introudction to qualitative research

Carson, D. Gilmore, A., Perry, C. and Gronhaug, K. (2001), *Qualitative Marketing Research*, London: Sage Publications

Yin, R.K. (1993), "Applications of Case Study Research", *Applied Social Research Methods Series*, Vol. **34**, Newbury Park, CA: Sage

Yin, R.K. (1994), "Case Study Research – Design and Methods", *Applied Social Research Methods Series*, Vol. **5**, 2nd.edn., Newbury Park, CA: Sage (3rd edition due 2003)

CHAPTER 8

Sampling

Synopsis
Having defined a research issue, and established what is currently known about this through secondary research by means of a literature review, it is usually necessary to collect new or primary data that will enhance our understanding of that issue. Such information is acquired through a survey of sources with knowledge/experience of the issue. However, where the numbers involved are potentially large it may not be possible or feasible to question every member of the relevant population. In these circumstances some form of selective questioning by means of a sample is called for. In this chapter we review some of the major matters relevant to this topic.

Keywords
Sampling; reliability; validity; probabilistic; non-probabilistic; random; stratified;, cluster; judgement; convenience samples

Introduction

There are three basic methodologies available to researchers - observation, experimentation and survey. All three methodologies are concerned with the systematic gathering and analysis of data with a view to informing decision-makers and enabling them to make a better decision than would be possible in the absence of that information. But the acquisition of additional information is a resource-hungry process which requires the decision-maker to balance some element of risk or uncertainty against the time and money which would be necessary to reduce this still further. Ideally, we would like to consult everyone likely to be influenced by or to have an effect on our decision but, in practice, we will usually have to compromise. Sampling offers us a means of doing this in an acceptable way, and in this chapter we shall look at the basic ideas underlying sampling, the different kinds of sample available, their various advantages and disadvantages, and the planning of a sampling operation. Such technical matters as calculating sample size, variability, error and bias are outside the scope of an overview of this kind but references to appropriate sources are provided for those who wish to explore these issues further.

The basis of sampling

As stated in the Introduction, ideally we would prefer to consult or measure everyone or everything which has a bearing upon the problem we are seeking to solve. Technically this totality of persons or things is referred to as the universe or population and one of the first problems to be addressed in sampling is the definition of the population to be researched in precise and unambiguous terms. For example, in the case of a manufacturing process the population to be sampled for quality control purposes could be every unit of output within a given time period, while for the provision of a social service for elderly persons it could be every individual aged 65 and over in a defined geographical area.

Under some circumstances it may be possible or necessary to survey or enumerate the complete population. Obvious examples are the counting of a country's population every ten years, the construction of a register of occupiers of property for purposes of the payment of rates, the electoral register, etc. Similarly, in some business-to-business markets, where the numbers of suppliers and/or users are small, a complete enumeration or census may be a viable proposition. However, in the case of very large populations it has to be accepted that a complete census is often unachievable - people will have died, moved, be out of the country, etc. - with the result that in some circumstances the results from a properly controlled sample may be more accurate than an attempted census.

Accuracy and precision are key concepts in sampling and fundamental to all good sampling design. Accuracy and precision, or reliability, means freedom from random error and the degree to which repeated administration of a sample will lead to comparable results between the samples (repeatability or reproducibility). In addition to reliability the other acid test of sample design is validity by which is meant the degree to which the survey measures that which it purports to measure. Validity is usually assessed and expressed in terms of the presence or absence of bias and a number of measures have been developed to identify sources of bias and their effect on validity.

The concepts of reliability and validity are a frequent source of confusion amongst students. A very clear and precise definition is offered by Martin and Bateson (1986).

1.   **Reliability** concerns the extent to which measurement is repeatable and consistent; that is, free from random errors. An unbiased measurement consists of two parts: a systematic component, representing the true value of the variable, and a random component due to imperfections in the measurement process. The smaller the error component the more reliable the measurement.

Reliable measures, sometimes referred to as good measures, are those which measure a variable precisely and consistently. At least four related factors determine how 'good' a measure is:

(a) **Precision**: How free are measurements from random errors? This is denoted by the number of 'significant figures' in the measurement. Note that accuracy and precision are not synonymous: accuracy concerns systematic error (bias) and can therefore be regarded as an aspect of validity (see below). A clock may tell the time with great precision (to

within a millisecond), yet be inaccurate because it is set to the wrong time.
(b) **Sensitivity**: Do small changes in the true value invariably lead to changes in the measured value?
(c) **Resolution**: What is the smallest change in the true value that can be detected?
(d) **Consistency**: Do repeated measurements of the same thing produce the same results?

2. **Validity** concerns the extent to which a measurement actually measures those features the investigator wishes to measure, and provides information that is relevant to the questions being asked. Validity refers to the relation between a variable (such as a measure of behaviour) and what it is supposed to measure or predict about the world.
Valid measures, sometimes referred to as right measures, are those which actually answer the questions being made. To decide whether a measure is valid ('right'), at least two separate points must be considered:
(a) **Accuracy**: Is the measurement process unbiased, such that measured values correspond with the true values? Measurements are accurate if they are relatively free from systematic errors (whereas precise measurements are relatively free from random errors).
(b) **Specificity**: To what extent does the measure describe what it is supposed to describe, and nothing else?

Both reliability and validity are highly dependent upon the accurate definition of the population to be surveyed, of the sampling unit to be surveyed and the specification of the sampling frame from which the sampling units are to be selected. A sampling unit (sometimes called an elementary sampling unit or ESU) is the specific individual or object to be measured in the survey. While the ESU will be drawn from the defined population its definition need not necessarily be precisely the same. For example, the population may be all households with a satellite television receiver, but the actual ESU might be specified as a particular member of that household in terms of age, sex, viewing habits or whatever. As noted, the sampling frame is a defined population from which the sample is to be drawn and so must be accurate, adequate, up to date and relevant to the purposes of the survey for which it is to be used. Ideally one would like a list such as the electoral register (even though we know this will be partially incomplete in terms of the population of persons aged 18 and over living in a given geographical area), the companies in a particular industry, the members of an organization and so on. In recent years many companies have come into existence specifically to offer such lists to persons or organizations wanting to reach a clearly defined audience, and these may provide an excellent sampling framework, particularly for mail surveys. In other circumstances one may wish to use location as the basis for a sampling frame, e.g. town, local government district, etc. and then sample from that area on a selective basis; or an airport for travellers, shopping centre for shoppers and so on.

Given a sampling frame, and having defined the sampling unit, the next step is to determine the most cost-effective way of selecting specific sampling units from the sampling frame. Basically the choice rests between a probability based or random sample or some kind of non-probability based design. Probability based sampling in its strictest sense means that every member of the defined population has a known and non-zero chance of being included in the sample. Where this condition is satisfied then one can make unequivocal statements about the accuracy and validity of the findings from the survey by reference to the degree of error and/or bias which may be present in it, as measured by well understood statistical methods. Similarly, if the purpose of the survey is to test hypotheses rather than estimation, e.g. the incidence of television viewing in a population, then one may use tests of significance to estimate the confidence one can place that a given hypothesis is correct, e.g. the likelihood that firms using marketing research will be more successful than those which do not is 0.95 i.e. the association between using marketing research and success is such that we would expect this relationship to hold good in 95 cases out of every 100 observed. There are several kinds of probability-based sample in addition to the 'pure' or simple random sample and these will be described in more detail in the following section.

In the absence of a sampling frame one cannot draw a probability based sample and so will have to resort to some judgemental or non-probabilistic method. Such sampling is often referred to as purposive and alternative approaches will be reviewed below.

Sampling techniques

The main sampling techniques available to the business and management researcher are summarised in Table 8.1.

Table 8.1. Sampling techniques

A	Probability-based samples	
	Random samples - unrestricted and simple	
	Stratified samples	
	Cluster samples	
	Systematic samples	
	Area	
	Multi-stage	
B	Non-probability based or purposive samples	
	Judgement	
	Quota	
	Convenience	

Random samples

An unrestricted random sample is one in which every unit has an equal chance of selection and where the selected unit is replaced before another is drawn, i.e. the same unit could occur more that once in a sample. Restricted random sampling is the kind to which most statistical theory refers and is suited more to static populations of inanimate objects than to dynamic populations of human being. Even so the requirements for replacement makes it unsuited to most real-life sampling operations of the kind used to assess and control quality in manufacturing industries. Accordingly, simple random sampling is generally preferred and has the added advantage that it 'produces more precise estimators' (Moser and Kalton 1971, 2nd edition 1985).

In the New Collins Thesaurus (1985) 'random' is shown to have the connotations of 'accidental, adventitious, aimless, arbitrary, casual, chance, desultory, fortuitous, haphazard, hit or miss, incidental, indiscriminate, purposeless, spot, stray, unplanned, unpremeditated'. It is unlikely that any procedure described by any of these words could meet the requirements of a true random sample that every member of a population should have an equal chance of selection, and so avoid the problems of selection bias. To achieve true randomness two procedures are available – the lottery method, in which each unit is assigned a number which corresponds to a ticket a sample of which is then drawn from a box or urn, and the random number method in which one selects the numbers from a table of random numbers. As anyone who has bought a raffle ticket knows the draw does not often convince one that the tickets were thoroughly mixed before drawing! (The reason why such elaborate steps are taken when drawing the balls for the National Lottery is to convince ticket holders that it is a truly random process.) Because of the practical problems of achieving a satisfactory mix, most researchers use tables of random numbers such as those prepared by Kendall and Smith or Fisher and Yates.

However, this procedure will only ensure a true random sample if the numbers have also been assigned to the sample units in a random way. As Moser and Kalton observe no ordinary list is constructed in a random fashion. 'Whether it is in alphabetical order, or seniority order, as is often the case with lists of the general population, in street and house number order, there is invariably some systematic arrangement'.

The great advantage of random sampling is the ease with which the sampling error may be calculated. Because of this the statistical efficiency of the method is seen as a benchmark against which to compare the efficiency of more complex methods and is assigned a coefficient of 1.0. That said, its disadvantages are almost overwhelming in applied fields like business and management research, namely:

1. The need to identify every single sampling unit.
2. The need to enumerate the sampling units.
3. The need to establish physical contact with the selected sampling units in order to measure or question them.

Stratified samples

To overcome these technical difficulties a number of restricted approaches to random sampling have been developed of which stratified sampling is one of the most popular. According to Mayer:

> Stratification is simply the process of splitting the population into strata (or smaller populations) according to factors that are correlated with the factor under study. The only requirement for stratification is that each item in the population must fall into one and only one stratum. Efficiency is gained through stratification by creating relatively homogeneous strata. The greater the correlation between the stratifying variable and the factor under study, the more efficient stratified sampling will be. Having set up strata, a simple random sample is drawn from within each stratum. The correct representation of the related factors in the sample assures a lower overall sampling error. (Mayer 1965)

From this description it is clear that defining the strata is critical to the sample design. Ideally, sampling units within each stratum should be as homogeneous as possible and each stratum should be distinctive from all the other strata. For example, we could stratify the population in terms of age, sex and education or use a composite factor such as socio-economic grouping or stage in the family life-cycle. If the subject of our survey is to do with shopping behaviour then perhaps we could stratify on the basis of food and non-food and further sub-divide or stratify in terms of independent and multiple retailers. In these cases one already has an *a priori* basis for stratification but in others this may not be readily apparent, and some exploratory research may be necessary to help define meaningful segments or strata for investigation.

In determining the representation of sampling units two approaches are possible, described as proportionate and disproportionate. As the term suggests, in the case of proportionate stratified sampling the amount of the sample drawn from each stratum is proportionate to the stratum's share of the total population, whereas in the case of disproportionate sampling one varies the proportion within each stratum in accordance with a criterion or criteria which reflects the variability within the strata. Suppose, for example, that one wishes to sample the opinions of employees about the desirability of a buy-out from the current owners and that the workforce comprises 700 manual workers, 150 technicians, 125 clerical and administrative workers, and 25 managers. Given a sample size of 200 then we would survey 140 manual workers, 30 technicians, 25 clerical workers and 5 managers using a proportionate design which, theoretically, is what we would expect from a truly random design but with the improvement that by stratifying the population we have eliminated the possibility of any variation between the strata.   While this is a technically satisfactory answer it is clear that by adopting a disproportionate sampling methodology we could greatly improve the quality and usefulness of the data for the same expenditure of effort. Given a sample size of 200 we would probably want to survey all 25 managers, all key technical and clerical workers up to a maximum of 105 and survey only 1 in 10 of the manual workers totalling 70 in all.

While a disproportionate sampling procedure increases the complexity of the statistical calculations necessary to arrive at an unbiased sample estimate, the improvement in efficiency (quality of output) is well worth the effort, for in addition to being able to make statements about the population as a whole, one can make statements about each of the strata individually.

Stratified sampling is used extensively in business for continuous research activities such as the Neilsen retail audit or the household consumption survey where the researcher has a sound knowledge of the population and the basic strata which comprise it. Even so the economics of data collection may make it unduly expensive to sample some strata on a truly random basis, and the researcher will look for a more cost-effective method such as that offered by cluster sampling.

Cluster sampling

Cluster sampling is similar to stratified sampling in that both techniques require the researcher to sub-divide a population into a set of mutually exclusive and exhaustive sub-groups. However, the methods differ in that in cluster sampling one samples the sub-groups whereas in stratified sampling one selects a sample from within each sub-group. It follows that in a cluster sample each sub-group should be a microcosm of the total population, while in a stratified sample each stratum represents a subset or segment of the population, each different from the other. The advantages of the cluster sample are that one does not require a precise sampling frame, and that it can be used where the population is widely distributed geographically. Because of this advantage cluster sampling is frequently used in conjunction with a geographic frame when the method may be referred to as area sampling. For example, one wishes to conduct a survey of the use of fertilisers by farmers in the UK then one approach would be to identify types of farming area - arable, pastoral, mixed, hill, etc. - choose geographic locations to reflect varying climatic conditions, and then interview every farmer within a radius of two miles of points selected within each area as the appropriate cluster. Similarly, with a household survey one might divide a town up into a number of areas each containing the same number of households and interview each householder in a sample drawn from all the areas. While cluster sampling is economically more efficient than other forms of random sample, it is statistically less efficient in that the standard error of the estimate is likely to be larger.

Systematic sampling

Another form of random sampling which is widely used is the systematic sample. This method has advantages over simple random sampling in that it is not necessary to number every unit in the sampling frame.   Instead one divides the population by the required sample size to determine the sampling interval {'k'} and then selects a random starting point whereafter every kth item is selected systematically, e.g.

Population = 2000, sample = 200

$$k = \frac{2000}{200} = 10$$

Random start = 7, therefore sample = 7, 17, 27, 37, 47..., 1997

On reflection, it is apparent that a systematic sample may be regarded as a one-stage cluster sample in the sense that in the above example we have really divided our population into 10 clusters and decided to sample the 7th. cluster.   Had we started at 5 (15, 25, 35, ...1995) then we would have sampled the 5th cluster. In addition, if there is no order in the list from which the sample is drawn a systematic sample would also qualify as a simple random sample. When drawing a systematic sample care must be taken to ensure that there are no hidden patterns or periodicities in the data as these could result in severe bias, e.g. a sample is drawn of daily sales receipts – if one numbers the days of the week 1-7 we would expect significant differences in the pattern of sales on a day to day basis such that selecting any day as representative would lead to distorted results.

While it has been convenient to describe the various types of probabilistic samples as if each could be executed as a single procedure, in reality most sampling is undertaken in a series of steps defined as multi-stage sampling. A multi-stage approach was implicit in our earlier example of a cluster sample of farmers' use of fertilizer. While there may exist a complete listing of the UK population of farmers, drawing a simple random sample could easily result in a widely dispersed and difficult to contact group of farmers. By stratifying farming into broad types – arable, pastoral, mixed, hill, etc., and selecting areas of the country where each is dominant, e.g. arable – Norfolk, Vale of York, Ayrshire, etc. one is able to focus one's interviewing effort in a highly cost effective way. Multi-stage sampling is widely used in national surveys of this kind, particularly when seeking to obtain information from the whole population of the country, e.g. voting intentions, opinions on an issue such as security at airports, etc. It is also the basis of omnibus surveys, although the actual selection of respondents for these may not always satisfy the random requirements of a probabilistic methodology to the satisfaction of a purist.

While the above description covers the main types of probability based sample, several other procedures are available (replicated, multi-phase, etc.), but are of more interest to the technician than the manager. They are also likely to be seen as important in student research projects using a quantitative methodology. Of more interest and importance to the manager and practitioner are a number of non-probability based sampling procedures which form the subject of the next section. These are also more suited to project work where limited resources are available.

Non-probability based or purposive samples

The obvious benefit of probability-based sampling procedures is that they allow one to draw inferences about the population from which the sample was drawn and state these with a known degree of confidence that any similarly chosen sample would yield the same results as that given by the present sample. The major drawback is that such procedures can be difficult, complex, time consuming and expensive to execute. Clearly, there is a need for a simpler methodology which can assist and inform decision making, albeit that it lacks the precision and accuracy of the probability based survey. Further, where resources are limited, as is the case with much student research, probabilistic methods may be unrealistic. The need for simpler and less expensive sampling procedures is largely met by judgemental approaches in which a sample is selected for a particular purpose (hence purposive sampling) with the two main techniques being quota and convenience sampling.

The essential difference between quota and random sampling is that in the case of quota sampling the interviewer selects respondents in accordance with some predetermined criteria such as age, sex and occupation, while in the random sample the respondents are selected (using the same criteria) by an objective methodology independent of the interviewer. While both approaches might yield very similar results the potential for bias in a quota sample is obvious – interviewers tend to select the most accessible individuals, both physically and in terms of their willingness to participate.

Consider, for example, a survey of airline passengers. Such persons are more likely to co-operate while killing time prior to departure than they are when going to an appointment on arrival, but their views on arrival might be more relevant. (Just to complicate matters the people with most time to kill are least likely to be important business people!)

The real problem is that while bias may exist in all survey research we cannot quantify it when using non-probability based samples and so do not know what allowance we should make for it. That said, a great deal of bias can be eliminated by using carefully specified and defined quota controls and using experienced interviewers. By doing so it is possible to obtain data which may be of greater practical use to the manager than that from a random sample owing to the greater focus on the particular types of respondents in whom they are interested. For example, if one is seeking feedback from persons who have used a new product it is unlikely that one has a sampling frame from which to select a random sample. But, for a quota sample, one would specify 'use/experience' as a basic criterion for selection.

The quota method, according to J. Desabie, is based on the following principle:

> Given that the various characteristics of a population are not independent of each other, a sample which is identical to the base population with respect to the distribution of certain base characteristics will not differ significantly from the base with respect to the statistical distribution of the other characteristics. (Desabie 1966)

In other words, if you select a quota from a population, provided the quota reflects the population in terms of factors such as age, income, education, occupation, etc. then it is reasonable to infer that other attributes discovered in the quota will reflect their distribution in the population.

Stocks (1973) quotes a number of definitions in his 'Review Paper on Quota Sampling Methods' which remains a basic reference on the subject. Thus Yates (1953) defines the quota method as:'...a variant of purposive selection. Interviewers are given definite quotas of people in different social classes, of different age-group, etc. and are instructed to obtain the requisite number of interviews in each quota.' Collins (1972) offers a similar definition when he states:

In this form of sampling, the interviewer received, instead of a list of names and addresses, a quota to fill. This will instruct her to conduct a set number of interviews with people in various categories, e.g. six interviews with women aged under 35 in the AB social grades.

Moser and Kalton offer a more extended definition when they observe that:

A wide variety of procedures go under the name of quota sampling but what distinguishes them all fundamentally from probability sampling is that, once the general breakdown of the sample is decided (e.g. how many men and women, how many people in each age group and in each 'social class' it is to include) and the quota assignments are allocated to interviewers, the choice of the actual sample units to fit into this framework is left to the interviewers. *Quota sampling is therefore a method of stratified sampling in which the selection within strata is non-random. [Emphasis added]* (Moser and Kalton 1971)

From these definitions it is clear that the reliability of a quota sample will depend very much upon the interviewer selecting respondents who correspond to the profile defined in the instructions for selecting a sample. Stocks (1973) cites several eminent statisticians who have criticized quota sampling on the grounds that the sampling variability of quota samples is several times as large as that found in random samples. Obviously the solution is to ensure that interviewers are properly briefed and supervised! The University of Strathclyde's Advertising Research Unit Fieldwork Guide gives precise instructions on the matter:

Quota sampling

This is used when we want to obtain a given proportion of respondents in all social classes, sex and age groups and is usually designed to match the overall proportion of respondents in all classes, sex and age groups. Your instructions will include a quota sheet stating how many men and women in each class, sex and age group are to be interviewed.

If the quota is INTERLOCKING, it will be necessary to ensure that each respondent fits the quota according to all three criteria, e.g. if you have to interview a male aged between 25 and 34 of social class C2, it is not adequate to interview a man aged 38 of social class C2 .

If the quota is PARALLEL, it is not necessary for each respondent to fit all three criteria simultaneously. Instead, you will be told the number of interviews to obtain, and within that total you will have to get a certain number of men and women, a certain number in each age group, and a certain number in each social class. The combination of the three criteria is not significant.

Of these two methods of quota sampling, the interlocking quota is the more effective in minimising error due to sampling in an on-going survey.

Method of finding quota

a) First deal with the class. Tour the area to find the streets where the property looks as though it will produce the classes you need. Council houses or houses close together in rows near factories, etc., will be C2Ds. Middle class homes are usually in better suburbs.

b) When you are getting towards the end of your quota, you will have to ensure against wasting time interviewing someone of the wrong age or class. You will have to modify your opening and say - Good morning ... we are interviewing a cross -section of people in different occupation groupings and different age groups. It's a survey among women in the 16-24 age group. Does that include you/is there anyone in that age group in the household. If not, ask if they know anybody nearby who does fit. If she does fit, you can then ask the occupation of the head of the household. 'I have to interview people in all sorts of occupations. Would you tell me what is the occupation of the head of household?

c)   After conducting a successful interview at an address you should always leave at least five houses before making the next call, unless otherwise instructed. Although the interval may vary, you never interview next door neighbours. If at the end of an interview, the respondent suggests that you interview his/her friend, you should avoid doing this.

d) Keep a constant check that you have the right kind of respondents for the quota. If someone is out of quota, write 0/Q in at the top of the questionnaire and tell your Supervisor. He/she may ask you to conduct a replacement interview so that you remain in quota.
    You should not, however, discard the questionnaire which is out of quota, as it may well still be used.

e)   Keep a tally of the number of interviews you have conducted on your Quota Sheet. It is important that you mark off each interview on your Quota Sheet immediately after it is completed so that you can see at a glance what type of respondents you still need to find. This also avoids the problem of doubling up on some interviews.

(See sample Quota Sheets, Figure 8.1 and Figure 8.2.)

Provided specific instructions such as these are followed then it is reasonable to accept Desabie's assumption that quota samples will yield reliable and valid data that is representative of the population from which the sample is drawn.

| Interviewer name | AB SMITH | | | Number of days | 5 | | |
| Interviewer code | 001 | | | Area | GLASGOW | | |

AGE	SEX & SOCIAL CLASS	NUMBER	TALLY CHECK	AGE	SEX & SOCIAL CLASS	NUMBER	TALLY CHECK
	Male	2	✓✓		Male	1	✓
	ABC1				ABC1		
	C2				C2	1	✓
	DE	2	✓✓		DE	1	✓
10-15	Female			35-44	Female		
	ABC1				ABC1		
	C2				C2	2	✓✓
	DE				DE		
	Male				Male	1	✓
	ABC1				ABC1		
	C1				C1		
	DE				DE	4	✓✓✓✓
16-24	Female			45-54	Female		
	ABC1				ABC1		
	C2	2	✓✓		C2		
	DE				DE	3	✓✓✓
	Male				Male		
	ABC1				ABC1		
	C2	3	✓✓✓		C2		
	DE				DE		
25-34	Female			55-64	Female	2	✓✓
	ABC1				ABC1		
	C2				C2		
	DE	1	✓		DE		

Figure 8.1. Sample interlocking quota sheet

| Interviewer name | AB SMITH | | Number of days | 5 |
| Interviewer code | 001 | | Area | GLASGOW |

SEX	Male	15	✓✓✓✓✓✓✓✓✓✓✓✓✓✓✓
	Female	10	✓✓✓✓✓✓✓✓✓✓
AGE	10-15	4	✓✓✓✓
	16-24	2	✓✓
	25-34	4	✓✓✓✓
	35-44	5	✓✓✓✓✓
	45-54	8	✓✓✓✓✓✓✓✓
	55-64	2	✓✓
	ABC1	6	✓✓✓✓✓✓
SOCIAL CLASS	C2	8	✓✓✓✓✓✓✓✓
	DE	11	✓✓✓✓✓✓✓✓✓✓✓

Figure 8.2. Sample parallel quota sheet

This expectation will be enhanced as the number of interlocking criteria is increased. Stocks (1973) proposed that the Market Research Society should adopt the following for its Code of Practice.

Quota set in terms of:

> Age
> Social class
> Working Status

> Geographical location, i.e. particular street

> Type of business

> Product usage

Place of interview:
> Home
> Street
> Work

Time of day of interview:
> Daylight
> Evening

Weekday or weekend:
> Weekday
> Saturday
> Sunday

Type of interviewer:
> Working individually
> Working as a team

Where a marketer has extensive experience of the customer, quota sampling may become very close to stratified sampling and the only issue is whether one selects respondents randomly or on the basis of judgement. Certainly, this is true of many aspects of household consumption where there is extensive documentation of the population in terms of its composition e.g. socio-economic classifications, and its location, e.g. ACORN. As in all other cases, the trade-off is between time/money and accuracy/reliability such that each case will have to be taken on its merits in terms of the perceived risk involved in the decision.

Another form of sample which involves neither probabilistic methods nor judgement is the convenience sample where the researcher takes a purely opportunistic approach and seeks information from a readily accessible sub group of the population. A classic example of such a sample was that drawn by Hastorf and Cantril whose paper 'They saw a game' had a major impact on defining the nature of selective perception. Following a major incident on the field between two college football teams the researchers interviewed spectators leaving the game and discovered that depending upon which team the respondent supported there were quite different interpretations of the incident itself. Sampling the opinions of a class of students or attendees at a management conference are also examples of convenience sampling, and can prove very valuable in helping to develop hypotheses which may then be tested by a more rigorous survey design if so desired. This is also true of quota sampling which may be an essential piece of exploratory research to provide information to define strata for subsequent random sampling.

Given the variety of survey methods available what factors should the manager/business researcher take into account in planning a sample survey? These are issues which will be addressed in the final section of this chapter

Planning a sample survey

The planning of a sample survey may be conveniently divided into seven steps, namely:

1. Define the purpose and objectives of the survey, i.e. what do you want to learn from the survey?
2. Define the relevant population or universe.
3. Identify the sampling frame and the elementary sampling unit (ESU).
4. Select a sampling procedure.
5. Determine the sample size.
6. Select the sample units.
7 Data collection.

The purpose or object of the survey will usually have been defined in a research proposal, as discussed in Chapter 3, when considering which of the three basic approaches – observation, experimentation, or sample survey – was the most appropriate to use. However, while the purpose should give a broad indication of the population to be surveyed it rarely defines it sufficiently precisely for the purposes of drawing a sample. An obvious requirement is that the population should comprise persons who possess the information which the survey is intended to secure, and time spent in defining precisely what this is will greatly improve the overall efficiency of the final survey. Of course, the precision with which one can define the intended respondents will depend very much upon how much one already knows about the subject under investigation.   For example, if one manufactures controls for use in a process industry such as steel or pulp and paper making it is likely that one will have a complete listing of all the firms in these industries, and so can easily define the universe. On the other hand if one operated a chain of international hotels almost anyone could be a potential customer, and it will be necessary to specify precisely the 'product' – business traveller, conference business, tour operator, etc. - in order to begin to define the population. Even so it is unlikely that one will come up with a sufficiently comprehensive listing that one could be confident that every single firm or individual who qualifies as a sampling unit is included within it. As we have seen, cluster sampling is the only probabilistic approach which does not require a list of the population as the basis for drawing a random sample, but all populations, e.g. business travellers, are not suited to this method.   It follows that one will often breach the rules of probabilistic sampling owing to an inability to identify fully the population from which a sample is drawn, but this does not seem to occasion too much concern in the case of many surveys which claim their results are representative of the population. Within reason it should not bother the practitioner either, but it does underline the spurious accuracy which statistical analysis can confer upon dubious data.

Selection of a sampling procedure will depend upon a number of factors not least of which is the existence or otherwise of a listing of the population as discussed above. Tull and Hawkins (1987) suggest seven criteria for judging which type of survey to use, namely:

1. Complexity
2. Required amount of data
3. Desired accuracy
4. Sample control
5. Time requirements
6. Acceptable level of non-response
7. Cost

Although these criteria are proposed in relation to the method of gathering data, i.e. by personal, mail, telephone or computer interview, they are equally applicable to the selection of a sampling procedure. Indeed, the selection of a sampling procedure will be influenced significantly by the preferred method of data collection, and vice versa, so that both will need to be considered together.

As a working generalisation, the more complex a subject the more likely it is one will use personal interviewing, and the less likely one will use a probabilistically based sample. With complex issues, qualitative research using in-depth interviews is usually more appropriate, although these may form the basis for simplified and structured questionnaires that can be administered to large samples.

Similarly, with the amount of data, the more information required the greater the likelihood that a respondent will discontinue an interview and so bias the results. Personal interviewing can help reduce this but its cost will restrict the number of interviews compared with other methods and so may incline one to a stratified or cluster sample in preference to a simple random sample. Conversely, where one only wishes to address a limited number of fairly straightforward questions a simple random sample would be preferred because of its greater accuracy and precision.

Sample control, time and cost are also closely interrelated. Clearly, the more rigorous the sampling procedure the greater the time and cost involved. From a pragmatic point of view the greater accuracy yielded by probabilistic methods may be unnecessary, particularly in a dynamic market which is changing rapidly, and so predispose the practitioner towards a purposive sample. Indeed a well-executed purposive sample may yield better and more timely data for decision making than a poorly executed random sample.

The determination of sample size is largely a technical issue concerned with the required reliability of the data to be collected, i.e. what is an acceptable level of error. Management invariably want little or no error until the budgetary implications of achieving this are spelled out. Much, therefore, will depend upon the overall importance of the decision for which the data is required. Given a budget, the sampling statistician will then use an appropriate mathematical formula to select the best design and sample size. Of course, this only applies to probability based samples; for purposive samples, judgement and experience will guide the decision.

The issue of non-response is one of the major problems facing researchers. Tull and Hawkins (1987) review a wide variety of sources which have addressed the topic and note that non-respondents 'have been found to differ from respondents on a variety of demographic, socio-economic, psychological, attitudinal and behavioural dimensions'. This is the crux of the issue - establishing contact and completing an interview will often yield initial response rates as low as 10 per cent (telephone surveys) 20 per cent (mail questionnaires) and 60 per cent (personal interviews) but, provided the respondents are similar to non-respondents in terms of the characteristics relevant to the survey, this will not prevent the drawing of valid conclusions, provided an adequate data base is collected. Various techniques have been devised to improve response rates and are described in more detail in Chapter 10. But, given the nature and size of the problem, it is unsurprising that managers question the time and effort involved in defining a population, developing a sample frame and selecting sampling units in a random fashion when a purposive sample involving much less cost could yield virtually equivalent data.

In the final analysis, it all boils down to the risk perceptions of those responsible for taking the final decision. Personal experience suggests that senior managers who are prepared to make major investment decisions on the basis of very limited evidence will often look for unreasonable, and often spurious accuracy on issues such as market share or sales forecasts, particularly for new products. Hopefully, increased exposure to marketing research as part of their career development will encourage the next generation of senior managers to invest more research effort on strategic issues and less on tactical matters and reverse the current emphasis. In the context of research project as an element in a formal course of study it is hoped that supervisors will also adopt a pragmatic approach to these issues.

Summary

In this chapter we have reviewed the ideas underlying the use of sampling as a means of improving our knowledge and understanding of the larger population or universe from which the sample was drawn. Save for very small populations, as may occur in some highly concentrated industrial markets, or otherwise narrowly defined populations, where it is possible to survey the whole population by means of a census, the sample survey is the only practical means of acquiring data on which one can base projections about the behaviour of the whole population.

Two broad approaches to sampling are available – probability based or random samples, and non-probability based or purposive samples. In a true random sample it must be possible to list every member of the population to be surveyed, and then select the sampling units (ESU) in such a manner that each has a known and non-zero chance of being included. A variety of techniques including simple random samples, stratified samples, cluster-samples and systematic samples were reviewed, as were judgement, quota and convenience samples as non-probability based approaches.

Each technique has particular advantages and drawbacks, nearly all of which require the user to compromise between costs and benefits in terms of accuracy, precision and reliability. Thus, in planning a sample survey it is necessary to balance the needs of the decision maker against the budgetary constraints. The responsibility of the researcher is to make explicit just what trade-offs are possible and what their implications are. To do this fully one must also consider carefully how the desired data are to be collected which is the subject of Chapter 10.

Recommendations for further reading

Collins, M. (1972), *Consumer Market Research Handbook*, New York, McGraw-Hill

Fink, Arlene (Ed) (2003), *The Survey Kit,* London: Sage Publications
   A 10 volume set covering all aspects of survey research.   Volume 7 deals
   specifically with sampling

Martin, Paul and Bateson, Patrick (1986), *Measuring Behaviour,* Cambridge, Cambridge
   University Press

Moser, C. A. and Kalton G. (1971), *Survey Methods in Social Investigation,* London:
   Heinemann (2nd Edition 1985)

Stocks, J.M.B. (1973), *Review Paper on Quota Sampling Methods,* Market Research Society
   Annual Conference Proceedings

Tull, Donald S. and Hawkins, Del I. (1987), *Marketing Research,* 4th Ed. New York,
   Macmillan (6th edition 1993)

Yates, F. (1953), *Sampling Methods for Census and Surveys,* London, Charles Griffin

CHAPTER 9

Questionnaire Design

Synopsis
In Chapter 8 we looked carefully at the means of selecting respondents from a population in order to ensure that they were representative of that population. One thing was particularly obvious – it takes time, effort and money to select an unbiased sample; yet all this investment will be squandered if one fails to design clear, relevant, meaningful and unambiguous questions for eliciting the desired information from selected respondents. This is the subject of this chapter. First we look at the design of questionnaires and questions, next at the issue of scaling and finally the construction of questionnaires.

Keywords
Questionnaires – planning, design, piloting; questions – design, phraseology; scales and scaling.

Introduction

Ask a silly question and you'll get a silly answer! While this may be a trite statement it contains a considerable element of truth. At numerous places in the text we have stressed the importance of objectivity, validity, reliability and the avoidance/minimisation of error. Nowhere is this more important than in the formulation of questions to elicit specific information from designated respondents.

In the previous chapter we described in some detail the steps necessary to ensure that any sample selected from a given population is representative of that population. If it is not then there is no way in which we can extrapolate findings from our sample with any degree of confidence that they reflect the characteristics/behaviour of the population as a whole. However, no matter how rigorous the sample selection , if the techniques used to elicit information are flawed then so will be the results. Given that questioning is a primary means of obtaining information from individuals concerning their attitudes, interests, behavioiur etc. it follows that defective questions will yield defective answers.

In this chapter we take a detailed look at some of the major issues encountered in developing clear, unambiguous questions and combining these into a 'test instrument' or questionnaire. To begin with we appraise some of the general matters involved in planning a questionnaire. This review leads naturally to a consideration of the actual questions to be used in a questionnaire and, specifically, their design, phraseology and structure.

In an earlier chapter (Writing a Research Proposal) we recommended the 'Kipling Test' as a check to ensure we have covered all the angles of a topic. This same test is equally important when constructing and evaluating a questionnaire and need to consider the 'Where, what, when, why, how and who?' of our subject matter. Five of these questions are concerned with objective data, but 'Why?' is a much more difficult issue to resolve as it requires respondents to account for their behaviour. Understandably, when presented with a direct question as to why we have behaved in a particular way there is a natural tendency to rationalise and offer generally acceptable explanations. If these were a true reflection of reality far fewer mistakes would be made in all aspects of business and management decision-making. To address this problem it is necessary to gain a better understanding of attitudes, beliefs, motivations and values. In part this may be established through the use of projective techniques and the development of various attitudinal scales. Several of the latter are discussed including Thurstone, Likert, Verbal Frequency etc.

Once we have developed robust questions the challenge is to combine these into a single, internally consistent questionnaire. This matter, and the testing or 'piloting' of the questionnaire, conclude the chapter leaving issues related to the interviewing of respondents and the completion of questionnaires to Chapters 10 and 11 respectively.

Questionnaire planning

Structured questionnaires are the principal means used for collecting data by means of a survey of a designated population or sample in which the researcher is interested. Inevitably, there is a potential conflict between the information the researcher wishes to obtain, and the respondents willingness to supply this information

In a paper given at an Esomar seminar in 1973 J. M. Bowen addressed this problem of the trade off between a desire to secure a maximum of information from a respondent, and the need to keep the interview clear, straightforward and of a reasonable length for ease of administration and maintenance of respondent interest. Clearly this trade-off has a major bearing upon questionnaire design in respect of at least four elements:

    Length
    Complexity
    Layout
    Wording

In order to keep the length of a questionnaire within reasonable bounds

Bowen suggests five possibilities:

> Learn to say 'No'.
> Ensure the results of every question can be used.
> Avoid duplication of information.
> Restrict the classification data asked for.
> Confine questions to the major issues.

The first two suggestions recognise that very often the buyers/users of research have not thought through precisely what it is they want to find out from a specific piece of research, and so have a natural tendency to include anything and everything which may have a bearing upon their problem. The role of the questionnaire designer is to inquire whether a question is really necessary and, if not, exclude it. This is especially the case when the researcher and designer are one and the same person. Similarly, one should avoid collecting identical information in response to what appears to be different questions, except when this is done intentionally as a test of internal consistency and a deliberate test of respondent accuracy.

The conventional wisdom with regard to classification data is that it should be left to the end of an interview so that if a respondent is unwilling to give the information (e.g. income) it will not prompt them to break off the interview. (Obviously this rule does not apply when one needs to ascertain whether the respondent conforms to the profile called for in a quota sample.) However, the fact that classification data is left to the end of the interview should not encourage the questionnaire designer to ignore the advice in 2 and 3 above.

Finally, one should avoid the temptation to try and obtain complete information when to do so might compromise the whole interview for very little improvement in one's understanding of the key issues. For example, four or five brands may account for 80-90% of total market share, with a further ten brands comprising the balance. To ask a respondent questions concerning all 15 brands could be counter productive, particularly if one intends to lump together all the minor brands as 'Others'.

Marton-Williams (1986 in Worcester and Downham) states that if a questionnaire is to be an efficient tool for collecting data then it must fulfil five functions:

> maintaining the respondent's co-operation and involvement;
> communicating to the respondent;
> helping the respondent to work out their answers;
> making the interviewer's task easy;
> providing a basis for data processing. (Marton-Williams 1986)

Depending upon the nature of one's research, the actual identity of a respondent will vary in importance. Where there is a very large population from which one is drawing a representative sample then it is usually possible to find replacements for individuals who decline to be interviewed. But, where the population is small, securing co-operation may be a major issue. Obviously, the more interesting the subject of the inquiry to the prospective respondent the more likely they will be to become involved However, you will have to maintain this interest for otherwise they make break off the dialogue, or else resort to giving incomplete or inaccurate answers in order to shorten the interview. It follows that the topic and the time required to complete an interview are major considerations when planning.

Effective communication depends very much on the design and phrasing of questions, which is discussed in some detail later. The main obstacles to clear communication are ambiguity, use of unfamiliar words, use of difficult and abstract concepts, overloading the respondent's memory and understanding with too many instructions, using vague concepts and trying to ask two questions at once. (Marton-Williams, op.cit.)

Clear and careful question design will also help the respondent answer in an accurate and meaningful way. This may involve the use of cue cards, multiple choice questions, rating scales, probing by the interviewer to help clarify their meaning, etc. These will be discussed in more detail later.

Making the interviewer's task easy only refers to those cases where the test instrument is to be administered by the interviewer. Advice on this will also be offered later but it is important to remember that the same issue also applies to self-administered questionnaires where the respondent has to navigate their own way, and cannot refer to another for clarification.

The final point about making a questionnaire suitable for easy data processing is very much a function of how structured the questionnaire is in the first place. Closed questions, where the options available are pre-specified, can also be pre-coded so that the data can be converted easily into a suitable database, often using optical character recognition and eliminating human error in transposition. In the case of open ended questions, or those offering the respondent the opportunity to "Write in", then the information will have to be processed either manually, where classification and interpretation are called for , or using appropriate software.

Question design

Tull and Hawkins' (1987) defined survey research as "the systematic gathering of information from respondents for the purposes of understanding and/or predicting some aspect of the behaviour of the population of interest". Such information may be factual or opinion based and the researcher's ability to secure it will depend heavily upon both the structure and the sequence in which they put questions to the respondent. In turn, the information received will be a function of the respondent's ability and willingness to respond (Moser and Kalton 1971). On ability it is recommended that:

> The surveyor should aim to ask questions only from those likely to be able to answer them accurately; to ask about past events only if he can reasonably expect people to remember them accurately (perhaps with the aid of recall methods); and to ask their opinions only if he can be reasonably sure that they understand what is involved and are able to give meaningful answers. It is always well to remember that most survey questions are addressed to a variety of people very differently qualified to answer them. (Moser and Kalton 1971)

It is also a well-established phenomenon that, once committed to a survey, respondents will answer questions even when they have no knowledge at all. Churchill (1987) cites the example of a question in a public opinion survey which sought the views upon a mythical piece of legislation. A total of 99.7 percent of the population expressed firm views on the desirability of the non-existent Metallic Metals Act with only 0.3 percent having 'no opinion'. Numerous other examples are to be found in the literature and it is common practice now to include a fictional item in a questionnaire as a control item to help establish actual knowledge or experience of the survey subject matter.

With regard to willingness to participate in a survey, this has been shown to depend very much on the prospective respondent's interest in the subject of the survey and on the method of administration (mail, telephone , personal interview or Internet). As noted in the previous chapter, non-response is a major problem in probabilistically based surveys and researchers devote considerable effort and ingenuity in reducing this to an acceptable minimum. In addition to facts and opinions research may be used to improve understanding of motivation, i.e. why people behave the way they do, and also to help predict behaviour.

Question phraseology

The actual phrasing of questions is critical to the quality of the data obtained and is a topic given extensive coverage in most specialist books on marketing research techniques. A sample of some of the better known of these is summarised in Table 9.1. Tull and Hawkins (1987) suggest that there are five general questions which must be addressed to ensure that both respondent and researcher assign exactly the same meaning to a question, namely:

> Are the words, singularly and in total, understandable to the respondents?
> Are the words biased or 'loaded' in any respect?

Are the alternatives involved in the questions clearly stated?
Are any assumptions implied by the questions clearly stated?
What frame of reference is the respondent being asked to assume?

To answer these questions it will helpful to review the major issues identified in Table 9.1.

Table 9.1. Issues in question phrasing

	Moser and Kalton	Alreck and Settle	Tull and Hawkins	Churchill	Chisnall
Focus or specific nature of question	√	√	√	√	√
Simple language	√	√	√	√	√
Ambiguity/clarity	√	√	√	√	
Vague or imprecisewords/vocabulary	√	√	√	√	
Leading question Overemphasis/bias	√	√	√	√	
Presuming questions	√				
Hypothetical	√				√
Personalised questions	√				
Embarrassing questions	√	√			
Social Desirability	√				
Questions on periodical behaviour	√				
Questions involving memory	√	√			√
Brevity/economy of language		√			√
Loaded questions		√	√		
Double-barrelled Questions		√		√	
Implicit alternatives/assumptions			√	√	

As noted earlier, a major factor influencing the quality of survey data is the respondent's ability to recall information accurately or else retrieve it from readily accessible records (applicable mainly to mail questionnaires). The problem with memory is that if people cannot recall accurately they are likely to guess, and so introduce an unknown error element into the findings.

Mayer (1965) points out that while memory decays over time the effect of recency may be influenced by two other 'laws of memory' – the intensity of the stimulus and the degree of association. In other words, we may forget trivial or minor events almost immediately but recall major happenings clearly years after the actual event, e.g. graduation day, wedding, birth of a child etc.

Because of the influence of association, we may also recall trivial events associated with major events long after they occurred. The message for the researcher is that one cannot assume an ability to recall accurately and so should take steps to select respondents for whom the topic is important and of interest (which will also improve response rates), and design questions which will aid recall or, alternatively, elicit qualitative statements which provide an indication of the strength, frequency, etc. of the behaviour which cannot be quantified precisely. Scaling and multiple choice answers are both of use in such situations and will be discussed in greater detail later.

Converse and Presser (1986) identify three techniques which have proved useful in enhancing the validity of the reporting of the past, namely: (a) bounded recall; (b) narrowing of the reference period; (c) cueing.

Bounded recall is useful in reducing over-reporting owing to people's tendency to lose track of time, and so include past events which happened before the time period under investigation. For example, in reporting the number of times my train or flight has been late in the past six months it is quite likely that I will include occasions extending over a longer period. To avoid this one should establish a baseline in an initial survey then re-interview the respondents at a later date and establish what has happened in the intervening period. Panels are particularly appropriate for collecting data in this way where one is especially interested in specific consumption behaviour over a defined period.

As the term suggests narrowing the reference period means inviting the respondent to report recent events rather than expecting prodigious feats of memory to recall trivial events that occurred weeks or even months ago. Converse and Presser (1986) offer the following example. 'Rather than asking "Do you get regular physical exercise?" (If yes), How many hours of physical exercise do you usually get in a week?" one can zero in on a narrow time period and ask "Did you get any physical exercise yesterday?" And, if yes, "How much?"'

However, such a question also raises the question as to whether 'yesterday' was a typical day. If asked on a Monday I would answer 'Yes, I swam half a mile' as I invariably do on a Sunday morning, but what would I say if asked on Tuesday through to Saturday? To overcome this type of problem one can ask respondents to average their behaviour, e.g. Q. 'On average how much exercise do you take a week?' A. 'I swim half a mile on Sunday mornings, walk to the station most weekdays and go hill walking every other weekend.'

The use of landmarks and cues is still regarded as experimental, but the thinking behind them appears sound. Landmarks are particular events or dates which are likely to have salience as reference points, e.g. major holidays, while cues amount to expanded explanations of the key word on which information is being sought so that respondents will not discard answers which they think might not fall within the definition of the key word.

Several of the issues identified in the table are dimensions of the same basic requirement – understandability. Thus ambiguity arises from vague, complex or imprecise words while clarity will come from focus, brevity and the use of simple language.

Question structure

Questions should be simple, intelligible and clear. It has been pointed out that, because questionnaires are usually written by educated persons who have a special interest in and understanding of the topic of their inquiry, and because these people usually consult with other educated and concerned persons, it is much too common for questionnaires to be over-written, over-complicated, and too demanding of the respondent than they are to be simple-minded, superficial, and not demanding enough.

While the generally accepted wisdom follows Payne's (1951) advice that questions should be kept short and not exceed twenty words in length Converse and Presser (1986) cite examples of longer questions proving more effective in eliciting more information. Possible reasons are that longer questions may stimulate respondents to talk more, may provide the respondent with longer to think of their reply, or may stimulate wider recall on the part of the respondent.

A major source of ambiguity is the so-called double-barrelled question. For example, if we asked the question, 'Have you flown to Glasgow on British Midland or the Shuttle?', the answer, 'Yes', would certainly inform us that the respondent has flown to Glasgow but we would not know if this was on British Midland or the Shuttle, or if both carriers had been used. To obtain the information the interviewer apparently wants we would be better advised to ask:

Have you flown to Glasgow?   Yes _____

                             No   _____

If 'Yes' can you tell me which airline you used?

                             British Midland   _____

                             Shuttle/British Airways   _____

                             Other (write in) _____

Double negative questions are also a source of ambiguity. For example, Oppenheim (1966) cites the question 'Would you rather not use a non-medicated shampoo?' (What does a negative answer mean here?)

Vague wording also leads to ambiguity even though the words themselves may be in common usage. For example, words expressing frequency such as 'often', 'occasionally', 'regularly', 'frequently' can mean quite different things to different people. For example, the answer 'Yes' to the questions 'Do you clean your teeth/brush your shoes/wash your car/regularly?' could mean 1 to 3 times a day/daily to weekly/weekly to monthly/respectively. Moser and Kalton (1971) counsel against the use of vague words and phrases such as 'kind of', 'fairly', 'generally', 'often', 'many', 'much the same' and 'on the whole' all of which are likely to yield vague answers. They also advise against 'why' and 'what' questions without some frame of reference to give focus to the question. Despite this advice many questionnaires do include such questions, and derive useful information from them.

To obtain useful information one needs to pre-identify the main responses one anticipates receiving, possibly with the intention of rank ordering these in terms of the spontaneous, top of the head reaction, e.g. Could you tell me why you prefer to fly British Midland to Glasgow?

          More convenient schedule   _____

          Better in-flight service   _____

          Easier check-in   _____

          More friendly   _____

          Cheaper   _____

          Other (write in) _____

          _____

Of course, many respondents may cite more than one reason but this can still assess which factor first comes to mind as the major benefit offered by British Midland by comparison with other competitors – its unique selling point. Alternatively, for self-completion questionnaires, you could ask the respondent to rank order their answer by noting the sequence in which factors are mentioned. Such a question can also provide a basis for probing on both the answers given and the factors not cited.

Equally confusing to respondents as non-specific questions are those which use words or phrases which are complex or not in common usage. One of the advantages cited for undertaking exploratory qualitative research through group discussions or unstructured/semi-structured interviews with individuals is that these give the researcher an insight into the vocabulary used by prospective respondents when thinking and talking about the research topic. In addition to helping to develop meaningful questions, such exploratory research may also throw up words or phrases which are particularly expressive to users and so can be used in developing a more effective selling/advertising message. The story is often told of a new floor polish developed by Johnson & Johnson which had a high resistance to traffic and so required less frequent buffing than other competitive products. Initial sales were disappointing so J & J commissioned some consumer research to help establish why their product had not achieved more success. The research showed that most users could not see any additional benefit from the new product, and so preferred to stick to the safety of their current brand. Probing on the traffic resistant property revealed that this was very attractive, but the housewives referred to the marking of polished floors as 'scuffing' so what they wanted was a 'scuff resistant' polish. Re-launched with this promise it was an instant success. (Perhaps the moral here is to do your research first!)

The above is an example of a word in common usage among respondents but unknown to the researcher. A much more frequent problem is that the well-educated researcher will have acquired a vocabulary which will let their peer group know they are well-educated, but may not be understandable to the audience to whom the research is directed. While this problem is especially acute in the case of technical terms (even when communicating with other 'experts' it is as well to define precisely what you mean by such technical terms), it is also aggravated by the use of complex words where simple ones would do. Specialist texts such as Payne's The Art of Asking Question (1951) or Selltiz et al. (1959) Research Methods in Social Relations give extensive examples of the use of simple language in place of a more pretentious and obscure phraseology while Gower's Plain Words is an essential vade-mecum for anyone seeking to communicate clearly with others. Other useful sources are Martin Cutts' *Plain English Guide* and Webster's Reference Library *Students' Companion*.

Focus and brevity will also help to reduce ambiguity and complexity. Focus will usually be achieved by constantly reminding oneself what is the fundamental purpose of the survey, i.e. what do we want to know. Alreck and Settle (1985) offer three examples of the right and the wrong focus but one will suffice to make the point about establishing purchase preference:

Wrong: Which brand do you like best?
Right: Which of these brands are you most likely to buy?

While the first question may help establish which brand has the highest reputation it does not necessarily tell you what you want to know, i.e. taking everything into account what do you actually buy?

Brevity will usually result if one sticks to one topic or issue at a time – a practice which will help avoid double-barrelled and complex questions. In addition to improving the likelihood that the respondent fully understands the question they are being asked to answer, the use of a series of sequential questions will often prove more economical as it is possible to skip questions which cannot apply given an earlier answer, or to probe in greater detail where a respondent possesses an attribute on which more information is required. Occasionally, one will have to use more than one idea to define an issue to which one wishes a reply. Wherever possible, use a separate sentence for each point rather than a compound sentence containing several clauses but, if this is not possible, careful attention to vocabulary and avoidance of superfluous words will help make the question clear. For example to determine the 'brand loyalty' of a British Midland flier travelling to Glasgow you might ask the following 'What would you do if you got to the airport and found that there was a 30-minute delay in your British Midland flight but there was a Shuttle leaving within that time?' This question would be better phrased as 'If your British Midland flight was delayed how long would you be prepared to wait before switching to an available Shuttle?' This is a compound question but yields better data from a simpler and more direct approach. Alternatively, you could have said, 'A 30-minute delay is announced on your British Midland flight. A Shuttle is due to leave before then. What would you do?'

To summarise, in order to phrase questions in a manner which is readily understandable to respondents you should:

> Use every day language
> Use simpler words rather than complex ones
> Use simple sentences rather than complex ones
> Keep the questions short and to the point
> Avoid double-barrelled questions
> Avoid double negatives.

Perhaps most important of all, once you have designed your questions pilot test them on persons of the kind who will be included in your survey to see if the questions are meaningful to them.

Loaded questions

Another fault to be guarded against in designing questions is the use of phraseology which 'leads' the respondent or is 'loaded' in a way which suggests a particular answer is being looked for. The problem arises most often with questions concerning people's attitudes, but is also possible with factual questions. For example, if you wish to establish people's preference for a particular brand you should either list all those available or none at all. If you asked, 'Which brand of baked beans, like Heinz or Crosse and Blackwell, do you buy?' it is likely that the aided recall effect of mentioning two brands will inflate the numbers claiming to buy them.

When seeking people's opinions questions which start, 'Don't you agree?' or 'Do you agree?' are likely to secure agreement, although subsequent words may counteract this initial invitation to support the proposition. For example, the statements 'Do you agree the Government should interfere in setting airline prices?' might yield a negative answer because of the loaded implication of 'interfere' while 'Do you agree the Government should get involved in setting airline prices?' is more neutral but has overtones that such involvement is a good thing. (Incidentally my Thesaurus offers 'get involved' as a synonym for 'interfere') Numerous examples of leading and loaded questions are given in the specialist texts referred to earlier, and these should be consulted for illustrations if required. Before leaving the matter, however, it must be recognised that on occasion a leading or loaded question may be included deliberately either to bias the result in the sponsor's favour or, alternatively, to help identify those with strong views in the opposite direction for further investigation. The ethics of the former are highly questionable and to be guarded against but, be warned, the practice does exist.

Many questionnaires incorporate questions which invite the respondent to 'Agree' or 'Disagree' with the statement made. This approach has been heavily criticised by numerous researchers on the grounds that it suffers from 'Acquiescence response set' whereby a proportion of all respondents will be found to agree with even directly contradictory statements. This tendency is the greatest among those with least education. In order to avoid bias from this source it is suggested that one should use forced-choice questions in which the respondent is required to choose one of two alternatives offered by the question or statement, rather than agree or disagree with a statement defining only one or other of the alternative choices. For example, the statement 'The Government should offer places in higher education to all those qualified to benefit from it' is likely to get a high level of agreement. So might, 'Young people wanting to benefit from higher education should be prepared to pay some of the cost themselves.' But, if our purpose is to determine whether our survey population is more or less in favour of fully government funded higher education, perhaps we would be better advised to ask, 'should the Government provide free higher education for everyone qualified to receive it, or should prospective students pay some of the costs themselves?' While this is a double-barrelled question in practice respondents have no difficulty in choosing one or the other !

The previous discussion of question phraseology has identified many of the pitfalls which face the researcher in their quest for clear, unbiased responses. Careful question design will do much to reduce bias arising from confusion or lack of understanding and will also help minimise the response bias which is a function of the respondent's perceptions and predispositions. Alreck and Settle (1985) provide a very helpful summary table of the major sources of response bias and this is reproduced as Table 9.2.

Table 9.2.   Sources of response bias

1	*Social desirability*. Response based on what is perceived as being socially acceptable or respectable.
2	*Acquiescence*. Response based on respondent's perception of what would be desirable to the sponsor.
3	*Yea-and nay-saying*. Response influenced by the global tendency toward positive or negative answers.
4	*Prestige*. Response intended to enhance the image of the respondent in the eyes of others.
5	*Threat*. Response influenced by anxiety or fear instilled by the nature of the question.
6	*Hostility*. Response arises from feelings of anger or resentment engendered by the response task.
7	*Auspices*. Response dictated by the image or opinion of the sponsor, rather than the actual question.
8	*Mental set*. Cognitions or perception based on previous items influence response to later ones.
9	*Order*. The sequence in which a series is listed affects the responses to the items.
10	*Extremity*. Clarity of extremes and ambiguity of midrange options encourage extreme responses.

Source: Alreck, Pamela L. and Settle, Robert B. (1985), *The Survey Research Handbook,* Homewood, Ill.: Irwin

The descriptions of the item are seen as self-explanatory but further detail is to be found at pages 112-19 in the original source.

Structured or unstructured?

The examples used to illustrate problems of question design have indicated that questions may be of two kinds – structured and unstructured or open-ended. The essential difference is that with a structured question one anticipates the possible answers and classifies the responses accordingly, whereas with open-ended questions one has no preconceived ideas of the responses and only seeks to classify the data post facto. As a working rule of thumb, unstructured questions are most appropriate in exploratory and qualitative research and enable one to develop structured questions which are best suited to survey and quantitative research.

The benefits of structured questionnaires in terms of speed of completion and analysis, accuracy and comparability of data are self-evident, always bearing in mind the sources of response bias discussed earlier. In terms of administration, structured questionnaires are ideally suited to self-completion as the respondent has a clear indication of the scope of possible answers to the question which helps to ensure that they are on the same wavelength as the researcher. While one should seek to ensure that the alternatives listed are mutually exclusive and exhaustive, this is sometimes neither practicable nor possible. However, it is standard practice to provide a space for 'others' with a short 'write-in' to define these. When administered personally in a face-to-face interview two basic options are available. First, one poses the question and records the spontaneous and unprompted answer of the respondent – probing for clarification if necessary. Given that the interviewer is assigning the respondent's answer to one of the predefined alternatives there is some danger of interviewer bias and this should be borne in mind both in briefing the interviewers and in interpreting the completed questionnaires. The second option is to show the respondent the possible alternatives and ask them to select the one which best fits their opinion or behaviour. Obviously, disclosing the options introduces problems of response bias but careful design and administration should keep these within acceptable limits. One advantage of the personal administration over the self-completion questionnaire is that with the former the respondent is unaware of the scope of subsequent questions, and so cannot modify their responses in anticipation of these. Of course, uncertainty as to the direction an interview may take may predispose a respondent to avoid committing themselves too strongly in case this causes dissonance later in the interview. We shall return to this issue in the final section on questionnaire construction.

As noted above, the design of structured questions requires one to predetermine the possible alternative answers ensuring that they are comprehensive but mutually exclusive. Designing such multiple choice or categorical questions requires considerable skill and can be very time-consuming – the benefits come, of course, at the analysis stage when the pre-classified responses can be transferred directly to the survey data base for analysis. Categorical questions are best suited to factual issues where it is possible to list the known alternatives. In some cases these will be limited to only two options – 'Yes' or 'No' – although such dichotomous questions should always make provision for a 'Don't know' category. In other cases there will be a wide spectrum of possible answers, and it will be necessary to group or classify these into an acceptable number of subgroups – usually not more than eight. Here the guiding principle is that one should opt for the minimum number of categories consistent with the level of detail required. In doing so one should also remember that it is always possible to combine or collapse categories but impossible to disaggregate them after the event. For example, in classifying respondents in terms of age the following categories might be provided

Under 16
16 - 24
25 – 40
41 – 60
Over 60

from which it is a simple matter to split the sample into persons over 40 and 40 and under. But, if you had asked: 'Could you tell me if you are over 40?' one has no means of analysing one's data to determine if there are any meaningful sub-groups or segments within these two broad groupings.

Where one is seeking to measure attitudes and opinions one is usually seeking to establish the strength and direction of the attitude. To do so the researcher will normally resort to some form of scaled measure and it is to the nature and scope of scaling techniques that we turn in the next section.

Before considering scaling methods, however, it may be appropriate to emphasise that a great deal of effort has been expended on determining what kinds of questions yield accurate, valid and reliable data. This being so the new researcher should not seek to reinvent the wheel and set out to design all of their questions from first principles of the kind which have only been lightly touched on here. Rather, you would be better advised to consult published compilations of survey questions.

In addition, the researcher should also consider the design of other extant questionnaires which may have addressed the same or similar issues as those of concern to them. Many such questionnaires are available in published research reports or will come one's way as a potential respondent.

Attitude measurement and scaling

While business and management researchers have a strong interest in facts about past events and the status quo, the primary concern of planners is the future. In order to help predict how people will behave in the future it is necessary to gather information on their prevailing attitudes and the factors which underlie and condition them. Although attitude has been defined as a predisposition to act it is no guarantee of actual behaviour. On the other hand, people rarely behave in a manner inconsistent with their attitudes/beliefs as this would create internal tension or dissonance. It follows that favourable or unfavourable attitudes provide the marketer with valuable information for planning the most effective marketing mix.

Churchill (1987) draws on the work of Summers and Engel, Blackwell and Miniard in proposing that there is substantial agreement that:

> Attitude represents a predisposition to respond to an object, not actual behaviour toward the object. Attitude thus possesses the quality of readiness.
>
> Attitude is persistent over time. It can change, to be sure, but alteration of an attitude that is strongly held requires substantial pressure.
>
> Attitude is a latent variable that produces consistency in behaviour, either verbal or physical.
>
> Attitude has a directional quality. It connotes a preference regarding the outcomes involving the object, evaluations of the object, or positive-neutral-negative feelings for the object. (Churchill 1987)

Given the multidimensionality of the concept it is clear that considerable thought and care will have to be given to the measuring of attitudes to ensure that the data secured from respondents is accurate and comparable. Scaling satisfies these criteria. However, as will become apparent, there are many types of scale, and one of the first considerations to be addressed in selecting one is to establish its measurement properties. In increasing order of sophistication four kinds of scale may be identified – nominal, ordinal, interval and ratio.

In the Westburn Dictionary of Marketing these are defined as follows:

> Nominal scales. This is the weakest form of scale in which the number assigned serves only to identify the subjects under consideration. Library classification schemes employ nominal scales, as does the Standard Industrial Classification (SIC) such that members of the same class will be assigned the same number, but each class will have a different number. By extending the number it is possible to achieve finer and finer distinctions, until a unique number is assigned to a specific object, e.g. a telephone number, a bar code.

> Ordinal scales seek to impose more structure on objects by rank ordering them in terms of some property which they possess such as height or weight. As with nominal scales, identical objects are given the same number, but the ordinal scale has the added property that it can tell us something about direction or relative standing of one object to another, e.g. 1 may represent the smallest member of a group such that we can safely say that 2 is bigger than 1, 5 is bigger than 2 and 17 is bigger than 5. However, this is all we can say (other than reversing the scale) and in order to be able to draw conclusions about difference between numbers we must know something about the interval between the numbers.

Interval scales have this property in that they are founded on the assumption of equal intervals between numbers, i.e. the space between 5 and 10 is the same as the space between 45 and 50 and in both cases this distance is five times as great as that between 1 and 2 or 11 and 12 etc. However, it must be stressed that while we may compare the magnitude of the differences between numbers we cannot make statements about them unless the scale possesses an absolute zero, in which case we would have a ratio scale

Ratio scales are the most powerful and possess all the properties of nominal, ordinal and interval scales, while in addition they permit absolute comparisons of the objects, e.g. 6 metres is twice as high as 3 metres and six times as high as 1 metre. (*http://www.themarketingdictionary.com*)

As noted there are many types of scales all of which have been tested and are of known reliability and validity in terms of measuring what they purport to measure. Among the more important scales which will be discussed here are the Thurstone, Likert, Verbal Frequency, Semantic Differential and Staple scales.

Thurstone scales

Thurstone scales were first introduced by L. L. Thurstone in 1928 and have been very widely used ever since. In essence, a Thurstone scale is an attempt to construct an interval scale by selecting a set of statements about a subject which range from very favourable to very unfavourable expressions of attitude toward the subject, with each statement appearing to be equidistant from those on either side of it. While the scales are easy to administer and easy to respond to – the respondent just indicates those items with which they agree – they are laborious to construct, and require the collaboration of a large group of judges who are required to assess the battery of items which consist of statements relating to the subject of the survey. Each statement is recorded on a card, and the judges are asked to sort these into piles with each pile containing statements expressing the same degree of favourableness towards the subject. The number of piles to be created equates with the number of points to be incorporated in the scale and is usually 7 or 9 with the central point – 4 or 5 – being seen as the neutral 'neither like nor dislike' middle of the continuum ranging from 'Dislike intensely' to 'Extreme liking', and each pile being judged as equidistant from its neighbours. Each pile is then numbered and the median value for each item is arrived at such that half the judges score the item higher and half lower than the median value. The items are then sorted again discarding those for which there is a wide range of opinion, and the remainder covering the whole range of opinions and approximately equally spaced along the scale; both as judged by median scores. Depending upon the number of items which survive the process the researcher may wish to divide these into two sets making it possible to administer a different battery to equal halves of his sample ('split–half method').

The selected items are incorporated into the questionnaire in random order. The respondent is asked to select all the items with which they agree, and their score is calculated as the average of the values (medians) of the items selected. Obviously the advantage of this method is that the respondent does not have to judge the distance between statements as this was done by the judges in constructing the scale. All the respondent does is select statements with which they agree, and so positions themselves upon the scale without having to reflect on the degree of agreement or disagreement with each item. Clearly, Thurstone scales require a considerable degree of effort to construct them, and some critics question whether the judges are representative of the ultimate respondents. Whether this effort is worth it depends upon the reliability the researcher is looking for and the time saved in administration – both of which help affect the time and effort required to develop Thurstone scales. As to representativeness the researcher should take this into account when selecting the judges in the first place.

Thurstone scales have been widely used to measure attitudes on a variety of topics and you may be able to find a validated battery of questions in a reference book such as the *Handbook of Research Design and Social Measurement* (Miller, D. C. and Salkind, N., 6th edition 2002, Thousand Oaks: Sage Publications).

Likert scales

These differ from Thurstone scales in that respondents are presented with a series of statements and asked to indicate their degree of agreement or disagreement by selecting a point on a 3, 5, or 7 point scale. Thus a 5 point Likert scale might appear as follows:

British Midland's in-flight service is better than British Airways:

Strongly agree   Agree   Uncertain   Disagree   Strongly disagree

_____   _____   _____   _____   _____

(NB. Some researchers use 'Neither agree nor disagree' as the mid point)

Data collected by using Likert scales may be presented as either a single, summated score or as a profile analysis.

If a single score is required then one can assign values of 1 to 5, 5 to 1 or +

2 to -2 to reflect the level of agreement or disagreement, with the sum of the individual scores being taken as a measure of the respondents' overall attitude toward the subject of the survey. In constructing the scale it is important to use items which invite the respondents to express a clear opinion, i.e. avoid neutral statements, and to vary the presentation between positive and negative statements in order to avoid the respondent getting into a mind set and automatically ticking the same box.

While a summated score has its advantages as a summary statistic its main disadvantage is that it loses the richness and detail which are obtained if one analyses the responses individually. Because each statement is a rating scale in its own right such analysis is possible with Likert scales but not with Thurstone scales. It must be remembered though that the Likert scale does not have interval properties, so no conclusion may be drawn as to the distance between the scale points. (While Thurstone scales are supposed to have interval properties Moser and Kalton (1971), inter alia, cast doubt upon this.) However, in addition to having good ordinal properties, Likert scales have a number of advantages, foremost among which is that they are comparatively easy to construct and easy to administer, especially in mail questionnaires. Some critics see ease of construction as a disadvantage and Chisnall quotes Worcester's comment that, 'All the overworked research executive has to do is to think up a few contentious statements, add a Likert agree-disagree scale, and hey presto, he has a ready-made questionnaire.' (As with all these techniques there is an extensive literature which deals with such issues in detail and those who wish to try their hands at constructing research instruments should refer to the recommended readings for further advice on the construction and wording of Likert scales.)

In addition to reporting summary scores, many researchers now use profile analysis as an effective and readily understandable means of presenting their results. In the case of a profile analysis one computes the mean or the median value for each item for each group that one wishes to compare, either with each other or with some 'ideal' profile. For example, suppose that in our airline survey we were seeking opinions on the following factors:

Age of equipment – Modernity
Check-in efficiency
Experience
Punctuality
Scheduling – Frequency, Convenience
Cabin comfort - leg room, décor
In-flight service – food, drink, entertainment
Friendliness

We could then ask respondents to rank our two airlines using a 5 point scale along the following lines:

1	2	3	4	5
Excellent	Very good	Good	Average	Poor

By summing the scores and deriving the average or mean score we could then plot the average score for each airline on each factor and construct a plot as in Table 9.3.

These factors or attributes can then be listed as in Table 9.3. and the mean scores for the two airlines reported giving an immediate visual picture of how they compare with one another.

Table 9.3. Profile analysis of two airlines

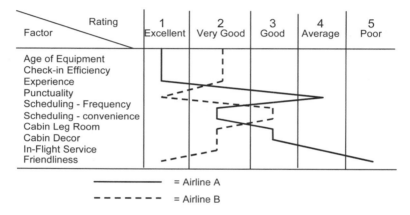

Verbal frequency scales

A major interest in nearly all research inquiries is determination of the frequency with which respondents behave or act in a given way.   Such interest stems very largely from the pervasive nature of the Pareto distribution as a description of actual behaviour in the market place. Simply put Pareto's law states that a disproportionately large fraction of a given phenomenon will be accounted for by a disproportionately small percentage of the total cases. In marketing it is often referred to as the 80-20 rule from the observation that in many industries 80 percent of the total output is accounted for by 20 percent or less of the producers in that industry (see the concept of concentration ratios in economics). Similarly, on the consumption side there is extensive evidence to indicate that a comparatively small number of users account for a significant amount of the total consumption as can be seen from Figure 9.1.

Clearly the attitudes and opinions of those who are heavy users carry more weight than those who are infrequent or light users.   Thus in our inquiry into attitudes towards British Midland and British Airways' service factors on the Glasgow – London route we would want to explore how attitudes might vary in terms of frequency of use, and we would ask a question to determine this in our own survey.

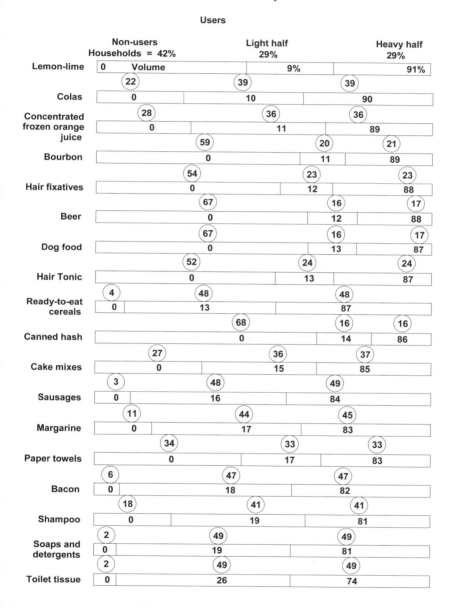

Source: Baker, Michael J. (2000), *Marketing Strategy and Management,* London: Macmillan

Figure 9.1. Annual purchase concentration in 18 product categories

However, in many cases, respondents may be unwilling or unable to specify a numerical frequency when we would still like to obtain some feeling for how often they have or might behave in a particular way. In such situations a verbal frequency scale will provide some data, though clearly not as substantive as that implied by a numerical frequency.

Verbal frequency scales usually comprise five alternatives, namely:

> Always
> Often
> Sometimes
> Seldom
> Never

Such a scale can be used in connection with a series of separate questions, when it is a useful technique for providing variety in a questionnaire and so aids involvement, or with a battery of questions concerning frequency of behaviour on a number of related topics, as suggested in Table 9.4.

Table 9.4. Frequency of behaviour – travelling Glasgow to London

Frequency Services	Always	Often	Sometimes	Seldom	Never
Bus					
Train					
Air – B Midland					
Air – B. Airways					
Book through a Travel Agent					
Pay by Cash					
Pay by cheque					
Pay by Credit Card					
Travel Off-Peak					
Travel 'Stand-By'					

Verbal scales of this kind are very useful in helping the researcher get a feel for the salience of a topic, or the likelihood of involvement in an activity. Their obvious disadvantage is that they lack the precision of numerical scales so that care must be taken not to read too much into the answers. For example, there is a world of difference between the businessman who travels to London every week and 'often' travels on British Midland and the student who travels up and down three times a year!

The semantic differential

This technique was devised by Osgood et al. (1975) as part of their study of semantics. The technique is straightforward in that respondents are invited to 'place' a concept or idea on a 7 point scale anchored by a pair of polar adjectives. As originally conceived by Osgood the objective was to measure the meaning of an object to the respondent in terms of "me as I would like to be", and "me as I am". This distinction is not seen very often in the application of Semantic Differential scales in most questionnaires where such questions are included.

Clearly, one of the key factors to be considered in devising a semantic differential scale is the selection of pairs of adjectives which are appropriate to the concept or object to be rated, are of interest to the researcher, and are meaningful to the intended respondents. To determine the latter it may be necessary to conduct some preliminary, exploratory research in order to establish just what are the relevant attributes. Obviously respondents can only rate the attributes presented to them. Equally, they will rate attributes which may be unimportant and so give the impression that they deserve equal attention to those that are.

Assuming one has identified a set of salient attributes, then the next task is to select appropriate adjectives, and their polar opposites. For example, Osgood et al. proposed the following:

Good	Bad
Kind	Cruel
True	False
Strong	Weak
Hard	Soft
Severe	Lenient
Active	Passive
Hot	Cold
Fast	Slow
Sane	Insane

In this listing all the 'positive' adjectives come first, and the 'negative ones second. When constructing an actual scale the designer should randomise the order so as to avoid response set developing. Figure 9. 2 gives an example of a semantic scale.

Two derivatives of the semantic differential scale are the adjective checklist and the Stapel scale, both of which are fully described in Alreck and Settle (1985). The benefit of the adjective checklist is that one can list a very large number of adjectives and simply ask the respondent to check those which they consider appropriate. As Alreck and Settle observe, 'Simplicity, directness, and economy are the major virtues of the adjective checklist'.

However, the output is nominal only, and gives no measure of distance between the descriptive adjective and the thing being rated as does the semantic differential. On the other hand, adjective checklists may be used as an input to the semantic differential scale, or combined with a numeric rating to form a Stapel scale (so called after its creator).

Soft		Hard
Dry		Wet
Scientific		Unscientific
Non-rigorous		Rigorous
Abstract		Realistic
Good		Bad
Analytical		Descriptive
Deductive		Inductive

Figure 9.2. A semantic scale

All three variants are particularly useful in marketing research in developing profiles of the image which a brand, product or service has in the minds of the public at large. In turn, this provides useful guidance on the development of messages, copy and unique selling propositions to enable sellers to communicate more effectively with prospective buyers.

To conclude this section, it has become obvious that the researcher has a wide selection of different scales available to help capture the attitudes, interests and opinions of respondents. In selecting the most appropriate, one could do worse than observe the ten commandments proposed by Alreck and Settle, namely:

> Keep it simple.
> Respect the respondent.
> Dimension the response.
> Pick the denominations.
> Decide on the range.
> Group only when required.
> Handle neutrality carefully.
> State instructions clearly.
> Always be flexible.
> Pilot test the scales.

Questionnaire design

At the beginning of this chapter we identified a number of factors to be taken into account when planning the content of a questionnaire. Having done this

,and developed appropriate questions observing the guidelines suggested, the next step is to structure the questionnaire to make it easy to administer, and acceptable to the intended respondents. Clearly, the four elements of length, complexity, layout and wording require careful attention

Bowen suggests a number of devices which may make the questionnaire seem shorter, essentially by keeping the respondent involved and interested. The techniques proposed are:

Varying the type of question asked.
Giving the informant things to do.
Use of visual aids.
Scattering questions on the same theme rather than bunching them.
Introducing interesting questions as soon as possible.
Making sure the questionnaire flows

By using devices such as these one can help reduce the natural tendency of respondents to economise by using the same information more than once, i.e. they get into a 'response set' and begin to tick the same end of a scale every time without paying attention to the actual question asked. Of course, such behaviour may arise from confusion which is a consequence of ambiguity and/or complexity in the design of the questionnaire.

On the same issue of complexity, Bowen (and others) counsel that you should always start a questionnaire with simple questions of fact or opinion in order to overcome the respondents' concern that they make a fool of themselves by being unable to answer the questions asked. Inevitably, some questions are bound to address complex issues. Many of the issues relate to the construction of scales and the choice of words touched on earlier.

With regard to layout, two distinct issues must be addressed – the order effect of questions and the actual physical layout of the questionnaire. Order effect was mentioned above in terms of varying the mix and construction of the questions in order to avoid a response set developing. However, it is clear that the problems cannot be avoided entirely, which makes it vital that the designer establish which is the most important issue and address this first. Bowen cites the example of a series of studies every six months designed to measure changes of image and attitude to a brand. Questions on this must precede questions on actual usage for otherwise the respondents may adjust their dimensions to all competitive brands, even though this is not actually the case.

In terms of physical layout, the first precept is to ask advice from someone with direct experience of the problems which occur in administering poorly designed questionnaires. Six basic principles are proposed:

• Make the questionnaire as clear as possible.

- Use a legible typeface and space the questions out. Some researchers mistakenly believe that by photo reducing their questionnaire they will make it less daunting. This may encourage the respondent to start but the sheer density and illegibility of such questionnaires will often prevent a respondent from completing them.
- Leave plenty of space for answers to open-ended questions.
- Ensure the instructions are crystal clear – particularly where it is intended that one should skip questions following a given response.
- Make certain all possible answers are provided for – otherwise the interviewer or respondent will be uncertain whether to classify a response such as 'pantry' as 'larder' or 'kitchen' if only these alternatives are provided.
- Keep instructions next to the question to which they apply. Listing them separately or at the beginning of a questionnaire is bound to result in confusion.

Bowen's fourth design element is wording and this was discussed in some detail earlier. In summary, however, the four golden rules for questionnaire design, especially those used for personal interviews are:

- Think through the use of each question and relate it to the research objectives to ensure it is absolutely necessary;
- Design the techniques and question methods used to maximise informant involvement;
- Cater to the interviewer in the worst possible conceivable situation;
- Pilot the questionnaire yourself.

Piloting the questionnaire

While all marketing research texts advocate the pre-testing or piloting of a questionnaire, the advice is often honoured more by the breach than the observance. However, when submitting a research report based on data obtained through a questionnaire the reader will expect to find a discussion of the pilot, and any changes made as a result of it.

Converse and Presser (1986) suggest ten purposes of pre-testing, the first four of which relate to specific questions, and the last six to the design of the questionnaire itself.

- Variation.
- Meaning.
- Task difficulty.
- Respondent interest and attention.
- 'Flow' and naturalness of the sections.

- The order of questions.
- Skip patterns.
- Timing.
- Respondent interest and attention overall
- Respondent well-being.

While many of these factors are self-explanatory some additional explanation may be helpful.

Variation refers to the degree of variation in actual responses to a question. Occasionally, where one is fairly certain of the distribution of the variation, a highly skewed response will help confirm one's expectations but, otherwise, such a pattern may well suggest that the question is not detecting the expected variation in the phenomenon under investigation. Of course the difficulty here is how many times should one pre-test a question to be confident the test is representative?

The importance of testing for meaning has already been addressed in the earlier discussion of ambiguity. Clearly, if respondents attach a different meaning to a word or phrase than that intended by the researcher then the results are unlikely to be relevant, although the data itself could be highly valid and reliable. Similarly, if questions are very complex , respondents are likely to simplify them and answer the question they think they were asked, which might be quite different from the researcher's original intention.

Task difficulty often arises because of low salience and difficulties of recall. Approaches to reduce these difficulties have been discussed earlier and may be further assisted by offering respondents open-ended, 'write–in', opportunities so they can qualify responses, or define the perspective from which they have answered the question.

Respondent interest and attention relates to both specific questions and the questionnaire as a whole, and will have a significant influence on the quality of the data provided. Once a respondent is committed to a questionnaire they will usually stick it out to the end, but if you have lost their interest, it is quite likely that they will take the path of least resistance in an effort to get through the exercise. The validity and accuracy of such responses is at best questionable.

The maintenance of interest depends heavily on both question and questionnaire design. Variety in the design of questions, the 'flow' or sequence of the questions, the use of 'skip questions' to avoid questions which are irrelevant to particular respondents, and the actual time required to complete an interview will all affect the quality of data. It is evident that questionnaire design is a skilled craft so that, while one may apply some 'scientific' tests to determine if basic principles have been observed, one must depend heavily upon the experience and expertise of the researcher. It should also be evident that our opening statement, that if you 'ask a silly question you'll get a silly answer', is likely to be the rule rather than the exception if questionnaire design is entrusted to an amateur. However, it is to be hoped that armed with some of the insights and issues reviewed in this chapter the new researcher will be able to avoid many if not all the pitfalls discussed.

Summary

In this chapter we have examined some of the major issues involved in designing a questionnaire. Clearly, the quality of data gathered will depend greatly upon the development of clear, unambiguous questions which convey the same meaning to all respondents, and so are likely to elicit comparable replies.

While designing questions and questionnaires is still something of an art, there is extensive advice on do's and don'ts for those wishing to try their hand at constructing a valid questionnaire. Similarly, there are extensive batteries of validated questions which have been thoroughly tested and shown to measure that which they seek to measure. Also, it is now possible to buy computer software to help design both questions and questionnaires, pilot them and produce hard copy or a computer-based guide as required.

Given that much business research is involved with seeking to measure attitudes and opinions as a basis for both explaining and predicting behaviour, considerable attention was given to various scaling methods for distinguishing the nature and degree of such attitudes and opinions.

Finally, we looked at some of the issues involved in combining questions into a questionnaire, and methods for pilot testing this prior to administration to the intended sample of respondents.

In Chapter 10 we look at the collection of data by means of various methods, involving questionnaires and interviewing, before giving advice on questionnaire completion in Chapter 11.

Recommendations for further reading

Fink, Arlene (2003), *How to Ask Survey Questions*, Volume 2 *The Survey Kit*, London: Sage Publications

Tull, Donald S. and Hawkins, Del I. (1993), *Marketing Research,* 6th edn. New York: Macmillan

Webb, John R. (2002), *Understanding and Designing Marketing Research*, 2nd Edition, London: Thomson Learning

Also look out for forthcoming November 2003:
Bulmer, M. (2003), *Questionnaires* 4 Volume Set, London: Sage Publications

CHAPTER 10

Data Collection – Interviewing

Synopsis

In the social sciences, a great deal of primary information is gathered by means of interviews with individuals or groups of people knowledgeable about the phenomenon under investigation. This chapter looks at the selection of respondents, and the various kinds of interview, both formal and informal, that may be employed in data collection.

Keywords

Interviews – unstructured, semi-structured, structured, mail telephone, drop and collect; focus groups; interviewer selection and control

---

Introduction

In Chapter 6 we reviewed the issues involved in selecting an appropriate research design and classified these into three categories – observation, experimentation and survey. In this chapter we are concerned primarily with the latter category and the collection of data using questionnaires, of the kind discussed in the preceding chapter, through the medium of personal interviews, mail and telephone surveys. However, the reader is reminded that the first step in developing a research design is to establish what is already known from existing published sources (the subject of Chapter 4) and that observation and experimentation will often precede any formal approach to respondents through survey research.

Interviewing

An interview is '1. A conversation with, or questioning of a person, usually conducted for television or a newspaper. 2. A formal discussion especially one in which an employer assesses a job applicant' (Collins Concise English Dictionary). While neither of these definitions addresses directly the nature and purpose of the interview in a research context they do establish the key elements, namely; an interview involves a personal exchange of information between an interviewer and one or more interviewees in which the interviewer seeks to obtain specific information on a topic with the co-operation of the interviewee(s).

Interviews vary considerably in their structure from highly formal exchanges in which the interviewer follows exactly a carefully designed and worded questionnaire, of the kind discussed in the preceding chapter, to highly informal exchanges in which the interviewer introduces the topic of interest and lets the discussion develop naturally by asking the respondent to expand or clarify points made. Between the former *structured* interview, which is sometimes called a *formal* or *closed* interview, and the *unstructured, informal, non-directive* or *conversational* interview are to be found three other kinds of interview. In the middle of the continuum is the *standardised open-ended* interview which consists entirely of formal open-ended questions in a pre-determined sequence. In turn we can distinguish two other kinds of interview intermediate between the standardised open-ended format and the ends of the continuum. First, there is the *semi-structured* interview which is a combination of both closed and open-ended questions and second, there is the *interview guide* approach where the interviewer has a checklist of topics they want to cover but interacts with the respondent and formulates *ad hoc* questions to get the desired information.

Clearly, unstructured and interview guide interviews are most appropriate in the early, exploratory phases of research where the researcher is seeking to gain an understanding of the topic and to formulate some preliminary working hypotheses. By the same token highly structured formal interviews ensure that each respondent is required to address exactly the same questions as all the others, so that the data collected can be aggregated and analysed, and regarded as representing the views of the population from which the sample respondents have been drawn. Sue Stone (1984) in her Crus Guide on *Interviews* makes the point that data derived from structured interviews is the most *reliable*, whereas that obtained form less structured interviews is more *valid*. The less structured the interview the more valid the data as the respondent has more and more freedom to express precisely how they think and feel about a topic being discussed.

Madge (1953) suggests there are nine kinds of interview situation to be found in social investigation, depending upon the type of person to be interviewed, and the purpose of the interview itself. In terms of the type of person, Madge identified three classes whom he labels *potentate, expert* and the *people*. A potentate is a person in a position of authority, an expert is a person who possesses special knowledge about other people or things, while people are members of a group in whom the social scientist is interested. Potentates may be regarded as opinion leaders (formal or informal) whose endorsement, co-operation and support is necessary in order for the research to proceed. For example, if one wishes to conduct multiple interviews with a firm to establish who is involved in organisational buying decisions then one will need the authority of the chief executive to proceed. Experts are persons with specialised knowledge or information of the subject of inquiry while people are persons whose attitude, interests and opinions are at the very heart of decision–making.

So, with three classes of persons, three purposes and five types of interview we have a basic repertoire of 45 interviewing 'treatments' available to us. In selecting between them, however, it will be helpful to stick with the basic distinction – class of person, purpose and type of interview – and we shall review each of these in more detail in the next few pages.

Type of respondent

In the introduction to his chapter on 'The Interview' Madge quotes Roethlisberger and Dickson's observation:

> It is commonly supposed, although there is little evidence to warrant such a supposition, that there exists a simple and logical relation between what a person says and what he thinks. (Madge 1953)

If this is so, and many would agree that it is, then the selection of respondents is as critical an issue as the selection and wording of questions, and the construction of questionnaires considered in the previous chapter. This is particularly the case in terms of potentates and experts as misidentification may well invalidate the totality of the data obtained. In the case of surveys of 'people' then the problem may be addressed quite successfully through the construction of the test instrument, control of its administration and care in the subsequent analysis and interpretation of the data obtained.

After all, we expect variability in our respondents and a primary objective of our research design and data collection is to ensure, insofar as is possible, that they are neutral and do not influence or bias our respondents. Of course, the same requirements also apply to interviews with potentates and experts, but given that these types of respondents are likely to be much fewer in number than is the case with broadly based consumer surveys, identification and selection are of the utmost importance. An example will help reinforce this point.

A colleague was undertaking research into the purchase of a flexible manufacturing system and wished to compare attitudes and practice in the UK and West Germany. Although able to speak conversational German this was not sufficient to conduct semi-structured technical interviews with German engineers actually responsible for selection and purchase decisions. He found that the respondent firms were nominating their public relations personnel to participate in the interviews because they spoke more English than their engineers. The fact that the PR people knew virtually nothing about the technical issues was considered secondary to the ability to communicate with an English-speaking interviewer. In this case the researcher appreciated the problem and got the linguists to act as interpreters, but he could just as easily have reported the views of the PR people as being those of the company.   Users of research should be unusually careful in checking out who the respondents were, and how they were selected – a point to which we will return when examining postal surveys.

Very often one will wish to interview potentates to gain access to other categories of respondents, as well as to establish their own views on the survey topic.   Access is probably the single biggest problem facing the researcher undertaking business to business as opposed to consumer research (although it can also be a problem in the latter area too!) This, of course, is quite understandable as information and know-how are very often the primary source of competitive advantage, and the owners of such are unlikely to want to share this with others. It follows, that if one is to gain access one will invariably have to convince a Chief Executive that the information supplied will be treated confidentially, that it is of no specific value and will only become so when aggregated with the replies form other respondents, and also that he and his organisation will derive some tangible benefits from the published survey.

Both potentates and experts can be very helpful in the early stages of developing a research design because their position and knowledge enables them to define what the key issues are. Also, they are usually able to point one in the direction of other sources of relevant information, and so help one structure the problem to be addressed. Further, in the realm of forecasting, potentates and experts are probably the best source of information about likely futures if for no other reason than it is their opinions and decisions which are most likely to influence future states. It is for this reason that the Delphi forecasting technique uses expert opinion as the basis for predicting significant future events, especially those involving technological change.

Ultimately, however, most research is concerned with people as it is their attitudes, interests and opinions that are central to the whole research process. Interviewing is the basic method of eliciting and establishing these factors. Further, as we noted earlier, when discussing the relative merits of qualitative versus quantitative research, the latter tends to carry more conviction and so has increased the incidence and scope of sample surveys many of which depend upon the personal interview as a means of data collection. Given the importance of interviews as a source of primary data, one needs to be sensitive to issues relating to the selection and control of interviewers as a basis for assessing the quality of a given piece of research. However, before looking at these factors in more detail we will examine more closely the type of interview as this will largely determine its suitability for different research purposes.

Type of interview

Earlier we identified a spectrum of interview types ranging from highly unstructured to highly structured. We shall now look at each of these more comprehensively with a view to establishing their basic characteristics, their advantages and disadvantages, the kind of data which they yield and any particular problems associated with their use. In that it is usual to proceed from exploratory research through to formal surveys we shall follow this order in our presentation.

Unstructured interviews

Unstructured interviews are also known as informal, non-directive or conversational. In Madge's view interviews of this kind owe their origin to the counselling techniques used by Sigmund Freud to elicit information necessary to diagnose his patients' problems, and prescribe appropriate courses of treatment. While Freud's counselling techniques may seem somewhat distant from commercial marketing research, aspects of them are still to be found in the field of motivation research of the kind developed and practised by Ernest Dichter. Similarly, they helped inform the development of the methodology used in the famous Hawthorne experiments which are a classic study in the evolution of social science research methodology.

Hawthorne was the name of the Western Electric Company's plant in Chicago and it was here that Harvard Business School Professor Elton Mayo undertook his famous studies into the importance of groups in affecting individual behaviour, and thereby discovered the importance of the informal organisation. In the course of these studies it was decided to conduct a series of directive interviews in which the interviewer was required to ask a series of specific questions of the employee respondents. However, considerable difficulty was experienced in keeping the interviewees on track, and led to the adoption of an indirect as opposed to direct approach which was very similar to Freud's counselling methodology. Madge quotes Mayo's colleagues Roethlisberger and Dickson (1939) who described this 'new method' as follows:

> After the interviewer had explained the program, the employee was to be allowed to choose his own topic. As long as the employee talked spontaneously, the interviewer was to follow the employee's ideas, displaying a real interest in what the employee had to say, taking sufficient notes to enable him to recall the employee's various statements. While the employee continued to talk, no attempt was to be made to change the subject. The interviewer was not to interrupt or to try to change the topic to one he thought more important. He was to listen attentively to anything the worker had to say about any topic and take part in the conversation only in so far as it was necessary in order to keep the employee talking. If he did ask questions, they were to be phrased in a noncommittal manner, and certainly not in the form, previously used, which suggested the answers.

Twenty thousand interviews were obtained over the next two years each lasting an average of one and half hours and led to the formulation of a code of conduct for interviewers which is entirely relevant to the use of the technique over fifty years later, namely:

1. The interviewer should listen to the speaker in a patient and friendly, but intelligently critical, manner.
2. The interviewer should not display any kind of authority.
3. The interviewer should not give advice or moral admonition.
4. The interviewer should not argue with the speaker.
5. The interviewer should talk or ask questions only under certain conditions.
   a. To help the person talk
   b. To relieve any fears or anxieties on the part of the speaker which might be affecting his reaction to the interviewer
   c. To praise the interviewee for reporting his thoughts and feelings accurately
   d. To veer the discussion to some topic which had been omitted or neglected
   e. To discuss implied assumptions, if this were advisable.

In its purest form the totally unstructured interview can be an invaluable source of ideas and insights from which working hypotheses may be developed. However, the information obtained is largely impressionistic and it is usual for the interviewer to follow rules 5(d) and 5(e) and 'veer' or *focus* the interview in order to ensure that it covers the topic with which the interviewer is concerned, and to clarify the basis or premises which underlie the respondents' answers. On this point Madge observes:

The Hawthorne interviewers steered the informant on to particular topics but not away from others. If the informant responds to a topic towards which he is guided, it is fairly reasonable to infer that he would have reached that particular topic without guidance in the course of a long enough interview. The distortion is in the sectors represented, and not necessarily in the internal content of these sectors.

Given that you are willing to endorse Madge's inference then, clearly, the focused interview offers significant advantages over the unfocused kind where the analyst may well have to review large amounts of irrelevant information (especially now that most depth interviews are tape recorded!) Merton and Kendall (1946) report one of the earlier uses of a focused interview in which respondents were asked to listen to a radio programme and then interviewed on it following the 'four canons of the focussed interview procedure... non-direction, specificity, range and depth and personal context.'

Non-direction is self-explanatory and can be achieved using a variety of both structured and non-structured questions, e.g. 'Could you tell me what you consider important about in-flight service?' to 'What did you think of the meal served on the flight?'

Both the above questions also satisfy the canon of specificity, as they require the respondent to describe what *they* think is important. Range is determined by comparing the scope and detail of the respondents' answers with the actual content or dimensions of the subject being discussed as predetermined by the researcher, i.e.. I have already defined the aspects of in-flight service I believe to exist/consider important and will regard the interviews to meet the test if they cover the same issues. Finally, depth and personal context must be judged by the degree to which the interview secures the involvement of the respondent to the extent that they are revealing their true feelings, rather than saying what they think the interviewer would like to hear, or that which would cast them in a favourable light.

From the foregoing overview, it is clear that the conduct of informal or unstructured interviews calls for considerable skills on the part of the interviewer. It follows that the user should inquire carefully into the background and experience of the interviewers used in work of this type so as to be able to form a judgement as to the quality of the data secured. Even more important, if you intend to conduct interviews yourself then you need to practice and rehearse until you have acquired the necessary skills yourself.

In recent years increasing use has been made of a variant of the one-to-one depth interview in which a *group* of persons are invited to discuss a topic. Here the moderator or interviewer can play a much less active role as the group will spontaneously generate ideas on its own and so reduce the likelihood of interviewer bias.

Group discussions*

(*This section draws heavily on an article, 'Group Discussions: A Misunderstood Technique' by Dr G. A. Fahad, a former colleague at Strathclyde University, which appeared in the *Journal of Marketing Management*, 1986, vol.1, no. 3(3), pp.315-27)

A recurring theme of this book is that researchers are invariably confronted with time and budgetary constraints and so must select the most appropriate and effective research method to help them resolve the problems facing them. In this quest they will frequently have to choose between the apparently factual and objective data yielded by a quantitative survey, and the more judgemental and subjective information generated by qualitative research. As a working rule of thumb, however, some qualitative research should always precede quantitative research when addressing a non-recurring problem where, by definition, the decision–maker has relatively little if any direct experience of the specific problem to be solved. In some cases this qualitative research will consist merely of a few unstructured or semi-structured individual interviews with a small number of persons believed to have some knowledge or insight relevant to the problem, while in others the researcher will wish to develop a more detailed and in-depth insight into the problem of interest. Under the latter circumstances, group discussions may well prove the most satisfactory approach. What then is a group discussion?

Put simply a group discussion is a 'research technique designed to study the interaction of group membership on individual behaviour, with a free exchange of ideas, beliefs and emotions helping to form a general opinion about the subject' (*Westburn Dictionary*). The origins of the method are to be found in the 'clinical laboratory' setting where many of the guidelines for its use were first developed. As a technique it is very flexible, and comparatively easy to organise and execute, which is in marked contrast with the administrative effort necessary to mount most sample surveys. Because of its clinical origins, it is widely held that group discussions must be moderated by a clinical psychologist. While this may add somewhat to the perceived credibility of the technique, experience suggests that while such professional advice may be helpful in diagnosing some of the data, e.g. of a projective kind, group discussions may be run successfully by moderators without any particular formal qualifications provided they have experience and are skilled in moderating discussions.

Black and Champion (1976) have defined the key attributes of a group discussion as being:

1. Questions are asked and responses given verbally
2. The interviewer rather than the respondent records the information elicited (Most group discussions are tape recorded for later detailed analysis).
3. The relationship between the interviewer and the respondent is structured in several specific ways, such as transitory or temporary relationship where participants are often unknown to one another, etc.
4. There is considerable flexibility in the format the interview takes.

To these attributes Sampson (1978) has added the following characteristics.

1. The group varies in number but has anything between 8 to 12 individuals.
2. Individuals in the group are known to have knowledge about the topic or issues being discussed.
3. Respondents are encouraged to express their opinions and attitudes

(freely) on issues being discussed.

4.   The interviewer's duty is basically to guide the direction and depth of the discussions.
5.   The underlying characteristic of the group situation is the need of the interviewer 'to learn about' the issues being discussed based on the respondent's own perspective.

As a methodology, group discussions are adaptable to a wide range of situations amongst which Smith (1972) has listed the following:

1.   For research concerned with motives, attitudes and opinions where social status and acceptance are involved.
2.   For bringing out ideas in the dynamic group situation which cannot be elicited by other methods.
3.   For attempting to answer the question 'why' in relation to behaviour.
4.   Valuable in the preliminary or exploratory stage of a research project.
5.   It enables a questionnaire to be constructed for piloting and pre-testing, which should include all the possible lines of enquiry.
6.   Useful for indicating the type of language people use when discussing the topic informally and ensures that in constructing a questionnaire, the wording of questions is meaningful.

Among other reasons cited in general literature Kinnear and Taylor (1987) listed the following:

1.   To generate hypotheses that can be further tested quantitatively.
2.   To provide overall background information on a product category.
3.   To get impressions on new concepts for which there is little information available.
4.   To generate ideas for new creative concepts.
5.   To interpret previously obtained quantitative results.

The last application is particularly important as it emphasises that qualitative research is an essential and inextricable element of the research process necessary to help structure formal data collection and inform the interpretation of the data collected.

Advantages and disadvantages

From his comprehensive literature review Fahad identifies a large number of advantages which have been claimed for the group discussion technique. First, he cites Gordon who listed the following advantages:

1. It enables the researcher to obtain the desired information more quickly than, for example, a questionnaire.
2. It ensures that respondents understand the questions being asked.
3. Its flexible nature allows the interviewer to adjust his line of questioning.
4. Much more control can be exercised over the context within which questions are asked and answers given.
5. Information can be more readily checked for its validity on the basis of non-verbal clues by the respondent. (Gordon 1969)

In addition to these advantages Fahad proposes ten others culled from a variety of sources as shown in Table 10.1.

TABLE 10.1. Advantages of group discussion

Synergism	Combined effect of the group produces a wider range of information, ideas, etc
Snowballing	A comment by an individual often triggers a chain of responses from other respondents.
Stimulation	Respondents become more responsive after initial introduction and are more likely to express their attitudes and feelings as the general level of excitement increases
Security	Most respondents find comfort in a group that shares their feelings and beliefs.
Spontaneity	As individuals are not required to answer specific questions, their responses are likely to be more spontaneous and less conventional.
Serendipity	The ethos of the group is likely to produce wider ideas and often when least expected.
Specialisation	Allows a more trained interviewer to be used and minimises the possibility of subjectivity.
Scientific scrutiny	Allows a closer scrutiny of the technique by allowing observers or by later playing back and analysing recording sessions
Structure	Affords more flexibility in the topics that can be covered and in the depth in which these are treated
Speed	Given that several individuals are being interviewed at the same time, this speeds up the process of collecting and analysing the data.

Of course, no technique is without its shortcomings and a number of disadvantages are associated with the group discussion technique. Fahad summarises these succinctly as:

1   Doubts about the validity of verbal responses particularly in relation to behaviour.
2   Interviewer variability means that the type and depth of information elicited can vary markedly.
3   In certain instances, respondents may have been recruited on the basis of a nominal fee, a present etc., and this tends to affect responses provided.
4   Interviewers may exercise a high degree of freedom, often resulting in short-cuts, carelessness in recruiting respondents and so on.
5   Sample size is often too small or not representative and so limits the generalisation of the data obtained.
6   Interaction between participants often biases responses provided.
7   Self-appointed leaders in the group may influence the opinions of the rest. (Fahad 1986)

However, many of the disadvantages may be minimised or even eliminated through professional practice (in recruitment, etc.) and skilled moderation. Certainly, the buyer of research would wish to satisfy himself on these points in both commissioning and evaluating the output of group discussions. Given these safeguards the benefits heavily outweigh the disadvantages.

Types of group discussion

Thus far the discussion has proceeded as if there were only one type of group discussion. In fact there are several each with its particular strengths and weaknesses. Fahad identifies three somewhat different approaches to classifying types of group discussion when he cites from Sampson (1978), Hartman and Hedblom (1979) and De-Almeida (1980).

Sampson (1978) suggests a three-way classification as follows:

1. *The group interview or discussion.* In this format, individuals are brought together under the direction of a group leader or moderator, who plays a more passive role than in the individual depth interview.
2. *Elicitation interview.* In this variant, the interviewer makes use of a battery of open-ended questions in the belief that the salient attitudes elicited may be more reliable measures of consumer behaviour.
3. *The repertory or Kelly grid technique.* In this format, stimuli are presented to respondents in the form of labels, written statements, drawings etc. and responses sought to these. (Sampson 1978)

By contrast, Hartman and Hedblom (1979) argue that classification can be made on the basis of structure, i.e.

1. *Highly structured:* involves the use of a standardised set of questions determined prior to the interview.
2. *Open-ended:* this is uncontrolled, unstructured and entails very little

guidance from the interviewer.

3. *Depth interview:* involves an 'intimate', long-term conversation with respondents in which the interviewer is allowed to probe, expand and periodically summarise what he/she understands respondents to have said.
4. *Group interviewing:* in this format, questions are posed to a group rather than to a single individual, more or less using the same format as an interview with single individuals. (Sampson 1978)

Based upon his own literature review De-Almeida (1980) came up with a four-way classification:

1. *Group discussions:* these tend to be mainly unstructured types of investigation of given topics, using small groups with basically non-directive moderation.
2. *Group interviewing*: in this format, questions are posed to a group rather than to a single individual, more or less using the same format as an interview with single individuals.
3. *Focused group interviewing:* individuals in the group are asked to base their responses on past subjective associations and emotions.
4. *Delphi group interviewing:* this format involves the group being asked to develop new ideas and insights based on knowledge of prior ones from other individuals, groups or even from the same group. (De-Almeida 1980)

While some observers regard the distinctions implied in the above classifications as being inconsequential, the evidence suggests that much of the reported dissatisfaction with group discussions as a technique is a direct consequence of the user failing to define precisely the kind of group discussion best suited to their problem.

However, choice of type of focus group is only one factor influencing the quality and value of the output from this method. Dickens (1982) identifies seven other factors likely to have a significant bearing on the success of a group discussion.

1. Preliminary planning
2. Respondent recruitment
3. Characteristics of the moderator
4. The venue
5. Format of the presentation
6. Management of the discussion
7. Analysis

The value of preliminary planning is axiomatic in all research design and execution and will not be discussed further. Similarly, selecting respondents able to respond to the issues on which the discussion is to focus is self-evident. As to whom should perform this task there appears to be little if any difference between letting the moderator recruit their own group(s), or having an agent recruit respondents for them in accordance with some broad definition of the characteristics required, e.g. single parents between 25 and 40 from ABC1 socio-economic groups.

All agree that the overall success of the group discussion method depends very heavily upon the characteristics of the moderator, and the literature provides copious advice on just what these characteristics might be. As Fahad comments 'The first-time user is often, however, left with the impression that a moderator is more an acrobat than an ordinary human being' – this in addition to being a paragon of all other virtues! We have already noted that the impression that all moderators should be trained clinical psychologists is erroneous – save for depth interviews exploring deeply-seated motivation the main requirement of a moderator is that they should be effective chairpersons – able to introduce the issues for discussion, to encourage participation from all the group members, to clarify ambiguities, to discourage a single person dominating the proceedings and knowing when to move the discussion forward when a topic has become exhausted, together with summaries of where the discussion has got to if appropriate.

The best advice on venues and format is that they should be appropriate to the topic and respondent mix. For example, our single parents would probably appreciate meeting in someone's home, whereas a group of purchasing executives would prefer a more business-like environment. The single parents once introduced could probably talk all day about problems they face when invited to do so, while the purchasing executives would probably want a clearer definition of the purpose of the meeting, a broad agenda and a time limit.

Running the group discussion is a function of its purpose and the moderator's skills touched on above.

Analysis may be *systematic* i.e. a factual summary of the content of the discussion using formal content analysis techniques on a recording of the interview, or *conceptual* in which the analyst identifies the key issues emerging from the discussion and, possibly, formulates these as hypotheses for subsequent testing. Most users will look for both kinds of analysis with emphasis depending upon the original objectives in using the group discussions in the first place.

While the subjective nature of the group discussions is likely to ensure that its primary use is for exploratory research to gain insight into and understanding of attitudes, opinions and behaviour, with the possibility of subsequent quantitative research to establish the strength and direction of these factors, there are strong indication that the method may also be a valid basis for actual decisions. There is extensive support for this view including the analysis of Reynolds and Johnson (1978) who reported a 97 percent level of agreement between the results from a group discussion approach and a survey on the same issue. Indeed where the results differed the group discussion data matched more closely the reality of actual sales. Provided the researcher clearly understands the advantages and shortcomings of the method it may well provide a relatively simple and cost effective aid to obtaining the information they are seeking.

Table 10.2. Interview guide

British industry and growth
- Definitions of growth and success in industries
- Prospects for British Industry
- Sunrise/sunset industries

Company performance
- Parameters of success
- Non-financial measures
- Specific companies

Attitudes to marketing
- Definitions of marketing
- Likert-type scale

Organisation of marketing in the company
- Inter-functional integration
- Responsibility for marketing; substance or trapping
- Organisational status of marketing
- Managerial background/marketing training

Corporate and marketing strategy
- Time horizon/strategic issues
- Formality of strategic planning; substance or trapping
- Strategies

Market research
- Information needs and sources
- Market research activities and uses
- Formality of market research; substance or trapping

Segmentation
- Typical customer versus groups of customers
- Product differentiation – proliferation of product ranges

The market mix
- Overall view of relative importance of mix factors
- Product quality – customer oriented versus absolute quality
- Product modification and NPD; market or technology driven?
- Service, selling, advertising and pricing

Interviewer guide

When addressing the issue of 'range' in unstructured interview it was stated that one could judge this by the actual content of the interviews with the researcher's prior expectation. Implicit in this statement is the belief that even in the most informal and unstructured interview one has some mental checklist to guide one through the interview. When committed to paper this checklist becomes the interview guide, and enables the interviewer to make sure that he has indeed covered all the issues believed a priori to be important to the research. Table 10. 2 is an example of an interview guide used by Baker and Hart (1989) when conducting the exploratory research with 'potentates' and 'experts' to validate the conclusions drawn from their wide-ranging review of the secondary data on the subject of factors associated with competitive success.

This kind of interview represents a further degree of formality beyond that of the interview guide which is simply a checklist or *aide-memoire* to ensure comprehensive coverage of the topic. As its name suggests a standardised open-ended interview uses predetermined questions which are put in precisely the same format and sequence to every respondent. Table 10.3 presents the second stage interview schedule developed by Baker and Hart after their first round of preliminary and exploratory interviews.

The obvious advantage of this approach is that it is possible to make direct comparisons of the answers which will all be given in the same order. Against this is the problem that some respondents will be loquacious and others taciturn, and that the meaning attached to their responses may vary considerably. However, the existence of a standardised set of questions makes it possible to use less well qualified interviewers as their role is simply to pose the questions and report accurately the answers. Here the skill requirement is centred on the *content analysis* of the responses.

Table 10.3. Semi-structured interview guide

British industry and growth

1.   How do you think British industry's performance should be evaluated? Please give reasons for your answer

> PROBE: sales, profitability, employee numbers and prospects, export achievement Reputation, IR record, etc.

2.   What is your opinion of the prospects for British manufacturing industry over the next 10 years?

> PROBE: overall growth rates
> Profitability, employment etc.

3.   Which industries do you consider to be:
  (a)   Sunrise industries (i.e. above average growth and profitability)
  (b)   Sunset industries (i.e. below average growth and profitability)
  (c)   What do you consider to be the average growth and profitability in
        these industries?

Company performance

4.   How do you think company performance should be evaluated?
       Please give your reasons for your answer.

> PROBE: innovativeness, reputation among
> customers, public reputation, IR record, environmental
> responsibility, etc.

5.   Do you think any non-financial measures of company performance
       should be incorporated into the study in hand?

> PROBE: reason for answer

6.   Can you suggest any outstanding examples of companies with
        above and below average performance?

> PROBE: contacts and possibility of introductions.

Attitudes to marketing
7.   What is *your* definition of marketing?

Organisation of 'marketing' in the company
8.   (a) Given your definition how do you think 'marketing' should be
           organised in a company?

> PROBE: Which functions are considered as the
> responsibility of marketing:
> sales, distribution/logistics, aftersales service, trade
> promotions, advertising, exporting, market research,
> product design, marketing staffing, marketing training,
> marketing planning, new product development, sales
> forecasting, pricing, packaging.
> NB. Usefulness of scale – full and sole responsibility – no
> responsibility.

(b)   Which of the above functions (if any) do you think should be part of the marketing department?

> PROBE: is the organisation and structure important at all?

(c)   Do you think that the personnel in the above functions should be involved in any marketing activities?

> PROBE: How this might be measured?
> e.g. number of personnel in each department with marketing responsibility/number of marketing department personnel involved in each functional area.

9.   In any company, how might you rank the importance of the following executives?

> PROBE: Production
> Finance/Accounting
> Sales
> Marketing
> R&D
> Personnel

10.   Do you consider that marketing as a department should be represented on the Board of Directors or chief decision-making executive committee?

11.   What is the function background of most managing directors and in your opinion, what should it be?

> PROBE: is this considered to be important?

12.   Do you consider it important for a managing director to have worked in a variety of positions and/or industries?

> PROBE: reasons for answer

13.   Do you think that Marketing Training is an important aspect of a company's operation?

> PROBE: formal marketing training programme (in-house, external), length of marketing 'apprenticeship', breadth of training, integration with other functions.
> NB. Limited to marketing personnel, or company-wide.

Corporate and marketing strategy

14.   What role and contribution has marketing to play in overall planning strategy?

> PROBE: 'Company mission' and how this might be included in a structured questionnaire.

15.   How would you define the time horizon of 'long-term' or strategic planning?

> PROBE: number of years and how important.
> Substance or trapping

16.   What do you consider to be the issues relevant to strategic planning?

> PROBE: definition of product market, long term investment, future sales volume, return on investment, cash flow/liquidity, forecasts of market size and share, mergers and acquisitions, company image/reputation, forecasting technological change, other.

17.   Do you consider processes and procedures for strategic planning to be important?

> PROBE: formal/informal meetings, written documents to guide planning, rules and roles; standardisation; centralisation. NB. Trappings and substance.

18.   Do you feel that strategic plans should be:
(a)   written down
(b)   accessible to others ?

> PROBE: reasons

19.   Who do you feel should be involved in the strategic planning process?

> PROBE: level of personnel (hierarchical) and functional
> department.

20.   Can you say which of the following strategies you consider to be most
      useful for achieving strategic objectives?

> PROBE: if respondent is industry-specific probe reasons
> for choice. If respondent is general clarify what the
> contextual influences on strategy might be.
> Check the following alternatives:
> (a) Increasing sales of current products in current markets.
> (b) Developing new markets for existing products.
> (c) Phasing out unprofitable products and markets.
> (d) Developing new products for existing markets.
> (e) Developing new products for new markets
> (f) Developing new products with higher value
>   added/lower value added to serve new markets.

Market research

21.   What do you consider to be a company's major information needs?

> PROBE: Market size, market share; market growth;
> future sales; competitive activity; customer requirements
> and preferences.

22.   What do you consider to be the most useful sources of these types of
      information?

> PROBE: Secondary sources (government data, trade
> associations data, company records) customer surveys,
> distributor surveys, qualitative research, field experiments,
> in-house (laboratory) experiments, omnibus survey data.

23.   In your view, which of the following marketing research activities are
      commonly undertaken (or commissioned) by companies?

> PROBE: industry research, motivation research, image
> research, advertising/ media research, pricing research,
> product competitive research, distribution research.

24.   In your opinion why might market research *not* be carried out (or
      commissioned) by companies?

25.   What do you consider to be the main uses to which market research might be put?

> PROBE: sales forecasting and planning, identifying product opportunities; evaluating customers' reaction to a product; selecting channels of distribution; advertising planning estimating market potential.

26.   Who is likely to be responsible for gathering and disseminating market research data in a company?

> PROBE: functional depts; in-house/ external. NB. Is this of any *real* importance. Substance or trapping.

27.   How formalised is market research in companies?

> PROBE: regularity of surveys; methodically carried out for specific purposes (e.g. NPD); use of MR techniques (are these a trapping?)

28.   How would you rate the following measures as indicators of how thoroughly a company researches its market?

(a)   the existence of an MR department
(b)   the size of the department
(c)   the amount of money spent on MR

Segmentation – (a) for industry – specific respondents only

29.   In your opinion, do companies in the industry divide up the market into groups of relatively similar types of customer?

> PROBE: segmentation   bases;   geography,   usage, customer size, purchase criteria.

30.   In your view, how different are the products of companies in the industry and how do they differ?

> PROBE: quality, style, features design performance, price, delivery, services, reputation.

31.   Has the overall number of products increased or decreased over the past 10 years?

32.   What do you consider to be the most successful products and what accounts for their success?

Segmentation – (b) for a general expert

29.   Do you think that markets should be divided into groups of relatively similar customers?

> PROBE: why

30.   In your view, how do products of competing companies differ from one another?

> PROBE: why

31.   Do you think there is a general trend to increase or decrease product ranges?

32.   What factors do you think explain a product's success?

The marketing mix

33.   In your opinion, what are the major factors in achieving competitiveness?

> PROBE: (for industry-specific respondents, probe for 1 industry only): product design, performance; range of products, aggressive marketing; increased manufacturing Investment; after sales service and spare parts; price, delivery, guarantees and warranties, sales liaison and information, advertising, technological progressiveness, knowledge of the market.

34.   In your opinion, what factors make up 'product quality'?

> PROBE: differentiation-number of products/choice; design; engineering and aesthetic; product performance – fitness for the task; quality of raw materials and components manufacturing/ technological progressiveness.

35.   Do you think an absolute quality orientation and a marketing orientation for quality can be distinguished? If so, how?

36.   In your industry, how often are products modified, and what form does the modification take?

> PROBE: style, features, variations, price, technology advancements, manufacturing/raw material/component change.

37.   In your view, what triggers product modification?

> PROBE: customer suggestion; technological progress, competitive activity; erosion of sales, general research for improvements.

38.   In your opinion, at what rate are new products introduced into the market?

39.   What do you think is the usual trigger for NPD?

> PROBE: customer suggestion; technological progress; competitive activity; erosion of sales, general research for improvements.

40.   What do you consider to be the essence of successful NPD or modifications?

> PROBE: good market analysis, product quality, product design, price, company image/reputation, wide distribution, good delivery and service; promotion, aggressive selling, product uniqueness, etc.

41.   What do you consider to be the main causes of new product failure?

> PROBE: as above and also the aspect of 'over-engineering – absolute quality'.

42.   In your opinion, what are the hallmarks of "good service" and which do you consider to be of importance in achieving company objectives?

> PROBE: parts availability, guarantees and warranties, speed of service calls; delivery, availability, installation/ demonstration/technical assistance, training operators, credit facilities, leasing, repair contracts.

43.   What do you consider to be the role of personal selling?

44.   What is important in the management of salespeople?

> PROBE: selection of representatives; Sales training; remuneration; control, etc. Probe *each* aspect separately.

45.   What do you consider to the role of advertising?

46.   What do you consider to be important in the choice of media strategy?

(a)

> PROBE: objectives; cost; competitive promotion; nature of the market, nature of the message.

(b)   In your opinion what is the most usual basis for choosing media strategy?

47.   What do you consider to be the role of pricing?

48.   In your opinion, what must be kept in mind when fixing prices?

> PROBE: the market, the competition, pricing objectives, profit sales mix, sales volume.

49.   What do you consider to the most common methods of pricing setting?

Compiled by the Author as part of a research project. A full discussion of Probing techniques is to be found in the next chapter.

Semi-structured interviews

These represent the halfway house between the partly and fully structured interview and comprise a combination of standardised open *and* closed questions in a predetermined sequence to be followed exactly by the interviewer.   Such questionnaires are widely used when sampling a population to ensure that one has the necessary factual information for determining its representativeness for ensuring that quotas have been filled, etc. when the primary purpose is to get a feel for attitudes, opinions, etc. as a preliminary to developing a fully structured interview using a carefully prepared and tested questionnaire of the kind described in the previous chapter.

Structured interviews

The major difference between the structured and the semi-structured interview is that in the former not only are the questions and structure predetermined but so also are the response categories. It should be appreciated that, other than for fairly short and straightforward questionnaires, very few interviews/questionnaires which are regarded as 'structured' conform exactly to the definition. Most structured questionnaires will contain 'Others' and 'Write-in' opportunities where it would be counter-productive or impossible to pre-identify and list all feasible responses, as well as the occasional open-ended question too.   However, the main distinguishing feature of the structured interview is that it generates *reliable* data which is amenable to statistical analysis and which can be collected by trained interviewers with little or no knowledge of the research subject – something which is increasingly important the less structured the interview. That said accurate and consistent questionnaire completion is vital to ensure the data is valid and reliable.

Telephone surveys

Long ago, in the 1970s, European texts felt compelled to point out that using the telephone to collect survey data was subject to considerable bias due to the fact that less than half the households had access to the technology, and that such access was mainly restricted to more affluent households. Today the picture is quite different. Not only do nearly all households have access to a 'phone but, with the advent of the mobile, very large numbers of individuals may be contacted personally at almost any time. As a consequence the use of the telephone for interviewing has increased significantly from the estimate of 30% of all interviews in the 1980s. (It has always been used extensively in industrial and organisational research). In this section we examine some of the key aspects of the telephone survey method.

Telephone interviewing first took off in the USA when home ownership exceeded the 70% level. Writing in 1983, James H. Frey attributed the significant shift to the use of the telephone to the 'rising costs and declining response rates by the face-to-face survey' reinforced by improved telephone technology, research procedures and the 'nearly complete accessibility of any population via the telephone'. That said, the telephone is not appropriate to all kinds of survey and its use should be restricted to those situations where it offers significant advantages over other interviewing methods in light of the usual time and budgetary constraints.   Frey offers a very useful table comparing mail, face-to-face and telephone survey methods which, although somewhat dated, is reproduced as Table 10. 4.

Table 10.4 Relative advantages and disadvantages of survey methods

	Personal	*Telephone*	*Mail*
Bias (from interviewer)	3	2	1
Control over collection	2	1	3
Depth of questioning	1	2	3
Economy	3	1	2
Follow up ability	2	1	3
Hard to recall data	2	3	1
Rapport with respondent	1	2	3
Sampling completeness	1	2	3
Speed of obtaining response	2	1	3
Versatility	1	3	2

Source: James H. Frey (1983), *Survey Research by Telephone*, Sage Library of Social Research, vol. 150 © 1983 and reprinted by permission of Sage Publications Inc.

The use of the telephone surveys has also grown in popularity with the introduction of Computer-Assisted Telephone Interviewing (CATI).   CATI has become the generic name for a number of proprietary systems developed by commercial firms and academic institutions each of which has specialist features that makes it particularly suited for a given kind of survey problem. However, all systems share the common feature that interviewing is undertaken using a CRT terminal. Frey describes the process as follows:

The interview is actually controlled by pre-programmed machine processes. Thus, in effect, the respondent talks to the computer through the interviewer. CATI directs the flow of each interview with exactly the right question – one question at a time. Pre-programmed editing instructions work to ensure that the responses are valid and consistent with answers to previous questions. If an interviewer keys in an inappropriate response, (for example, not included in response categories) an error message automatically appears on the screen and corrective measures can be implemented immediately. When the correct response is entered the computer determines which question should be asked next. The next question will not appear until the previous question has been answered with an appropriate response category. At the end of an interview, all respondents' replies are automatically and instantaneously entered into the computer memory.

The ability to check for consistency and validity, to ensure precise and correct administration, to drop questions once sufficient data has been collected and so shorten succeeding interviews, and to create a database in one step in real time are all significant advantages of CATI. Unfortunately, the increase in telephone selling and in direct mail are resulting in respondent resistance and the problems of securing participation in surveys of all kinds are likely to become increasingly acute. (Reference to packaged software available to devise and execute CATI is contained in Chapter 12).

If a preliminary analysis indicates that a telephone survey is preferable to personal interviewing or mail questionnaire in terms of likely cost and speed of response, then two major issues must be addressed. First, how to remove or reduce sources of bias and, second, what modifications are necessary to make the questionnaire suitable for administration without the use of visual cues that can be incorporated into mail and personally administered questionnaires?

Given that 'phone ownership now exceeds 90% it is likely that telephone listings provide as complete a record of the population as do Census data. It follows that one can use probability based methods of sampling and generate a random sample of the population so eliminating a major source of bias as compared with non-random samples in terms of the representativeness of the sample. Using telephone directories, one can draw a random sample by selecting a start point, and then using a fixed interval based on the total number of entries to achieve a sample of the desired size. Such a sample may be stratified or unstratified. Of course, some phone owners are ex-directory and will be excluded from the sample. One way of getting round this problem is to draw the numbers and then add one to them on the assumption that the first number does exist, and that the new number may be either a listed or unlisted number.

Alternatively, one may already have a listing of a population of interest together with phone numbers and this may be used as sampling frame.. (A detailed description of Telephone Sampling is to be found in Worcester and Downham).

Having established contact one immediately encounters the cardinal problem with all survey techniques – will the contact agree to respond? Securing collaboration may well be difficult given that many firms use the telephone for selling, and the respondent may well be sceptical about your intentions and find it easier to ring off than listen to your explanation. When used as a survey technique, effective telephone interviewing calls for experienced interviewers and specially designed questionnaires. Novice researchers are unlikely to possess either! Texts such as Worcester and Downham do contain advice on questionnaire construction and administration and should be consulted by those who feel this is still the best method. (This is quite different from recognising that the telephone is a very useful research tool for undertaking exploratory research, making contact with possible subjects for further study, checking out data collected by other means and so on.)

Mail surveys

While documented evidence is hard to come by, many researchers believe that the data secured from a properly designed and executed mail survey is as good as that which may be obtained from face-to-face personal interviews ,and/or telephone surveys with the in-built checks described as above.

Among the advantages and disadvantages of postal surveys Wilson (2003) lists the following:

advantages:
national and international coverage
low cost
no interviewer bias
respondent convenience
piggybacking

disadvantages
low response rate
biased response
lack of control of questioning
lack of control of respondent
limited open-ended questions
pre-reading of questionnaire
response time (Wilson 2003, p.131)

The obvious and major advantage of the mail survey is that every firm and household in the country can be reached for the same basic cost, with the result that mail surveys are estimated to cost one third as much as personally administered questionnaires (See Lindsay Brook, 'Postal Survey Procedures' Chapter 7 in *Survey Research Practice*, Gerald Hoinville and Roger Jowell, Heinemann Educational Books, 1978). Postal surveys also have the advantage that they are completed at the respondents' convenience so that participation may occur which would have been impossible or rejected if initiated by a personal approach or telephone call. This facility also allows the respondent to reflect on their answers, check records or consult with others if appropriate.

As with most things, however, the particular strengths of the mail survey are also regarded as weaknesses by critics of the methodology. Perhaps the strongest criticism raised is that of respondent self-selection, i.e. only those willing to go to the bother of completing the questionnaire will make a return. Given that in many postal surveys the return is 20 percent or less, it is understandable that one should be concerned as to whether the respondents are in fact representative of the sample which itself was designed to be representative of the target population.   Users of research should probe deeply on this issue.   Most published reports contain the claim that 'an examination of the respondents' characteristics revealed no significant differences from the characteristics of the sample'.   Fair enough, but ask for the comparative information to satisfy yourself that this is indeed the case.   Better still, ask for a sample of the non-respondents to be interviewed face-to-face or by telephone to see if their responses are in line with the 'volunteer' respondents.

Of course, the real problem is to secure better rates in the first instance, and there are a number of techniques to help achieve this. Perhaps the most successful technique is the careful identification and selection of respondents in the first place. By choosing persons for whom the issues are salient, and addressing the survey to them personally, very high levels of response may be achieved.   While there is   possibly a 'halo' effect around academic institutions, which make extensive use of mail surveys for reasons of economy, the author has supervised numerous surveys with response rates of 50 percent or better involving chief executives and directors of major firms. Most text books offer extensive advice on techniques for increasing response rates from the use of adhesive postage stamps (how many chief executives open up their mail?)   through use of incentives to follow-up letters or telephone requests. (see Brook, 'Postal Survey Procedures' for example). As with other technical matters the users best defence is to select a reputable and experienced practitioner, and to ask them to justify the use of a particular technique or method.

Drop and collect surveys

While comparatively little has been written about this technique it is likely to become more popular in future because it combines the low cost of the mail or telephone survey with an element of personal involvement which encourages respondent participation. In an article in *Marketing Intelligence and Planning* (vol. 5, no. 1, 'Drop and collect Surveys: A Neglected Research Technique') Stephen Brown reviews the method and reports a simple experiment to demonstrate its effectiveness. As Brown explains:

> The drop and collect technique involves the hand delivery and subsequent recovery of self-completion questionnaires though several other variants may exist. These include hand delivery and postal return and postal delivery and personal pick-up. By combining the strengths and avoiding the weakness of face-to-face and postal surveys, drop and collect provides a fast, cheap and reliable research tool. The speed stems from the fact that the questionnaire is completed in the respondent's own

time not the interviewer's.   Comparisons are obviously difficult but Walker estimates that one agent can deliver approximately 100 questionnaires per working day. This incidence of contact is not far short of that achieved in telephone surveys and, depending on the circumstances, considerably more than that attained by personal interviewing. (Brown 1987)

A significant advantage of personal collection is that it encourages both high response rates and timely completion, with up to 70 percent of questionnaires being available at the agreed collection time. Because of this high response rate it has been estimated that 'in terms of cost per completed questionnaire drop and collect surveys (is) ...on average... 20-40 percent less expensive than postal surveys and around half the cost of face-to-face interviews' (Brown, 'Drop and collect Surveys'). In part the lower cost than personal interviews is because one can use relatively unskilled 'delivery agents' in place of trained interviewers, and because the actual personal contact is much less. However, response rates of up to 90 percent almost match those achieved by face-to-face interviews, are equivalent to the best telephone survey returns, and are considerably in excess of the response to mail surveys.

In addition, as Brown comments, because respondents can complete the questionnaire in their own time it is possible to use longer and more detailed questionnaires than in most face-to-face or telephone surveys. Also, when collecting the completed questionnaires the collection agent can check that they have been completed correctly, clarify any points as required by the respondent as well as ask supplementary questions if desired. But, because the interaction between agent and respondent is limited the possibility of interviewer bias is greatly reduced.

A third factor in favour of the technique, cited by Brown is its reliability because of the control it gives over the sample selection process. On delivery the agent can ensure that the questionnaire is given to the intended respondent and, in the case of non-response, establish reasons for this – e.g. unable to contact, doesn't satisfy the sample criteria (e.g. non-user), unwilling etc.

As one would expect the technique also has a number of weaknesses. In common with all self-completion questionnaires there is a bias towards literate respondents, there is no guarantee that the claimed respondent actually completed the questionnaire (although personal delivery and collection helps minimise this risk), and the personal nature of the method requires one to depend on highly clustered samples compared with mail or telephone surveys (but not with face-to-face interviews).

On balance, however, the advantages outweigh the disadvantages, and Brown reports the design and the implementation of an experiment to determine its effectiveness amongst retailers in Lisburn, Northern Ireland.

The experiment confirmed the advantages of speed, low cost and high response rates, and also showed that the nature of the covering letter, questionnaire length and sex of the delivery agent had little effect on the overall response rate.

Summary

In this chapter we have examined a wide range of issues involved in the collection of data through various kinds of interview. The uses and advantages/disadvantages of the various approaches have been looked at in some detail as have the issues to be taken into account when administering questionnaires. Further, if the administration of structured questionnaires is delegated to a professional field force, an appreciation of what is involved will enable the user to ask meaningful questions on the subject and assess how well the fieldwork has been executed on their behalf. However, if you are to administer your own questionnaires you should read Chapter 11 carefully.

In Chapter 13 we will review some of the methods and techniques used to interpret the data gathered by the various methods discussed here.

Recommendations for further reading

Fielding, N. G. (2002), *Interviewing*, 4 volume set, (London: Sage)

Fink, Arlene (Ed) (2003), *The Survey Kit*, 10 volume set, London: Sage Publications, volumes 3, 4 and 5.

Gubrium, J. F. and Holstein, J. A. (Eds) (2001), *Handbook of Interview Research* (London: Sage)

Krueger, Richard A. and Casey, Mary Anne (2000), *Focus Groups*, London: Sage Publications

CHAPTER 11

Questionnaire Completion

Synopsis
In this chapter we present the guidelines issued to interviewers administering questionnaires developed by the Centre for Social Marketing at Strathclyde University as part of its continuing programme of research into health education and other social issues. While the guidelines are designed to ensure consistency in data collection involving multiple interviewers, the procedures and methods are equally relevant for students and other individuals engaged in administering a formal questionnaire.

Keywords
questionnaire administration – routing, coding, probing, show cards, scales

Introduction

The results of a survey are based on the collection of data, which must be valid. This means that the interviewer must record the information given by the respondent in every interview with accuracy. In order to ensure that sufficient accuracy is achieved, the following points should be observed:

(1) General points to observe when asking questions

(a) *Each question should be asked exactly as it is written on the questionnaire.*
The questions have been worded very carefully by the research worker in charge of the survey and piloted by experienced interviewers. Every interview is an exchange of communications between two individuals. Words are the essence of this communication. Some words may have quite different associations and if different words are used we shall have the wrong response.

   If we cannot be sure you have asked the questions in exactly the same way, we cannot compare your results.

(b) *You should always read out the introductory phrase you are given on each survey in the exact words given to you at the top of the questionnaire.*

(c) *If you use a 'probe' which is really a supplementary question, you should use this in the exact words given to you for that type of probe.* (These probes are given later in the section.)

(d) *You should not explain any of the questions.*

The reason for this is that if you give your interpretation of the question, this may be different from that of another interviewer. So, in effect, you are asking a different question.

(e)   *You should ask each and every question you are required to ask, and in the order in which it is written.*

Often it may seem to you that the respondent has already given you the answer to a question by a comment she has made during the interview, or even, you may feel, in answer to a question which has already been asked. But you must still ask every question as you come to it, because the answer a person gives at one stage of the interview may be quite different from the one he/she gives at another.

  We very carefully arrange the questions in a certain order so that a train of thought is made. If you start rearranging the questions this train of thought is changed. Sometimes too, a question is repeated on purpose, as a sort of check question. If the respondent changes her mind about something or remembers something later on which she was trying to think of earlier, then you must not change the original answer you have recorded. Taking each question individually, the answer you get to a question at the time you ask it *is the correct answer.*

(f)   *You should not put in any supplementary question on your own.*

(g)   *You should always follow all the procedures given on the questionnaire for asking questions, showing cards, visual aids, scales, etc.*

  (i)   We shall often ask you to handle a question in a certain way. There may be a procedure given to you about rotating the order of asking different sections of the question, or we may ask you to work through the sections in a certain way. This procedure should be followed meticulously. Otherwise you are doing the same as if you were to change the wording of the question – you are asking another question.

Similarly, if there is a procedure for the respondent about what you want her to do – for example, explaining the meaning of a scale card, or choosing one of a series of statements – you should read out the appropriate instructions *exactly as written* on the questionnaire. These instructions can be easily identified as they always appear in block capitals.

These procedures and instructions are *part of the question,* and are very carefully planned and worded by the research worker, who needs to be sure that every interview has been conducted in the same way, and that the same question has been asked in every case.

(ii) On many of the surveys you will be asked to show a *card*. On the card there may be a list of opinions from which you would like the respondent to choose one, or a list of opinions which you want the respondent to go through with you one by one, or a sort of thermometer scale on which you want the respondent to show you his opinion of something.

Remember that we always have a very good reason for asking you to show a card, and it is *not the same at all* if you do not show the card: you are in fact changing the question again.

(h) *'Don't know responses'.*

If a respondent gives a 'Don't know' response to a question you should try to elicit some kind of answer from him. At all times respondents, should be aware that we are not testing their knowledge, merely interested in their opinions. A good way of dealing with this type of response is to say 'What do you think?' or 'We're interested in your opinions.' Try at all times to avoid recording a 'Don't know' response.

(2) Routing

These questions filter out respondents. On questionnaires there are usually some questions which do not have to be asked of some respondents or if previous questions are answered in a particular way. In this case you should skip the questions until you come to the question indicated in the routing column, e.g. if 'No' got to Q4, if 'Yes' ask Q3. You should pay particular attention to these routing instructions when going through the questionnaire at home, as you can create a very bad impression on the respondent if you fumble back and forth and ask unnecessary questions.

An example of a routed question is given below

Q19 Do you ever take an alcoholic drink?		(76)
	Yes	①
	No	2
	DK	3

IF 'YES' CONTINUE, if 'NO' GO TO Q22

Q20 Usually how often do you have a drink?		(77)
SHOW CARD 29	More than once a week	1
	Regularly every week	②
	2 or 3 times a month	3
	About once a month	4
	Only very occasionally	5
	DK	6

Q21   Last time you had something to drink
        what did you have?
        PROBE FOR DETAILS OF WHAT WAS DRUNK
        Ask Anything else?

	BEER/ LAGER (½ pints)	SPIRITS (single measures)	WINE/ SHERRY (glasses)	COCKTAILS (glasses)	
CODE NUMBER OF DRINKS OPPOSITE					(78)
No of drinks	--*2*--	---*1*---	--------	--------	(79)
					(80)

(3)   Coding of answers

(a)   *Precoded* In this type of question, we have anticipated all or most of the answers you are likely to get, and written these answers on the questionnaire opposite some 'code' numbers. All you have to do is put a circle round the appropriate code number. For example:

Q18   (a) On an average day, how many cigarettes/   (72)
            cigars do you smoke?

	Less than 1 daily	1
ACTUAL NUMBER ----*12*---	1-15	②
(cigarettes)	16-20	3
	21+	4
	None	5

(73)

ACTUAL NUMBER _____	Less than 1 daily	
(cigars)	1-15	2
	16-20	3
	21+	4
	None	⑤

(b) In an average week, how many ounces of   (74)
      cigarette/pipe tobacco do you smoke?

	Less than ½ oz weekly	1
	½ - 1 oz	2
ACTUAL NUMBER............	1 – 4 oz	3
(ounces of cigarette tobacco)	5 - 8 oz	4
	More than 8 oz	5
	None	⑥

(75)

ACTUAL NUMBER............	Less than ½ oz weekly	1
(ounces of pipe tobacco)	½ - 1 oz	2
	1 – 4 oz	3
	5 – 8 oz	4
	More than 8 oz	5
	None	⑥

There are several points to be remembered when you are recording pre-coded answers:

(i)   You should always record something for each question you are required to ask. If the answer is something like 'none' or 'never' and there is no code for this type of answer, write in 'none' or 'never'. If you have not filled in a code we cannot give you the benefit of the doubt; in other words, we will have to assume that you have not asked the question at all.

(ii)   If the answers given do not seem to fit into any of the coded answers, do not force them into one of them. We would far rather you wrote out the answer in full, so that we can decide into which code it should go, than that you should code it wrongly. A 'golden rule' you should remember is *If in doubt, write it out.*

(iii) *Never* read out the answers to a pre-coded question unless you are instructed to do so. These answers are printed in to help you, not because we want to respondent to be forced to choose between them, or to know what the choices are. If we had wanted this we would have put the answers on a card for the respondent to look at and choose between.
       The only exception to this is when you get a vague answer on timing and need to fit it into a specific category of the pre-codes. See later in this section – Prompt Probe (page 260).

(iv)   Sometimes there is a code for 'others' for answers that cannot be put into the pre-codes. In this case you should write in the answer and code the 'others'. For example:

Q11	All the advertisements and leaflets we have been talking about were produced by the same people. Who do you think produced them?		(33)
		HEBS	1
		Another health education body	2
		Other health bodies	3
		The Government	4
		Health Authority	5
		Anti-smoking pressure group	6
		Anti-drinking pressure group	7
	WRITE IN _____		
		Anti-drugs pressure group	8
		Sports company	9
		Magazine/newspaper publisher	0
		Cigarette company	X
		Drink company	V

MULTICODE POSSIBLE   (36)

Drugs company		1
Other .... *Schools*		②
Don't know		3

(b) *Open-ended* An open-ended question is one where we cannot anticipate the answers and we want you to record exactly what was said as fully as possible.

In most open-ended questions you should record answers verbatim, *in the exact words used by the respondent*. It does not matter if you think you can express what you know the respondent means much better than she can; we want you to take down, as if in dictation, her exact words. The reasons for this are two-fold. First, it is very interesting and useful for campaign development to know exact words which people use to describe things. Second, you will not be tempted to record only that which you think is important (this leads to tremendous bias). Also it is much easier for us to grade the exact shades of meaning in what a respondent says if you give us her words.

Think of the following answer, and how important the words used are:

Q27   When you said there were things you can do to help improve your health, what things did you have in mind?

PROBE FULLY, ASK ANY OTHERS?

Well I don't know, some people might   (30)
just say you should just give up   (31)
smoking but I think doing a little   (32)
exercise and watching what you   (33)
eat helps

The answer is quite typical of the sort of thing you can expect. The respondent may not have thought about this subject before. Faced with the question she fluffs around a little, and she is thinking aloud when she tells you what other people might think. But remember that the fact she is hesitant is interesting to us. If she had answered immediately and definitely, 'Give up smoking', we would have known that the subject aroused pretty strong feelings.

Let us consider the way this answer might have been recorded if the interviewer did not record everything. A really poor interviewer could probably cut the respondent off after the first sentence 'Well I don't know', recording 'I don't know'.

The technique of verbatim reporting is something which comes with practice, but there are two hints we can give you:

- start writing immediately the respondent starts to speak;
- when she outstrips you, as she probably will unless she sees you writing and slows up (she often will), it is a good idea to repeat what she has said to you *as you write it* which invariably has the effect of slowing her down to your pace

(4) Probing

Probing is a way of getting a respondent to:

- answer you in terms of the question
- say more, or
- explain herself

Probing, unless skilfully done, can introduce a great deal of bias. The interviewer is only human, and it is natural that she will probe more fully on points which appeal to her, or which she agrees with, or which she thinks are important. This is why we often do not think it is a good idea to let you know what we expect from a question: you may find yourself only recording what you think we want to know. It is impossible to gauge the importance of any point until the survey is finished. So always follow the probing procedures printed on the questionnaire faithfully.

There are *three main types of probe,* and these are described below:

A. BASIC PROBES – used to get the respondent to answer in terms of the question.

The respondent, if she has misunderstood the question or does not know the answer, may do one of five things:

(a) She may answer so far off the point that you can tell she has not grasped the meaning of what you are asking.
(b) She may ask you what you mean.
(c) She may ask you what your opinion is.
(d) She may refuse to answer because she feels she does not know enough.
(e) She may not answer you properly in terms of the card or scale which you are showing her.

Basic Probe (I) (always used first before other probes) Repeat the question.
When the respondent answers so far off the point that you can tell she has not grasped the meaning of what you said, record the first answer she gives and then use basic probe (I), viz. *Merely repeating the question, perhaps putting emphasis on different words.* Repeat the question or part of the question slowly and clearly. You may think this makes you sound foolish but this is not so.

The point is that a carefully piloted question can stand up to this treatment. You should, as an interviewer, be able to rely on your question to get the information you require.

Basic Probe (I) is supposed to get you the answer you want, and should always be tried first, before you use any other probe.

e.g. You said you did get involved in sport/physical activity. Could you tell me the sorts of things that you are involved in?
   A. I like watching football.
   Q. Could you tell me the sorts of things that *you* are *involved* in?
   A.   Oh, I go swimming occasionally and long walks with the dog.

Basic Probe (ii) – 'What do you mean?'
This is used if the respondent asks you what you mean. This is, admittedly, a difficult one to parry, and you will probably only annoy her by repeating the question too many times. The way to deal with this is as follows: try repeating the question or part of the question, as in Basic Probe (I) and if the respondent still asks what you mean, say 'I would like to know what you understand by...'

   e.g.Do you ever get involved in any sport/physical activity
   A. Are you counting walking?
   Q. Any sport/physical activity.
   A. I am not sure what you mean by physical activity.
   Q. I would like to know what *you* understand by physical activity. Do you ever get involved in any sport/physical activity?
   A. Oh well, I suppose I would count walking. In that case I do get involved in sport/physical activity.

If a respondent gives you an answer which you know to be incorrect, however preposterous it may seem to you, you must never correct her. It is most revealing to us if the respondent is in fact misinformed. Do not ever say something like, 'But you said before that you thought so-and so', or 'had used so-and-so'. Take each answer down as it comes, when it comes.

Basic Probe (iii) – 'What is your opinion?'
Another thing which happens often is when a respondent cannot make up her mind, and asks you for your opinion. Here you should throw the ball back into her court by saying, 'I would like to know what you think'. You should *never* express your own opinion.   This would bias your respondent completely.

Basic Probe (iv) – 'What do you think?'
On some questions respondents may be asked to give an opinion on some subject to which she has not given much thought before. In this sort of case you often find a respondent reluctant to answer. She may say something like, 'I can't tell you, as I've never really thought about it before'. In this case you should repeat the question, emphasising the word 'think', and then if she still says she does not know, use the following probe question:

'Would you tell me what you think, from what you have heard or seen about...?'

and, as a last resort: 'Would you make a guess?'

These last probes are only to be used if all else fails. Do try repeating the question or part of the question (Basic Probe (I). You should usually be able to get an answer from this. If not, go on to use Basic Probe (v).

Basic Probe (v) – Getting the respondent to answer in terms of a show card.
    If you are asking the respondent to choose one of a series of statements or opinions on a card, you must be sure that she answers by using one of the words on the card. If she does not you must draw her attention back to the card by using the basic probe, 'Would you tell me which of these words or phrases on *this card* comes closest to what you think?', or 'would you show me on this card?'

> e.g.   I have a card here with some statements on it. (READ OUT CARD)
>   I would like you to tell me which of them applies to eating salt?
>   (VERY GOOD, QUITE GOOD, GOOD, NEITHER GOOD NOR
>   BAD, QUITE BAD, VERY BAD.)
> A.   I think eating salt is all right in moderation.
> Q.   Would you tell me which of the phrases on this card comes closest
>   to what you think?
> A.   Oh, 'NEITHER GOOD NOR BAD' I would say.

B. PROBES FOR OPEN-ENDED QUESTIONS – to get people to say more. There are three kinds of probes used here:

(a) *Continuing Probe.* The next important probe to master, and possibly the most difficult, is the continuing probe. Briefly, what we are trying to do is to get people to say as much as possible, without leading them in any way. Ideally, no probe except this and the basic probe should be used.

    (i) The first continuing probe may not sound to you like a probe at all, but simply the normal thing you would do in any interview. It involves looking expectantly at the respondent with your pen posed over the paper, as if she were about to say more.

(ii) You may also repeat the last words she has just said, in exactly the same words as she has used. If you change the words, you may introduce bias.

(iii) You can say, 'mm' or 'yes' in an anticipatory manner.

Written down, these 'continuing probes' sound very strange, but once you have practised them for a time you will find they come quite easily and naturally. It is essentially a conversational probe. You should look upon all your interviews as a conversation between you and the respondent. Always draw her out sympathetically, without giving any opinions of your own.

(b) *What else/Any other probe.*   This is the final probe used on open-ended questions.

The way you ask this is as follows:

'What else can you tell me about…? Inserting the appropriate question, and recording fully any other information you are given.   Never ask 'anything else?' as this usually elicits the answer 'no'. Rather ask a positive question – 'What else?' because, although it might not be as socially acceptable, it produces results.

e.g.   Could you tell me the sorts of sports/physical activity that you are involved in?'
PROBE FULLY

A.   I take exercise three times a week.
Q.   Exercise?
A.   Yes swimming, walking, that sort of thing.
Q.   Mm?
A.   That's all really.
Q.   Any other kinds of physical activity you do?
A.   I do a lot of gardening I suppose
Q.   Mm?
A.   That's all.

(c) *Explanatory Probe.*   This is used to get people to explain themselves (only to be used if instructed).
On an open-ended question, when the respondent has said as much as she can, there may still be some points which are incomplete, or incomprehensible. If this happens, do not interrupt the respondent as she

is speaking to you, as you may interrupt her train of thought. Wait until she has stopped speaking after all the continuing probes, and *then* use one of the following two probes:

(i)   If the respondent's answer is ambiguous, incomprehensible, or incomplete then you should repeat exactly the words she has said, and then ask:

Either   - 'What do you mean by that?'
Or   - 'In what way was that?'
Or   - 'What makes you say that?

(ii)   e.g. When you said there are things you can do to help improve your health, what things did you have in mind?

PROBE FULLY, ASK ANY OTHERS?

A.   Have a good diet.
Q.   What do you mean by diet?
A.   Eating the right kinds of food.
Q.   Mm?
A.   Like fruit and vegetables and brown bread.
Q.   What makes you say that?
A.   They've got lots of fibre in them.
Q.   Mm?
A.   Isn't that enough? I can't think of anything more to say.

This is the sort of thing people often say. In open-ended questions, you should record verbatim even these 'finishing up' statements, so that we know you have got absolutely all you can from that person. If you use a 'continuing' probe and get no response, you should *always* record that you have used a probe.

C   SPECIFIC PROBES – used to get the exact information you want.

(a) *Amplifying Probe.* On some questions, especially pre-coded ones, you may not get exactly the information you require. For instance, if you were asking someone about physical activity, and she told you she did 'exercise', you might want to know what sort of exercise. In this case you would *not* prompt her by asking her something like, 'Would that be running or aerobics or swimming?' This would be prompting, putting your own interpretation of a word into the respondent's mind, instead of letting her give you her interpretation. You should deal with this question in this way. Ask 'What kind of/sort of…?' *Do not* use any other phrase except those.

(b) *Playback specific probe.* This probe is used mainly on questions of frequency or time. If the answer given is not given to you in the terms you want, you 'play back' what the respondent has said to you.

e.g.How often these days do you take an alcoholic drink (if at all)?

A. Only on special occasions.
   (Here the interviewer should not interpret the answer herself – after all your idea of what constitutes a 'special occasion' may be quite different from that of another person).
Q. How often is that?
A. How often do special occasions occur?

(c) *Prompt probe.* This is only to be used if all else fails, and it must *only be used in questions of frequency or time* – 'How long ago?' or 'When did you?' It is sometimes very difficult to get an accurate answer to these questions without using the prompt probe, in which you offer a series of pairs of alternatives to the respondent

This prompt probe is the only exception to the rule that you must never prompt – i.e. put something into the mind of the respondent that is perhaps not there – and should be used with great restraint, and only as it is written above.

The way to proceed with this sort of probe is as follows:

Look at your questionnaire and find which is the least frequent or the longest ago and taking that, ask one of these questions:

(1) *On frequency* – 'Would it be once in…or more often than that?' and work down to the right answer.
(2) *On questions of 'how long?'* – Would it be within the last…or longer ago than that?' and work down until you get the right answer.

e.g. When did you last take an alcoholic drink?

A. Ages ago
Q. Would it be within the last 12 months or longer ago than that?
A. Oh, within the last year.
Q. Would it be within the last six months or longer ago than that?
A. Oh, within the last six months.
Q. Would it be within the last month or longer ago than that?
A. No, it is longer ago than a month.

SUMMARY OF PROBES

(a) *Probes to get respondent to answer in terms of the question*

    Basic probes:

(i) When she answers off the point	Repeat the question or part of question.
(ii) When she asks what you mean	Basic probe (I) first and then 'I would like to know what *you* understand by ...?'
(iii) When she asks what you think	Basic probe (I) first and then 'I would like to know what *you* think. We are interested in your views.
(iv)'Last ditch' probes if respondent will not answer because she feels she does not know enough	Basic probe (I) first and then 'Would you tell me what you think from what you've heard or seen?' then 'Would you make a guess?'
(v) Basic probes on showing a card	Basic probe (I) first and then 'Which of the words/phrases/brands on this card comes closest to what you mean?' 'Would you show me on the card?'

(b)   *Probes to make people say more*

    Continuing probes:

(i)   Looking expectantly
(ii)   Saying 'mm' or 'yes'
(iii)   Repeating the last words of what the respondent has said in an anticipatory manner.

    What else probes

    Explanatory probes:

(i)   What did you mean by that?
(ii)   In what way was it...?
(iii)   What makes you say that?

(c)   *Probes to get specific information*

(i)	Amplifying probe	What sort of/kind of…?
(ii)	Playback probe	Playback what respondent has said in order to get *specific* answer required
(iii)	Prompt probe	How long ago? Or When did you?

HOW TO INDICATE PROBES

Write (P) beside each comment where you have asked the respondent for more.

e.g. What sort of things can you do to improve your health?

> Everything in moderation (P) cut down drinking and smoking (P) don't eat too many fatty foods (P) a little exercise (P) nothing else

You carry on probing until the respondent has nothing more to say and then end with '(P) nothing else' to indicate that you did try to probe further but the respondent had nothing more to say. This is called probing to a negative.

(5) Show cards

These are cards showing lists of words or phrases. They are used to prompt answers to certain questions e.g. what advertising is respondent aware of. They also help to make the respondent define his attitude to some element of a campaign. Make sure cards are shown and that the respondent reads them properly, and if necessary wait until he fetches his glasses! Explain that here is a list of items we would like him to consider, and he is to choose one or two, depending on the instructions. If he does not appear to understand the card or perhaps cannot read, read out the items and make a note on the questionnaire of what you have done.

When there is more than one show card attached to each other, you must take the cards back before the next question to prevent the respondent leafing through. Reading the cards prematurely can be fatal to some types of questions.

Here are three important points about card showing:

> (i) Unless the respondent is blind or says he cannot read, you must *always* show the card. If you cannot show the card for these reasons, then you must record this on the questionnaire.
>
> (ii) When you show the card you should read out the words on it *before* you ask the questions. Many people read carelessly or incorrectly;

there is much more semi-literacy in the country than you might think.

(iii) If you are asking the respondent to choose one of a number of statements or opinions on a card, you should be sure that he answers you exactly in terms of one of the words on the card.

Questionnaires should indicate which 'show' card should be used with each question thus, e.g. 'SHOW CARD 12'. Photographs, pictures, leaflets, booklets, posters, stickers, etc. are referred to as 'VISUAL AIDS' with an appropriate number. The system of numbers used for both show cards and visual aids runs consecutively, so 1, 2 and 3 might be show cards; 4, 5, and 6 visual aids, and 7, 8, and 9 show cards.

(6) Scales

We often need to know how significant a respondent perceives a given concept to be. Commercial Market Research companies often need to know how a respondent rates a brand or product, either against other brands or against other products, or with regard to specific attributes required from that kind of product. In this case we use some form of scale, of which there are three main types.

(a) *Verbal scale* Here the degrees of the scale are expressed in the form of words, for example:

How well do you think the advertisements we have been talking about manage to get across the point that being healthy is not just a matter of giving up smoking and drinking? Choose a phrase from this card which best describes your answer.

Very well
Reasonably well
Not really well
Not at all well

(b) *Marks.* In this case the respondent is asked to award marks, usually out of 10, to an advertisement or brand for a specific attribute, e.g. how many marks out of 10 would you give the *Daily Mirror* for being a newspaper that gives you all the health news you want?

(c) *Semantic differential scales.* These scales, described in Chapter 9, consist of a number of alternative responses to a statement. The responses at either end of the scale are more or less opposite in meaning. There are usually about 10-12 statements per question (see example below).

Q 31   Here is a list of things that other people have said may be good for health. READ OUT WHOLE LIST
How important do you think each of them is for health?
SHOW CARD 35, READ OUT EACH STATEMENT INDIVIDUALLY AND OBTAIN RESPONSE
ROTATE START

	Very important	Quite important	Not very important	Not at all important	DK	
Give up smoking	①	2	3	4	5	(56)
Eating more fibre	6	⑦	8	9	0	
Drinking less alcohol	1	②	3	4	5	(57)
Losing weight	6	7	⑧	9	0	
Eating less sugar	1	②	3	4	5	(58)
Taking exercise	6	⑦	8	9	0	
Getting the doctor's advice on how to stay healthy	1	2	③	4	5	(59)
Relaxing/getting plenty of sleep	6	7	⑧	9	0	
Eating less salt	1	②	3	4	5	(60)
Using medicines	6	7	8	⑨	0	
Easting less fatty foods	1	2	③	4	5	(61)

The respondent chooses her response from a show card. The interviewer circles the code number which applies to the respondent's reply

We use this type of scale because, if *administered properly*, they give us information that we cannot easily obtain in any other way.

Sometimes these scales will consist of five or seven boxes placed between two words or phrases. The words at either end of the boxes are more or less opposite in meaning. There are usually about 20 or so scales set out on a page. At the top of the page is a *concept*, which the respondent is being asked to rate. Usually the concept will be a brand of some product field, but sometimes it may be the respondent's own opinion of herself, or a company, or just about anything.

Where this 'empty box' type scale is used, respondents are required to tick the scales as quickly as they can, and if they do put down their first objective opinions, the results will be some measure of their subconscious motivations and attitudes.

You can appreciate that clients find such information extremely useful to improve their products and advertising.

The only alternative technique to obtain this kind of psychological information is 'in-depth' interviewing. Such methods are difficult to carry out on a large scale and tend to give somewhat misleading results if the samples of respondents involved are small.

The proper administration of semantic differential scales is a more advanced skill than simple interviewing techniques. The interviewer must be aware of the purpose of the technique, and must strive to create the proper milieu, or 'psychological atmosphere'.

The most important thing to get across to the respondent is that we do not want a slow, considered opinion. Their first impression is the thing we are after.

Some people are naturally cautious and will be slow. Others may try to ponder over the 'correct answer' in a misguided attempt to be as helpful as possible. If it is explained properly the speed element of the administration of the scales can be conveyed to most respondents. Interviewers will have to experiment a bit to find the best way of dealing with people who go too slowly.

On average, about four seconds per scale should be allowed as a reasonable speed. Some respondents will be much faster, but others will try to drag on beyond this point.

If much more than four seconds per scale is being taken, the respondent is getting bored and the information being obtained is actually of less value. If possible, the interviewer should interject to try to speed things up.

(7) Rotate and tick start

On some questions it is not possible to rotate the actual statements or list of products, and then the researcher asks the interviewer to rotate the order and TICK START. In this case the interviewer ticks the statement she starts with.

On the first interview she would tick the first statement. On the next interview, she ticks the second statement, reading out the statements starting from the second statement and ending with the first one and so on. In most cases it is possible for the interviewer to tick the appropriate statements at home before doing the interviews, as it is sometimes difficult to remember in the middle of an interview which statement was ticked at the last one, e.g.

Q 28   Now I'm going to read a list of things people do.
READ OUT THE WHOLE LIST
Could you tell me how good or bad you think they are for your health, giving your answer from this card.
SHOW CARD 35, READ OUT EACH STATEMENT INDIVIDUALLY AND OBTAIN RESPONSE

ROTATE START, TICK START_____

		Very bad	Quite good	Neither good nor bad	Quite good	Very good	DK	
1.	Go to the pub for an occasional drink	1	2	3	4	5	6	(35)
2.	Eat high fibre food	7	8	9	0	X	V	
3.	Take gentle exercise once or twice a week	1	2	3	4	5	6	(36)
4.	Smoke cigarettes occasionally	7	8	9	0	X	V	
5.	Eat sugary food	1	2	3	4	5	6	(37)
6.	Run in marathons regularly	7	8	9	0	X	V	
7.	Eat fatty food	1	2	3	4	5	6	(38)
8.	Spend most evenings in the pub	7	8	9	0	X	V	
9.	Drink a lot of milk	1	2	3	4	5	6	(39)
10.	Smoke heavily	7	8	9	0	X	V	
11.	Eat salt	1	2	3	4	5	6	(40)

(8) Summary of points on the interview

Important points to remember when asking questions:

(a) Each question should be asked exactly as it is written on the questionnaire. Do not add words to try to soften the question. The questionnaires have been worded very carefully, to make sure that all interviewers have asked the same question in the same way. In order that we can compare results, you must be very scrupulous about this ruling.

(b) You should always read the introductory phrase given at the beginning of each survey as it is written.

(c) Each and every question should be asked in the order in which it is written on the questionnaire. This ensures that no questions are omitted. Bear in mind that the questionnaire has to follow a certain pattern and that we sometimes ask the same question again and again on purpose, as a sort of check. If you are routed past a question put a line through it to show it was not asked. Never leave a question completely blank.

(d) The respondent may change her mind in the course of an interview because of something you have been discussing. You should not change an answer previously given, even if the respondent contradicts herself, or asks you to change the question. The ruling is that whatever the respondent answers at the time of being asked the question is the correct answer to that question. Make a note on the questionnaire if she has changed her mind.

(e) You should never explain the question. If the respondent does not understand, make a note of this on the questionnaire and go on to the next question. Never change the wording or ask a supplementary question, except one of the standard probe questions.

(f) Write legibly and always use blue or black biro. All answers must be recorded at the time of the interview.

(g) There must be an answer recorded for every applicable question on the questionnaire. Unless you explain why there is no answer recorded at any question, the questionnaire is incomplete and we cannot use it. The questionnaire will be returned to you.

(h) Make a note beside any question where odd circumstances prevented you from asking the question as instructed, e.g. respondent was blind and you read out from show card etc.

(i) Cross out a wrongly recorded code with two diagonal lines. Never cross it out with an X as this causes confusion.

(j) Where you have been given a vague answer, do not make a guess. If you are not sure what to code, throw the question back at the respondent until you get a definite answer.

(k) Instructions in capital letters are addressed to you and should not be read out to the respondent. Only where the writing is in ordinary small letter do you read this out to the respondent.

(l) Record replies accurately and swiftly. Control the interview by asking questions at a speed to suit the respondent. If you are too slow they get irritated, if too fast they will not understand.

(m) Give adequate thanks to the respondent for their co-operation when the interview is concluded.

Interviewer selection and control

From the above discussion of questionnaire completion it should be clear that the role of the interviewer is critical to the effective administration of a questionnaire. No matter how much effort has been put into the structuring and design of the questionnaire poor administration can invalidate all the data collected and render the survey useless. It follows that interviewers must be trained and qualified for the task in hand.

As we have seen, the level and kind of qualification will depend very much upon the type of interview. For in-depth, informal and unstructured interviews one requires a person with knowledge of the subject matter, interpretative skills and judgement as the scope and content of the interview and the explanation of this will depend entirely upon the interviewer. Conversely, in the case of semi-structured or structured interviews using a questionnaire, the interviewer will not require specific knowledge or interpretative skills, but they will require personal skills in initiating and conducting the interview if one is to secure the desired information from the intended respondents. Because of these demands, and the fact that few organisations undertake a sufficient volume of field research to keep professional interviewers fully employed, specialist divisions or firms have developed to undertake field interviewing on a sub-contract basis.

In the *Consumer Market Research Handbook* John F. Drakeford and Valerie Farbridge deal with the subject 'Interviewing and field control' in considerable detail. Much of this is more relevant to the professional practitioner than the user but in concluding their chapter they offer the following checklist for buyers i.e. persons employing others to administer a questionnaire for them.

Research planning and design:

(a)   Is the right degree of emphasis placed upon the interviewing phase of a project, compared with the other phases through which the project has to go?

(b)   How are the questionnaires, recording forms, diaries or inventories laid out, and by whom are they designed?

(c)   Has the designer any interviewing experience, and has he or she at any stage piloted the questionnaire?

(d)   Are the instructions to interviewers comprehensive; and who drafted them?

(e)   Are the sampling procedures to be used in the project feasible in the field?

(f)   How are the interviewers instructed on these sampling procedures and under what circumstances, if any, are they allowed to deviate from instructions?

(g)   What checks are imposed to ensure that a sampling plan is followed?

Field control

(a)   How is the field management at head office organised in general and in relation to the implementation of a particular project?

(b)   How much contact is there between head office staff and the supervisors and interviewers?

(c)   What documentation exists as a control on contact rates, interviewing rates etc?

(d)   How is supervision in the field organised and how are queries that arise in the field dealt with?

(e)   What is the ratio between supervisors and interviewers and what responsibilities have the supervisors for maintaining adequate interviewer standards?

(f)   What procedures are followed in briefing interviewers, either personally, by post or telephone?

(g)   How well are these procedures supported by written material of a general kind (e.g. interviewer manual) or a kind specific to the survey (e.g. instructions, call sheets, etc.)

The interviewers

(a)   What is the composition of the field force and how has it been built up?

(b)   How are the interviewers initially selected?

(c)   How are they trained, either at formal sessions or in the field?

(d)   How frequently are the interviewers seen by head office staff and supervisors?

(e)   Are they aware of the nature and depth of the quality control procedures conducted?

(f)   What are their terms of employment and how are they paid?

(g)   How regularly do the interviewers work also for other organisations?

(h)   To what extent do they work also for other field forces?

(i)   What methods of identification are carried?

Quality control

(a)   What checks are imposed on interviewers while work is in the field and how are the problems and queries resolved?

(b)   How often and at what level are supervisor spot checks, postal checks, revisits to respondents conducted as further control measures?

(c)   What are the check-editing procedures once work has been returned to head office and how are queries and suspect interviewing dealt with?

(d)   Has the organisation been able to build up a data bank on individual interviewer performance; if so, what does this data bank comprise?

Source: Drakeford J.F., Farbridge V. (1986), "Interviewing and field control", pp.147-166 in Worcester R. and Downham J., (Eds), *Consumer market research handbook*, third edition, London: McGraw-Hill,

As a further check the buyer might also ask to see the kind of fieldwork guide issued to interviewers and check its scope and clarity against the extract on questionnaire completion given above.

Summary

The advice given in this chapter is primarily intended for situations where more than one interviewer is involved in administering a formal questionnaire. That said, the instructions/advice are equally applicable to the individual interviewer to minimise the possibility of respondent bias being introduced by the interviewer. As such, the guidance is also relevant to other forms of interviewing where the objective is to obtain unbiased information from respondents.

Recommendations for further reading

Drakeford J.F., Farbridge V. (1986). Interviewing and field control. In: Worcester R. and Downham J., editors. *Consumer market research handbook*, third edition. (London: McGraw-Hill), pp.147-166

Also look out for forthcoming November 2003:
Bulmer, M. (2003), *Questionnaires* 4 Volume Set (London: Sage Publications)

CHAPTER 12

Conducting Primary Research Online
Anne Foy

Synopsis
This chapter is designed to describe to researchers the potential for conducting primary research online, and the factors which need to be considered when choosing this kind of research methodology. Ethical considerations, including the importance of data protection will be discussed, as well as technical and logistical requirements. Suggestions will also be made about how to proceed if you do decide to go ahead with an online piece of primary research.

Keywords
computer mediated communications (CMC); ethics; email; web survey; log file analysis

Introduction

Several of the chapters in this book are concerned with determining and constructing a research methodology. Whilst many of the rules and guidelines given in these chapters are applicable to doing primary research online, using the Internet to conduct research does throw up its own set of variables. Thus this chapter highlights both the advantages and disadvantages of doing primary research online, as well as the methodological considerations of the electronic world.

There are a number of ways one can research in the online world, and these reflect those survey methodologies found in offline research. For example researchers can use the Internet to conduct interviews, to use focus groups , to observe behaviours and to use survey methodology.

In this chapter we shall look at the ethics and 'netiquette' of doing this kind of research in the online environment, as well as the technical issues which researchers will encounter.

Computer mediated communications

Computer mediated communication (CMC) is a growing force in qualitative research. Mann and Stewart (2000) describe nine ways in which the Internet is currently used to communicate:

1.   Web pages
2.   Email
3.   Chat
4.   Mailing lists
5.   Usenet groups
6.   Focus groups
7.   Conferencing
8.   MU* Environments
9.   Multi-media environments

In Chapter 5 we have already described the first 5 categories, all of which someone using the Internet for secondary research might come across. The last four categories are more specialised, and tend to be used in primary research.

Focus groups
Online focus groups act much like those offline, and are generally conducted by professional focus group facilitators such as VRROOM or W3Resources. Participants do not need special software to join in, instead they use a web site to sign in to the group. (Mann and Stewart 2000) Online focus groups can act either *synchronously* (real-time, like a chat room) or *asynchronously* (users can respond at their leisure – more like an email group). (McAuley 2003).

Conferencing
Essentially online conferencing uses special software to allow participants to post messages on a given topic . Whilst using similar functionality to email, all messages are held in a secure central repository.   A well known example of this is LotusNotes Groupware (Mann and Stewart 2000)

MU* environments
MU* are virtual text based environments, and MUDs (Multi User Domains/Dungeons) are the most common form of these (Mann and Stewart 2000)

Multi-media environments
Environments which allow real-time audio and visual communication, e.g. *http://www.thepalace.com* (Mann and Stewart 2000)

The last two categories are typically those where observational research would take place. (See Chapter 7 for more on observation as a research methodology.) At the moment the Internet is still mainly a text based environment, which limits its potential for observational research, but the use of emoticons and other electronic markers do offer some non-verbal cues (for example, surrounding a word with asterisks stresses the *importance* of that word), and there is the potential of the Internet for auditory and visual communication in the future. One of the main considerations for observational researchers online is how 'natural' can a virtual community be? (For a summary on doing observational research online see Chapter 4 Mann and Stewart 2000, or C. Hines (2000), *Virtual Ethnography* (London: Sage)). There is a huge amount of primary material online for observational researchers. However, as with other kinds of research, there are several important ethical issues which need to be addressed.

Ethics of online research

If you are researching within a formal institution such as a University, you may well find that they have a code of ethics which should be followed, and you should make sure that you have complied with your institution's requirements in this regard. A good starting point for ethical queries is 'Marketing Ethics – an overview' by Paul Whysall (2000), which gives general advice.

There are a number of basic ethical tenets specifically applicable in conducting primary research online. The most basic of these, and one which we have discussed in Chapter 5, is copyright. Remember that whilst information online may not carry a copyright statement, it is still copyrighted to its author. The second basic ethical tenet all researchers should consider, is the principle of **data protection**. Whilst each country has its own laws concerning data protection, every researcher must acquaint themselves with this aspect *before* beginning their research. Again, when researching within a formal institution you may well find that your University or College has a data protection policy in place, and you may be expected to sign a document to make sure your research is covered by the Institution's data protection registration. Basically, data protection principles mean that any person should have access to data collected about themselves, and this data may not be shared without the subject's consent. For more information on the UK data protection provision, visit *http://www.dataprotection.gov.uk/*, and for an outline of the 8 basic principles of data protection in the UK see *http://www.hmso.gov.uk/acts/acts1998/80029--l.htm#sch1* Some funding councils, for example the ESRC, also carry advice on issues like data protection, copyright and duty of confidentiality - see *http://www.esrc.ac.uk/public/guide.html*

In ethical terms, this translates into giving all research subjects what can be termed 'informed consent'. That is, all potential subjects should be given full information about the purpose of the research, the kind of data to be gathered, and the security of that data once gathered, before deciding to take part. Researchers may think that if they do not keep any kind of personal information about a subject, for example, by applying anonymous identifiers to respondents, that it may be possible to circumvent these requirements. This would be a mistake. Say, for example, that respondents fill out an online survey, and submit their responses which the researcher transfers into an offline database. Participants are given a number when they respond, and there are no personal identifiers requested (for example, name, gender, email address). Thus no 'personal' information is held. However, further along in the research process you discover a very interesting follow up question which could clarify an important part of your study. If you have no personal details about your respondents, how can you contact them to follow up your research? Whilst it may seem easier to try and circumvent the data protection system, not only could it harm your research itself, it would also be seen as a glaring omission by any examiner, and implies that you have not understood the process of research. In the UK, recent changes in the legislation mean that all records, not just those in electronic format, are now covered by the Data Protection Act (1998) at *http://www.hmso.gov.uk/acts/acts1998/19980029.htm*.

Some sources recommend that researchers make sure that they receive a record of the consent of the participant, for example in the form of an email explicitly agreeing their participation. Another way to do this with an online survey may be to have a screen at the beginning of the process which requires the user to click on a button stating that they 'agree' with the text on that screen regarding data and consent, before enabling them to complete the online questionnaire. This is much like clicking on the 'I agree' button when loading a new piece of software. However, you have no way of guaranteeing that the participant has read the statement, or that this process will not frighten off potential respondents. The issue of consent in online research is one which is constantly being debated, and researchers must make sure that they have checked up on the latest legislation in this area. Again, your university should be able to give you guidance on this.

Observational researchers must be very careful to consider the aspect of consent. For example, it is not ethically sound for researchers to take part in an email list and quote from that list without identifying themselves to the list and asking permission to quote. However, there are situations where a researcher identifying themselves can immediately affect the environment they are trying to study. One way round this may be to 'observe' the list for a set time period, and at the end of that period to choose the quotations necessary, and then contact the individual authors involved to request their permission. Of course, this does not guarantee a favourable response, as it is entirely possible that list participants may feel that they have been 'spied' upon. Another place to seek guidance on this aspect of Internet life is in the rules of lists and groups themselves. Most list and group hosts will have an 'acceptable use policy' which will outline clearly what behaviour is expected of users of the list/group, and this should always be consulted. Google specifically states that using their groups for surveys of any sort unless the group is specifically set up for that purpose is not acceptable (*http://groups.google.com/googlegroups/posting_terms.html*).

Whilst the following suggestions of information researchers should give to potential subjects are by no means exhaustive, they offer some initial ideas about ethical considerations in conducting primary research online. Information the researcher should give includes:

- Information and contact details (including institution) for the researcher
- The purpose of the research, and the qualification the research may lead to
- If using email, how the email address of the subject was gained (see the next section for further guidance on finding respondents)
- The anonymity of the respondent
- The security of the data gathered
- The use to be made of the data gathered, including any potential transfer of that data
- The commitment required from the respondent (for example, estimated time to complete an online survey, if there are likely to be follow up emails), and any recompense the respondent may receive for their participation
- The deadline for completion of the research
- Information about the data protection and ethical position of the researcher (e.g. that the researcher has fulfilled their legal requirements in this regard)
- If using email, whether the recipient may pass on the email to other people
- You should assure recipients that if they choose not to respond or take part in your research, they will not be contacted by you again.

If you are sending out multiple contact emails, you can use the BCC function of your email programme. This means that email recipients can not see the addresses of other recipients on the email list, again preserving anonymity.

Online interviewing

Email can be used to conduct interviews, although the lack of immediacy and non-verbal cues are factors which may hinder this kind of research. On the other hand, the associated anonymity, and time to consider answers, as well as the increased access to internationally based respondents, can be advantageous. On a more immediate level, researchers can use 'chat' software (for example ICQ (I seek you) technology allows two users to have a direct real-time conversation, Hewson et al. 2003). These online methods of interviewing also carry advantages in that they keep costs down and as all the communication is by nature textual, the data is automatically recorded (Hewson et al. 2003). CAPI (Computer Assisted Personal Interviewing) has already been used in the offline world and shares many of the same methodological advantages and disadvantages as online interviewing and survey methodology. Studies using this technique are a good place to learn about how other researchers have addressed the problems of using computer technology in research – see Sainsbury, Ditch and Hutton (2003) or Miller and Brewer (2003) for an introduction to this method of interviewing.

Future developments in the use of web video software will bring back the 'personal touch' where researchers would prefer to observe non-verbal cues and establish more of a rapport with their participants. Current limitations and differing availability of bandwidth, as well as differing software for audio and video broadcasting mean that this level of communication is not yet widely available. So, if you want to include a piece of video in your research for subjects to respond to, make careful consideration of the file size and quality. If you do include something in your research which needs specialised software to view or use, make sure you use a commonly available piece of 'freeware', so that should users need to download software to view part of your research, it will not cost them anything! Also, provide a link to download. However, requiring your respondents to download software is not likely to encourage participation, so think carefully about the simplest way to use visual and audio cues if this is what is required for your research project.

Finding participants

Unlike telephone numbers there is no way to do a random sample of email addresses (McDaniel and Gates 2002). Established mailing lists are a common place to start in Internet surveys. (For a summary and comparison of research conducted so far using different methodologies see Mann and Stewart 2000, particularly Chapter 4, pp.65-98). Essentially a researcher can use lists to post a request to participate to large numbers of list members simultaneously. However, there are a number of factors which should be considered before using them. Mailing lists are generally populated by 'lurkers', and one study showed that 83% of list members had never contributed anything, whilst only 6% had sent more than a couple of messages. (Kawakami cited in Kitchin 1998). Like webpages, lists wither and die but still live on in cyberspace. For this reason, Ó Dochartaigh recommends that lists need over 100 subscribers for there to be any traffic while lists over a 1000 members will be very active. This is an effective method of narrowing the field when researching lists, and a visit to a resource such as CataList at *http://www.lsoft.com/catalist.html* can show you lists by number of subscriber, for example, lists with over 1000, or even 10,000 subscribers.

Whilst these kinds of groupings have been used by other researchers, there are limitations. No email lists which satisfy these criteria may be found, particularly in specialised research areas. There are ethical reasons for not choosing this route. Some research has borne out the fact that requests for help with academic research can be seen as intrusive by particular online groups, for example Diani and Eyerman (1991). When some lists, such as Roots-L, are as large as 10,000 people, that is a lot of ill will which could be generated by not using the lists as requested.

Furthermore, as someone who does not frequent these lists, steaming in with your first message being a survey, without offering any information or help to others first would be a serious breach of 'netiquette', and likely to result in a 'flame war', in which your inbox could be flooded by emails from people criticising you – again a lot of ill-feeling. This, of course, could also prompt people to fill in the questionnaire with malicious motives, or even in extreme cases, to hack the online survey to make it unusable, or to crash the server by multiple simultaneous submissions. There is also the possibility that people who are not really the ideal target population will be found this way. Multiple approaches to people across different lists are not a welcome form of email behaviour, so learn about the netiquette of cross-posting (p.118).

It is important to make clear to people you are 'cold-calling' how you got their address. Spam is a tricky subject. Some people may consider the contact email as spam (unsolicited and unwanted email) because they did not specifically sign up to retrieve it. You can purchase email lists from various suppliers, but again, this is likely to give a very large yet unfocused sample.

The email address used to generate the initial contact message is important. Email software can easily be configured to automatically junk emails from certain, or even simply unknown, addresses before it even gets to the inbox. Unsolicited emails with file attachments are also often trashed unviewed purely because of the risk of computer viruses within attachments. Sheehan (2001) also suggests that the email suffix itself could have an effect on response rates. For example, spammers – senders of junk mail - often use passport accounts like Hotmail so they do not receive responses to their private email accounts, and this also enables them to dodge persecution by Internet Service Providers (ISPs) for sending out content which is against netiquette. It is easy to set up a Hotmail account, use it once to send out spam, and then shut it down and start up a new one with a different identity, although email accounts can be tracked down eventually by experts.

However, this does not automatically guarantee a welcome reception for the right suffix. Many people may not recognise the significance of such suffixes, whilst it is easy to forge email addresses. Furthermore, the existence of different protocols across countries muddies the waters, for example the

.edu vs *.ac.uk* difference highlighted in Chapter 5. Something for an online researcher to consider is to register their own domain name.

Using a domain name to provide the email address for the original 'hook' to the site may encourage someone to open an unsolicited email. Even if someone is not quite sure about opening your email, they can always find your web page from your address to see what it is you might be affiliated with.   You should carefully consider your email 'handle' to hide any possibility of potential bias according to gender or country of origin. It has to be carefully thought out. You must also consider what to put in the subject line of the message – leaving the subject line blank can sometimes also be an indication of spam, so this is not an option, nor would it be ethical. Furthermore, the domain name suffix itself is important. For example, you may choose not to use a *.com* domain name for two reasons. Firstly, *.com* can imply the site is a commercial site, something which could potentially prejudice people against filling out a survey, and secondly, .com is associated with many users with specifically American websites. Thus, the content and presentation of the initial email is important.

Although researchers may wish to collect data from a specific numerical sample, due to the very nature of the web it is unrealistic to assume that this will limit the survey to that sample. This kind of effect, where the sample takes on a life of its own, is known as 'snowball sampling' (Snowball sampling is not restricted to online research, and has its own advantages and disadvantages – for a summary see Atkinson and Flint 2003). In 1999 a Canadian primary school class of 17 children sent out one email each to a friend, asking them to pass the message on to as many people as they liked, so the class could track where the emails got to in a 2 month period. Within one day 208 responses were received, increasing to 150 per hour until the email account had to be closed down. (Coombes 2001) Some researchers have tried to use access controls to prevent people outside the initial sample from responding, or to minimise multiple responses from the same person. These include using password protected systems, (see for example Heerewegh and Loosveldt 2002) or placing cookies on an individual's browser to see if they come back for a return visit. Cookies are in fact seen by some as an invasion of privacy, as sites, without your permission, are placing information onto your machine which allow them to identify you, and consequently your shopping or browsing habits – see Chapter 5 for a brief explanation of how cookies work.

Alternatively of course, instead of posting an email to potential respondents, researchers can use other methods to gain participants, including posting a request for respondents to mailing lists or newsgroups, or on specific web pages, and not forgetting that offline methods can also be used to gain a sample. Whichever method a researcher uses to find a sample, the usual rules of research apply – you must be wary of factors which can skew the sample.

You also need to consider how you are going to administer your research with your sample, and a popular method covered elsewhere in this book is to use a survey methodology.

Survey methodology

There are two main ways in which researchers can currently administer surveys online. *Email surveys* are those in which questionnaires which are sent out directly to potential subjects as part of an email, so the respondent can simply click "reply" and fill out the questionnaire ready to send back to the researcher. *Web surveys* are those in which a questionnaire is posted on a web page and users visit the page, fill out the survey and then submit it, preferably electronically.

Email survey

When using the email survey methodology, the first question is whether to send out the questionnaire to potential respondents directly, or to send out an initial contact email to establish the sample. Whilst the second method has ethical advantages, one of the methodological flaws identified with this is the skewed sample that ensues, although you could ague that any survey suffers from self-selection because any person can decline to take part. Email does have some distinct advantages over traditional postal survey methods – there are lower costs involved, it is less labour intensive for the researcher and as email is a more immediate medium, responses can be very quick.

Another consideration is the data format of the email. The lowest common denominator in email is TXT (text) files, which give little flexibility in formatting. This is important when a survey includes elements where respondents have to choose one or more elements from pre-prepared lists. Because the email would essentially be re-formatted by each user, it would make it more difficult to automatically pull the data gathered into any kind of database; an important factor when dealing with potentially large numbers of respondents. Although you could attempt to get round this by sending an email questionnaire in an attachment to the basic email, there are a number of reasons against this. Software compliance means that not all users would have the same software, and furthermore, sending unsolicited attachments is likely to scare off potential respondents for computer virus reasons.

There are other disadvantages to email surveys. Multiple email addresses and 'churn' (users changing their service provider and consequently their email address) provide problems in identifying the exact independent numbers in a sample. (Bradley 1999, cited in Sheehan 2001). Using email to survey individuals has other downsides; respondents may try to draw you into correspondence which could impact upon their survey responses. Sheehan (2001) "attempted to identify as many e-mail surveys done for academic purposes as possible, and only 31 surveys could be identified that contained sufficient data to perform this analysis. This minimal adoption of e-mail surveying to date, combined with falling response rates, may indicate a less than promising future for e-mail surveys."

Other considerations include remembering that the Internet is a global phenomenon.   In language terms, the prevalence of English speaking countries on the Internet was echoed with, in 2001, a significant 73% of sites having English as their main language, with German the closest language with 7%. (*http://www.wcp.oclc.org/stats/global.html* and *http://www.wcp.oclc.org/stats/size.html* on 24 February 2002.) Swoboda et al. (1997) performed a world-wide email survey, and achieved 90% of their 20% response rate within four days from all areas of the world, showing that the English language did not appear to be a barrier to response rates, and developing nations did not seem disadvantaged in their access to email.   However, researchers should be careful in their use and choice of language, and remember that this can be a factor.

The drawbacks outlined above mean that email survey is not always the best online research methodology, particularly if you have a long survey or a large potential sample, or you need to strictly control the sample population. However, it can still be useful. For example, most researchers are advised to run a pilot study of their research to iron out any potential problems before the proper research study is performed (see Chapter 9 questionnaire design). You could use email survey to conduct a small pilot study prior to your main research, and this is particularly useful when preparing an online web survey.

Web surveys

Web surveys are hosted on a web page, and respondents visit the page using their Internet browser where they can fill out the questionnaire and electronically submit it to the researcher.

There is a temptation for online researchers to succumb to "Field of Dreams" Syndrome (FDS) – if you build it, they will come, they being potential respondents. On the Internet this is a common failing of many worthwhile sites. However, in simple terms this means that just building a website with a questionnaire on it will not generate respondents. Whilst there are numerous things one can do to publicise a website, for example using metatags (specific pieces of code in the document programming), and registering with search engines, there are also reasons not to follow this path. Unless the survey can be left to run for several months, the site will not rise up the rankings of most search engines. Linking from other websites skews responses to the people that can find and visit those particular websites. One of the biggest and most annoying factors on the web is the increasing number of dead links – links to pages which are out of date but have never been deleted. Surveys which are relatively short lived but hang around in search engine caches and listings for some time will also generate a lot of ill will towards the particular research project, and also to Internet research in general.

Potential criticisms for online researchers

The Internet is a rapidly growing medium. The OCLC (Online Computer Library Centre) is one organisation which has been tracking the growth of the web (The 'State of the Domain' webpages can be found at *http://www.sotd.info/*) Their tracking software "harvests" sites open to public access to analyse content and statistics. With a few provisos this project shows that between 1997 and 2001 there has been a growth of 457% in the number of websites online, and that the top five nations for country of origin of web sites in 1999 were the US (49%), Germany (5%), UK (5%), Canada (4%) and Japan (3%).

A criticism often levelled at web surveys is the possibly skewed population, concerning socio-economic class, sex, age, language and geodemographics. The assumptions are that the web is the domain of young western males of above average education and socio-economic status. Furthermore, on a global scale there are questions of language and accessibility. However, Yun and Trumbo give a variety of statistics which show that in 1999, the female population of the web was up 16% to 46 % from 1995, and that in December 1999, 20% of the online population was aged 45-64. More recent data shows that 'Women now account for 52 percent of home Internet users, or 55 million people, up from 50.4 million last year. There are 49.8 million male home users, up from 48.2 million in December 2000 (Neilsen 2002). It should also be noted that some researchers highlight that compared to traditional methods of surveying populations, the Internet can offer increased geodemographic and socio-economic diversity within samples. For more on this see P. Desai, *Methods Beyond Interviewing in Qualitative Market Research*, (London, 2002).

What this data tells us is that traditional stereotypes of Internet users are not necessarily borne out by research. However, to confirm this fact it is important that any survey includes questions which will ascertain if respondents represent a reasonable distribution in terms of age, gender and geography, so that individual researchers can justify the validity of their sample population, or at least identify any potential skew factors.

Furthermore, there are still questions over the comparative merits of traditional and web-based survey methods. For a recent summary see "Web Survey Bias: sample or mode effect?" by Grandcolas et al. (2003).

Technical architecture

Many researchers will feel that they do not have the time or the expertise to construct their own online survey, and may ask other people to help them with this aspect of their research. However, it is important to have a basic understanding of how online surveys work and the technical possibilities to ensure that the researcher gets the information they want in the format they want. This section discusses the main factors which any researcher wishing to run an online survey should consider in their design.

Data handling of responses

One of the best things about using an online questionnaire is the improved efficiency in data handling. If the 'submit' tag on the online form is correctly set up, you can store replies on your web server and then download all the data at the end of the survey period directly to a pre-built database so that responses are automatically filled in to the database, rather than having to re-enter data manually. (Although you should ensure that every questionnaire response is emailed to you in text format automatically as it is submitted as a back-up procedure). One way to get around the technical difficulties of setting up a form to 'submit' is to invite users to print out the form and send it in by post. There are of course numerous reasons to try and avoid this approach, for example, the costs and effort involved for the participant in printing off and posting the form, and the technical aspects of making sure the form will print out onto different sizes of paper (e.g. A4 or letter).

Specialist software such as NUD*IST, NVivo, MAXqda or Atlas.ti can be used to analyse data. They are commonly used to analyse data gathered in large-scale interview surveys, but the researcher needs to have experience of the software to use it properly. These products are essentially fancy database programs and some of the functionality they provide, for example, categorising responses, can be replicated in standard database software such as Microsoft Access. Each program offers different advantages, for example ATLAS.ti helps in visual analysis of text, audio and graphical data, whilst NUD*IST (the latest version is called N6) is specifically aimed at code-based qualitative analysis. Researchers must have a clear idea of what kind of data they wish to collect (e.g. numerical, graphical or textual) and how they want to analyse this data, before choosing their research methodology. Some software can help you to set up questionnaires, for example SphinxSurvey, whilst there are also online providers of this kind of service, (for example, *http://www.hostedsurvey.com/*). However, there are of course cost implications in this approach. A good website to visit to compare different kinds of research software is Scolari, at *http://www.scolari.co.uk* which has lots of different types of program, with downloadable demonstrations.

Many researchers may find that commonly available web design software is sufficient for their purposes in building an online survey. For example, Microsoft Frontpage has many built-in capabilities to allow online interactive forms to work simply, without the need for complex programming. (These capabilities need to be supported on the server by the availability of Microsoft Frontpage Server Extensions, and will need to make sure your server environment supports these). For example, these functions allow the user to specify that responses are received as delimited text. The reason for this is that most database software can use user-determined import specification rules to recognise the selected limiters, for example quotation marks, as field breaks and automatically assign the data to the correct fields in the database without manual data entry being required. Then the database can easily be utilised to analyse the data collected.

This may sound complicated, but what it means is that the researcher has to make sure that the data they collect online can be easily converted into their chosen offline storage and analysis system. Researchers need to consider how to collect their data, and web forms, by their nature, can limit participants into responding in a way that suits the researcher. This can be done by using check boxes, radio buttons and text fields.

There are square 'check' boxes which when clicked appear to be 'ticked' and round 'radio' buttons which when clicked show a 'dot'. All of these should be set to their 'unchecked' state on beginning the questionnaire – that is, the default value of each response is at zero. Therefore there is no skewing of results by having the default value as 'No', although it does of course mean that people can decline to respond to certain questions. However, this is also ethically a more sound model.

Radio buttons are the round symbols, and these are used when you want to elicit a single response only. For example, from the choice, Yes, No, Don't know, (and of course no response) you would only want respondents to be able to choose one alternative. This is done by linking these three radio buttons together with coding, so that the computer knows that if one of them is checked, by default, all the others must be unchecked.

Check boxes are slightly different. Although they are again grouped by coding, any number of the boxes can be checked, and these are used when the respondent may choose more than one answer to a question. Then there are drop down lists. These are used when you would like the respondent to select one response from a long list. The visible comment is 'Please select one of the following', so although there is a 'default' entry, it is not one of the actual items on the list, there is a clear instruction to at least look at the other options. Always consider the order in which potential responses appear on a list, and keep this consistent throughout the site. Any terms used in the survey should be defined. The questionnaire should also follow each question with a specification of what the respondent was required to do. For example:

Q 9 Name the first three famous Scots that come to mind (Type in, Firstname Lastname)

1. [_____]

2. [_____]

3. [_____]

Hosting and design

When designing an online questionnaire simplicity is the key. Not only does this reduce technical errors, it also decreases download time. Dillman et al. (1998) identified a correlation between higher quit rates and fancy designs, and surmised this was possible due to the increased time to download for such complicated designs. Whilst some researchers have suggested that using surveys that 'unfold' on screen according to what responses are given can produce much more finely targeted data, there are several reasons against this. First of all, on a technical level, this means there are more things to go wrong, particularly as the java scripting required for such interactivity is not a feature of older browsers. Furthermore, Dillman (2000) found that novice web users were put off by such aspects as pull down menus and unclear instructions.

Researchers using online surveys need to keep things simple. Clear and uncluttered design is important – consider the population you are surveying, do not use too many colours or fonts, and always work to the lowest common denominator (and remember that different colours and types of layout have different cultural connotations – see Marcus and Gould 2000). For example, if you use a particular font on your website, this will only work on other machines with that font installed, otherwise it will turn into a font that machine does have. Therefore it is best to stick to simple fonts like Arial. If you need to use a symbol, insert it as a graphic rather than just putting it in the text, so if a different machine doesn't have the same font, you don't lose your symbols as well. Use tables to structure your web page – most web pages use hidden tables to hold text and graphics in position. For example to make sure that if the page is printed out onto A4 paper, the text will fit and not run off the edge of the page (and this is something to check for when you print out pages from other websites). This also ensures that your survey holds its appearance. Work on the assumption that your users have a monitor of resolution 600 x 800 to make sure all your survey fits on the screen and your users do not need to scroll sideways to read your web page. Try and limit the size of your web pages so they are quick to download. All of these are simple instructions which make sure your survey looks the part and you do not alienate potential respondents.

Questionnaire structure

Questionnaire design was covered in depth in Chapter 9 of this book. Whilst many of the same principles apply to surveying online, there are a few other factors to consider. For example, whilst some guides recommend placing personal information at the end of a survey so as not to 'scare off' potential responses (Coombes), some online researchers have found this not to be the case – for example, Frick, Baechtinger and Reips (1999) found there to be a significantly lower quit rate when personal questions were at the beginning as opposed to the end of the online questionnaire(10.3% versus 17.5%). It has been suggested that this is due to the prevalence of web forms asking for this information up front making people used to this approach. However, it is just as likely that we base the assumption that personal questions should come at the end of a questionnaire on interview based surveys where it is often felt it is better to build up a rapport with a subject before asking 'personal' questions. Furthermore, the addition of a clear data protection statement could improve the drop out rate regarding personal questions.

From an ethical standpoint there should be the possibility for the respondent to quit the survey at any time. It is therefore also useful to make sure a button is available to clear the respondent's answers from the entire form.

Cross-platform usability

Although there are technical difficulties in online interactive questionnaires, the growing standardisation of the web can help to overcome this. The site should be tested using a variety of versions of Internet Browser such as Internet Explorer or Netscape Navigator. It should also be tested on both PCs and Macs. So that respondents do not lose their answers if they want to check something on another web page, PC users can be instructed to 'right click' on links and choose to open them in another window. Mac users, who only have one mouse button, find that other windows automatically open when a link is clicked. However, this kind of functionality, and other coding shortcuts such as pop-up windows, are dependent on the age of the browser. As with any questionnaire, you should pilot the survey before 'going live'. This not only checks the validity of the data gathered, it makes sure that technically the survey works properly. You should time your test subjects and use this information to give potential respondents an approximate time to complete the survey.

Log file analysis

Researchers should ensure that their site is monitored whilst it is online. Smith (1997) recommends that log file analysis is something that all web surveys should consider for the extra data generated. For a more detailed analysis of the use of log files in web site data analysis, see Burton and Walther (2001).

Obviously, completed questionnaires submitted would give an idea of this, but it is potentially more revealing and accurate to use Log File Analysis to monitor site traffic. Not only will this tell the user how many hits a site has had, but where these hits have originated, if they have come through particular search engines, what kind of browser the respondent is using etc. To analyse this data, the researcher can make an FTP (file transfer protocol) connection to the website, and download the automatically generated log files. These can then be run through software such as FastStats Analyser to analyse the log data. Alternatively, many hosting companies now offer online log file analysis as part of their hosting package.

Whilst such usage statistics can indicate response rate, a number of factors should be noted. If users were accessing the site from different IP addresses each time they visited this could account for a false increase in the number of users. Sites also can receive 'hits' from webcrawler software used by search engines, again falsely inflating the number of visitors to the site.

Potential disadvantages of electronic data collection methods

There are invariably problems with data collection from the web. For example, a user could be identified as someone with their own computer with Internet access. However, many people share computers, and on another measurement level, even email addresses are not an accurate indicator. One email address may have a number of users, and conversely, one user can have a number of email addresses. Indeed it is common for many users now to have at least two email addresses, one belonging to their home computer account, and another account which can be logged into from anywhere in the world, for example Hotmail or Yahoo email. This is also of course true of IP addresses as you can have many users from one IP address, and conversely, a single user can be assigned different IP addresses every time they log on depending on their ISP.

There are other reasons researchers should be wary of information gathered in Internet studies. It is relatively easy for someone taking part in an online study to deceive the researcher, for example, it is easy for participants to lie about their details, such as age, gender etc. which may of course have a specific bearing on the research (Hewson et al. 2003 p. 52). One good way to test whether a respondent is bona fide is to send an automated 'thank you' email to them on completion of the study, using the email address they have specified (Keller et al. 1998). If this bounces back as unrecognised, then this is an indication that the respondent is not reliable – however, there are numerous reasons for bounce back. If you took the advice earlier in this chapter about using an Internet mail account for taking part in surveys, and used for example, a Hotmail email address, if your account inbox becomes full, Hotmail bounces back your emails until you make some space in your account, and there are of course other technical reasons why an email may bounce, down to human error in typing in the address in the first place.

If your research project requires that you measure response times to certain questions, these times can be affected by the speed of the Internet connection and how busy the server is, and over longitudinal studies, participants may forget passwords or change email address (Hewson et al. 2003).

The Internet is also a constantly developing medium. If researchers propose to undertake a long-term study online they should be aware that the technology could change over the period of their research.

Advantages of online surveys

Whilst there are many aspects of conducting primary research online which require extra thought and planning, the benefits can outweigh the disadvantages covered in this chapter.

There is the obvious advantage of a very large and diverse survey population. Costs in conducting research can be lower than traditional survey methods, especially if a large or geographically diverse sample is required. Whilst there are initial set up costs, the automation of data-handling can save researchers money, and often more importantly, time. Response times are generally very short for Internet research. The anonymity of online surveying can be an advantage depending on the kind of research being done. If researchers are concerned about respondents to an online survey deliberately disguising their identity and providing misleading information, I would recommend that they pilot their research in an offline environment. Not only will this test the reliability of the survey itself, it will also provide a comparative baseline for the validity of the responses gathered.

There are other, more specific, reasons to use web surveying; for example, web surveys take advantage of immediacy in that users tend not too mull too long over answers. Kiesler and Sproull (1986) found that people participating in e-surveys were 'more likely to be self-absorbed and uninhibited' and consequently may concentrate more on the questionnaire. Furthermore, respondents are more likely to give long and self-disclosing comments on open ended responses , with Schaefer (1998) showing a four-fold increase in length of open-ended responses using electronic methods. It has been suggested this is due to the speed of typewriting over handwriting (Schaefer and Dillman 1998).

Because Internet research is a constantly developing area, other advantages, and disadvantages, are constantly coming to light. As more and more people use the Internet to conduct primary research, more information will become available. Researchers should make sure that they review the most up-to-date literature available before starting to use the Internet, and should not rely on references even a couple of years old, due to the evolving nature of the technology.

Summary

The purpose of this chapter was to make researchers aware of some of the issues they may face should they choose to conduct their primary research online, and each research project will require different considerations. As we have highlighted, these factors are not exhaustive, and researchers must make sure they have consulted the most up-to-date resources before finalising their research strategy. However, researchers should not be put off by these caveats. The potential advantages of Internet research outweigh the disadvantages, and the rules of keeping on top of the current literature, and considering ethical and technical implications of research strategies would need to be followed in any kind of offline research project.

Recommendations for further reading

Desai, P. (2002), *Methods Beyond Interviewing in Qualitative Market Research*, Book 3 of Qualitative Market Research: Principle & Practice, Seven-Volume Set, London: Sage Publications Ltd

Hewson, C., Yule, P., Laurent, D. and Vogel, C. (2003), *Internet Research Methods: a practical guide for the social and behavioural sciences*, London: Sage Publications Ltd

Mann, C. and Stewart, F. (2000), *Internet Communication and Qualitative Research: A handbook for researching online*, London: Sage Publications Ltd

McAuley, C. (2003), 'Online methods', pp. 217-220 in R. L. Miller and J. D. Brewer (eds), (2003), *The A-Z of Social Research: a dictionary of key social science research projects*, London: Sage Publications Ltd

CHAPTER 13

Data Interpretation

Synopsis
In this chapter we give an overview of the major techniques and methods used in the interpretation of data. To a large extent the researcher's choice will have been pre-determined when developing a research design (Chapter 7) and selecting a methodology (Chapter 6). Thus the placing of this chapter was dictated by the implementation sequence – design – data collection- data interpretation – rather than the planning sequence when methods/techniques comprise an integral element of both design and methodology. Beginning with a consideration of basic principles of data interpretation we look next at coding and classification as primary steps in analysing qualitative data. Then we discuss the concepts of confidence limits and statistical significance before moving on to look at a variety of descriptive and inferential statistics widely used in analysing quantitative data.

Keywords
data–analysis, interpretation; classification, coding; descriptive and inferential statistics.

Introduction

In earlier chapters we have emphasised strongly that a major purpose of research is to shed light on areas of uncertainty in order to enable the researcher or decision-maker to achieve better understanding within the inevitable constraints of time and money. To this end we have examined at some length the need to define research issues in a clear and unambiguous way, and to the development of a research design best suited to the collection of the necessary data. Implicit to the whole process is the assumption that the researcher has considered carefully the analytical techniques and methods appropriate to the interpretation of the data once it has been collected. Thus, while it is convenient for the logical development of a text book to examine procedures for analysing data at this juncture, *in reality* consideration of this matter should emerge at an early stage in the research process.

Where complete data is available one is entitled to make substantive statements about the relationships between variables revealed by data, e.g. the relationship between income and purchase behaviour, or the findings from a carefully controlled experiment. In the great majority of cases, however, it will be necessary to make do with partial data collected by means of a survey or some other kind of observed data. In these circumstances one will be able to draw inferences concerning the relationship between variables but will be uncertain of the confidence which one may place upon these inferences unless some satisfactory technique exists which allows us to make meaningful pronouncements on the matter which are verifiable by and acceptable to other researchers. Fortunately, statistical techniques provide this capability when it is possible to quantify one's data in an acceptable way, and the purpose of this chapter is to review the methods and procedures available. The point we are seeking to make here is that knowledge of these methods and procedures should guide and inform the formulation of hypotheses, and the design of the research through which the data is to be collected. To begin with we consider some of the procedures and conventions developed in other social sciences for the interpretation of data. Then, given the prevalence of qualitative data in business research, we examine the issues involved in classification and coding before considering the issue of confidence and statistical significance. This consideration leads naturally to a discussion of the salient differences between descriptive and inferential statistics.

In the case of descriptive statistics we shall look at plotting, tabulation and averaging. For inferential statistics the main topics will be cross tabulation, correlation, differentiation and pattern analysis. We conclude the chapter with a review of the main multivariate methods of analysis which have gained widespread acceptance in the analysis of complex business and management data in recent years.

Data interpretation

While business and management are comparatively new disciplines they have the advantage that they can draw upon many other disciplines in advancing their own interpretation of the nature of the phenomena in which they are interested. In doing so, however, they are bound by the principles and conventions of the social sciences on which they are founded, and some knowledge of these principles and conventions is essential if one is to draw meaningful conclusions from the information generated by business and management research. But this is not the place for an exploration of the philosophical foundations of the nature of truth, and the discussion will be confined to a selective and somewhat simplistic review of some key ideas and concepts.

If we take marketing as one of the business disciplines then we may assert that it is concerned with 'mutually satisfying exchange relationships'. If this is so, then our primary concern must be with the question of how individuals and organisations make such decisions. A cursory review of a number of the longer established social sciences – economics, psychology, anthropology, sociology, social psychology, etc. – quickly reveals that each adopts its own particular perspective and thus draws a rather different interpretation as to the nature of exchange relationships. John Madge (1953) in his excellent analysis *The Tools of Social Science* (Longman) addresses this problem when he observes that the underlying theories which underpinned the economics of the then superpowers of the USA and USSR were both derived from that propounded by Marx and Engels. Madge suggests that Karl Mannheim has helped both to explain this apparent contradiction and develop a more constructive approach through his 'sociology of knowledge' in which:

> He renounces the abstract concept of objective knowledge, but shows that in given circumstances it is possible to arrive at reliable decisions in factual disputes. These decisions are limited by the observers' incomplete perspective, *but when members of a group have aims in common, they will also tend to reach agreement on questions of fact.* [emphasis added].(Madge 1953)

In other words our interpretation of the 'facts' or 'reality' is a product of our beliefs, experiences and knowledge, all of which are the product of our background and upbringing. Armed with this insight it is clear that while disagreement may arise because the parties have access to different information it is just as likely to arise because they place a different interpretation upon the same information. This possibility is to be seen daily in case discussions in Business Schools where all the participants start with the same information as recorded in the case study but come to quite different conclusions as to its interpretation, and as to the most appropriate course of action to solve the problem described. Thus, if one has studied economics it is likely that the desire to impose order and structure through quantification will encourage one to suppress subjectivity and so regard the unit of analysis – people – as homogenous. Conversely, the behavioural scientist in spite of John Donne's observation that 'No man is an island', will regard the individual as the unit of analysis and start from a belief in heterogeneity. Given the start point and orientation of economists and behavioural scientists both groups can survive amicably by agreeing to disagree, but this does not help marketers with a pragmatic interest in groupings of people which are less than the total demand for a given product or service. To develop a marketing mix to meet the particular needs of a market segment we need an explanation of group behaviour which incorporates elements of both disciplinary approaches.

While we are the product of our experience, and it is unlikely that we will be exposed to a blinding revelation such as Saul on the road to Damascus which will totally change our *perception* of the world, if we are aware of the possibility of alternative interpretations then we will have a significant competitive advantage over those who will not admit to such a possibility. Thus business researchers should recognise that theirs' is a synthetic discipline, which seeks to pull together concepts and ideas from a variety of other disciplines in an attempt to develop a *holistic* interpretation of business behaviour, in just the same way as a doctor draws on both the physical and social sciences in developing an understanding of health as a concept. It follows that knowledge and understanding of the key concepts 'borrowed' from other disciplines is a pre-requisite to the analysis of business problems, and the interpretation of information pertaining to them. In addition, one needs an understanding of the methods employed by social scientists in gathering and interpreting data and it is this topic which we shall address in this chapter. Specifically, data analysis using descriptive and inferential statistics.

Business and management research is rarely, if ever, undertaken out of sheer curiosity. Its initiation is purposive, and usually directed to 'reducing the areas of uncertainty surrounding business decisions'. In turn, business decisions are concerned with future courses of action with the result that most business research is an attempt to understand current behaviour better as the basis for predicting future behaviour. As pointed out in the introduction to this chapter, it is inevitable that subjectivity will influence the whole process. Indeed, it is doubtful if there can be such a thing as value-free social research. That said it is vital that in collecting and interpreting data one should seek to do so *objectively* in terms of the prevailing conventions designed to satisfy the needs of accuracy, validity and reliability.

While prediction is a basic goal of social science research, all are agreed that this is much more difficult than is the case in the physical sciences. As discussed in Chapter 2, where we looked at some of the philosophical issues underlying prevailing attitudes to research, this may be the result of two interpretations:

> Some people conclude that human and social behaviour is not wholly subject to determining factors, but that every individual has some capacity of choice which enables them to vary their conduct in partial independence of the forces operating upon them. Others believe that, although human behaviour is fully determined by circumstances, these circumstances in all their ramifications are so numerous and so unknowable that we can never hope to predict how any individual or any group will respond to a given situation. (Madge 1953)

But, for operational purposes, we can ignore the metaphysical arguments concerning free will or determinism. What is needed is that 'the principle of causality be applied to social phenomena'. (Durkheim (1938) – quoted by Madge). In other words we undertake research to determine if there is a causal relationship between antecedent and consequent events of a kind which will enable us to make predictive statements about their future occurrence. For example, if we observe that a 10 percent change in price is accompanied by a proportionate increase or decrease in demand on every occasion that such change is made, then it is reasonable to infer that it is the change in price which causes the change in demand. Of course, the problem for the marketer is that it is very difficult, if not impossible, to emulate the physical scientist and seek to establish the causal relationship between changes in the marketing mix and buyer behaviour, owing to his inability to control all the other factors likely to influence the outcome. (See section on Experimentation, pp.128 ff).

Of course, it is not all plain sailing for the physical scientist either as the controversy over Pons and Fleishman's 'discovery' of cold fusion in 1989 clearly shows. The announcement of this finding polarised opinion between chemists who accepted the possibility and physicists who did not. However, all agreed that Pons and Fleishman did not follow the accepted protocol of the scientific method, nor did they publicise their findings according to normal conventions. As such their claims did not satisfy the criteria for acceptable scientific research.

The basic problem in business (as in other social sciences) is highlighted by the debate over qualitative versus quantitative research. As we have seen (pp.20-26) qualitative research provides insight and a richness of information but lacks the conviction and credibility which are associated with quantification. Ideally, the researcher should use both approaches – qualitative research to inform one of the nature and parameters of the problem, and quantitative research to derive empirical generalisations which may be used to determine future courses of action. Madge endorses this view when he writes:

> While, however, it is proper to guard against the misuse of quantification, it cannot be implied that there is very much choice in the matter if we aim at empirical generalisation. At their very least, statistical techniques expose the principal assumptions underlying the generalisations arrived at and provide some stable measure of the degree of confidence with which it is reasonable to accept them. The statistical method gives precision and system to the more or less unconscious inductive processes constantly used in every day life. When a man attempts to generalise from his own unrepresentative selection of data, and perhaps even openly rejects statistical method you may at best regard his generalisation as a brilliant and illuminating piece of guesswork. He may have lighted on an inspired hypothesis, but he has certainly proved nothing. (Madge 1953)

It is in this spirit that we now review the methods and procedures which will be encountered most often in the analysis of business and management data. Before doing so, however, it will be useful to say something about the analysis of the kind of unstructured data yielded by most qualitative research methods, and particularly ethnography and grounded theory. Because of its unstructured nature the first task of the analyst must be to establish if there are patterns or logical groupings within the data which will enable the researcher to interpret its meaning more efficiently and effectively. This may be achieved by means of *classification* and *coding*.

Classification and coding

Once data has been collected it has to be analysed and interpreted. The less structured the original data collection the more complex and time consuming the task becomes and the greater the benefits of seeking to collect original data in a more structured way in the first place. However, irrespective of whether one develops a structure in advance, as with a survey, or waits for one to emerge through analysis as with grounded theory, two activities are of especial importance – *classification* and *coding*.

Classification is concerned with the creation of categories while coding is the technique used to assign the raw data to the correct category. We will deal with them in this order.

Classification

The purpose of classification is to group together bits of information that share common characteristics. As well as defining the similarities that allow us to place an object or bit of information into a given category, classification also enables us to distinguish between categories. According to the number of criteria used in our classification system it may be very simple or highly complex. For example, one might wish to classify living organisms and start by distinguishing between those that are earthborne and those that can fly. This is obviously a very crude classification. If I told you that I was thinking of a living organism it might be your first question to try and establish exactly what I am thinking about. If I answer 'earthborne' then your next question might well be "Does it live on the land or in the sea?". If I say 'On the land' then you might ask "Is it warm or cold blooded?" and so on, and so on until, through a process of elimination and the identification of more and more classificatory factors or variables, you are able to identify specifically what it is that I am thinking about.

Classification is the foundation upon which all knowledge is based, and is fundamental to learning and understanding. But, while all subjects or bodies of cognate knowledge have developed classificatory systems, there are important differences between the physical and social sciences. Riley et al. summarise the main difference succinctly when they write:

> All branches of science have developed classification systems bases (sic) on the discovered differences and similarities of their subject material. By contrast social research does not possess natural categories based on secure definitions. Therefore categorisation in social research is itself a social process which requires a consensus and yet which is biased by subjectivity. (Riley et al. 2000, p.51)

Riley et al. qualify this assertion by pointing out that some of the material used by social scientists, like demographic data, is factual and that there are sufficient regularities in some patterns of behaviour to enable the construction of robust classificatory systems, such as the definition of socio-economic groups. Careful and agreed classification is important, as without it one will be unable to generalise and confirm or otherwise the association between observed data and its association with a defined population. Scientific 'proof' is much simpler to demonstrate because precise definitions exist for the objects under investigation.

Given that we can define a population from which the data under investigation has been drawn, then it is possible to use agreed statistical procedures to analyse it. Further, in accordance with the procedures and conventions related to a given statistical technique, we will be able to make generalisations about patterns within our data and their relationship with the population from which the data was obtained. In turn this will allow us to predict the likelihood of such patterns occurring in the future with varying degrees of confidence. It is clear why agreed principles of classification are vital to research in the social sciences.

To begin with it is important to recognise that there are several approaches to the development of classificatory systems. Riley et al. distinguish four broad types:

- *Scientific classes* (the result of cumulative scientific enquiry).
- *Classes laid down by social research* (the result of social science good practice)
- *Classes set by social norms* (classes accepted by society).
- *Psychological classes* (the mental processes of categorisation and evaluation). (Riley et al. 2000 p.52)

In essence, this list represents a classification itself. Although not explicitly stated by the authors, inspection suggests that this list has been compiled in terms of an underlying concept of formality or objectivity with Scientific classes being the most objective and formal and Psychological the most subjective and informal.

Now this may not have been the authors' intention but, as an observer, it appeared to me to be a reasonable principle to use with this data set. Herein lies the essence of classification – what is the crux or core of the topic in which we are interested? In this case it is *classificatory systems* and the definition of the four categories appeared, at least to me, to be based on the constructs of formality/objectivity and informality/subjectivity. It follows that using these constructs I could establish parameters or boundaries for each of the four categories which would enable me to assign any piece of research into one or other of them.

The previous paragraph also points to the importance of **precision** in the use of language when developing definitions. In normal usage class and category are synonymous – in social science research they have rather different connotations as a category would be considered a sub-set of a class. You will have observed that I have reclassified Riley *et al's* 'classes' as 'categories' simply by adopting a different classificatory principle. They use generalised and basically undefined descriptors to create their classes. I have chosen to use a dimension that I can operationalise through formal definition that will enable me to classify pieces of research in a consistent and reliable way that will satisfy the requirements of good research practice. If I follow Riley et al.'s suggested division than I have a *category set* containing four distinct categories as defined by them. However, as Selltiz et al. point out, a category set must meet certain basic rules which may be summarised as:

1. The set of categories should be derived from a single classificatory principle.
2. The set of categories should be exhaustive; that is, it should be possible to place every response in one of the categories of the set.
3. The categories within the set should be mutually exclusive; it should not be possible to place a given response in more than one category within the set. (Selltiz et al. 1959 p.392)

To satisfy these rules one would need to spell out the relevant criteria in considerable detail either *post facto,* when presented with an unstructured data set, or in advance if one proposed to gather data using some kind of structured questionnaire. In the latter case the specified criteria would constitute the coding scheme.

By now you may feel like Alice in Wonderland when Humpty Dumpty advised her that words meant what he wanted them to mean. Herein lies the problem with much social science research, and the property that distinguishes it from 'scientific' research – an inability to replicate a study. Often this inability may be due to the fact that social scientists are concerned with animate objects whereas scientists are concerned with inanimate objects. But, in many cases, the inability arises from either a lack of precision in specifying one's classificatory criteria, or the unwillingness of a subsequent researcher to adopt the same criteria when investigating the same phenomenon.

The message is unmistakeable, whether you are a student submitting work for formal examination, or a researcher subject to peer review, you must be crystal clear in spelling out what you have done, how and why. If you do so, and your reasoning is logical and based on accepted principles, then your work cannot be dismissed simply on the grounds that someone else might have preferred a different approach.

Coding

Coding is "A general term used to describe the procedure for classifying objects in terms of some predetermined principle. In market research, it refers to the classifying of data to make it amenable to subsequent analysis". (www.westburndictionary.co.uk)   It usually involves tabulation and quantification, or the assignment of numerical values, that allow statistical procedures to be used in the interpretation of the information represented by the data.

As noted above, in the case of unstructured data or data collected for another purpose, the coding will take place after the data has been collected, which is usually the case with exploratory research, especially grounded theory. However, when collecting data using structured research designs, and especially surveys with formal questionnaires, the researcher will define the categories of data to be obtained in advance and create codes to define these categories.

Coding after data collection is the first step in *data reduction* where the researcher is seeking to identify any patterns, sequence or system in the recorded information. It is often referred to as *content analysis*. Usually, one will have a research topic in which one is interested, and this will inform the selection of material to be analysed as well as suggesting the principles to be used. Occasionally, as happened to the author when a doctoral student, someone will present you with a data set and invite you to comment on it. In my case I was presented with a record of almost half a million respondents to a self-completion questionnaire published by *Good Housekeeping* in the USA in the 1960s and told to "do something with it". In addition, as I was only one of several students, my analysis was required to be different from that of everyone else. To begin with however, we all took the same step to make the problem more manageable – we sampled the sample and selected some 1200 questionnaires from the population using probabilistic methods.

Having drawn my sample I then looked for a simple classifying principle and discovered that the questionnaires asked whether the respondent was male or female, or was a joint effort by both a male and female. Once the data had been sorted in this way it became possible to examine similarities and differences in the response patterns between the three groups in terms of their reported behaviour. One of the interesting findings provided support for a theorised relationship that had not been tested at that time; namely, that in mixed gender dyads there are defined areas of authority and responsibility for purchase decisions. When asked "Who decides the brand of household remedies?" the females said "I do"; the males said "My wife does" and the joint respondents said "The female does". Conversely, for objects like car tyres and batteries, by common agreement this was almost exclusively a male domain. In the case of decisions on major items, like white goods and furnishings, then shared decision making was the norm. At the time these findings were unsurprising. Whether they apply today is another matter, and could well be an interesting study if the issue has not been the subject of published findings in recent years. However, the real point is that, while gender is a classificatory variable in almost all research, few researchers actually make use of this factor in their subsequent analysis. There must be many published data sets available that might yield interesting findings if analysed using gender as the classificatory factor for exploring the categories of data covered in a questionnaire.

Confidence limits and statistical significance

When Lord Kelvin observed that unless you can measure a thing you know nothing about it he was expressing not merely a scientific opinion but a common aspect of human nature. Numbers, of course, are a language and a very powerful one in that through them one can communicate highly complex ideas in a very succinct way. But, as with Arabic and Chinese, unless the intended receiver of the communication can speak the language there will be no understanding. It is ironic, therefore, that in many aspects of business one is invited to quantify the existence or otherwise of a relationship, but then has to resort to verbal interpretation in order to communicate the meaning of the quantification to those who asked for the quantification in the first place. However, as our earlier discussion of qualitative versus quantitative research revealed, quantified data carries more conviction even though many readers cannot interpret the numbers generated by such research.

This belief in the credibility of numbers is not wholly misplaced for, provided the data is accurate, valid and reliable, then an understanding of the language of statistics will enable us to make quite precise statements about the interpretation which may be placed upon it which will conform exactly with the interpretation made by any other statistically literate person. It follows that while the user of research findings need not be wholly fluent in the language of statistics, they should have a sufficient familiarity with it to understand the basics and know when to call upon the service of an interpreter to explain nuances beyond their own comprehension. In this context the nature of *confidence* and *significance* are particularly important.

Technically, confidence limits and statistical significance are two sides of the same coin. This will become clearer when we look at particular statistical techniques later in this chapter, but it will be helpful here to consider briefly their role in data analysis. In the first chapter of this book we defined the aim of business research as being 'to reduce the areas of uncertainty surrounding business decisions'. It follows that, having conducted a piece of research, one would like to know how much confidence can be placed in the results. In other words how likely is it that the outcome indicated by the research results will be the correct one? The answer to this question will almost invariably be expressed in probabilistic terms such as 'It's ten to one/a hundred to one against this happening' or 'It's 95%/99% certain that the real outcome will be the same as the test result'. The first pair of statements are of the kind which 'ordinary' people use when making statements about the likelihood of an outcome and usually represent a subjective probability. The second pair of statements are of the kind which a statistician would make based upon the sampling of a population, and so are objective probabilities. However, the first statements are also statements of significance while the latter two are statements of confidence. Both measures are derived form the concept of the continuous or *normal distribution* which itself is a convenient substitute for the *binomial distribution*.

It will be recalled that the normal distribution defines the relative frequency or probability with which given values occur. For example, suppose that we are interested in monitoring the retail price of a particular washing machine, then sampling of a variety of outlets in different locations yields 100 observations which range from £180 to £220. If the prices are distributed normally then we can use the parameters of the normal distribution (the mean and standard deviation) to predict that 90% of the prices will be in the range from £189-£211, 95% of the prices £187-£213 and 99% in the range £183-£217. These are confidence levels.

When it comes to reporting significance then the parameters are used rather differently and, by convention one would only report that an observation was 'significant' if it was more than 1.96 standard deviations from the mean. In our washing machine example 95 % of all cases lie within +- 1.96 standard deviation of the mean – only if the price was less than £189 or greater than £211 would it be regarded as statistically significant. In other words *observations are regarded as significant if they are unusual*. By the same convention an observation is said to be *highly significant* if its likelihood of occurrence is less than one in 100 which means that it will be at least +-2.58 standard deviations from the mean, which applies to prices of less than £189 or greater than £217. In this example both exceptionally high and low prices were considered in determining whether they were significant or not on the grounds that the manufacturer would probably want to explore further what factors, e.g. town centre or out of town outlet, were associated with them. Accordingly a two-tailed test of significance was applied. But if the manufacturer was only concerned that discounting by some of his customers was undercutting other outlets, because his product was being used as a loss leader, he may only have been concerned with prices below a certain limit and applied a one-tailed test of significance. We return to this issue later in the chapter.

In sum, a confidence level will indicate the likelihood that an observed relationship will occur with a given frequency on future occasions so that the decision-maker can decide what level of confidence is acceptable to them as the basis for taking future courses of action. By contrast, the occurrence of statistically significant findings signals something out of the ordinary which may merit further investigation and analysis. Once again it is up to the decision-maker to decide at what level of occurrence they would wish to have exceptions drawn to their attention – $p<0.05$, $p<0.01$, $p<0.001$, etc.

Having established this distinction, it will be useful now to look at the nature of descriptive statistics before moving on to the more sophisticated area of statistical inference.

Descriptive statistics

With increased access to computers, and the development of more and more sophisticated data analysis software, there has been a growing tendency in recent years to neglect the use of basic descriptive statistics in favour of 'more powerful' techniques. Without in any way wishing to diminish the value of these new techniques this author would wish to affirm the value of descriptive statistics, both in their own right and as a precedent to more technically sophisticated methods and procedures. Further, and as a broad generalisation, it is probably true to say that the more obvious and robust relationships on which action decisions may be based will often emerge from an evaluation of the basic data. By contrast, relationships which can only be detected through the use of complex and sophisticated procedures are most often useful in formulating further hypotheses for detailed and focused analysis, rather than making action oriented decisions.

Given a body of data, the first task is to structure and organise this in a manner which will make it amenable to further analysis. With quantitative data, tabulation and plotting are invariably the first steps in this process.

Where data has been collected using a properly designed test instrument of the kind discussed in Chapter 9, then the *tabulation* of information should be largely a formality of summarising the responses to the questions asked.

For example, a furniture manufacturer is interested in determining what kind of furniture respondents have purchased within the past five years. Having determined that a purchase has been made within this period he asks:

'Could you tell me what kind of furniture you have bought in the last five years' and provides the following listing for the interviewer.

Lounge suite   _____
Dining room suite   _____
Bedroom suite   _____
Fitted kitchen   _____
Bed   _____
Table   _____
Chair(s)   _____
Settee/sofa   _____
Wardrobe   _____
Dressing table   _____
Others (write in)   _____

....
....
....

Table 13.1. Furniture purchases in the past five years

Type of furniture	No. mentioning	%
Lounge suite	311	67.6
Dining room suite	104	22.6
Bedroom suite	127	27.6
Fitted kitchen	54	11.7
Bed	222	48.3
Table	85	18.5
Chair(s)	116	25.2
Settee/sofa	82	17.8
Wardrobe	35	7.6
Dressing table	109	23.7
Others (e.g. TV cabinet, coffee table, chest of drawers)	449	97.6
Total respondents	460	100

Once coded this information can be transferred direct on to database, and it is a simple matter to print out the number of mentions of each kind of furniture and convert these into a percentage of the total respondents to the survey as in Table 13.1.

A table of this kind summarises 'what' has occurred. While one may draw some broad conclusions from it concerning the relative popularity of different kinds of furniture further analysis would obviously be desirable. For example, is furniture purchase correlated with age and/or income? Methods for answering such questions will be addressed later in this chapter.

In Table 13.1 the data is presented in exactly the same order as the alternatives were listed on the questionnaire. While perfectly understandable in this format the impact of the table would be improved if one were to restate it in terms of rank order according to the number of mentions as in Table 13.2.

Table 13.2. Furniture purchases in the past five years

Type of furniture	No. mentioning	%
Others (e.g. TV cabinet, coffee table, chest of drawers)	449	97.6
Lounge suite	311	67.6
Bed	222	48.3
Bedroom suite	127	27.6
Chair(s)	116	25.2
Dressing table	109	23.7
Dining room suite	104	22.6
Table	85	18.5
Settee/sofa	82	17.8
Fitted kitchen	54	11.7
Wardrobe	35	7.6
Total respondents	460	100

In turn this data would have even greater impact if presented as a bar chart as shown in Figure 13.1.

Plotting data in this manner greatly enhances the readability of a report as one gets an immediate visual impression of the size and relative importance of the data classes being reported. The ability to plot data as bar charts, graphs or pictograms is a feature of most basic computer-based analysis programmes and can literally be achieved at the 'touch of a button'. Given such a capability the analyst can easily afford to try more than one approach to see which form of presentation has the most impact. Figure 13.2 reproduces the output of a typical package (Microsoft Excel) for a simple data set.

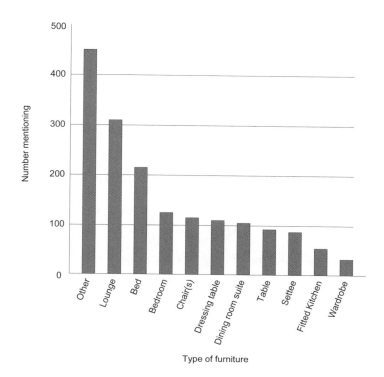

Figure 13.1. Furniture purchases in the past 5 years (bar chart)

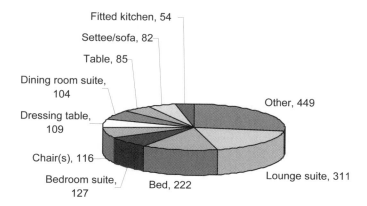

Figure 13.2. Furniture purchases in the past 5 years (pie chart)

However, although tabulation and plotting will provide some 'feel' for the data they are relatively crude in terms of what they can communicate, and more sophisticated methods are called for if one is to derive the full benefit from a database. Selltiz et al. (1959) suggest that given a database the analyst will typically want to do one or another, or several of the following things.

1. To 'characterise' what is typical in the group.
2. To indicate how widely individuals in the group vary
3. To show other aspects of how the individuals are distributed with respect to the variable being measured.
4. To show the relation of the different variables in the data to one another.
5. To describe the differences between two or more groups of individuals. (Selltiz et al. 1959)

To accomplish these tasks the analyst has access to a number of basic tools which for convenience may be classified as *univariate, bivariate and multivariate* analysis. As the name suggests, bivariate analysis deals with pairs of variables, while multivariate analysis can deal with three or more variables simultaneously. In general, and as Selltiz et al.'s (1959) list implies, it is usual to progress from description and analysis of a single variable, to an examination of relationships between pairs of variables and finally to the much more complex task of exploring relationships between three or more variables at once.

Descriptive statistics are of particular value in describing databases containing a large number of values. Selection of the appropriate statistic(s) will depend upon the nature of the data to be analysed; specifically nominal, ordinal, interval or ratio in character? It will be recalled that in Chapter 9 when discussing the nature of scales, the basic differences are that:

(a) Nominal data is the weakest kind in that the number assigned serves only to identify the subject, e.g. library classifications.
(b) Ordinal scales seek to impose more structure on objects by rank ordering them in terms of some property which they possess such as height or weight.
(c) Interval scales have greater power in that it is assumed that the distance between numbers is known and constant so that one can draw conclusions about the meaning of differences between numbers.
(d) Ratio scales are the most powerful and possess all the properties of nominal, ordinal and interval scales, and also permit absolute comparison between objects.

Given that one knows the type of data then one can easily select the most appropriate statistics as shown in Table 13.3 taken from Alreck and Settle (1985).

Table 13.3 Tool selection for descriptive statistics

Scale type	Average	Spread	Shape
Nominal	Mode		
Ordinal	Median	Range	
	Mode	Maximum	
		Minimum	
Interval	Mean	Standard deviation	Skewness
	Median	Range	Kurtosis
	Mode	Maximum	
		Minimum	
Ratio	Mean	Standard deviation	Skewness
	Median	Range	Kurtosis
	mode	Maximum	
		minimum	

Source: Alreck, Pamela L. and Settle, Robert B. (1985), *The Survey Research Handbook*, Homewood, Ill.: Richard D. Irwin

Descriptive statistics serve two basic purposes, they provide a measure of central tendency and of dispersion. In every day speech we refer often to 'the average' in the sense of 'the typical or normal amount, quality, degree etc.' (*Collins Concise English Dictionary*). In other words it is used to convey the idea of the most commonly or frequently occurring event. However, while the 'average' – be it expressed as the mean, median or mode – may be the most typical value, in and of itself it provides only limited insight into a database unless we also possess some knowledge of the dispersion or spread of data about this most typical value. Such information is provided by statistics such as the range, standard deviation and shape of the distribution itself (kurtosis, skewness). A brief description of these various measures will help clarify the point.

As indicated in Table 13.3 three 'averages' are in common use – the mode, the median and the mean. Of the three the mode is the weakest in that it simply defines the category which appears most frequently – in the furniture purchase survey referred to earlier. 'Others' were mentioned by 98% of the respondents and so this is the mode for this particular distribution and tells us that the most likely purchase is likely to be a smaller piece of occasional furniture outside the range in which the manufacturer was primarily interested. Such information may be particularly valuable as a strategic insight in that it might encourage the manufacturer to make some of these smaller items as a means of keeping his brand name in front of customers so that they will recognise it when making the larger but less frequent purchase of say a lounge suite. However, in many distributions several categories may occur with equal frequency giving rise to multiple modes and difficulty in interpretation.

When data is ordinal, interval or ratio the analyst will also be able to refer to the median a as measure of central tendency. The median is literally the middle case in a data set organised in terms of the 'value' of the object being measured. Thus, in Table 13.2 there are 11 categories rank ordered in terms of number of mentions so the median category is dressing tables with five other types of furniture each receiving more or less mentions. Perhaps its most important characteristic is that it is unaffected by extremes although, in the context of the furniture data, this is largely irrelevant!

The third commonly used measure of central tendency is the arithmetic mean which is computed by adding up the sum of the values and dividing this by the number of categories. For example, in the furniture case the total number of responses from the 460 respondents was 1694 so we could recalculate Table 13.2 on the basis of number of mentions with the result given in Table 13.4.

Table 13.4. Furniture purchases in the past 5 years

Type of furniture	No. of mentions	% of all mentions
Others	449	26.5
Lounge suite	311	18.4
Bed	222	13.1
Bedroom suite	127	7.5
Chair(s)	116	6.8
Dressing table	109	6.4
Dining room suite	104	6.1
Table	85	5.0
Settee/sofa	82	4.8
Fitted kitchen	54	3.2
Wardrobe	35	2.1
Total respondents	460	100

The arithmetic mean for the number of mentions is $\overline{X} = 1694/460 = 3.68$. Obviously the mean is heavily influenced by the high scores for others, lounge suites and beds, with the 'others' exercising a particularly strong effect. To summarise the distribution of values around the measures of central tendency we need to compute a number of other measures of dispersion. For nominal data measures of dispersion are inappropriate, but for all other categories of data our understanding will be considerably enhanced if we know the *range* of values. The range is calculated simply by taking away the lowest (minimum) value from the highest (maximum) value. In our survey of furniture purchases the range is:

$$449 - 35 = 414$$

If we compare these data – maximum, minimum and range – with the mean we will begin to get some feel for the overall distribution of values. This understanding will be greatly enhanced if we also calculate the *variability* or spread of the observations around the mean. The most frequently used statistic for this purpose is the *standard deviation*. It will be recalled, from the discussion of the characteristics of the normal distribution as the basis for sampling, that the standard deviation is in fact the square root of the variance, and provides a single value of the spread of data about the mean in the same units as the mean. Clearly, the smaller the standard deviation the more tightly the observations are clustered around the mean and vice versa.

All distributions do not assume the shape of the normal distribution and two measures are used to describe how much the actual distribution departs from the normal. These statistics are *skewness* and *kurtosis*. As the term suggests skewness is the degree to which the distribution is biased towards one or other side of the mean. In the normal distribution data are distributed symmetrically around the mean and the skewness is zero. In a skewed distribution the distribution of observations is asymmetrical. Where the distribution is skewed to the left as in Figure 13.3(a) then the coefficient of skewness will be positive and when to the right, as in Figure 13.3(b), it will be negative.

The importance of calculating the coefficient of skewness is that it helps interpret the value of the standard deviation as a measure of the spread of the distribution, i.e. if it is zero we can assume a normal distribution and proceed accordingly. Otherwise, depending upon the sign and the size of the coefficient, we would recognise that the distribution was asymmetrical.

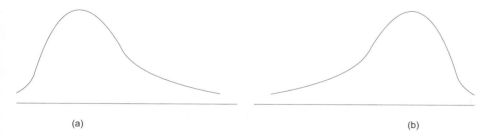

(a)   (b)

Figure 13.3. (a) Positive skewness   (b) Negative skewness

Kurtosis measures whether a distribution is more (positive) or less (negative) peaked than a normal distribution.

Most of the measures touched on here – variance, standard deviation, skewness and kurtosis – are laborious to compute manually but we can produce them on command using packages such as SPSSX. Given their value in helping to interpret a database they should be provided routinely in any formal data presentation.

Descriptive statistics are concerned with just that – the description of variables in a data set. Because we look at one variable at a time, such as the high street price of a washing machine or the frequency of purchase of different items of furniture, useful and informative as such *univariate* analysis is, the description of *what is* provides only limited understanding as to *why it is* so. To determine why things are as they are we need to examine the relationship *between* variables and it is to this topic which we now turn.

Inferential statistics

Univariate or *marginal* analysis is an essential first step in data interpretation and will give the researcher a good feel for their database. But, as noted, it is usually the relationship between variables which is of primary interest as it is these which may enable one to infer why things occur in a particular way. The conditional 'may enable' in the previous sentence is essential for the mere fact that two events are associated or correlated does not necessarily mean that they are causally related. Indeed the relationship between two events may be entirely spurious, as is the case with the thesis that amputation causes deafness, a proposition which a professor attempted to prove to his students as follows. First, he placed a flea on the laboratory bench and clapped his hands. The flea jumped. Next he cut off the flea's legs and clapped his hands again. The flea did not move, prompting the professor to declare triumphantly that it was clear amputation causes total deafness in fleas!

Real world examples of the drawing of incorrect inferences abound. Recently, a report appeared in which it was claimed that Germans eat twice as many bananas as the British. This conclusion was based on the responses to the question 'How often do you eat a banana?' As neither Britain nor Germany produce bananas it is a relatively simple matter to determine their consumption of this fruit by dividing recorded imports by the populations of countries – an analysis which reveals that Britons and Germans consume nearly the same average volume per capita. The report is both true and false depending upon how one measures consumption. Most researchers would infer that a statement stating someone did something twice as often meant they consumed twice as much. In this case, however, it is clear that the average 'German' banana is half the size of its 'British' counterpart so that the actual consumption in volume/price terms is virtually the same. The finding does point to different sources of supply (e.g. the Canaries (small) versus Colombia (large)) but not to the major differences in consumption behaviour which could have been inferred from the first statement.

The two examples, given above are by way of a caveat as to the interpretation of the inferential statistics to be reviewed in the next few pages. The purpose of inferential statistics is to facilitate comparison of two or more variables, and to determine the strength of any relationship and the likelihood, especially when it is based on sample data, that is representative, i.e. that a replication of the study/analysis would yield the same result.

Having reviewed the marginal or nominal data through univariate analysis the next step in the process is to seek to establish whether there is any association between pairs of variables through bivariate analysis. The first step in this process is usually to distinguish between dependent and independent variables. A *dependent variable* is one which, as the name suggests, is affected by another *independent variable*. In other words, when one defines a dependent variable it is hypothesised that changes in it will be caused by changes in the independent variable(s) with which it is associated. Suppose, for example, that one hypothesise that the speed of adoption of an innovation is a function of Everett Rogers five characteristics of relative advantage, complexity, compatibility, communicability and divisibility, then the five characteristics (which would need to be defined with some precision for purposes of data collection) are independent variables in that it is anticipated that a change in any one of them will result in some change in the speed of take up of the innovation. It is necessary for the researcher to hypothesise the existence and direction of causality, e.g. the more complex an innovation the more slowly it will be adopted, in order to be able to select which of the various measures of association will be most appropriate.

In some circumstances, however, the researcher may have no preconceived ideas or hypothesis about causality. In such cases it is not necessary to specify whether a variable is dependent or independent but fewer statistical techniques are available for analysing the data. In deciding which technique to use Alreck and Settle (1985) provide the very useful summary table reproduced as Table 13.5. In order to use the table one must be able to determine whether variables are categorised or continuous, and which is to be treated as the independent variable and which the dependent variable. It will be recalled that categorised or 'discrete' data consists of data which is classified into separate or discrete categories. In other words it is nominal data in which the categories are not related to one another. By contrast, and as the name implies, continuous data is any form of numerical data that is arrayed or distributed on some continuum. While continuous data may be represented in categories in order to summarise it more effectively, e.g. age groups, income bands, the underlying distribution is

continuous and it is this which matters.   It will also be recalled that
categorical data results from the use of nominal scales whereas continuous
data may be derived from ordinal, ratio and interval scales. Having defined
the variables in this way it is a simple matter to select the most appropriate
statistical measure(s) from the table.

Table 13.5. Statistical measures of association

INDEPENDENT

		Categorical	*Continuous*
D E P E N D E N T	Categorical	Cross-tabulation (contingency) [Chi-square]	Discriminant analysis [F ratio]
	Continuous	Analysis of variance [F ratio] Paired T-test [Value of *t*]	Regression analysis [F ratio] Correlation Analysis [Probability of *r*]

Source: Alreck, Pamela L. and Settle, Robert B. (1985), *The Survey Research Handbook*,
Homewood, Ill. Richard D. Irwin

Cross-tabulation

Of the methods cited cross-tabulation is the most common and widely used.
The reason is not hard to find – both variables may be categorised and it does
not matter which is classed as dependent and which independent. Thus if
we are in doubt as to whether our data is continuous or not we can still use
cross tabulation to determine the presence and degree of association between
any pair of variables we choose to analyse. For this reason it is commonplace
to compute the cross tabulations for all possible combinations of the key
variables in a survey. (Given the power and speed of modern computers one
should be wary of comparing everything with everything when one is likely
to be overwhelmed by a mountain of print-out. One of the reasons for
marginal analysis is to select those variables whose distribution looks
promising for further analysis, and to reject those which lack this property.)
    Probably the best way to explain cross tabulation is through an actual
example. Twenty years ago (1983), when interest first began to develop in
the potential market for multichannel cable TV, the author was involved in a
survey into the likely reaction to such a service in the West of Scotland. The
following description was given to respondents:

    For a basic monthly subscription charge, you can get access to over 20
    separate channels. These channels will include all the normal BBC and

ITV channels, the new satellite ITV and BBC television, and also channels with full length feature films, sport, news and local community programmes. Such a service could cost about £14 per month.

A total of 985 responses were received to the questionnaire. Table 13.6 gives two examples of cross tabulations in which intention to subscribe is compared with the age and social class of the respondents. Look at the table relating age to intention. This table comprises two *rows* – non-intenders and intenders and five *columns* – representing age groupings – giving a total of ten *cells*. Each cell contains three *values* the first of which is the actual number of persons/respondents who satisfied the age and intention criteria for that cell. The second value is the column percentage and the third is the row percentage which may be compared with the total values provided. Thus the top left hand cell in the table tells us that 47 respondents aged between 16 and 24 said they did *not* intend to subscribe to the service which was equivalent to 59.5 per cent of all respondents in the age group and 5 per cent of the total sample. So what does the table as a whole tell us? The key values to look at are the distribution of column percentages in each cell compared with the row total. For the sample as a whole 681 respondents said they did not intend to subscribe, representing 72.3 per cent of all respondents, i.e. 261 or 27.7 per cent said they would subscribe to a new service. Now look at the column percentages for each age band from which it is immediately apparent that the younger the respondent the more likely it is that they will subscribe to the new service.

If you would like to see if you understand this look at the table comparing intention with social class and write down your interpretation of it. Then turn to the end of the chapter to see how your analysis compares with the author's.

In undertaking cross-tabulation analysis it is important to keep the number of categories within reasonable proportions, otherwise it becomes very difficult to interpret and can also result in cells with very low frequencies or values e.g. a cross-tabulation of age (five categories) and social class (seven categories) would give a table with 35 cells. It is important to ensure that the cell frequencies satisfy a minimum *expected* value as otherwise it will not be possible to calculate the chi-square statistic which is used to measure the significance of the reported distribution against the likelihood that it could have occurred by chance, even if there were no differences in the sample from which the sample was drawn.

As Alreck and Settle (1985) explain, computer programs will calculate chi-square statistics 'regardless of whether or not the expected cell frequencies are of adequate size' with the result that if the expected values are below the required minimum the statistic generated will be invalid. Thus the researcher must check the cell frequency to ensure it meets the minimum

Table 13.6. Intentions to subscribe to cable TV

Cross tabulation of intention to subscribe to TV by age group of respondents

Count Col % Total %	16-24 years	25-34 years	35-44 years	45-54 years	55 years and over	Row Total
Non-intenders	47	152	169	111	202	681
	59.5	62.6	72.8	70.3	87.8	72.3
	5.0	16.1	17.9	11.8	21.4	
Intenders	32	91	63	47	28	261
	40.5	37.4	27.2	29.7	12.2	27.7
	3.4	9.7	6.7	5.0	3.0	
Column Total	79	243	232	158	230	941
	8.4	25.8	24.6	16.8	24.4	100.0

Cross tabulation of intention to subscribe to cable TV by social class of respondents

Count Col % Total %	Social Class A	Social Class B	Social Class C1	Social Class C2	Social Class D	Social Class E	Unemployed	Row Total
Non-intenders	7	125	116	164	98	93	47	650
	58.3	74.4	67.4	67.8	67.6	90.3	78.3	72.1
	0.8	13.9	12.9	18.2	10.9	10.3	5.2	
Intenders	5	43	56	78	47	10	13	252
	41.7	25.6	32.6	32.2	32.4	9.7	21.7	27.9
	0.6	4.8	6.2	8.6	5.2	1.1	1.4	
Column Total	12	168	172	242	145	103	60	902
	1.3	18.6	19.1	26.8	16.1	11.4	6.7	100.0

expected size requirement of five cases. The important point here as Alreck and Settle underline is that it is the *expected* not the *actual* cell frequency which counts, and this cannot be determined by inspection alone but must be calculated, i.e. you could have a cell frequency of 0 and it would not affect the chi-square statistic so long as the expected frequency was 5 or more. To determine the expected value of the cell with the smallest frequency one must find the smallest row total, divide it by the total for the table and multiply it by the smallest column total. Thus in the table comparing intentions with age the cell to examine is 'Intenders' aged 16 to 24. The relevant numbers are 261/942 X 79 = 21.88. The smallest cell value is 28 for 'Intenders' 55 years and over which is above this so chi-square statistic for this table would be invalid. You might like to try your hand on the intention by social class table to see if this is also acceptable, or whether it might be necessary to recode the data in order to achieve larger cell frequencies, e.g. by combining the A and B categories. The answer is at the end of the chapter.

As noted above, given the distribution of responses yielded by our survey, what we need to know is whether these reflect genuine differences in the population, or whether the same distribution could have arisen purely by chance, i.e. sampling error. To compare observed and expected values one needs to calculate the chi-squared (x^2) statistic. A description of this statistic and the procedure for calculating it will be found in any basic statistics textbook and most marketing research texts with an emphasis upon techniques and so need not detain us here. What the user needs to know is how to *interpret* the statistic.

Basically, the larger the chi-square value the greater the relationship between the variables to which it relates. However, the size of the x^2 is also a function of the size of the distribution itself so that the larger the number of items in a distribution the larger the x^2 is likely to be. In order to allow for this one must establish the number of ways in which the two sets of data – expected and observed – may vary. This is known as the *degrees of freedom* and is usually provided by most statistical analysis programmes. If not, for contingency tables it is simply calculated by multiplying the number of rows minus 1 times the number of columns minus 1. Hence, for our intentions data the degrees of freedom or d.f are 4 for age and 6 for social class. The reason we need this information is that the chi-square distribution varies according to the number of degrees of freedom and in order to establish the significance of our x^2 value we will need to refer to the appropriate table of values (to be found in most statistics books). However, most computer packages will provide a probability value which will indicate the likelihood that the observed values could have occurred by chance. In the case of our two tables the values are:

Intentions by age $x^2 = 46.0424$ d.f 4 prob = 0.0000
Intentions by social class $x^2 = 25.2367$ d.f 6 prob = 0.0003

As we have observed, the great advantage of cross-tabulation or contingency tables is that we can use them to compare both categorical and continuous data and need have no prior hypothesis about relationships between variables, i.e. which are dependent and which independent. (In practice one would establish a null hypothesis so as to be able to confirm or infirm it.) Much can be learned from such analysis but this can be greatly increased if one or both of the variables represents continuous data. Where this is so a number of other techniques are available as indicated in Table 13.5. A brief description of these techniques follows.

Analysis of variance (ANOVA)

As Table 13.5 indicates the appropriate technique to use when the independent variable is categorical and the dependent variable is continuous is analysis of variance or ANOVA. Analysis of variance is measured using the F-test with the objective of determining whether there is one or more significant differences among the sample groups represented in the table. The statistic is derived by examining the significance of the difference between means by comparing the variability of values both within and between groups.

As with chi-squared and student $-t$ (which is a special case for measuring variance when only two distributions are involved) the F-test is a standard test included in most computer programs and so easily obtained 'on command'. However, its use is only appropriate where the samples all have similar distributions, where the dependent variable data have been derived from an interval or ratio scale (not ordinal) and from *different* respondents. Provided the data satisfies these requirements the F-test will generate values which indicate whether or not significant differences exist, the degrees of freedom present in the table and the probability associated with the measurement. (Where the program does not provide d.f. and p. these may be obtained from tables for F in the same way as for x^2.)

Correlation

Correlation analysis is a technique for measuring the strengths of the linear relationship between two variables. If observations of the relationships were plotted graphically on a scatter gram then we might find the patterns shown in Figure 13.4.

Correlation is measured by the statistic r and may have values ranging from +1, meaning a perfect positive correlation, and –1, meaning a perfect negative correlation, with the value 0 meaning that there is no correlation between the two variables at all.

As our summary Table 13.5 shows correlation analysis is appropriate where both variables are continuous, e.g. sales and advertising expenditures. However, one does not need to specify which variable is dependent and which independent. By the same token one cannot use correlation to *prove* causation, although given results may provide evidence to support such an inference. For example, in the case of the sales-advertising relationship if the firm fixes its advertising budget as a percentage of sales then advertising spend would go up and down with sales but sales would be regarded as the independent variable and advertising spend as the dependent variable. Conversely, if one varies the advertising spend and detects parallel movement in sales up and down it would seem reasonable to infer that advertising expenditures have an effect on sales i.e. advertising spend is independent and sales are dependent upon them. This would be shown by a positive correlation – the higher the value the stronger the relationship.

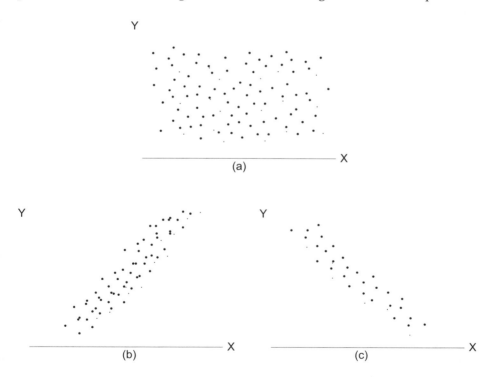

Figure 13.4. (a) No correlation, (b) high positive correlation, (c) high negative correlation

Negative correlations indicate that an inverse relationship exists so that an increase in one variable – say, immunisation against diphtheria – results in a decrease in the other – the number of reported cases of the disease.

While high values of r indicate a strong relationship, low values may give a misleading impression of the strength of the association between the two variables. This is so because r does not represent the proportion of a perfect ($\pm$ 1) relationship which the two variables share. To establish this one must compute the *square* of the correlation coefficient to yield R^2 which is know as the *coefficient of determination*. Thus values of r and R^2 would be as follows:

$$r = 0.10 \quad R^2\ 0.01$$
$$r = 0.20 \quad R^2\ 0.04$$
$$r = 0.30 \quad R^2\ 0.09$$
$$r = 0.40 \quad R^2\ 0.16$$
$$r = 0.50 \quad R^2\ 0.25$$
$$r = 0.60 \quad R^2\ 0.36$$
$$r = 0.70 \quad R^2\ 0.49$$
$$r = 0.80 \quad R^2\ 0.64$$
$$r = 0.90 \quad R^2\ 0.81$$
$$r = 1.00 \quad R^2\ 1.00$$

Thus a correlation of 0.5 means that only 25 per cent of the variance between two items is shared between them, and even a 'high' correlation of 0.7 indicates that less than half the observed variance is shared by the two variables concerned.

As with other tests described earlier, the significance of a correlation coefficient will usually be produced automatically by computer analysis programs but, if not, it can be determined by reference to statistical tables.

Finally, it should be noted that there are two main types of correlation analysis: the Pearson product – moment correlation (Product-Moment or PM) which is appropriate for interval or ratio scaled data, and Spearman's rank correlation which may be used for interval or scaled data, but is mainly used for ranked or ordinal data.

Regression analysis

Regression and correlation are closely related concepts. As we have seen, correlation analysis measures the degree of association between two or more variables. By contrast *regression* analysis examines the nature of statistical dependence between a dependent variable and one or more independent variables. According to Claycamp:

The basic measures produced by regression techniques are of two types:

1. The parameter values of a mathematical model – called a regression equation – that can be used to calculate expected values of the dependent variable as a function of specific independent variable values.
2. Measures of the deviations, or variance, between the original and expected values of the dependent variable.

Correlation techniques, on the other hand, produce standardised summary statistics to measure the goodness-of-fit of the regression equation to the data as well as to analyse the relative strength of statistical relationships among alternative combinations of variables. (Claycamp 1974)

When there is a single independent variable the technique is referred to as *simple* or *linear regression;* where there is more than one independent variable it becomes *multiple* regression. Like correlation analysis, regression analysis produces a summary statistic r^2 (*r*-square) which measures the proportion of variance in the dependent variable that is explained by the independent variable(s).

To compute a regression equation it is necessary for both the dependent and independent variables to be derived from interval or ratio scales. Normally the relationship between the variables should be linear, but it is possible to convert curvilinear relationships to linear ones where desired as is often the case when one wishes to predict from observed data, e.g. when forecasting.

Discriminant analysis

Discriminant analysis is the last technique proposed in Table 13.5 from which it can be seen that it is appropriate where the dependent variable is represented by categorical data, and the independent variable(s) by continuous data. However, as Alreck and Settle (1985) point out 'If the researcher wishes to measure the relationship between two variables *that need not or cannot* be identified as independent and dependent, analysis of variance is recommended…'[my emphasis]. Quite simply this is because Anova programmes are much more commonplace than discriminant analysis ones and are easier to understand. If, however, one wishes to predict the category of a dependent variable when it is not known, but the value of the independent variable is, then one must use discriminant analysis. Users presented with a discriminant analysis should invite the analyst to explain its use, and the justification for preferring it, in the context of the database to be analysed.

Multivariate analysis

[Many of the examples given in the following pages relate to marketing issues for two reasons:

1. The author is more familiar with them than other business/managerial settings;
2. Quantitative data of the kind amenable to analysis using the described techniques is more common in a marketing context than most other kinds of managerial problems.]

In Chapter 1 we claimed that the problems facing managers are difficult to resolve because they contain many variables interacting dynamically with one another, often simultaneously. As a consequence it is rarely possible to undertake experiments of the kind familiar to scientists in which one varies one factor while holding all others constant in order to determine what effect such variation may have. In the preceding sections we have reviewed techniques appropriate to the analysis of a single factor (univariate) and to the interaction of two factors (bivariate analysis). In this section we will look briefly at some of the techniques available to the analyst concerned with more than two variables – multivariate analysis – which, given the complexity of most business problems, has become increasingly popular in recent years, particularly because of the enormous increase in computing power which is now readily available.

Some years ago Hooley (1980) wrote a paper in which he referred to multivariate analysis as 'the academic's playground but the manager's minefield'. The allusion is apt – the mathematical complexity underlying most multivariate techniques is high, but much of the output appears convincingly simple. The result is that the non-statistician is likely to be persuaded that powerful techniques, which can apparently reduce a large and dense matrix into a simple summary statistic plot or diagram, must be right.

We can only reiterate the caveats introduced at the beginning of the chapter:

(a) Before setting out to collect any data you should have clear objectives as to precisely what it is you wish to discover or clarify;
(b) Data analysis should proceed methodically from marginal analysis, or univariate analysis, and then bivariate analysis by which time you should have a good understanding of the relationships within the data set.

As Ehrenberg (1963) has argued, when discussing the uses of factor analysis, a perceptive analyst is probably able to derive as much information from looking at a correlation matrix as can be derived by using such a matrix as an input to a factor analysis.   That said, multivariate analysis techniques represent an important device in the researcher's tool kit and can be of great value when applied to the correct problems.

The paper referred to earlier by Graham Hooley was in fact the introduction to a special edition of the *European Journal of Marketing* (vol.14, no.7, 1980), 'A Guide to the Use of Quantitative Techniques in Marketing', which remains one of the most 'user-friendly' overviews of the topic available to the non-mathematician. It will be referred to extensively in the following pages!

Hooley (1980) follows Heenan and Adelman (1975) when he classifies multivariate techniques as falling into two categories – predictive and descriptive.   Among the best-known and most widely used predictive techniques are multiple regression, principal components analysis, multiple discriminant analysis, conjoint analysis and automatic interaction detection (AID).   In the descriptive category factor analysis, cluster analysis and multidimensional scaling have now become commonplace.   A brief discussion of each of these is given below.

Multiple regression

As the name implies multiple regression involves analysis of the relationship between a dependent variable and two or more independent variables. This technique was described briefly in the preceding section.

Principal components analysis (PCA)

Cliff Holmes in the *Consumer Market Research Handbook* (1986) introduces PCA with the following explanation:

> In the statistical analysis of relationships between variables it is often important that the variables are uncorrelated (orthogonal) with one another. This is particularly true in multiple regression techniques and in the interpretation of factors in factor analysis. The method of principal components analysis is a technique for obtaining new 'artificial' variables which are uncorrelated with one another. (Holmes 1986)

If one were to visualise one's observations plotted in a three-dimensional space then a principal components analysis proceeds by selecting those grouped around the longest axis plotted through the centre of the plot and represents the component or factor which accounts for the highest amount of the total variance in the data set. The second component is then derived by selecting the next longest axis orthogonal, i.e. at right angles, to the first, and so on. While there are as many components as there are variables most analysts will content themselves with selecting only the first few which account for the majority of the variance and discard the remainder as individually they explain relatively little of the total variance.

Holmes discounts PCA as having much practical use in interpreting marketing data (although he cites examples of its use in selecting test market locations, classification of towns, and the stratification of local authority areas for sampling purposes) but stresses its value as an input to factor analysis.

Multiple discriminant analysis (MDA)

Rob Lawson (in Hooley (1980) defines MDA as:

> A technique employed to discover the characteristics that distinguish the members of one group from another, so that given a set of characteristics for a new individual, the group to which he should be assigned can be predicted. MDA was originally developed in the botanical sciences as a way of discovering distinguishing features of generic plant groups, on the basis of criteria such as leaf size and type, so that new species could be subsequently classified.
>
> In marketing the technique is perhaps most useful as a method for identifying the characteristics that discriminate between market segments – the segments are defined prior to the analysis based on whatever criteria are of interest to the particular study.

For example, if one wishes to segment the market on the basis of usage one would categorise the population as say heavy, medium, light and non-users and then use MDA to determine how independent factors such as age, income and occupation vary according to these categories, as the basis for developing the most appropriate marketing mixes to exploit the maximum potential from the market.

Lawson explains that 'MDA works by providing maximum separation between the groups. This is obtained by maximising the difference between the means of the groups in relation to the standard deviation within the groups'. As such MDA proceeds in much the same way as multiple regression analysis. Lawson provides both a worked example and an analysis of Evans's (1959) classic use of discriminant analysis to try and predict car purchase for those wishing to explore the technique in greater detail.

Conjoint measurement (CM)

According to Hooley (1980), 'conjoint measurement seeks to identify the relative importance of each product attribute in creating overall desirability for the product. This information can then be used to suggest ways of improving the product or even new product possibilities. Similarly, the information can be used to estimate how respondents would trade-off one attribute against another in approaching an "ideal" brand or product.'

Antilla et al. provide a useful review of the method together with a detailed analysis of its application in the Finnish market for colour televisions in the Hooley monograph. In their view a particular advantage of CM 'over the more traditional multivariate marketing research methods lies in its ability to take into account the trade-off phenomenon and to provide operative information on the utilities the decision-maker relates to product attributes'. In the TV example six attributes are used – price, brand name, size, colour reproduction, guarantee and design – with 4,3,3,3,2 and 2 'levels' or categories respectively. This yields 431 possible alternative combinations to which the conjoint analysis yields answers to the four key questions identified by Wind et al. (1978) namely:

1. What is the utility of each attribute level?
2. How important for the buyer is each attribute?
3. What kind of trade-offs can be made between attributes?
4. How do answers to the above questions vary across respondents and can they be segmented in a meaningful way?

However, as Antilla et al. explain, 432 combinations of attributes would make ranking an impossible task, and a key skill of the analyst wishing to use the technique is to reduce the number of combinations to feasible proportions. As with all multivariate techniques the mathematics are off-putting to the less numerate but the value of the output is readily apparent in Table 13.7 reproduced from Antilla et al.'s study.

Table 13.7 Relative attribute importance for three utility segments

Attribute	Price sensitive segment N=59 (%)	Quality prone segment N=71 (%)	Design-size conscious segment N=35 (%)
Price	44	9	5
Tube size	15	12	24
Brand name	14	24	12
Colour reproduction	20	38	25
Guarantee	5	16	4
Design	2	1	30

Source: Antilla, Mai, Van Den Heuvel, Rob and Mollor, Kristian (1980), "Conjoint Measurement for Marketing Management", *European Journal of Marketing,* Vol. **14**, No. 7, pp.397-408

As the authors explain:

The results clearly indicate the differences in relative attribute importance between segments. Although colour reproduction is an important factor for all groups, (also shown by the high level of relative importance for the entire sample) the quality-prone segment would be characterised by its strong willingness to trade-off price against colour reproduction (i.e. to pay more for the better colour-reproducing sets). This group is also much more sensitive to changes in attributes considered to be related to quality such as guarantee and brand name. A characteristic of the second segment is the extreme importance of price relative to the other attributes. A preference for modern design and small-tube-size television sets is common among the third segment. (Antilla et al. 1980)

Clearly, analysis of this kind provides valuable pointers to the marketing decision maker plotting strategy and planning the marketing mix. Unless one is qualified to discuss the technical aspects of the method perhaps the safest test of its suitability is to ask the common-sense question, 'Are the respondents being asked to make realistic comparisons?' If they are, and the researcher(s) is reputable and has prior experience of using the technique, then the method offers obvious benefits to managers wishing to segment markets and develop differentiated marketing mixes.

The automatic interaction detector (AID)

Although AID is 'not strictly a multivariate technique (as the independent variables are not examined simultaneously)' (Hooley, 1980) it is usually considered as one. AID is used often as a preliminary to cluster analysis (see below) and represents an intermediate step between it and cross-tabulation, and so is of particular value when seeking to reduce large databases to manageable proportions. It was developed for this purpose by Sonquist and Morgan (1964) and represents a development of the 'Belson sort' which was first proposed in 1959.

In the Hooley monograph Cliff Holmes describes the technique as follows: The technique is essentially very similar to that of Dr. Belson. It divides a sample through a series of binary splits across a set of independent variables which produce the greatest discrimination in the dependent variable. The computation steps are:

1. Take each candidate variable, one at a time and split into all possible dichotomies.
2. For each dichotomy calculate the between sums of squares (BSS) and select that split which maximises BSS.
3. Next the dependent variable is split into two categories on the independent variable which explains the maximum amount of

variance.

4. Repeat step (3) treating each of the two new groups independently.

While this may sound complicated the procedure yields an easily understandable 'tree' diagram of the kind shown in Figure 13.5.

As with all techniques AID has its strengths and limitations. As noted above it is particularly useful as an exploratory device for detecting patterns within large data sets, but against this must be set its potential to generate spurious results particularly because it does not distinguish correlated variables.

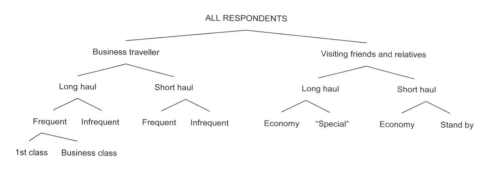

Figure 13.5 Aid analysis of airline usage decisions

Factor Analysis

Essentially, factor analysis is '… a statistical technique which can analyse the relationship between any number of variables and produce a set of "factors" each factor being a composite of some cluster of the original variables' (Harvard University Computation Center 1967). Because of its ability to reduce very large and complex databases into a smaller set of explanatory factors, and its easy availability in programs such as SPSSX, factor analysis is a widely used analytical technique. However, a great deal depends upon the interpretive skill of the analyst, and one must be wary not to be 'seduced' by the simple descriptive labels used to identify factors which are obviously a composite of several complex and interacting variables. For example, in a major survey of the principal factors underlying design success in international markets Ughanwa and Baker (1989) identified 34 contributory elements. A factor analysis reduced these to 11 principal components which between them explained 75.5 per cent of the variance of the data.

Cluster analysis

[This technique is described in some detail in *Marketing Strategy and Management* (Baker 2000) in the chapter on marketing segmentation. Rather than re-invent the wheel, and for the sake of convenience, that description is reproduced here.]

The marketer's interest in segmentation is particular example of a general problem faced by analysts and decision-makers in virtually all areas of activity, namely: 'Given a sample of N objects or individuals, each of which is measured on each of p variables, devise a classification scheme for grouping the objects into g classes. The number of classes and the characteristics of the classes to be determined.' (Everitt 1974 p.1)

Everitt continues:

> These techniques have been variously referred to as techniques of *cluster analysis*, *Q-analysis*, *typology*, *grouping*, *clumping*, *classification*, *numerical taxonomy* and *unsupervised pattern recognition*. The variety of the nomenclature may be due to the importance of the methods in such diverse fields as psychology, zoology, biology, botany, sociology, artificial intelligence and information retrieval. (Everitt 1974 p.1.)

In addition to the many fields of study in which different approaches to clustering have been developed, it is also important to recognise that such methods can be used for a number of different purposes. Thus Everitt cites Ball's (1971) list of seven possible uses of clustering techniques as follows:

(i) Find a true typology
(ii) Model fitting
(iii) Prediction based on groups
(iv) Hypothesis testing
(v) Data exploration
(vi) Hypothesis generating
(vii) Data reduction

In market segmentation studies each of these different objectives may be appropriate.

Ideally clusters should be self-evident and capable of identification simply by reviewing a set of data and distinguishing natural groupings within it e.g. classifying people as male or female. However, for most purposes decision-makers require a much finer discrimination than is possible using the two or three dimensions, which is the maximum which most of us can conceptualise simultaneously. Because of this need for greater sophistication there has been a proliferation of techniques, which Everitt classes into five types:

Hierarchical
Optimisation – portioning

Density or mode seeking
Clumping
Others

Hierarchical clustering techniques may be either *agglomerative* or *divisive* in nature. Under the former procedure one would start from the stance of the behavioural scientist in our earlier description of approaches to market segmentation and regard each individual as a potential market in his or her own right.   In most cases such an assumption would be unrealistic in economic terms so one would begin to combine individuals into groups. Conversely, the economists' undifferentiated demand schedule would be the logical starting-point for a divisive approach to segmentation.   Everitt observes: 'Both types of hierarchical technique may be viewed as attempts to find the most efficient step in some defined sense, at each stage in the progressive subdivision or synthesis of the population.

Partitioning techniques differ from hierarchical techniques in that they allow for adjustment of the original clusters, created on the basis of a predetermined criterion, through a process of reallocation. Thus, if one's *a priori* expectations as to the optimum way to segment a market leads to groupings which look less than ideal, or do not perform as expected, one can relocate individuals until an optimum segmentation is achieved.

Density search techniques are, as the name suggests, methods which seek to emulate the human observer's ability to distinguish clusters of high density surrounded by spaces with a lower density.

The fourth main type of technique, *clumping*, is seen as necessary where overlapping clusters are desirable. The case cited by Everitt is language where, because words tend to have several meanings, they may belong in several places. Finally, there is a number of other techniques such a 'Q' factor analysis, latent structure analysis, etc., which do not conform to any of the previous categories. These techniques, and many more from the other categories, are described at some length in Chapter 2 of Everitt's book.

The existence of so many different clustering techniques is itself evidence of the fact that there is no clear 'best' method and that one can anticipate arguments for and against any given approach. Everitt provides a useful summary of problems associated with cluster analysis *per se* and then in the context of the five-fold analysis discussed above. General problems include those of the precise definition of a cluster, the choice of variables, the measurement of similarity and distance and deciding the number of clusters present. These are technical matters beyond the scope of a book of this kind, but Everitt points out that there are various intuitively reasonable ways for validating clusters, namely:

Firstly, several clustering techniques, based on different assumptions, could be used on the same set of data, and only clusters produced by all or by the majority of methods accepted. Secondly, the data could be randomly divided into two and each half clustered independently. Membership assignment in the partitioned samples should be similar to that of the entire sample, if the clusters are stable. A third method of establishing the underlying stability of groups produced by a clustering program is to make predictions about the effect which the omission of some of the variables would have on the group structure and then to check that the predictions are verified.

The final word should also be given to Everitt, who reinforces the adage that any interpretation of data is only as good as the person making it when he comments that:

> Cluster-analysis is potentially a very useful technique, but it requires care in its application, because of the many associated problems. In many of the applications of the methods that have been reported in the literature the authors have either ignored or been unaware of these problems, and consequently few results of lasting value can be pointed to. Hopefully future users of these techniques will adopt a more cautious approach, and in addition remember that, along with most other statistical techniques, classification procedures are essentially descriptive techniques for multivariate data, and *solutions given should lend to a proper re-examination of the data matrix rather than a mere acceptance of the clusters produced.* [My emphasis] (Everitt 1974)

John Saunders provides an extended discussion of the method in Hooley (1980), as does Holmes in the *Consumer Market Research Handbook* under the heading 'Numerical Taxonomy'.

Multidimensional scaling (MDS)

Derived from a set of techniques developed originally in the field of mathematical psychology MDS has now been applied extensively in the marketing domain. According to Hooley (1980):

> While MDS techniques can operate on a variety of different types of data they have a common set of objectives:

> To produce a representation of the relationships between objects (in the marketing context usually brands) and/or between variables (often product attributes), and/or between evaluators of the objects or variables (respondents). (Hooley 1980)

The relationships discovered are used to build a picture of brand images in the minds of the respondents and an indication of individual respondents' product requirements. In essence MDS techniques seek to represent these relationships in a spatial configuration or model so that the relationships between brands and variables can be used for product positioning purposes (see, for example, Doyle, 1975) and the locations of respondents' product requirements can be used as a basis for market segmentation (see, for example, Johnson, 1971).

Hooley describes a variety of algorithms which have been developed to address different kinds of problem and provides an analysis of the UK market for king-sized cigarettes to illustrate their application.   His conclusion, which applies to the output of most multivariate analysis, is that:

> While MDS has yet to be fully accepted by marketing management as a definitive, strategic management tool, it has gained wide acceptance as an exploratory tool to enable a feel for a market to be developed. Findings and suggestions are then further investigated using some of the more familiar, tried and tested techniques.   It is probably in this latter, exploratory role, that the major value of MDS will be realised. (Hooley 1980)

Conclusion

To begin with we can do no better than imitate Hooley who cites Sheth's (1977) seven commandments to the researcher:

1. *Do not be technique orientated.* Focus the problem on the needs of management, then selects the appropriate analytical tool – not vice versa.
2. *Consider multivariate models as information for management.* Any model produced from multivariate techniques is an aid to managerial decision making and not a substitute for managerial judgement.
3. *Do not substitute multivariate methods for researcher skill and imagination.* Use common sense to evaluate the results of multivariate analyses. Do not rely on statistical measures of robustness alone.
4. *Develop communication skill.* Learn how to communicate findings to management in a non-technical way wherever possible. Adoption of findings as information inputs to decisions depends on management feeling confident about how that information was derived.
5. *Avoid making statistical inferences about parameters of multivariate models.* Beware of generalisations to populations where the nature of a sample is unclear.
6. *Guard against the danger of making inferences about market realities when such inferences may be due to the peculiarities of the method.* Do not take results at face value.   Even where high levels of statistical significance can be attached to findings ensure that results have a sound theoretical and common sense basis. Where possible, use split

samples to validate models developed on fresh data.
7. *Exploit the complementary relationship between descriptive and predictive methods.* Do not use techniques in isolation where other techniques may add to the information obtained, or further validate findings. Often techniques can helpfully be used in sequence. (Hooley 1980)

Most important we must remember that the techniques are not a panacea in themselves. This has been neatly put by Young:

The danger we must always avoid is becoming peddlers of techniques in search of problems rather than the problem solvers in search of techniques.

The primary consideration of any study must be the basic problem that it sets out to solve. This will lead to a search for specific types of information rather than a preference for particular analysis techniques. The various techniques available do, however, form a comprehensive set of tools to aid the interpretation and presentation of that information. (Young 1973)

Answers to Questions (pp.227-8, 311, 313)

The interpretation of part 2 of Table 13.6 ('Intentions to subscribe to Cable TV by social class of respondents') is that the intention is influenced by both income and usage dimensions of social class. Thus social classes C1, C2, D and the unemployed (heavy users) have stronger intentions to subscribe than class B (light users). In the case of class A high incomes increases the intention to subscribe for a light user category whereas low incomes debar class E (heavy users of TV).

The chi-square statistic for the table would be valid as the calculation is $252/902 \times 12 = 3.35$ and the smallest cell value of 5 exceeds this.

Recommendations for further reading

Sage Publications have an extensive and up-to-date list of books covering all aspects of data analysis and ranging from introductory to advanced texts.   Visit *http://www.sagepub.co.uk*

Diamantopoulos, A. and Schlegelmilch, B. (1997), *Taking the Fear Out of Data Analysis*, London: Thomson Learning

Moutinho, L. and Meiden, A. (2003), "Qualitative methods in marketing", chapter 9 in M. J. Baker (ed), *The Marketing Book* 5th Edition, (Oxford: Butterworth Heinemann)
This chapter gives a comprehensive overview of the subject and contains many useful summaries of the most widely used data analysis techniques.

Oakshott, Les (2001), *Essential Quantitative Methods for Business, Management and Finance,* 2nd Edition, London: Palgrave

CHAPTER 14

Writing Up and Getting Published

Synopsis

*While the title of this chapter, and its positioning might suggest that "writing up" is something to be addressed at the conclusion of a piece of research, it is something that began the moment one put pen to paper (or finger to keyboard) in developing a research proposal. Of course "Getting Published" **is** something that can only happen once one has converted one's ideas into a permanent record accessible to others. It is publication, the act of making one's ideas and thought a matter of record, that probably accounts for the fact that so many of us postpone the act for as long as we can. Spoken words lack the permanence of written ones, and are much easier to amend or retract. They can be excused or withdrawn on the grounds that they reflect preliminary thinking, and not one's conclusion on a matter of importance. Written words, especially when submitted for publication, are a quite different matter.*

In this chapter we address two major themes. First, we look at the issues and potential problems encountered in preparing a formal record of our work. Second, we explore the matters involved in submitting work for publication, especially in a scholarly or academic journal.

Keywords
Writing; theses; dissertations; articles; structure; content; peer; reviewing; publication; guidelines

Getting started

Ask any experienced writer about their craft and they will invariably tell you at least two things: getting started is the biggest hurdle to be overcome in successful writing, and that those who publish most have received many more rejections than those who publish little or occasionally. On closer inspection it is possible to identify two quite distinct sequence of events – one a virtuous circle the other a vicious circle as represented in Figure 14.1.

In determining which path you will follow, two apparently contradictory aphorisms should be borne in mind:

Time spent in reconnaissance is seldom wasted
Procrastination is the thief of time

The first aphorism is a military maxim which summarises the belief that marshalling the available and relevant information about a problem is more likely to lead to a successful outcome than rushing into action. We offer some explicit advice about this below.

The second aphorism identifies one of the major impediments to the successful completion of a project – procrastination. As suggested in Figure 14.1 procrastination is usually a consequence of anxiety.

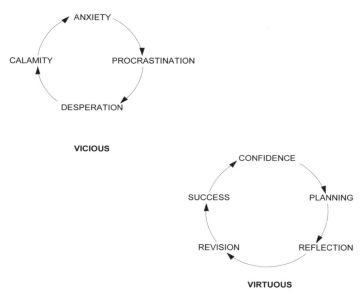

Figure 14.1 Vicious and virtuous circles

Silverman (1999) lists a number of reasons why writing for publication can cause anxiety:

Risk of Failure	Rejection
Being Wrong	Not Enough Time for Scholarly Activities
Professional Envy and Jealousy	Perfectionism
Scholarly Activities Interfere with Teaching or with Teacher-Student Relationships	Lack of Self-Confidence as an Independent Scholar
Lack of Self-Confidence as a Writer	Scholarly Activities Hurt Relationships with Family and Friends
Procrastination	Writer's Block
Not Identifying a Niche for Research and Publication	Not Securing Adequate Funding or Support
No Longer Being Able to View Oneself as 'a Giant in Chains'	Completing a Project and Having to Find Another

Faced with problems such as these it is hardly surprising that one puts off the act of writing for as long as one can! Further, the inclusion of procrastination as a source of anxiety itself reinforces the vicious nature of getting into this circle. To avoid, or break such a circle one needs self confidence in one's ability. Past achievement – you wouldn't have got this far if others hadn't a regard for your abilities – should help bolster the ego, as should discussion with your supervisor or mentor.

The second step in the virtuous circle should also help build your confidence. While planning is not the same as doing it is a form of doing, and should reassure you that the task to be attempted can be broken down into a series of smaller and more manageable steps which are much less daunting than the task as a whole. As discussed in Chapter 3 there are agreed protocols and conventions concerning the structure of a research project. The finished report should conform closely with this structure viz:

Introduction
Literature Review
Research Design
Data Analysis
Conclusions and Recommendations.

The **Introduction** will draw heavily on the original Research Proposal suitably modified to reflect changes made as the project ran its course. Similarly, the **Literature Review** and **Research Design** will have been drafted as they progressed and should require little more than editing. Much the same applies to the **Data Analysis** which means that when we talk about 'writing up' we usually mean the final part – the drawing of **Conclusions and Recommendations** from our analysis and relating these back to the original research issue, and findings from our secondary research. Usually, the drafting of conclusions and recommendations will require us to revisit earlier material, but this should be a question of tidying up, not of wholesale revision. If your findings show that your original conceptualisation was wrong this can still be regarded as a contribution to knowledge and understanding, and provide the basis for another piece of research. (This assumes the original conceptualisation was not based on flawed reasoning, and took cognisance of the extant literature on the topic – but this should have been determined before you embarked on primary research.)

The message is clear – start writing at the earliest opportunity. In developing the Research Proposal it is helpful to visualise what the finished document might look like. A cursory examination of some successful theses/dissertations, or journal articles, will quickly reveal that most are written to a formula that experience has shown to cover the essential elements. By following this 'formula' it is possible to complete parts of the work as one proceeds, as well as ensuring that a vital step has not been overlooked. In the next section we provide an example of what the Contents page of a Thesis might look like.

Outline structure and content

Abstract
A succinct summary of the work as whole. The description or 'blurb' you would find in a book catalogue or the cover of a book.

Chapter 1. Introduction

1.The Research Issue or Problem
What is it? Why is it important/significant? e.g. identifying the early adopters of new industrial products.

2.Theoretical Foundations
What are the disciplinary foundations of the Research Issue ? i.e. Discipline(s), Field and Sub-Field. e.g. Sociology, Psychology and Marketing; Adoption and Diffusion of Innovations; New Product Development, Organisational Buying Behaviour.

3. Working Proposition/ Hypotheses
"The early adopters of new industrial products may be pre-identified in terms of organisational and personal characteristics. Such identification will accelerate the adoption and diffusion of new industrial products."

4. Definitions.

5. Boundaries/Scope of the Study.

6. Overview of the structure of the written document.

7. Summary and link to the next chapter.

Chapter 2. The literature review

1. Introduction/Overview
A synoptic review of the sources and origins of the research in the field (Adoption and Diffusion of Innovations) and Sub-Field(s) (New Product Development, Organisational Buying Behaviour) as identified in Chapter 1.
The substance of this review is the agreed status of knowledge as would be found in recent, major and established text books dealing with the Field,

e.g. Everett Rogers' *Diffusion of Innovations,*(1995) 4th, Edition; and the Sub-Field e.g. Michael Baker and Susan Hart, *Product Strategy and Management,* (1998).

2. Research on the Topic

An in-depth inquiry into the sources that deal directly with the specific topic to be investigated. Some of the sources may be dated, e.g. Baker published his doctoral dissertation on this topic as *Marketing New Industrial Products* in 1975. However, the main thrust of one's research should be in the immediate past, especially publications that post-date the text books. In addition to searching the published literature one should also scan the abstracts of unpublished dissertations.

Once the relevant sources have been identified one should obtain copies, and critically review them following the procedures described, inter alia, by Chris Hart (1998).

3. Cognate Research

A major criticism of much research in an interdisciplinary and hybrid subject like marketing is that it fails to take cognisance of parallel research in cognate fields. For example, Rogers identifies eleven "traditions" that have undertaken major research into the adoption and diffusion of innovation. In Europe there are two quite distinct "schools" with an interest in innovation and new product development – one focuses on engineering, the other on marketing and managerial issues. It is rare for members of one school to attend meetings of the other! With honourable exceptions like Rogers, the paradox is that there has been little diffusion between the schools and traditions.

4. Conclusions

Drawn from the literature review and summarising what is known about the Research Issue. Equally, if not more important, what is **NOT** known, i.e. the *information gap* that needs to be addressed to illuminate the Research Issue/solve the Research Problem.

5. Summary and link to the next chapter.

Chapter 3. Research methodology

1. Introduction.

Link to previous chapter and overview of the structure and content of this chapter. (As explained   in an earlier chapter, 'Methodology' includes all aspects of the design and implementation of a piece of research.)

2. Statement of the Research Issue/Problem

This may take the form of a general proposition or hypothesis elaborated into a series of linked propositions/hypotheses. Alternatively, where the research is exploratory, the problem may be specified as a question or series of research questions. It is these hypotheses etc. that need to be 'answered' to bring the research to a satisfactory conclusion.

3. Overview of the Methods Available

While one is not required to describe the advantages/disadvantages of all the options available, the reader needs to be persuaded that the writer was aware of these, and has made an informed choice best suited to the needs of the project.

4. Operationalisation

This must include definitions of the population to be surveyed and the procedures to be used in sampling this population.

Next, one must define precisely the variables – dependent, independent and intervening – that are to be examined and the relationships (hypothesised) between these variables.

5. Data Collection

The procedures to be used should be described in general, supported by a Table or Diagram to summarise how these will be implemented.

The nature and design of the instruments to be used in collecting the data, e.g. interview schedule, questionnaire, should then be described in detail. Next, one must describe and justify the analytical techniques to be used.

6. Implementation

A description of the implementation of the research, the outcomes, e.g. response rates, and a commentary on this.

7. Summary and link to next chapter.

Chapter 4. Data analysis and findings

1. Introduction.

Link to the previous chapter and overview of structure and content of this chapter.

The structure of this chapter should follow that proposed in section 1 of Chapter 3 (Statement of the Research Issue/Hypotheses) unless there is a very compelling reason for varying this,

2. Overview of the Primary Data

An evaluation of the data set in terms of its representativeness, validity and the extent to which it measures what it purports to measure.

3. Analysis

A description of the techniques used to analyse the data and the extent and degree to which the findings confirm or infirm the hypothesised relationships.

With the advent of powerful software, such as SPSS, there is a tendency to go directly to complex, multivariate procedures without first conducting a marginal analysis (descriptive statistics), analysis of variance and correlation. Where strong relationships (meaningful findings?) exist these simpler techniques will reveal them, and help inform the interpretation of more complex analyses. If such relationships are not apparent the merits of sophisticated statistical manipulation are questionable.

Summary and link to the next chapter

A reprise of the principle findings and results.

Chapter 5. Conclusions and recommendations

1. Introduction

Link to the previous chapter and overview of the structure and content of this chapter.

2. Conclusions

The conclusions drawn from the findings of both the secondary and primary research. These should include a critical commentary covering the strengths and weaknesses of the study and possible alternative explanations.

3. Implications

An assessment of the potential impact of the study and its findings in terms of:

  i)   Its contribution to knowledge/ understanding;
  ii) Its contribution to theory and theory development;
  iii) Its contribution to practice and application;
  iv) Its implications for future research.

Recommendations

Specific recommendations that arise from the preceding section in terms of the implications of the findings.

Summary

Reprise of the Research Issue and the principal findings.

Appendices

Bibliography

A Checklist for Evaluating Dissertations

(This checklist is taken from the advice given to Honours students in the Department of Marketing at Otago University in New Zealand. It is reproduced by permission of the Head of Department, Professor Rob Lawson).

8.1 The Problem

- Was the problem clearly stated and defined?
- Was the problem researchable? What logical or practical limitations of the research should be considered?
- Was the problem important? Would the solution or partial solution of this problem make a contribution to knowledge or practice; or has this same problem been researched a number of times in the past.
- Was the problem properly delimited? A thorough investigation of a narrow problem is superior to a cursory examination of too broad a problem.
- Were the limitations inherent in the study recognised and stated? Most studies are limited by one or more of the following; data-gathering techniques and instruments, sources of data and the ability of the researcher. Both the researcher and the reader should be aware of these limitations in interpreting the data.
- Were special terms, and general terms used in a special way, clearly defined? (Provided that precise definitions are required. This may not always be necessary or even possible).
- If the researcher made any assumptions, were these clearly stated? Frequently, a researcher will actually have certain assumptions in his mind while doing his study and he may feel the assumptions would be obvious to a reader but this feeling itself may be a false assumption.
- Where applicable, was the background or historical development of the problem adequately described?
- Were the hypotheses to be stated or questions to be answered clearly stated? These should be developed from the theoretical framework of the study.

8.2 Review of Related Literature

- Was the emphasis on literature pertinent to the problems or was the impression given that the researcher included almost everything he read on the problem?

- Was the relationship between the previous research on the problem and the current research described? A critical review of previous research emphasising the strengths and weaknesses is important but it is even more important to point out the similarities and differences when previous research is compared with the current research.
- Did the researcher review research and literature in related disciplines that might have implications for the present study?

8.3 Procedures

- Was the research method used appropriate to the solution of the problem?
- Were the procedures described completely and clearly? If so, another investigator should be able to repeat the study without difficulty.
- If applicable, were all variables that might influence the study recognised and controlled by the research design?
- If applicable, were valid and reliable instruments used to collect the data?
- Was there evidence of care and accuracy in recording and summarising the data?
- Were appropriate methods used in analysing the data and were the methods correctly applied?

8.4 Discussion and Conclusions

- Were the findings and conclusions supported by the data presented? No matter how logical or important a statement may be, it has no place in the conclusions if it is not supported by the data presented in the study.
- Were the findings compared with findings of similar studies reported in the review of related literature?
- Were the findings and conclusions free of the bias of the researcher? Bias may be shown both in what is said and in what is not said.
- Were recommendations made for further research? No one has worked as closely with the problem as the researcher and undoubtedly, he or she has seen possibilities for further research that another person may not see.
- If applicable, were the implications of the study for practice stated completely and clearly?

8.5 General Considerations

- Was the title clear, complete and concise?
- Was the organisation of the report logical and clear to the reader? Chapter headings and subheadings are particularly helpful to the reader.

- Was the dissertation correct in terms of "mechanics" - typing, spelling, grammar, tables footnotes and bibliography? Carelessness in mechanics may indicate the attitude the researcher took toward all of his work. At the least, careless errors distract the reader and may prevent one from receiving the important message reported.

8.6 Summary
- Did the summary give a concise and clear statement of the important parts of the study?
- Did the summary include any new material not previously reported? Often new material that should have been reported in previous chapters of the report is included in the summary.

Fleshing out the outline

ALL agree that one needs to start committing ideas to paper at the earliest opportunity; to discipline oneself to write on a regular, programmed basis; and of the benefits of revision.

Experience show that many students behave in exactly the opposite way to that recommended. They will find innumerable reasons (excuses) for delaying the start of the writing up process; will find all kinds of other activities that must take precedence to sitting down with the proverbial blank sheet of paper in front of them and, consequently, find they have no time left to review and revise what they have eventually committed to paper. They also delude themselves into thinking that by amassing copious raw materials (frequently large numbers of unread journal articles obtained via the internet or simply notes?) they will be able to transform straw into gold overnight. In practice the reverse usually happens. Faced with a mountain of straw and a rapidly approaching deadline panic sets in and we are into the vicious circle described earlier.

The first thing to remember is that a report, thesis or dissertation is a *written* document and its value will be judged largely on its content and presentation. To be sure many such documents will be subject to discussion with the author and/or formal oral examination. However, in the case of work submitted for a formal award a major purpose of the viva is to establish the intellectual ownership of the work, and the candidates' ability to justify and defend what they have done. The acid test of any written document is the extent that it exists in its own right, and does not leave questions unanswered or unresolved. Very few readers of written documents like books, papers and dissertations will have the opportunity to discuss their content with the author. It follows that a primary responsibility of the author must be to anticipate the readers information needs and satisfy them.

As with other stages in the execution of a research project, one should carefully observe any specific requirements governing the submission of a written report of it. In the case of formal qualifications the examining body will usually publish its own guidelines. An example of these together with an indication of the weighting given to the various elements is given in Appendix 1. Similarly, Conference Organisers and the Editors of scholarly publications will outline their expectations and requirements in line with those set out in Appendices 2 and 3 respectively. It goes without saying that failure to comply with these guidelines and advice is likely to result in an unsatisfactory outcome.

There are many conventions that govern written communications of all kinds. A number of these are discussed here, particularly those that are viewed as necessary conditions for successful writing. Issues such as grammar, punctuation and spelling should have been inculcated as part of one's formal education, and not call for a great deal of conscious thought. That said we all develop bad habits and, as I write, my word processing program continually reminds me of mine! In most instances I am more than happy to follow the advice offered. On occasion I choose not to, and this is a matter of *style*. While conventions also apply to many aspects of style (see, for example, Strunk and White *The Elements of Style*) one should not be afraid to use a word or expression that one feels better communicates one's idea or meaning than the conventional one. The acid test must always be *clarity* – is your meaning clear and unambiguous? But, more than that, what you write must be *interesting* and hold the reader's attention. In some cases, especially that of the formal examiner or reviewer, one has no option but to read the material.

The difference between the Inland Revenue's *Tax Return Guide* and J.K Rowling's Harry Potter books is not hard to discern. We have to read the former, and try to understand its obfuscations as best as we can, but it is unlikely we will get much pleasure or interest from the exercise. As for Harry Potter, most people can't wait to turn the page and discover what is going to happen next. The scarcity of best sellers testifies that this is a rare gift, but this should not distract us from trying to write more like J.K Rowling and less like the faceless bureaucrats responsible for many opaque government publications. (This despite the advice to be found in Sir Ernest Gower's *Plain Words* written specifically for Civil servants to encourage them to write clearly and accessibly.)

The point we are seeking to make here is that, while conventions may apply to the structure and presentation of different kinds of written communications, the whole essence of the exercise is *communication.* Complex sentences, jargon and poly-syllabic (long!) words are to be avoided wherever possible. The aim should be to say what has to be said in the clearest and most succinct way that one can achieve.

Often guidelines will be suggested for the length of a piece of work. Preece (1994) suggests that the maximum number of words for dissertations is, on average:

Bachelors 12,000words
Taught Masters 20,000 words
Research Masters 50,000 words
Doctoral Thesis 75,000 words.

Similarly, Editors of journals and Conference Organisers will indicate a preferred length of between 4000 and 6000 words. However, such recommendations are usually qualified to indicate that shorter or longer submissions will be acceptable, provided that they achieve the objectives set by the work itself. (A word of warning to students writing dissertations as part of a taught course, your tutors will have a lot of assessment to perform within a very limited time, and will not look kindly on submissions that greatly exceed the suggested upper word limit unless they are exceptionally good).

While writing too much is to be avoided, as we have hinted the more usual problem is "writer's block" – the inability to get started at all. To overcome this Silverman (1999) suggests several "Coping Strategies" viz:

Write Daily
Compose First, Worry Later
Accept Your Need for Rituals and Totems
Provide Opportunities for Experiencing a Feeling of Accomplishment
Talk with Persons Who Are Good Listeners and Who Are Not Threatened by Your Projects
Work on Several Journal Articles or Book Projects at the Same Time
Avoid Projects You Might Not Be Able to Complete
Avoid Projects That Are Unlikely to be Publishable
Incorporate a Jenga Philosophy (Jenga is a strategy game)
Getting into the "Zone"

As someone who has written quite a lot, I can confirm that this is excellent advice. The most important thing of all is to do something. Once you have committed some ideas to paper you can revisit and review them; amend, eliminate or elaborate upon them; share them with others and seek comment and advice. The important thing is you have started, and overcoming the inertia this requires is one, if not the most difficult aspect of writing anything.

To summarise this section of the chapter we can do no better than summarise Sharp and Howard's **Rules for Writing** viz:

1. **Plan.** You should develop a detailed outline first to ensure that your material will be presented in a logical and coherent way.
2. **Introduce.** Tell the intended reader what your purpose and objectives are and how you intend to achieve them in a formal Introduction.
3. **Motivate.** Make clear what benefits the reader will gain if they read the paper. It is a cliché but true that you only have one opportunity to make a first impression. Some people (examiners, reviewers) have to read your work, even if it is dull and uninteresting, but the rest of the world doesn't.
4. **Hold.** Maintain interest by concentrating on substantive issues and don't allow yourself to be distracted by lacunae.
5. **Discuss.** Demonstrate how the points you are making are relevant to your purpose and objectives, as set out in the Introduction.
6. **Break.** Use headings and sub-headings to break up the text into manageable 'bites'.
7. **Illustrate.** Use graphics to present complex data.
8. **Illuminate.** Give examples to reinforce the argument.
9. **Summarise.** Remind the reader of the key issues with which you have dealt, and any conclusions and recommendations arising from them.
10. **Conclude.** Indicate how your findings may be used in practice, and any new issues that deserve further research.

(Adapted from Sharp and Howard 1996, pp.224-5)

Writing for a purpose

Probably the best advice one can give about writing is to treat it as a marketing exercise – start with the need of the reader and organise your material to meet their needs. As noted, many of the readers needs have been formalised in terms of the structure and content as exemplified by the Appendices. Taken together these guidelines suggest that one must:

1. State the *Objective* or *Purpose* of the thesis, paper or report.
2. Demonstrate familiarity with the body of knowledge, theories and ideas that summarise what is already known about the field of inquiry that your topic falls into.
3. That a genuine research issue exists that is worthy of investigation.
4. That you are familiar with research methodology and have selected an approach and techniques most likely to yield new information relevant to the research issue.
5. That you have operationalised the research issue in a meaningful way and collected valid and reliable data germane to it.
6. That you have interpreted the data in accordance with the

conventions and procedures developed to ensure objectivity and validity in analysis and that the conclusions drawn accurately reflect the data and would have been arrived at by another independent investigator following the same protocols.

7.   That you are able to integrate the findings of the primary research with the secondary information derived from your literature review and show how the former illuminate and add to what was previously known.

8.   That, based on this synthesis, you are able to draw conclusions that are relevant to the purpose of the research.

While these guidelines are applicable to all kinds of writing they will need to be tailored to meet the precise needs of the intended audience. Effectively, these may be divided into two groups:

a) Examiners;
b) Editors, Conference Organisers, Publishers.

In the case of Examiners who are assessing a submission for the formal award of a degree Mauch and Birch (1993) suggest that Chairpersons look for the following characteristics when evaluating student research writing:

The problem is clearly stated and well conceptualised.
Ideas are communicated in clear, readable language.
The student demonstrates significant analytical skills.
The writing is succinct, not verbose.
The presentation is well organised.
The thought processes are well defined and internally consistent. (Mauch and Birch 1993, p.246)

It is important to remember that, in general, examiners wish candidates to succeed. They have all been through the experience themselves and know how stressful the process can be. Their role is to ensure that the work submitted is genuinely that of the person presenting it, and that it is of a sufficient standard in terms of the explicit and implicit criteria to merit an award. It is important also to remember that there is a minimum standard that has to be achieved, but there is no upper limit to the actual achievement. While we would all like to change the world view of our topic, in reality knowledge accumulates slowly and incrementally. Obviously, you must make a contribution but, in the great majority of cases, the examiners are more concerned to establish that you have served an apprenticeship in the formulation and execution of research, and are now fit to practice without supervision, than they are in the magnitude of the contribution *per se*.

Much the same criteria will be applied by the second group of Editors etc. However, persons evaluating material for publication will often enlist the services of expert reviewers, and supply them with specific guidelines against which a manuscript is to be assessed. In Appendix 4 we reproduce the forms issued to reviewers for the *Journal of Marketing Management* and the British Academy of Management Annual Conference.

Nowadays, students writing research degrees are actively encouraged to try and publish their work at Conferences and in academic journals. Such publication is an intrinsic element of the professional academic's career and plays an important part in promotion decisions. Hence, "publish or perish"! In the second part of this chapter we look briefly at some of the key issues involved.

Getting published

A major publisher of academic journals, including the prestigious *European Journal of Marketing,* is MCB Press based in Bradford, England (now Emerald). During the 1990s they introduced a newsletter designed specifically for Editors, Reviewers and Authors offering comment and advice and some of the earlier articles have now been made available on-line at *www.literaticlub.co.uk* Two of these articles – 'The Peer Review Process' and 'Write Right First Time' contain particularly useful advice which conforms with much that has been written on these topics. Accordingly, they have been adopted as the primary sources for this section.

In his article "Write Right First Time", Robert Brown argues that a major reason behind the rejection of papers submitted to academic journals is that the authors have failed to test their ideas out on others before offering them for formal peer review. To counter this failing, Brown proposes the use of Action Learning Sets, and summarises the essential differences between the two processes in Table 14.1.

Brown suggests (Table 14.1) several key differences between Expert Reviewing and Action Learning Set Review. Expert Reviewing is usually at arms length; Action Learning calls for collegiate, face-to-face interaction. The process will be enhanced if the members are not expert in each other's fields as they "lack pre-conceptions about the content of a paper or its context" (Brown: 4). Such action learning reviews should be complemented by parallel expert reviewing.

An action learning set should be diverse, with 5 members, including a Set Adviser whose role is to keep discussion focused and ensure constructive criticism.

Table 14.1. The different characteristics of expert and action learning set reviews

Expert View	Action Learning Set Review
Usually remote	Always face-to-face
Often anonymous	Never anonymous
Sometimes misinformed, ill-considered or even vindictive and all this can be obscured by the anonymity	Face-to-face feedback makes all of these problems much less likely to arise
Sometimes combative and adversarial	Always supportive and collegiate
Feedback focuses primarily on content of article	Feedback focuses primarily on structure of article
Often gets 'captured' by expert perspective and so focuses on what an expert would want to tell a reader, thus leaving the benefit for the reader implicit	Review by educated laymen makes it easier to help the writer take a marketing perspective and so focus on presenting what a reader would find valuable and to make such benefit explicit
Only rarely is there opportunity for follow-up or further explanation	Follow-up and elaboration is an integral part of the process
No synergism between reviewers because reviewers don't meet	Strong synergism between reviewers because reviewers work together
Individual effort	Team effort
Rarely leads to deeper insights beyond the content of the paper under review	Often leads to deeper insights about careers and life

The argument in favour of Action Learning is that it follows a cycle:

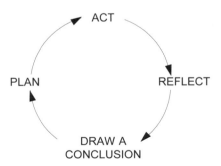

Figure 14.2 The cycle of action learning

In this cycle it is the reflection and drawing of conclusions which is important Too many people just oscillate between Planning and Action. The problem is compounded because many authors do not seek external advice before submitting for publication and so are restricted to their own, limited, self-perception of what is right or wrong. As any student of TQM will tell you, trying to inject quality at the end of the production process is likely to be counter productive

In Brown's experience as an editor, two major sources of failure are:

1. Lack of originality
2. Unclear/poor presentation

The latter is the more common problem. While an editor (or supervisor) may help, this is not their primary role. The remedy is to get authors to express their ideas clearly in the first place.

Brown (op. cit 5) asks authors to provide explicit answers to the following 8 questions:

A. who are the intended readers? - list 3 to 5 of them by name;
B. what did you do? (limit -50 words)
C. why did you do it? (limit -50 words)
D. what happened? (limit - 50 words)
E. what do the results mean in theory? (limit -50- words)
F. in practice? (limit - 50 words)
G. what is the key benefit for your readers? (limit - 25 words)
H. what remains unresolved? (no word limit)

(G) is probably the most important question, but all 8 need to be answered.

These answers should be reported at the beginning of every draft and provide an agenda for comparing intention with execution. Once all discrepancies have been removed, the draft is ready for submission.

For a set to perform effectively it is important that everyone:

(a) comes fully briefed;
(b) focuses on the big picture of what the author is trying to say;
(c) asks 'dumb' questions when they genuinely don't understand;
(d) is willing constructively to confront their own and their colleagues fears;
(e) is honest with themselves when they reflect;
(f) openly discusses the fruits of their reflections.

For the experienced author who is "committed to making a concerted effort to ensure that their next manuscript submission to a journal (and the research it is based on) is better than their last one" there is excellent advice offered by

Rajan Varadarajan (1996: p.6). In a reflection on his extensive experience as Editor of the prestigious American journal, the 'Journal of Marketing', he identified common weaknesses in the many papers reviewed and offered guideposts to authors. For those aiming at having their work accepted by the more prestigious journals this is an essential read.

Peer reviewing

> Essentially, the peer review process is a quality control mechanism for academic or learned journals and, to a lesser extent, professional or practitioner journals. ("The Peer Review Process", Paul Evans, *Literati Newsline*, 1994/1995)

The Editor is responsible for the policy of a journal and acts as the first screen in determining whether an article is suitable in terms of the journal's objectives and positioning, and of an appropriate standard.

Most journals operate double blind refereeing under which all information relating to an author is removed, the paper is coded and sent to reviewers known to be experts in the field covered by the paper. Reviewers are usually invited to rate a submission against a number of criteria, such as originality, contribution to knowledge, and provide a confidential note for the editor. In addition, reviewers normally provide advice to authors, especially when recommending revision. The length of reviews varies enormously from *a* paragraph or two to several pages.

The decision is either to accept as is - for most journals less than 10% achieved a straight acceptance - to revise and resubmit (15/20%) or to reject (70/80%). Obviously rates vary by journal, and provide a crude guide to the popularity of a journal (number of submissions) and its standards. In some cases, revisions are accepted by the Editor but, where extensive revision is called for, the original reviewers may be asked to look at a paper for a second time.

Evans suggests 6 benchmarks for judging an article:

1. Does the article add to what is already known?
2. Is the article demonstrably related to what has been previously written?
3. Are the arguments employed valid in terms of the body of knowledge?
4. Is the article easy to read?
5. Do the arguments flow logically?
6. Are the conclusions strong?

Evans also summarises the advantages and disadvantages of the peer review process as follows:

Advantages
1. Refereeing allows an author to claim priority to an idea.
2. Validation of the author's work.
3. Protection from plagiarism.
4. Assurance of authenticity.
5. It may contribute towards obtaining a job or promotion, or funding.
6. Quality assurance.
7. Improves scholarship by ensuring relevant literature is cited.
8. Work receives added value by the process of revision.

Disadvantages
1. Some reviewers find it difficult to be truly impartial and allow their own opinions to show through their critiquing of an article.
2. Reviewers are human and can make factually incorrect judgments.
3. Reviewers may often disagree on the merits of the same paper.
4. Anonymity of reviewer means that the author has little recourse.
5. Time - the major delay in publications is often the peer review process.

It is largely the Editor's responsibility to eliminate or reduce these disadvantages.

In addition to action learning sets, many academic departments publish working paper series so that authors may obtain feedback on their work prior to submitting it to a journal. Submission of papers to conferences also provides an opportunity for comment and feedback in real time. Evans also suggests the use of electronic media by using the BITNET.

A survey of MCB editorial review board members confirmed that successful articles are usually required to meet 8 criteria, namely:

1. Originality and innovativeness (is it interesting?)
2. Relevance to previous work.
3. Building on and relevance to body of knowledge.
4. Evidence and objectivity.
5. Clarity of writing.
6. Quality and logical progression of argument
7. Theoretical and practical implications.
8. Meets editorial objectives

These criteria apply to all academic material that is to be submitted for publication whether it be conference paper, journal article or a book. They are either explicit or implicit in the guidelines reproduced in the Appendices.

Summary

In this chapter we have explored two important and related issues – the writing up of a piece of research and submitting it for publication. All students required to complete a thesis or dissertation must present their findings in written form and we have addressed some of the main issues that need to be taken into account. Even more detailed advice will be found in the references that follow.

Not all students will be expected to publish their research, even though copies of it will usually be lodged in a library or other archive. However, given the increasing pressure to "publish or perish" in academic circles, more and more supervisors are encouraging their students to publish with them. Some knowledge of and familiarity with the conventions associated with publication will clearly be useful in determining how to structure and present one's work, and the criteria to be satisfied. As these criteria also apply to theses and dissertations submitted for formal examination this information should be useful to all students too.

Recommendations for further reading

Day, Robert A. (1998), *How to Write and Publish a Scientific Paper*, 5th Edition, Cambridge: Cambridge University Press

Germano, William (2001), *Getting It Published*, Chicago: The University of Chicago Press

Mauch, James E. and Jack W. Birch (1993), *Guide to the Successful Thesis and Dissertation*, Third Edition, New York: Marcel Dekker Inc

Perry, chad, Carson, David and Gilmore, Audrey (2003), "Joining a conversation (writing for EJM)", *European Journal of Marketing*, Vol. **37**, No. 5/6, pp.652-667

Rudestam, Kjell Erik and Rae R. Newton (2000), *Surviving your Dissertation*, London: Sage Publications

Seely, John (2000), Series Editor, *One Step Ahead*, Oxford: Oxford University Press. This series comprises a series of monographs (9currently) covering all aspects of written and spoken communication,   Essential reference for anyone writing for publication.

Appendices

These appendices illustrate the Guidelines published by the organisations for the benefit of their students/contributors. **The Golden Rule** in every case is that you must obtain and observe the specific guidelines that apply to your work.

1. MA Dissertation Notes for Guidance – *Nottingham University Business School.*
2. Conference Organiser Guidelines for Submission – *BAM 2001.*
3. Editorial Guidelines – *Journal of Marketing Management.*
4. Reviewers Guidelines - *AM Conference 2001.*
5. Reviewers Guidelines - *Journal of Marketing Management.*

Appendix 1. Nottingham University Business School – MA Dissertation Notes for Guidance (Reproduced with the permission of Professor Caroline Tynan, Nottingham University Business School)

The University of Nottingham Business School
MA Dissertation Notes for Guidance

1. Dissertation Requirement and Assessment

All MA students undertake a dissertation. This dissertation is written in the summer just before the course ends. Students must achieve a minimum mark of 50% in the dissertation and a 50% average across all courses modules to be awarded the degree of MA.

2. Objective of Dissertation

The purpose of the MA dissertation is to provide students with the opportunity to undertake independent research in a topic which falls broadly under the heading of the title of the degree registered for. In undertaking the dissertation, students should look to draw on and extend material covered in the course. Normally dissertations should have a significant empirical component (whether quantitative or qualitative) which should be aimed at providing further understanding of key theoretical concepts The typical dissertation therefore is likely to be structured around a review of relevant literature, outline of methodology and a presentation of empirical analysis. This does not preclude the use of alternative formats for the dissertation, nor does it preclude students from undertaking a project based on conceptual development in the context of a detailed literature review. Further guidance on the suitability of dissertation topics can be provided by supervisors or the Course Director.

3. Choice of Topic

Students are encouraged to begin thinking about a suitable topic for their dissertation as soon as possible. Some members of staff will put forward dissertation topics in relation to areas in which they are specifically interested and a list will be circulated; others will be available to supervise projects which fall broadly within their subject area.

In general, the dissertation would be expected to include both conceptual and practical analysis. While it is possible to prepare a dissertation based exclusively on conceptual analysis or one which relies purely on desk research, students are advised that dissertations of this nature depend upon thorough analysis and criticism and are by no means an easy option.

To complete a dissertation successfully students must check that the topic is realistic in terms of the time available for completion, the scope of the problem and the availability of information and other resources. It is important at an early stage to define the specific problem to be addressed and the methods to be adopted.

Where a particular topic requires primary research (interviews, questionnaires, group discussions) from external sources, students should be explicit about their purposes and affiliations. In particular if a dissertation topic is being sponsored by an external organisation, the student should make this clear in any external information collection. The use of the University affiliation should not be used to facilitate the collection of commercially sensitive information. Any doubts about the ethical aspects of information gathering should be discussed with the supervisor.

4. Supervision Arrangements

In general it is the *responsibility of the student* to identify a dissertation area and contact an appropriate supervisor. Students are required to submit a dissertation proposal form (see appendix 1) to the MA Office no later than 2nd May. This form consists of a cover sheet which states the dissertation topic name of the supervisor, an initial dissertation outline and should be signed by the student and countersigned by the supervisor. Students having difficulty in contacting an appropriate supervisor should contact the Course Director. While the dissertation is an individual piece of work, the supervisor will undertake the following:

(i) offer guidance in the specification of the dissertation topic and the formulation of the problem as well as providing some suggestions for preliminary reading;
(ii) offer assistance in outlining an appropriate structure for the dissertation and generally expect to see, at a fairly early stage, a detailed outline of the dissertation; and
(iii) help in relation to any specific problems encountered in the course of the research and discuss ideas of possible approaches with the student.

The supervisor will also be the person who marks the dissertation. Students whose first language is not English and have some doubts about the clarity of their written work should approach their supervisor who may be willing to read some of their dissertation and advise on style.

Contact your supervisor early and agree topics and structure. Most supervisors have research commitments over the summer as well as holiday time; they cannot therefore guarantee to be available for the whole of this period, so it is important to organise the work early to ensure that the dissertation structure and method have been agreed at the start of the study.

5. Presentation and Length

When preparing the dissertation take note of the following requirements:

(i) The dissertation should be in the order of 20,000 words in length up to a maximum of 25,000 words. It should be typed (10, 11, 12, point font), double or one and a half spaced on A4 paper with margins of approximately 2.5 centimetres (1 inch). Pages should be numbered straight through, not on a chapter by chapter basis.

(ii) Binding. Dissertations should be hard bound in a black binder with gold lettering. The front of the dissertation should contain:

University of Nottingham
Title of Dissertation
Student Name
Title of MA Course

The spine of the bound copies should read:

Title of MA Course   Student Name   Year

iii) The first page of the dissertation should be a title page, formatted as shown below:

Competitive Advantage
in Small Service Businesses
by
AN Other
2001

A Dissertation presented in part consideration for the degree of *"Title of MA Course"*.

The title page should be followed by a one page summary, the table of contents and the acknowledgements (if any).

(iv) A clear chapter structure is important in reinforcing the line of argument; appendices can be used for the presentation of certain types of factual material mathematical/statistical proofs, survey results etc. where to include these in the text would distract from the general argument. All work done by other people - either published or unpublished - must be acknowledged and clearly referenced, as should the source of any published data, diagrams or photographs. *Failure to do so constitutes the academic offence of plagiarism.*

(v) References to the work of others should be made in the text, citing author and date (for example: 'Porter, (1980) argues that ...'). A comprehensive bibliography, with references sorted alphabetically should be included at the end of the dissertation. It is important that these references should be accurate and include all the information required to enable a reader to find the references cited.   The Business School recommends that students follow the Harvard system for referencing.   This entails author name cited in the text (as above) and a list of references at the end of the dissertation in the form shown below. Where possible the use of footnotes should be avoided when referencing.
The following should be acceptable:

Journal: Tellis, G. J. (1986) 'Beyond the Many Faces of Price: An Integration of Pricing Strategies' *Journal of Marketing* Vol 50 pp. 145-60.
Book: Kotler, P. (1980) *Marketing Management Analysis*, Planning and Control, Prentice Hall, New Jersey.
Edited Book: Binks, M. R. and Coyne, J. (1986) 'Financing Entrepreneurship' in Carter et al (Eds), *Personal Financial Markets*, Philip Allan, Oxford.
Conference Paper: Knight, J. A. G. and Lebrecht, H. M. (1979) 'Tool control and distribution and workholding requirements in flexible manufacture'. Proceedings of the second Joint Polytechnic Symposium on Manufacturing Engineering, Coventry, Guilford, IPC, pp. 14-24.

More detailed statements on referencing systems and practices are available in University Libraries.

(vi)   While the use of footnotes is not generally encouraged, they may be used to highlight important points which would break the flow of the text. They should be identified numerically and presented at the foot of the page to which they refer.

(vii)   Diagrams and tables should normally be included in the text as close as possible to the point at which they are discussed. In the case of dissertations which use an unusually large number of diagrams, it may be preferable to group these diagrams at the end of the relevant chapters or in an appendix.

(viii)   There is provision for dissertations considered commercially sensitive to be classified as confidential.

(ix)   Two copies of the dissertation, hard bound in black with gold lettering, should be handed in by September 28th-to the MA Office; one for the supervisor and one for the Business School Library. Non-submission by the due date may mean the award of a mark of zero and failure to obtain the degree of MA.

Appendix 2. Conference Organiser Guidelines for Submission BAM 2001
(Reproduced with permission from Dr Carolyn Strong, Conference Organiser)

Paper Submission Guidelines

There are three different formats; working papers, refereed papers, and new for Cardiff 2001, a 'best paper track'. Please indicate when submitting your paper under which one of the following categories you wish it to be reviewed.

1. **Working papers** represent research that is in the initial or mid stages and an abstract is to be submitted for review. If the working paper is accepted a fuller document can be prepared and submitted. The abstract should be not more than two sides of A4, between 300-500 words.

2. **Refereed papers** represent research that is in the final stages and is very well developed; the complete paper is required for submission to conference referees. There is no word or page limit, although perhaps 7000-8000 words might be the usable maximum. Papers submitted to this track will not be considered for publication in the British Journal of Management.

3. New for Cardiff 2001, the **best paper** track will represent outstanding papers submitted specifically by authors who wish their conference paper to be considered for publication in the British Journal of Management. To be considered for review in the best paper track, papers must contain work of an exceptionally high quality and originality. Authors intending to have their paper considered for this track must provide a concise 60 word summary (in addition to an abstract), outlining why they consider their paper to be appropriate for consideration as a best conference paper and for review in the BJM. Papers accepted for this track will be subjected to a more stringent selection process, incorporating standard BJM review procedures and criteria.

Submission of a paper implies that it contains original work which has not been published previously, and that is not under consideration for publication elsewhere. A brief abstract of the paper (50-100 words) will also be required for inclusion in the programme.

Preparation of all manuscripts must conform to the BJM guidelines.

(These are ©Blackwell Publishers and can be found at their website: *http://www.blackwellpublishers.co.uk/asp/journal.asp?ref=1045-3172&src=sbm*)

Appendix 3. Editorial Guidelines – Journal of Marketing Management

In accordance with its policy, the *Journal of Marketing Management* welcomes contributions from theoreticians and practitioners in the following areas:

- **State of the art papers on particular topics**
e.g. portfolio planning, sales management, pricing

- **Management of the marketing mix**
the practical issues of managing product, price, place and promotion efficiently and effectively

- **Customer behaviour**
how and why both corporate and ultimate customers behave in the way they do

- **Marketing intelligence**
the establishment and maintenance of marketing information systems and everything associated with them

- **Case studies**
how an organization has tackled an important marketing problem

- **Meta marketing**
how marketing ideas and techniques are applied to the less- or non-traditional areas of services, public and non-profit organizations

In addition to these core areas the journal also attracts
- Marketing education and training papers
- Conference reports and commentaries
- Books reviews and abstracts
- Letters

Submissions (3 copies) should be of 4000-6000 words (excluding display material and references) typed double-spaced on A4 paper. The first page should consist of the title, authors' names, addresses and an indication of author for correspondence with his/her telephone/fax number. The second page should comprise an abstract of the paper (c. 150 words) and a biography (c. 150 words) detailing the authors' background, affiliations and interests. Display material must be numbered, captioned and cited in the text. Authors should avoid identifying themselves in the main body of the text.

References

References are indicated in the text by either "Recent work (Wensley 2000, 1999; Katsikeas et al. 2000)"   or "Recently Wensley (2000) has found ..". All such references should then be listed in alphabetical order at the end of the paper in accordance with the following conventions:

1.Books
Baker, Michael J. and Hart, Susan J. (1998), *Product Strategy and Management,* London, Prentice Hall Europe

2. Journal Articles

O'Malley, L. and Tynan, C. (1999), "The Utility of the Relationship Metaphor in Consumer Markets: A Critical Evaluation", *Journal of Marketing Management*, Vol. **15**, No. 7, pp. 587-602

3. Contributions in books, proceedings, etc.

Kotler, Philip and Andreasen, Alan R. (1999), "Strategic marketing for non-profit organisations". In: *The IEBM Encyclopedia of Marketing* (Ed.) Baker, Michael J., London, Thomson Learning, pp. 668-681

Copyright offprints: Authors submitting a manuscript do so on the understanding that if it is accepted for publication, copyright in the paper exclusive shall be assigned to the Publisher. In consideration of the assignment of copyright a PDF of the paper and a copy of the *Journal* will be supplied to each author. Further reprints may be ordered at extra cost, The Publisher will not put any limitations on the personal freedom of the author to use material contained in the paper in other works. Papers are accepted for the Journal on the understanding that they have not been or will not be published elsewhere in the same form, in any language.

Manuscripts on Disc

When supplying the **final** version of your article please include a disc of your manuscript prepared on PC- compatible or Apple Macintosh computers along with **one** hard copy print-out. 3.5" sized discs, CDs, 100MB Iomega Zip Discs and most word processing packages are acceptable, although any version of Microsoft Word or Wordperfect is preferred.

Please follow these guidelines carefully

- Include **one** copy of the word processed article in its original format (e.g. Word), including figures and tables.

- Also include an .rtf copy of the file (Rich Text Format), with all the diagrams etc. included. If the article includes a figure which is a photograph, or a particularly complex illustration, this should be saved in a separate .tif file. All diagrams and figures should be in black and white.   If prepared on an Apple, include the file in ASCII format.

- Ensure that the files are not saved as read-only.

- Manuscripts prepared on discs must be accompanied by one hard copy, including all figures, printed with double spacing and which may be used if setting from the disc proves impracticable.

- Ensure the final version of the hard copy and the file on disc are the same. It is the author's responsibility to ensure complete compatibility. If there are differences the hard copy will be used.

- The directives for preparing the paper in the style of the journal as set out in the Instructions to Authors must be followed; i.e. ensure the document is in the following order: Title; Authors; Addresses; Abstract; Running heads; Introduction; Materials and methods; Results; Discussion; Acknowledgements; References; Appendices; Figure legends; Tables; Footnotes; Abbreviations.

- The operating system and the word processing software used to produce the article should be noted on the disc (e.g. Win XP/Word 2000), as well as all file names. The disc should be labelled with the journal reference number (if known) and author name(s).

- Do not include copyright material, e.g. word processing software or operating system files, on the disc because this can create difficulties with Customs clearance.

- Package floppy discs in such a way as to avoid damage in the post.

Additional points to note

- Use two carriage returns to end headings and paragraphs.
- Type text without end of line hyphenation, except for compound words.
- Do not use lower case "l" for "1" or "O" for "0". (They have different typesetting values.)
- Be consistent with punctuation and only insert a single space between words and after punctuation.
- Please include a list of any special characters you have had to use, e.g. Greek, maths.

Please note that all articles should be submitted to the Editor for review:

Professor Susan Hart
Editor, Journal of Marketing Management
Department of Marketing, University of Strathclyde
173 Cathedral Street
Glasgow, G4 0RQ, Scotland

All other enquiries and accepted papers and accompanying disks should be directed to:
Westburn Publishers Ltd
50 Campbell Street
Helensburgh, Argyll, G84 9NH, Scotland

All of this information and more can be found on our Website at:
http://www.westburn.co.uk

Appendix 4. Reviewers Guidelines AM/BAM
(Reproduced with permission from Dr Carolyn Strong, Conference Organiser)

Name
Address

Date

RE: Academy of Marketing Conference 2001

Dear

Thank you for agreeing to act as a paper reviewer for the AM 2001 Conference at Cardiff University.

Attached are the papers I would like you to review; along with the copy of the paper (which does not have to be returned) are a reviewer information sheet and a reviewer evaluation form. Please complete the reviewer evaluation form and fax it to Carolyn Strong on 029 20 XXXXXX or mail it by post to the above address.

I would appreciate the return of your review as soon as possible, but no later than 12 April 2001.

Many thanks for your time and input into the AM 2001 Conference.

Yours sincerely

Dr. Carolyn Strong
AM 2001 Conference Chair

Reviewer   _____

Paper Title   _____

Track	
Arts and Heritage Marketing	
Business to Business Marketing	
Consumer Behaviour and Consumer Marketing	
Cross-cultural Marketing	
Direct Marketing	
Electronic Marketing	
SIG's	
Ethics and Social Responsibility	
International Marketing and Export Marketing	

Marketing Communications and Promotion Strategy	
Marketing Education	
Marketing Research	
Marketing Strategy	
Relationship Marketing	
Retailing	
Sales Management	
Services Marketing	
Social Marketing, Not for Profit and Greener Marketing	

Reviewer Evaluation Form
Academy of Marketing Conference 2001
Cardiff Business School

Fax to: Dr Carolyn Strong 020 20XXXXXX

Paper Title:

1. To what extent is the problem formulation of the parameters of the research developed?

A Small Extent   **A Large Extent**
              1   2   3   4   5   6   7

2. To what extent does the literature review draw on previous theoretical and empirical studies?

A Small Extent   **A Large Extent**
              1   2   3   4   5   6   7

3. To what extent are data collection procedures rigorous and appropriate to the problem formation?

A Small Extent   **A Large Extent**
              1   2   3   4   5   6   7

4a. *CONCEPTUAL/THEORETICAL PAPERS.*

To what extent does this paper contribute to the development of the concept/theory within its area of research interest?

A Small Extent   **A Large Extent**
              1   2   3   4   5   6   7
4b. *EMPIRICAL PAPERS:*

To what extent will the acceptance of this paper contribute to the presence of a broad variety of methodological approaches and research issues at the conference?

A Small Extent   **A Large Extent**

         1   2   3   4   5   6   7

5. To what extent is this paper likely to stimulate research in the future?

A Small Extent   **A Large Extent**

         1   2   3   4   5   6   7

6.   Would you recommend this papers to be considered for a conference 'best paper' award? (Please tick)

Yes	No

Overall Recommendation (please tick):

Accept without revision	
Accept subject to minor revisions (as outlined below)	
Accept subject to major revisions (as outlined below)	
Reject	

Please state below any comments you wish to make about this paper which may be used as a basis for revision of the paper:

Please return to: Dr Carolyn Strong, AM 2001 Conference Chair Cardiff Business School.

Appendix 5. Reviewers Forms – Journal of Marketing Management

Reviewer: _____

Date: _____

Title: _____

The enclosed manuscript has been submitted to the *Journal of Marketing Management*. I would greatly appreciate you reviewing this for us. We aim to provide authors with a timely response and thus would appreciate having your review by (Insert Date Here)

If it is not possible to complete the review by this date, could you please return the manuscript and telephone me so that I can make alternative arrangements.

Thank you for your assistance. Please send your review to the Editor:

Professor Susan Hart
Department of Marketing, University of Strathclyde
173 Cathedral Street, Glasgow G4 0RQ, Scotland

Summary Evaluation

1.   Please indicate your opinion of the manuscript in terms of:

	Excellent	Good	Average	Poor	Not applicable
Originality	☐	☐	☐	☐	☐
Conceptual Development	☐	☐	☐	☐	☐
Readability	☐	☐	☐	☐	☐
Managerial Implications	☐	☐	☐	☐	☐
Research Method	☐	☐	☐	☐	☐

2.   What is your general evaluation of the manuscript?

Excellent	Good	Average	Poor	Belongs Elsewhere
☐	☐	☐	☐	☐

3.   What is your publication recommendation?

Accept in   Accept with   Accept with   Reject
present form   minor alterations major alterations

☐   ☐   ☐   ☐

Please detail necessary alterations on the next page.

Please note here comments intended for the Editors only:

```



```

Please type your comments concerning specific reasons regarding your recommendation, and identify those revisions necessary to make the manuscript suitable for publication.

```
(Full A4 page given for this)



```

CHAPTER 15

Making a Presentation

Synopsis
Although it is frequently said that "The pen is mightier than the sword" the spoken word is much more commonplace. It is also more likely to have an immediate impact on more people than written communication. Indeed, in societies with low levels of literacy, spoken communication may be the only effective means of mass communication. Further, with the development of broadcast media and telecommunications it is now possible for a single speaker to address an audience of millions simultaneously. It is for these, and many other reasons, that effective oral communication is considered an essential skill in most walks of life, and nowhere more so than in academic and business communities.

In this chapter we outline some of the important factors to be borne in mind in preparing and delivering an effective oral presentation. While the primary emphasis is upon structure and content, reference is also made to the use of audio-visual aids, the actual delivery and the handling of questions.

Keyword
Presentations; structure; content; audio-visual aids; delivery

---

Introduction

In the Beginning ...

When preparing an oral presentation (hereafter simply a 'presentation') two basic scenarios may be encountered. First, one has prepared a written report and has been asked to present it orally to a specific audience. Second, one has been invited to make a presentation on a specified theme to a specified audience. In the first case one already has a structure and content; in the second the proverbial blank sheet of paper!

In the previous chapter we offered advice on the structure and organisation of written reports. While this was intended primarily for students preparing theses and dissertations the same advice is generally applicable to persons making written reports for other purposes. The key points will be repeated here as the same advice is also relevant to persons preparing an oral presentation *de novo* as, invariably, one will need to prepare a written draft or script to ensure that the presentation covers the essential points in a logical and interesting way within the time limits set down.

Like Caesar's Gaul, all effective communication may be divided into three parts – the *beginning, middle* and *end*. In primary school, when being told how to write our first essay, the teacher will stress the importance of following this structure. And, in telling us, the teacher will usually:

Tell us what they are going to tell us;
Tell us, and
Tell us what they have told us.

In other words, there should be an introduction or agenda informing us what is the subject of the communication and how it is to be developed. Next, there is the communication itself – that which the communicator wishes to convey to us and, presumably, what it is we came to hear about. Finally, there is a summary reminding us of the key points made, and the conclusion the speaker wishes us to draw from the presentation.

While all presentations should conform to this basic structure, depending upon the circumstances the *length* of a presentation will vary enormously. Doctoral theses often have a word limit of 80,000 words and Master's dissertations a limit of 20,000 words. A major textbook may well have half a million words or more! Lectures are rarely more than an hour long and conference presentations 15 to 20 minutes. Obviously, the number of words or time limit is a major determinant of the scope and content of a presentation. Further, with an oral presentation one cannot set it aside and come back to it later, nor refer back to remind oneself of an earlier point that has a bearing on new information. Indeed the rule of thumb for a 'presentation' is that it should contain no more than *five* pieces of information.

This advice is derived from two important and related concepts – the *attention span* and *short-term memory*. According to Foxall et al. (1998) "In psychological terms, *attention* refers to the amount of mental effort or cognitive capacity allocated by an individual to the stimulus environment or task in hand." (80). To begin with it is reasonable to assume that persons being addressed will pay attention to a communication. But, if the communication is not sufficiently interesting to hold their attention then other stimuli – both internal and external – are likely to distract them so that effective communication ceases to occur. The longer a presentation, the more difficult it becomes to retain the audiences' attention.

The main reason that one's attention begins to wander is that the short-term memory can hold only a limited number of bits of information before it begins to suffer from overload. To make room for new, incoming information it has to discard some of the existing content, either by sending it to long-term memory, from which it may be recovered later, or by rejecting the information altogether. According to research by Miller (1956) the short-term memory has a capacity of between five and nine bits of information with seven – the 'magic number' – representing the average. It is probably for this reason that experienced presenters suggest that one confine a presentation to five key points or issues as this should be within the information processing capacity of all members of an audience. Of course this assumes your bits of information are more interesting than other available stimuli!

The recommendation that a 'presentation' contain five bits of information is echoed by Chad Perry's advice on the writing of a five chapter PhD (2000). According to Perry there are five major parts in a PhD each of which will be the subject of at least one chapter, namely:

The Introduction
Literature Review
Methodology
Findings and Results
Conclusions and Recommendations

As we shall see, most academic presentations will need to address the same five issues. It is also apparent that the introduction will outline what the presentation is about while the conclusions will remind us what the presentation was about. The remaining three elements are the heart of the presentation and should cover:

1. What is already known about the subject and what it is desired to know in addition to this?
2. The methods and techniques used to acquire the information necessary to fill the perceived 'gap'.
3. The scope and nature of the actual information acquired and the interpretation to be placed upon it.

From this brief review it is clear that our presentation should comprise *five* elements organised into *three* parts – introduction or agenda, the substance or subject matter, and the summary – and our blank sheet of paper should be divided into three sections with approximately 10% of the space for both introduction and summary and **80%** for the subject itself.

If you already have a written report then you can disaggregate it into the three sections. If you haven't then we will have to begin by addressing **four** main questions (you should also bear these in mind if you have already prepared a written report as the guide as to what to include and what to leave out.) These questions are:

1. What is the topic or subject to be presented?
2. To whom. I.e. who will comprise the intended audience?
3. With what objective in mind?
4. Within what constraints in terms of Time, Place, available Aids etc.?

We will deal with each of these in turn.

The topic

If you have been invited to make a presentation there is an implicit assumption that you know something about the subject and that this is worth listening to because this knowledge is not widely known. Alternatively, the subject matter may be familiar, but you are offering a new or different interpretation of it. Yet a third scenario is that, as someone who has written authoritatively about the subject, the audience is keen to listen to the pearls of wisdom from the author him/herself (few of us achieve this 'guru' status!)

There is, of course, yet another scenario – you don't know much about the subject but have been selected to research it and present your findings. Those of you preparing student assignments will be familiar with this situation.

In all cases you will have been given a word or phrase that defines the subject matter on which you have been invited to speak. For the purpose of this paper let us assume the subject is 'Market Segmentation'. If your name is Hooley, Saunders or Piercy then you fall into the 'guru' category as you have written a definitive text book on the subject, and your problem is going to one of data reduction – how to select from all you know that limited subset of information that best answers the other three questions posed above. If you work for a market research company that has just developed a new technique, then it is likely that it is this that you are expected to talk about. For most of us it will be a question of establishing what is known about market segmentation, and then researching and selecting those parts that satisfy the other three questions. However, in order to satisfy the first requirement of 'telling what you are going to tell', the best way to start is by defining just what your presentation on Market Segmentation' is going to cover. To do so it will be helpful to offer a generic definition – preferably from an established and well-known authority – and then any qualification you wish to make to describe the intended scope of your treatment. Thus, Kotler (2000) offers the view that:

> Market segmentation represents an effort to increase a company's targeting precision. (Kotler 2000)

Actually, this is not a very helpful place to start. It doesn't tell you what market segmentation is and it invokes another concept that you may or may not know anything about – targeting. Sorry Phil!

The *Westburn Dictionary of Marketing* (available **free** at *www.themarketingdictionary.com*) is rather more helpful when it tells us that:

> ...the concept of market segmentation rests upon recognition of a differentiated demand for a product, while its use as a marketing tool depends upon identification of the most appropriate variable or variables with which to subdivide total demand into economically viable segments.

On the other hand, you may prefer to go back to the original source, which first identified market segmentation as an alternative to a strategy of product differentiation. This view had dominated thinking for decades since the Industrial Revolution and the introduction of mass production. In a seminal article published in 1956 Wendell Smith specified the primary features of a 'production orientation' and its strategy of product differentiation, which is "concerned with the bending of demand to the will of supply. It is an attempt to shift or to change the slope of the demand curve for the market offering of an individual supplier". By contrast market segmentation reflects the sovereignty of the customer, the marketing concept and a marketing orientation in that "*Segmentation* is based upon developments on the demand side of the market and represents a rational and more precise adjustment of product and marketing effort to consumer or user requirements". Simply put, market segmentation is concerned with identifying groups of consumers with similar tastes and preferences who differ in these requirements from other groups of customers, and for whom it is worthwhile developing a differentiated product or service that meets their needs precisely. If this makes sense, then the problem, as usual, is 'How do I do that?' Presumably, this is one of the things your audience will wish to know.

The audience

If you have read the preceding paragraphs about market segmentation carefully, and you subscribe to the marketing concept, then it is clear that your potential success in making an effective presentation will depend heavily on putting these ideas into practice. If we can pre-identify the specific interests and information needs of the intended audience then we should design our presentation to satisfy these. Are these volunteers or pressed men? Do they really want to be there or has someone told them to attend? How much, if anything, are they likely to know about the subject already and how interesting/important is the subject to them? As advised in previous chapters, we should apply the 'Kipling Test' and remind ourselves that there are six basic questions that call for an answer – who, what, why, where, how and when?

It will be helpful if you write down your answers to these six questions and keep referring to your list as you develop your presentation, and as a final check before you deliver it. If you can summarise the answers into a pen portrait of the audience, so much the better.

Where the subject of your presentation has been spelled out clearly in advance, and attendance is voluntary, you may be lucky and attract a homogeneous audience. Otherwise, it is unlikely that a single pen portrait will describe all the members of your audience and you will have to decide who is the primary audience for whom the presentation is mainly intended, and what interests are represented by the remainder; and how you can try to meet these without compromising your dominant theme. To solve this dilemma it will be useful to consider the third point …

The objective

Obviously, the objective of a presentation will depend upon the needs of the audience and the purpose of the presenter. Suppose that one is preparing an introductory lecture to introduce the topic to persons with little or no prior knowledge of it. In this case the objective(s) might be stated as:

1. Definition of the concept of market segmentation.
2. Overview of the main bases for segmenting markets – demographics, geo-demographics, preferences, benefits, social character, social grading, industrial and international.
3. Methods for segmenting markets.
4. The selection and use of segmentation techniques.
5. When *not* to segment.

For a more advanced class, or executive development seminar, the focus might be on a specific technique such as perceptual mapping, in which case our objectives might be:

1. Definition of perceptual mapping.
2. The use of perceptual mapping in strategic marketing planning.
3. Qualitative and quantitative approaches
   - Visual product mapping
   - Attribute profiling methods
   - Multidimensional positioning analysis
     KYST
     Kelly Grids
     Cluster analysis
     PREFMAP
     MDPREF
4. Selecting the 'ideal' segment.

And, for an even more specialised presentation, one might focus on just one of the techniques identified under point 3.

However, while the detailed objectives will vary considerably, all should begin with a definition of the topic to be dealt with, followed by a listing of the objectives which constitute the agenda or Table of Contents for the presentation. As to what is feasible, then we must answer the fourth of our original questions …

What constraints apply?

In addition to the needs of the audience, their existing state of knowledge and the desired objectives to be achieved, a number of other physical constraints will have to be taken into account. Of these the most demanding is the actual *time* available.

Initially, most inexperienced speakers wonder how on earth they are going to find sufficient to say to occupy the time allocated to them. However, once they begin to develop an outline for their presentation, and collect material the problem tends to become "how on earth can I fit all this into the time available?" We will return to this issue below, when discussing the Content in more detail.

The *size* of audience is also an important factor to be taken into account when preparing your presentation. As a rule of thumb, the larger the audience the more formal your presentation will have to be, and the greater the use of audio-visual aids. It follows that you need to establish what is the expected audience size, what kind of room will the presentation be made in, and what facilities will be available?

When the audience is small it may also be necessary to prepare quite a formal presentation, e.g. a report of work done for a sponsor, a conference paper, an executive briefing. But, with a small audience, it is much more likely that the audience will want to interact with the speaker, ask questions etc. Such audiences are also more likely to expect a copy or summary of your presentation, often distributed in advance of it. Clearly, these expectations present their own challenges, and a formal lecture to 500 first year undergraduates may well appear much simpler once you have overcome the initial stage fright. We offer some tips for dealing with interactive audiences later in the chapter. First, we must decide what to include in our presentation, in other words the content.

Content

In the introduction we suggested two possible scenarios – you have a paper or written report and need to convert it into a presentation; or you have been asked to prepare a presentation from scratch. In the first case most of your effort will consist of eliminating the 'padding' used in written communications to lend emphasis, provide continuity and link new points to old ones. In the second case, your first task will be to write a report! However, if you have taken the steps recommended earlier, you should have a much clearer idea of what is expected of you, and not have to cater for the needs of a heterogeneous and totally self-selecting audience that might constitute the readership of a written communication. Accordingly, your research and data collection should be much more focused and selective. However, you should still follow the advice relevant to the development of a written communication discussed in Chapter 14.

Two aphorisms summarise succinctly the best advice for anyone embarking on a new venture:

> Look before you leap
> Time spent in reconnaissance is seldom wasted

While there is always a great temptation to rush into activity, experience shows that thinking things through before taking action almost always leads to a better end result. This belief is reflected in the observation that problem definition can account for as much as 90 per cent of problem solving. Only by establishing clearly and precisely what is required can we define what needs to be done to achieve the desired outcome. Thus, our 'Objectives' for a first year undergraduate lecture on Market Segmentation was based upon a review of the contents pages of some of the leading introductory marketing textbooks that have been widely adopted for such courses. This examination revealed a high level of agreement on both the key topics, and the sequence in which to present them. Accordingly, this served to define both the scope and structure for our presentation. The body of knowledge is well established and well known; the presenter's role is to communicate this in a clear and interesting manner using examples familiar to the audience of students to help reinforce the points being made, and encourage further independent exploration of the subject by them.

The above example describes a situation where the presenter is helping to transfer 'old' information to a 'new' audience. Our second scenario is where the presenter has 'new' knowledge and a 'new' audience. In order to express new ideas clearly one should ask, and provide answers to the following questions:

1. What is the issue or topic to be addressed?
2. Who is likely to be interested in it? (Remember the pen portrait).
3. What benefits will they gain –i.e. 'What's in it for me?
4. What did you do? Why?
5. What new knowledge, insight or explanation has emerged?
6. What implications do your findings have for future practice, research?
7. What, if anything, needs to be done now?

Obviously, the amount of material necessary to answer each of these questions will depend very much on issues raised earlier, such as the size and composition of the audience, their state of prior knowledge, time available etc. For example, if you are presenting an academic paper then, in answering Question 1, you will need to establish your familiarity with the subject and earlier work by citing the work of others active in the field. On the other hand, if you are making a report on a problem you have investigated that is already familiar to your audience, a simple statement of the known problem will probably suffice.

To begin with, Jennifer and Mike Rotondo (2002) recommend that one perform a "Brain Dump" which they define as "The act of getting out into the open everything you know about something. In terms of preparing for a presentation, the brain dump would include whatever your participants should already know about the subject, what they need to get from your presentation, how they are going to use what you present, what's likely to interest them, and what questions they might have," (14). Of course, you must not take 'everything' literally – keywords will do. The aim is to see what raw materials you have so that you can begin to develop clear-cut answers to the questions set out above. Where gaps appear, then further research is called for. The Rotondo's also suggest that in collecting content you should organise it into two categories – Need-to-know and Nice-to-know. The 'Need-to-know' information will appear in the presentation, and will probably form the basis of any visual aids or notes to be circulated to participants. The 'Nice-to-know' information is just that. It is useful to flesh out the key need-to-know points, to demonstrate your command of the topic, meet the needs/interests of the audience etc. It will be included in your own script or notes, but not in the materials given to participants.

Once the raw materials have been collected and classified the next step is to prepare an **Outline.**

Outlines

The outline is the skeleton that will determine the form and structure of the presentation. The Rotondo's suggest three main outline styles in common use, and four others that might be appropriate, namely:

- **Chronological**
- **Narrative** (story telling)
- **Problem/solution**
- **Cause/effect**
- **Topical** – divides the topic into several sub-topics
- **Journalistic questions** – answers Kipling's questions
- **Spatial** – follows a linear logic based on location, direction and space

The five Objectives listed earlier for a presentation on Market Segmentation also constitute an outline. They also satisfy the recommendation that a presentation should contain only five key points as this is all an audience is likely to remember. But, bearing in mind the earlier discussion of attention and short-term memory, this advice should not be taken at face value. Several reasons support this view.

To begin with while you may have an opinion on five key points this does not mean that they correspond with everyone else's view of what the five key points should be. While it may be true that if you offer ten key points only five will be remembered, it is probable that different people will have quite different lists of the five that are important for them. Hence, you should build some redundancy into your presentation. Similarly, each key point may provide a 'peg' on which to hang a series of sub-topics each of which may also cover a number of points. The balance between insufficient information and overload is a delicate one, but it is better to have too much material than too little. You can always leave something out, but ad hoc improvisation can seriously compromise a formal presentation.

Once you are satisfied with your outline then you can assign the content from your 'brain dump', or the written document and other sources, to the appropriate heading/sub-heading. Remember to cluster your material in terms of what the audience needs to know, and what it might be nice to know if time permits. You now have the substance from which to craft your **Script.**

Scripts

Reading from a prepared script can be an extremely boring business – particularly for the audience! In most cases the audience would prefer to have the script and read it themselves. Yet the paradox is that, however spontaneous they may appear, most oral presentations are word-perfect deliveries of pre-prepared scripts. So, other things being equal, it is not the script that comes between a presenter and an audience, it is the quality of the delivery. We return to this later. The first task is to ensure that we have a quality script.

In the previous chapter we summarised Sharp and Howard's 'Rules for Writing' as follows:

1. **Plan.** You should develop a detailed outline first to ensure that your material will be presented in a logical and coherent way.
2. **Introduce.** Tell the intended reader what your purpose and objectives are, and how you intend to achieve them in a formal Introduction.
3. **Motivate.** Make clear what benefits the reader will gain if they read the paper. It is a cliché but true that you only have one opportunity to make a first impression. Some people (examiners, reviewers) have to read your work even if it is dull and uninteresting, but the rest of the world doesn't.
4. **Hold.** Maintain interest by concentrating on substantive issues and don't allow yourself to be distracted by lacunae.
5. **Discuss.** Demonstrate how the points you are making are relevant to your purpose and objectives, as set out in the Introduction.
6. **Break.** Use headings and sub-headings to break up the text into manageable 'bites'.
7. **Illustrate.** Use graphics to present complex data.
8. **Illuminate.** Give examples to reinforce the argument.

9. **Summarise.** Remind the reader of the key issues with which you have dealt, and any conclusions and recommendations arising from them.

10. **Conclude.** Indicate how your findings may be used in practice, and any new issues that deserve further research. (Adapted from Sharp and Howard, pp.224-5)

Assuming that you have followed this and the other advice offered here, you should now have a script for conversion into a presentation.

Conversion and delivery

Nearly all presentations contain a visual element. The most basic but often most compelling visual element is the presenter themself. Why otherwise do people watch television, go to the cinema or theatre? Unfortunately, few people who are called upon to make oral presentations possess the skills or personality of the professional performer and, to compensate, most of us use visual aids and props to make up for this. The challenge is to prevent the technology overwhelming the content.

This salutary lesson was brought home some years ago when delivering a module on an Executive MBA on a Saturday morning. The computer crashed, and with it all my carefully pre-prepared PowerPoint slides. In the absence of a technician there was nothing for it but to resort to 'chalk and talk'. At the end of the session the very well qualified and senior executives were kind enough to say it had been the most enjoyable session they had had in a long time. By comparison with the resources they had for developing high-powered, audio-visual shows most academic presentations were distinctly amateurish and homemade. In fact the audio-visual trappings detracted from the substance of the content. By contrast, having an academic 'create' diagrams and crude drawings in real time, while delivering his script was real theatre, and held their attention and involvement far better than a 'canned', 'here's one I made earlier' delivery.

Clearly, the message, once again, is that you must tailor your presentation to the needs of the audience. In a participative workshop type of environment, with well-prepared and motivated participants, a rigid structure with lots of slides is not the best approach (although they still wanted copies of handouts that went with a formal presentation!). If you were presenting your latest competitive paper at an Academic conference to your peers, you would be ill advised to think that you could do this without carefully selecting what you want to say, and supporting this with appropriate visual materials.

So, just what is 'appropriate'? The answer, I'm afraid, is "That depends". Probably the lowest common denominator/key-limiting factor of all the suggestions made so far is *time*. Clear speech could be anything between 120 and 180 words a minute – less is ponderous, more a 'gabble'. So take an average of 150 and multiply by the number of minutes available and you have your word limit. Now go to Tools and get the word count for your draft script – don't be surprised if it's way over the limit!

An alternative approach if you intend making extensive use of slides is to bear in mind the advice given by Rotondo:

No more than 2 slides per minute;
One concept per slide;
Use key words and phrases (noun and verb);
Stay within the 8 x 8 rule;
Make your bullet points consistent in structure;
Capitalise properly.

(The 8 x 8 rule means that you should have no more than 8 lines of text per slide and 8 words per line).

By applying this advice we come up with $2 \times 8 \times 8 = 128$ words a minute. While this might be OK for a spoken presentation, it would be a disaster if you tried to deliver 30 slides of this kind in 15 minutes. Given that your audience is literate, reading out the content of your slides will soon irritate and then alienate them. It is likely to be even worse if you try delivering an alternative text, while they are trying to read what is on the slides. It follows, that you should use slides in moderation – they are not intended as an autocue!

If restricted to Key points, text on a slide can be a useful aide-memoir for both the presenter and the audience. When used to summarise data in Tables, Graphs, Diagrams they can convey much more information, and more clearly than trying to describe the data without a visual aid. Similarly, illustrations photographs and video clips can all enliven a presentation in a way no amount of words can do.

Bearing in mind that an audience has come to hear the presenter, my own view is that slides should be used in moderation and only to summarise, emphasise and complement the speaker's text. It follows that unless you are a very experienced and accomplished speaker you need to **learn your script**. If you don't you are very likely to digress, extemporise, overlook something important and, worst of all, run out of time before you can bring the proceedings to the intended climax. I know – I've done it often!

By 'learning your script' I do not mean literally memorising it word for word, although this does help you get over the first couple of minutes when you will be feeling most under pressure. Rather, we need to memorise enough to ensure continuity without losing some appearance of spontaneity. Of course, if you give a presentation several times you will probably get to know it by heart, and also learn how to vary the delivery to achieve the most effect.

The best way to learn your script, and help commit it to memory is to rehearse. Rehearsal is important to get the timing right. If you have prepared a PowerPoint presentation with notes, then the first run through can be done at your computer, scrolling through the slides and speaking the script, while keeping a careful note of the elapsed time. Once you have done this a few times, and adjusted the content to fit the time allowed, then you should try to get a rehearsal in the actual location where the presentation is to be made, or one as similar to it as possible. Conference and other organisers will be able to tell you what kind of room you will be in and what audio visual aids are available.

On the day itself you definitely need to recce the actual room in which you will be performing. What kind of projector is to be used? Do you need to connect it to your laptop, or can you load your material onto the system's own hard drive? What controls are there? In many modern lecture theatres/conference suites you will find a podium with sufficient knobs and switches to launch a space shuttle. Find out what they are, and practice using them. If there is a technician supplied, ask for and take their advice. And, finally, if there is time, go through your presentation again using the actual facilities on site.

While natural ability is a godsend, all of us can improve our oral presentation with practice. Perhaps the first thing to do is see if you can get someone to video you actually delivering a presentation. (Most academic institutions offer this as part of the induction training offered to probationary lecturers. It is less common in my experience for research or other students who will be called on to make such presentations as part of their study programme). Viewing yourself in action can be a salutary experience, but one from which much can be learned.

Two aspects deserve particular attention – speech and gesture.

The Rotondos discuss four important voice qualities – volume, pitch, intonation and enunciation. If a room is wired for sound you should use the microphone – having tested beforehand how sensitive it is to movement. If the microphone cannot cope with movement, and you have to remain rooted to the spot, then you might try without it and get someone else to let you know if they can hear you clearly from different places in the room. Nowadays, however, most microphones can cope with a certain amount of movement. The pitch of your voice will also have an important bearing on how easy it is to hear you. Once again, you will need someone else to advise you what is most acceptable from the audience's point of view.

Intonation is important in giving emphasis: enunciation in ensuring clarity. Both can be improved with practice, and listening to tape recordings of you own voice will indicate where improvements can be made. (The help of a friend is also valuable. Apparently, I do not pronounce 'g's' on the ends of words – something of a liability for a Professor of Marketing – but I was completely unaware of this until someone else told me).

The analysis of speakers' effectiveness has confirmed that gesture is very important in enhancing the impact of the spoken word. While politicians, such as Bill Clinton and Tony Blair, have a repertoire of hand movements and facial expression to emphasise the point they are making, such movements may not be appropriate to presentations other than political speeches. Under different circumstances gestures may become a distraction and, if repeated frequently, an irritant. Tom Peters may get away with shambling round a stage – I wouldn't recommend you try it.

Remember it is the **content** of what you have to say that is of primary interest – all else is trappings that may or may not add value.

Interactive or not?

An important consideration with any presentation is if, and when, to take questions. Whatever your decision, you should make it clear in your opening statement what the ground rules are.

Taking questions as they occur to the audience can break up the flow and totally destroy your carefully prepared time schedule. On the other hand, a question may indicate a fundamental misunderstanding of what it is you are trying to say, and call for immediate correction. Probably the best solution to this dilemma is to tell the audience that you will be pleased to take questions at the **end** of your presentation, **unless** there is something of vital importance that cannot wait. By emphasising that an interruption must be of 'vital importance' most members of the audience will wait until the end before asking a question.

Questions usually fall into one of two categories – those that you are dreading and those to which there is a simple answer. Now, if you are dreading a question it suggests that you can anticipate it – if you can, then perhaps you should try and head it off by incorporating the answer to it in the original presentation. If not, then you should prepare an answer in advance and hope you may not have to use it!

Anticipating possible questions is an important part of preparing a presentation. Indeed, trying to anticipate what an audience would like to know about a topic should be part of your initial research and inform the selection of the content. If you are presenting 'old' knowledge to a 'new' audience – e.g. a lecture – then questions may occur on any part of it. However, if you know your stuff, answering such questions should not be too much of a problem. But, if you don't know the answer to a question then admit it. You could ask your audience if any of them know the answer, or offer to find out if you can and contact the questioner with the answer later. Don't prevaricate – things will only get worse, and put in question the validity of everything else you've said.

Where you are presenting 'new' information then it is this that is likely to prompt questions. Again, you should try and anticipate these, and prepare answers. For example, you will probably only have presented your most important findings. If so prepare some slides/notes covering the less important outcomes, and have them ready.

An important 'trick of the trade' when fielding questions is always to repeat the question. This serves several purposes. First, the audience may not have been listening as intently as you, so this gives you the opportunity to tell them what you believe the question to be, i.e. the one which you are going to answer. This also provides you with an opportunity to rephrase a question in terms you can answer, or to defuse it if it is hostile! Second, it allows the questioner to clarify or restate the question if they think you have misunderstood them. And, third, it gives you a few seconds of precious thinking time.

If no one has any questions you may wish to encourage them, especially if you have allowed time for feedback. You could say something to the effect that   "In my opinion the big question is ....."   "What do you think?" Or "Where do you think we might go from here?" On the other hand, you may sense everyone is as keen for a break as you are so, thank them for their attention, and leave while you are in front.

Summary

In this chapter we have addressed some of the more important issues to be taken into account when preparing an oral presentation. To begin with we identified two possible scenarios. First, you have written up a report or other formal document, such as a thesis or dissertation, and have been asked to make an oral presentation of this to a defined audience. Second, you have been asked to make a presentation on a specific topic, but will have to prepare this from scratch. In the first case we are going to have to reduce a possibly voluminous written document into a short, and highly focused series of points; in the second we are going to have to prepare a script from which to develop the presentation.

All presentations should be divided into three parts – a beginning, middle and end. We need; briefly, to tell the audience what we are going to tell them – the subject of our presentation. Then, occupying about 80 percent of the total time available, there is the middle, which contains the substance of what we want to communicate, and, finally, like this, there is a short review of the key points to remind the audience what these were.

The content of a presentation should be restricted to about **five** main points; otherwise we are likely to exceed both the interest and attention span of the listeners. However, we suggested that as it is unlikely each member of an audience will have exactly the same interests, or information needs, as every other, then some redundancy should be built in. Specific advice was offered as to how you might do this.

Stress was laid on the importance of preparing a clear **Outline** based on the perceived needs of your audience, i.e. what is it they have come to hear about? Ideally, this should comprise our five or more key points organised into our three sections. Then, each of the key points should be amplified by a series of sub-headings or points necessary to explain and reinforce them. Subsequently, if you are preparing audio-visual aids, these are likely to be the key elements of such aids.

The Outline also forms the basis for our **Script.** In our view preparation of a written script is essential. Only by doing this can we ensure that we will take maximum advantage of the time available. Scripts are not for reading from (unless you are making a radio broadcast!), they should be memorised and rehearsed until you can deliver them spontaneously. If the worst comes to the worst and you dry up, then they are there to get you back on track.

Once you have refined your script, then you have to consider how you are going to deliver it – who will be in the audience, what are their expectations, how much time have you got, where will the presentation take place etc.? Most presentations will benefit from the use of visual aids, but it was recommended that too many may distract rather than inform your audience.

Finally, we looked briefly at the question of audience participation and the handling of questions.

While very few of us will achieve the presence or delivery we take for granted in top actors and actresses, we can do a great deal to ensure that our oral presentations are effective. Preparation, rehearsal and practice will go a long way towards achieving the desired outcome – an interested and satisfied audience.

Recommendations for further reading

Perry, Chad (2000), "Presenting a Thesis", *www.literaticlub.co.uk/writing/ theses.html*
Comprehensive discussion of the 'Five chapter PhD' and writing up

Riley, Michael, Wood, Roy C., Clark, Mona A., Wilkie, Eleanor and Szivas, Edith (2000), *Researching and Writing Dissertations in Business and Management,* London: Thomson Learning
Contains a Chapter on 'The oral presentation of dissertation findings'

McCarthy, Patsy and Hatcher, Caroline (2002), *Presentation Skills*, London: Sage Publications
A guide for students combining practical tips and case studies

Rotondo, Jennifer and Rotondo, Mike Jr. (2002), *Presentation Skills for Managers,* New York: McGraw-Hill
Offers lots of practical advice on preparation and delivery, including the use of PowerPoint

References

Agre, P. E. (2001), "Infrastructure and institutional change in the networked university", *Information, Communication and Society*, Vol. **3**, No. 4, pp.494-507

Alexander, J. E. and Tate, M. A. (1999), *Web Wisdom: how to evaluate and create information quality on the web*, Mahwah, NJ/London: Lawrence Erlbaum Associates

Alreck, Pamela L. and Settle, Robert B. (1985), *The Survey Research Handbook*, Homewood, Ill: Richard D. Irwin

Antilla, Mai, Van Den Heuvel, Rob and Mollor, Kristian (1980), "Conjoint Measurement for Marketing Management", *European Journal of Marketing*, Vol. **14**, No. 7, pp.397-408

Atkinson, R. and Flint, J. (2003), "Sampling, snowball: accessing hidden and hard-to-reach populations", pp.274-280 In: Miller, R.L. and Brewer, J. D. (Eds.), *The A-Z of Social Research: a dictionary of key social science research projects*, London: Sage Publications Ltd

Bachmann, D. and Elfrink, J. (1996), "Tracking the progress of e-mail versus snail-mail", *Marketing Research*, Vol. **8**, No. 2, pp.31-35

Baker, Michael J. (2003), *The Marketing Book*, 5th Edition, Oxford: Butterworth - Heinemann

Baker, Michael J. (2002), "A Composite Model of Buyer Behaviour", *Journal of Customer Behaviour*, Vol. **1**, No. 1, pp.85-109

Baker, Michael J. (2000), *Marketing Strategy and Management*, London: Macmillan

Baker, Michael J. (1999), *The IEBM Encyclopaedia of Marketing*, London: Thomson Learning

Baker, Michael J. (1995), *Marketing: Theory and Practice*, 3rd Edition, Basingstoke: Macmillan

Baker, Michael J. (1975), *Marketing New Industrial Products*, London: Macmillan

Baker, Michael J. and Hart, Susan, J. (1989), *Marketing and Competitive Success*, Oxford: Philip Allen

Baker, Michael J. and Hart, Susan J. (1998), *Product Strategy and Management*, Hemel Hempstead: Prentice Hall

Barzun, Jacques and Graff, Henry F. (1977), *The Modern Researcher*, 3rd Edition, New York: Harcourt Brace Jovanovich Inc

Bell, C. (1969), "A Note on Participant Observation", *Sociology*, Vol. **3**, pp.417-18

Black, J. A. and Champion, D. J. (1976), *Methods and Issues in Social Research*, New York: John Wiley

Blaikie, Norman, (2003), *Analyzing Quantitative Data*, London: Sage Publications Ltd

Blaikie, Norman, (2000), *Designing Social Research,* Cambridge: Polity Press

Blaxter, Loraine, Hughes, Christina and Tight, Malcolm (1996), *How to Research,* Buckingham: Open University Press

Blois, Keith (2000), *The Oxford Textbook of Marketing,* Oxford: Oxford University Press

Bonoma, T.V. (1985), "Case Research in Marketing: Opportunities, Problems, and a Process", *Journal of Marketing Research,* Vol. **22**, No. 2, pp.199-208

Bosnjak, M. and Tuten, T. L. (2001), "Classifying response behaviours in web based surveys", *Journal of Computer Mediated Communications,* Vol. **6**, No.3

Bradley, N. (1999), "Sampling for Internet surveys. An examination of respondent selection for Internet research", *Journal of the Market Research Society,* Vol. **41**, No. 4, pp.387-395

Brook, L. (1978), "Postal Survey Procedures", Chapter 7, in Hoinville, Gerald and Jowell, Roger, *Survey Research Practice,* London: Heinemann Educational Books

Brown, Robert (1995), "Write Right First Time", *www.literaticlub.co.uk/writing/articles/write.html*

Brown, S. (1988), "Information seeking, external search and 'Shopping' behaviour", *Journal of Marketing Management,* Vol. **4**, No. 1, pp.33-49

Brown, S. (1987), "Drop and collect Surveys: A Neglected Research Technique", *Marketing Intelligence and Planning,* Vol. 5, No. 1

Bryman, Alan (2001), *Social Research Methods,* Oxford: Oxford University Press

Burton, Mary C. and Walther, Joseph B. (2001), "The Value of Web Log Data in Use-Based Design and Testing", *Journal of Computer Mediated Communication,* Vol. **6**, No. 3, *http://www.ascusc.org/jcmc/vol6/issue3/burton.html* downloaded 8 May 2002

Hines, C. (2000), *Virtual Ethnography,* London: Sage Publications Ltd

Campbell, D. T. and Stanley, J. C. (1966), *Experimental and Quasi-experimental Design for Research,* Chicago: Rand McNally

Carson, D. Gilmore, A., Perry, C. and Gronhaug, K. (2001), *Qualitative Marketing Research,* London: Sage Publications Ltd

Censorware project web page, "Size of the Web: A dynamic essay for a dynamic medium" at *http://censorware.org/web_size/,* visited 19 May 2000

Churchill, Gilbert A. (1987), *Marketing Research – Methodological Foundations,* 4th Edition, New York: Holt, Rinehart and Winston

Claycamp, Henry J. (1974), "Correlation and Regression Methods", In: Ferber, Robert (Ed.), *Handbook of Marketing Research,* New York: McGraw-Hill

Cohen, M. R. and Nagel, E. (1934), *An Introduction to Logic and Scientific Method,* New York: Harcourt

Collins, M. (1972), *Consumer Market Research Handbook,* New York: McGraw-Hill

Converse, J. M. and Presser, S. (1986), *Survey Questions,* Beverley Hills: Sage

Publications Inc.

Coombes, Hilary (2001), *Research Using IT*, Basingstoke: Macmillan

Cooper, P. and Branthwaite, A. (1977), "Qualitative Technology: New Perspectives on Measurement and Meaning Through Qualitative Research", *Market Research Society Annual Conference*, March, pp.79-92

Cresswell, John W. (1998), *Qualitative Inquiry and Research Design: Choosing among Five Traditions*, Thousand Oaks, CA: Sage Publications Inc.

Cutts, Martin (1996), *Plain English Guide,* Oxford: Oxford University Press

Davis, Gordon B. and Parker, Clyde A. (1997), *Writing the Doctoral Dissertation,* Hauppauge, NY: Barron's Educational Series Inc

Day, Abby (2001), "How to Write Publishable Papers", *www.literaticlub.co.uk/ writing/publishable.html*

Day, Robert A. (1998), *How to Write and Publish a Scientific Paper*, 5th Edition, Cambridge: Cambridge University Press

De-Almeida, P. M. (1980), "A Review of Focus Groups Methodology", *European Research*, Vol. **8**, No. 3, pp.114-20

Desabie, J. (1966), *Theorie et practique des sondages*, Paris, Dunod

Desai, Philly (2002), "Methods Beyond Interviewing", Volume **3**, *Qualitative Market Research: Principle and Practice*, London: Sage Publications Ltd

Diamantopoulos, A. and Schlegelmilch, B. (1997), *Taking the Fear Out of Data Analysis*, London: Thomson Learning

Diani, M. and Eyerman, R. (Eds.) (1991), *Studying Collective Action*, London: Sage Publications Ltd

Dickens, J. (1982), "The Fresh Cream Cakes Market: The Use of Qualitative Research as part of a Consumer Research Program", In: Bradley, U. (Ed), *Applied Marketing and Social Research,* New York: Van Nostrand Reinhold, pp.4-43

Dillman, D. A. (2000), *Mail and Internet surveys: The tailored design method*, New York: John Wiley and Sons

Dillman, D., Totora, R. D., Conradt, J. and Bowker, D. (1998), "Influence of plain versus fancy design on response rates for web surveys", Paper presented at annual meeting of the American Statistical Association, Dallas, TX

Dooley, David (1990), *Social Research Methods*, 2nd Edition, Englewood Cliffs, NJ: Prentice-Hall (4th edition 2001)

Drakeford, John F. and Farbridge, Valerie (1986), "Interviewing and Field Control", In: Worcester R. and Downham J. (Eds.), *Consumer market research handbook, third edition*, London: McGraw-Hill, pp.147-166

Durkheim, Emile (1895), *The Rules of Sociological Method*

Dyer, W.G. Jr. and Wilkins, A.L. (1991), "Better Stories, Not Better Constructs, to Generate Better Theory: A Rejoinder to Eisenhardt", *Academy of Management Review*, Vol. **16**, No. 3, pp.613-619

Easterby-Smith, Mark, Thorpe, Richard and Lowe, Andy (1991), *Management*

Research, London: Sage Publications Ltd

Easton and Araujo, (1997), "Management research and literary criticism", *British Journal of Management*, Vol. **8**, No. 1, pp.99-106

Ebersole, S. (2002), "Uses and Gratifications of the Web among Students", *Journal of Computer Mediated Communication*, Vol. **6**, No. 1, *http://www. ascusc.org/jcmc/vol6/issue1/ebersole.html* downloaded 25 February 2002

Ehrenberg, A.S.C. (1963), "Some Queries to Factor Analysis", *The Statistician*, Vol. **13**, No. 4

Eisenhardt, K. M. (1991), "Better Stories and Better Constructs: The Case for Rigor and Comparative Logic", *Academy of Management Review*, Vol. **16**, No. 3, pp.620-627

Eisenhardt, K. M. (1989), "Building Theories from Case Study Research", *Academy of Management Review*, Vol. **14**, No. 4, pp.532-550

Evans, F.B. (1959), "Psychological and Objective Factors in the Prediction of Brand Choice: Ford verses Chevrolet", *Journal of Business*, Vol. **32**, No. 4, October, pp.340-369

Evans, Paul (1995), "The Peer Review Process", *www.literaticlub.co.uk/ writing/articles/peerreview.html*

Everitt, Brian (1974), *Cluster Analysis,* London: Heinemann

Fahad, G. A. (1986), "Group Discussions: A Misunderstood Technique", *Journal of Marketing Management*, Vol. 1, No. 3, pp.315-27

Fisher, David and Hanstock, Terry, *Citing References,* 4th Edition, Nottingham: Library and Information Services, Nottingham Trent University

Fowler, H.W. (1994), *Modern English Usage,* Ware: Wordsworth Editions Limited

Foxall, Gordon R., Goldsmith, Ronald E. and Brown, Stephen (1998), *Consumer Psychology for Marketing,* 2nd Edition, London: International Thomson Business Press

Frey, James H. (1983), "Survey Research by Telephone", *Sage Library of Social Research, Vol.* **150**, London: Sage Publications Ltd

Frick, A., Bächtinger, M. T. and Reips, U-D. (1999), "Financial incentives, personal information and drop-out rate in online studies", In: Reips, U-D. et al. (Eds.), *Current Internet science. Trends, techniques, results,* Zürich, Online Press, Available: *http://www.dgof.de/tband99/pdfs/a_h/frick.pdf,* cited in Bosnjak and Tuten, *Classifying response behaviours in web based surveys*

Gabbott (2002), Address to the Academy of Marketing Doctoral Colloquium

Gans, H. J. (1968), "The Participant Observer as Human Being: Observations on the Personal Aspects of Field Work", in Becker, H.S. (Ed), *Institutions and the Person: Papers Presented to Everett C. Hughes,* Chicago: Aldine

Germano, William (2001), *Getting It Published,* Chicago: University of Chicago Press

Giarrusso, Roseann, Richlin-Klonsky, Judith, Roy, William G. and Strenski, Ellen (1998), *A Guide to Writing Sociology Papers,* 4th Edition, New York: St.

Martins Press Inc

Giddens, A. (Ed.) (1974), *Positivism and Sociology*, London: Heinemann

Gill, John and Johnson, Phil (1997), *Research Methods for Managers,* 2nd Edition, London: P. Chapman

Glaser, B. (1998), *Doing Grounded Theory. Issues and Discussions,* California: Sociology Press

Glaser, B. G. and Strauss, A. L. (1967), *The Discovery of Grounded Theory: Strategies for Qualitative Research*, New York: Aldine

Glatthorn, Allan A. (1998), *Writing the Winning Dissertation*, Thousand Oaks, CA: Corwin Press Inc

Gold, R. L. (1958), "Roles in Sociological Fieldwork", *Social Forces*, Vol. **36**, pp.217-23

Gordon, G., Kimberley, H.T and MacEachran, A. (1975), "Some considerations in the design of effective research programs on the diffusion of medical technology", in Abernathy, W.J., Sheldon, A. and Prahalad, C.K. (Eds.), *The Management of Health Care*, Cambridge: Ballinger

Gordon, R. L. (1969), *Interviewing Strategy, Techniques and Tactics*, Homewood, Ill: Dorsey Press

Gordon, Wendy and Langmaid, Roy (1988), *Qualitative Market Research: A Practitioners and Buyers Guide*, Aldershot: Gower

Gower, E. (1954), *The Complete Plain Words*, London: HMSO

Graham, P. (2003), "Intellectual property rights", pp.156-160, In: Miller, R. L. and Brewer, J.D. (Eds.), (2003), *The A-Z of Social Research: a dictionary of key social science research projects*, London: Sage Publications Ltd

Grandcolas, U., Rettie, R. and Marusenko, K. (2003), "Web Survey Bias: sample or mode effect?", *Journal of Marketing Management*, Vol. **19**, pp.541-561

Griffiths, R. T. "History of the Internet, Internet for historians, (and just about everyone else)", at *http://www.let.leidenuniv.nl/history/ivh/frame_theorie.html* visited 5 June 2003

Guba, E.G. and Lincoln, Y.S. (1994), "Competing paradigms in qualitative research", Chapter 6, pp.105-117, In: Denzin, N.K. and Lincoln, Y.S. (1994), *Handbook of qualitative research,* Thousand Oaks, CA: Sage Publications Inc.

Gummesson, E. (1988), *Qualitative Methods in Management Research,* Lund: Studentlitteratur

Gummesson, E. (1991), *Qualitative Methods in Management Research*, Newbury Park, CA: Sage Publications Inc.

Hair, J. F., Anderson, R., Tatham, R. and Black, W. (1995), *Multivariate Data Analysis with Readings*, Englewood Cliffs, NJ: Prentice Hall

Halfpenny, P. (1979), "The Analysis of Qualitative Data', *Sociological Review*, Vol 27. No. 4, pp.799-825

Hamlin, R. (2003), "Induction, Deduction and the Pig Headed Decision

Maker: Why we should learn to love them all", *The Marketing Review*, Forthcoming

Hart, Chris (1998), *Doing a Literature* Review, London: Sage Publications Ltd

Hart, Susan J. (1987), "The Use of the Survey in Industrial Market Research", *Journal of Marketing Management*, Vol. **3**, No. 1, pp.25-38

Hartman, J. and Hedblom, J. H. (1979), *Methods for the Social Sciences: A Handbook for Students and Non-Specialists*, Westport Conn., Greenwood Press

Harvard University Computation Centre (1967)

Hastorf, A. M. and Cantril, H. (1954), "The Saw a Game: a Case History", *Journal of Abnormal and Social Psychology*, Vol. **49**

Heenan, D.A. and Adelman, R.B. (1975), "Quantitative Techniques of Todays Decision Makers", *Harvard Business Review*, July/August

Heerewegh, D. and Loosveldt, G. (2002), "Web Surveys: The effect of controlling survey access using PIN numbers", *Social Science Computer Review*, Vol. **20**, No. 1, (February), pp.10-21

Hewson, C., Yule, P., Laurent, D. and Vogel, C. (2003), *Internet Research Methods: a practical guide for the social and behavioural sciences*, London: Sage Publications Ltd

Holmes, C. (1986), "Multivariate Analysis of Market Research Data", In: Worcester, R. and Downham, J. (Eds.), *Consumer Market Research Handbook*, 3rd Edition, Ch. 13, New York: McGraw-Hill

Hooley, Graham (Ed.), (1980), "A Guide to the use of Quantitative Techniques in Marketing", Special Edition *European Journal of Marketing*, Vol. **14**, No. 7

Hooley, Graham (1980), "The Multivariate Jungle - The Academic's Playground but the Manager's Minefield: An Introduction to the Special Edition", *European Journal of Marketing*, Vol. **14**, No. 7, pp.379-386

Hooley, Graham J., Saunders, John A. and Piercy, Nigel F. (1998), *Marketing Strategy and Competitive Positioning*, 2nd Edition, London: Prentice Hall

Hughes, John and Sharrock, Wes (1997), *The Philosophy of Social Research*, 3rd Edition, Harlow: Addison Wesley Longman Limited

Irving, Ray and Smith, Cathy (1998), *No Sweat: The Indispensable Guide to Reports and Dissertations*, Corby: Institute of Management Foundation

Jankowicz, A.D. (2000), *Business Research Projects*, 3rd Edition, London: Thomson Learning

Keller, F., Corley, M., Corley, S., Konieczny, L. and Todirascu, A. (1998), "Webexp: a Java toolbox for Web-based psychological experiments", *Tech Rep HCRC/TR-99*, University of Edinburgh, referenced in Hewson et al. 2003

Kennedy, A. M. (1982), "Longitudinal Research Methods: Applicability in Industrial Marketing", *Working Paper*, Department of Marketing, University of Strathclyde

Kiesler, S. and Sproull, L. (1986), "Response effects in the electronic survey", *Public Opinion Quarterly*, Vol. **50**, pp.402-413

Kinnear, T. C. and Taylor, J. R. (1987), *Marketing Research: An Applied Approach*, New York: McGraw-Hill

Kipling, Rudyard (1902), 'The Elephant's Child', *The Just So Stories for Little Children*, Macmillan and Co. Limited

Kitchin, R. (1998), *Cyberspace: The World in the Wires*, Chichester: Wiley

Kotler, Philip (2000), *Marketing Management: Analysis, Planning, Implementation and Control*, 10th Edition, Englewood Cliffs, NJ: Prentice Hall

Kotler, Philip, (2000), *Marketing Management*, 19th Edition, Upper Saddle River, NJ: Prentice-Hall

Kuhn, T. S. (1970), *The structure of scientific revolutions*, 2nd Edition, Chicago: The University of Chicago Press

Lawrence, S. and Giles, C. L. (1999), "Accessibility of Information on the Web", *Nature*, Vol. **400**, no. 6740, pp.107-109, in Censorware project web page, *Size of the Web*

Lawrence, S. and Giles, C. L. (1998), "Searching the World Wide Web", *Science*, Vol. **280**, pp.98-100, in Censorware project web page, *Size of the Web*

Levitt, Theodore (1960), "Marketing Myopia", *Harvard Business Review*, July-August, p.45

Likert, R. (1967), *The Human Organisation*, New York: McGraw-Hill

Littler, D., Hogg, M. K. and Lewis, Barbara R, (2003), "Editorial: Developing Research on 'Customers'", *Journal of Customer Behaviour*, 2003, Vol. **2**, pp.1-9

Luecke, Richard (1994), *Scuttle your Ships Before Advancing, and other lessons from history on leadership and change for today's managers*, New York: Oxford University Press

Lyons, D. J., Hoffman, J., Krajcik, J. and Soloway, E. (1997), "An investigation of the use of the world wide web for online enquiry in a science classroom", *Paper presented at the meeting of the National Association for research in science teaching*, Chicago, Ill: March

Madge, J. (1953), *Tools of Social Science*, Lara, London: Longman, Green

Malinowski (1921), "The Primitive Economics of the Trobriand Islanders", *Economic Journal*, Vol. **31**, pp.1-16

Mann, C. and Stewart, F. (2000), *Internet Communication and Qualitative Research: A handbook for researching online*, London: Sage Publications Ltd

Marcus, A. and Gould, E. (2000), Cultural dimensions and global web user-interface design: What? So what? Now what? *6th Conference on Human Factors & the Web*. Accessed 5 June 2003: *http://www.tri.sbc.com/hfweb/ marcus/hfweb00_marcus.html*

Martin, Paul and Bateson, Patrick (1986), *Measuring Behaviour*, Cambridge: Cambridge University Press

Marton-Williams, J. (1986), "Questionnaire Design", In: Worcester Robert and Downham, John, (Eds.), *Consumer Market Research Handbook*, 3rd edition, Chapter 5, London: McGraw-Hill Book Company

Mauch, James E. and Birch, Jack W. (1993), *Guide to the Successful Thesis and Dissertation*, 3rd Edition, New York: Marcel Dekker Inc

Mayer, Charles S. (1965), "Marketing Research Sec 24 and Statistical and Mathematical Tools Sec 25", in Frey, Albert Wesley, *Marketing Handbook*, 2nd edition, New York: Ronald Press

Mayo, Elton (1933), *The Human Problems of Industrial Civilization*, New York: Macmillan

McAuley, C. (2003), "Online methods", pp.217-220, In: Miller, R.L. and Brewer, J. D. (Eds.), *The A-Z of Social Research: a dictionary of key social science research projects*, London: Sage Publications Ltd

McDaniel, Carl and Gates, Roger (2002), *Marketing Research: the impact of the internet*, 5th edition, Hoboken, NJ: Wiley

Mcleod, P.L., Baron, R.S., Marti, M.W. and Yoon, K. (1997), "The eyes have it", *Journal of Applied Psychology*, Vol. **82**, No. 5, pp.706-718

McNair, M. P. and Hersum, A. C. (1954), *The Case Method at the Harvard Business School*, New York: McGraw-Hill

Meade, Margaret (1942), *Growing Up in New Guinea*, Harmondsworth: Penguin Books

Menabney, N. (2003), "Internet" pp.160-164, in Miller, R. L. and Brewer, J. D. (Eds.), *The A-Z of Social Research: a dictionary of key social science research projects*, London: Sage Publications Ltd

Merton, R. L. and Kendall, P. L. (1946), "The Focussed Interview", *American Journal of Sociology*, Vol. **51**, pp.541-557

Miles, M.B. and Huberman, A.M. (1994), *Qualitative Data Analysis – An Expanded Sourcebook*, Newbury Park, CA: Sage Publications Inc.

Miller, D. C. (1991), *Handbook of Research Design and Social Measurement*, 5th Edition, Newbury Park CA: Sage Publications Inc

Miller, D. C. and Salkind, N. (2002), *Handbook of Research Design & Social Measurement*, 6th edition, Thousand Oaks: Sage Publications Inc.

Miller, George A. (1956), "The magical number seven, plus or minus two: some limits on our capacity for processing information", *Psychological Review*, Vol. **63**, (March), pp.81-97

Miller, R. L. and Brewer, J. D. (Eds.), (2003), *The A-Z of Social Research: a dictionary of key social science research projects*, London: Sage Publications Ltd

Mintzberg, Henry (1973), *The Nature of Managerial Work*, New York: Harper and Row

Moser, C. A. and Kalton G. (1971), *Survey Methods in Social Investigation*, London: Heinemann (2nd Edition 1985)

Murphy, E., Dingwall, R., Greatbatch, D., Parker S. and Watson, P. (1998),

"Qualitative research methods in health technology assessment: a review of the literature", *Health Technology Assessment*, Vol. **2**, No.16, pp.1-272

New Collins Thesaurus (1985), Glasgow: Collins

Ngai, E. W. T. (2003), "Internet Marketing Research (1987-2000): a literature review and classification", *European Journal of Marketing*, Vol. **37**, No. 1/2, pp.24-49

Nielsen NetRatings dated 21 January 2002, *http://www.nua.ie/surveys/index. cgi?f=VS&art_id=905357576&rel=true*, visited 26 February 2002

NUA Internet Surveys, "E-mail driving growth of office workload", [Online], (2000a), *http://www.nua.ie/surveys/?f=VS&art_id=905355873&rel-=true*, in Sheehan, K., *Email survey response rates*

Ó Dochartaigh, N. (2002), *The Internet Research Handbook: a practical guide for students and researchers in the social sciences*, London: Sage Publications Ltd

Oakshott, Les (2001), *Essential Quantitative Methods for Business, Management and Finance* 2nd Edition, London: Palgrave

Odlyzko, A. (2001), "Content is Not King", *First Monday*, Vol. **6**, No. 2, (February), *http://www.firstmonday.org/issues/issue6_2/odlyzko/* downloaded 12 August 2002

Oppenheim, A. N. (1966), *Questionnaire Design and Attitude Measurement*, London: Heinemann

Osgood, Charles E., Suci, George J. and Tannenbaum, Percy H. (1967), *The Measurement of Marketing*, Urbana: University of Illinois Press

Paccagnella, L. (1998), "Getting the seat of your pants dirty: strategies for ethno-graphic research on virtual communities", *Journal of Computer-Mediated Communications*, Vol. **3**, No. 1, *http://www.ascusc.org/jcmc/vol3/issue1/paccagnella.html* downloaded 23 June 2002

Payne, S.L. (1951), *The Art of Asking Questions*, Princeton University

Perry, C. (2001), "Case Research in Marketing", *The Marketing Review*, Vol, **1**, pp.303-323

Perry, Chad (1998), "Processes of Case Study Methodology for Postgraduate Research in Marketing", *European Journal of Marketing*, Vol. **32**, No. 9/10, pp.785-802

Perry, Chad (2000), "Presenting a Thesis", *www.literaticlub.co.uk/writing/theses. html*

Phillips, E.M. and Pugh, D.S. (1994), *How to Get a PhD: A Handbook for Students and their Supervisors*, 2nd Edition, Buckingham: Open University Press

Popper, K. R. (1968), *The Logic of Scientific Discovery*, Rev Edition, London: Hutchinson

Preece, Roy (1994), *Starting Research*, London: Pinter Publishers

Relevant Knowledge, cited in the Wall Street Journal of 15 September 1998, and referenced at *http://new-website.openmarkt.com/intindex/99-02-s.htm*, The Internet Index No. 23, compiled by Win Treese on 28 February 1999

Reynolds, F. K. and Johnson, D. K. (1978), "Validity of Focus Group

Findings", *Journal of Advertising Research, Vol.* **18**, No. 3, pp.21-24

Riley, M. J., Wood, R. C. and Szivas, E. (2000), *Researching and Writing Dissertations in Business and Management,* London: Thomson Learning

Riley, Michael, Wood, Roy C., Clark, Mona A., Wilkie, Eleanor and Szivas, Edith (2000), *Researching and Writing Dissertations in Business and Management,* London: Thomson Learning

Robson, C. (1993), *Real-world Research: A Resource for Social Scientists and Practitioner Researchers,* Oxford: Blackwell

Roethlisberger, F. J. and Dickson, W. J. (1939), *Management and the Worker,* Cambridge: Harvard University Press

Rogers, Everett M. (1995), *The Diffusion of Innovations,* Fourth Edition, New York: The Free Press

Rosenberg, R. S. (1997), *The Social Impact of Computers,* 2nd Edition, San Diego CA: Academic Press Inc.

Rotondo, Jennifer and Rotondo, Mike Jr. (2002), *Presentation Skills for Managers,* New York: McGraw-Hill

Rudestam, Kjell Erik and Newton, Rae R. (2000), *Surviving your Dissertation,* London: Sage Publications Ltd

Russell, B. (1948), *Human Knowledge: Its Scope and Limits,* Reprinted 1962, New York: Simon and Schuster

Sainsbury, R., Ditch, J. and Hutton, S. (2003), "CAPI (Computer Assisted Personal Interviewing)", pp.18-22, in Miller, R. L. and Brewer, J. D. (Eds.), *The A-Z of Social Research: a dictionary of key social science research projects,* London: Sage Publications Ltd

Sampson, P. (1978), "Qualitative Research and Motivation Research", In: Worcester, R.M. and Downham, J. (Eds.), *Consumer Market Research Handbook,* 2nd Edition, New York: Van Nostrand Reinhold

Saunders, Mark, Lewis, Philip and Thornhill, Adrian (2002), *Research Methods for Business Students,* 3rd Edition, London: FT Prentice Hall

Schaefer, D. R. and Dillman, D. A. (1998), "Development of standard e-mail methodology: Results of an experiment", *Public Opinion Quarterly, Vol.* **62**, No. 3, pp.378-397

Seiler, R. E. (1965), *Improving the Effectiveness of Research and Development,* New York: McGraw-Hill

Selltiz, Claire, Jahoda, Marie, Deutsch, Morton and Cook, Stuart W. (1959), *Research methods in Social Relations,* Rev. One-volume Edition, New York: Holt, Rinehart and Winston

Sharp, John A. and Howard, Keith, (1996), *The Management of a Student Research Project,* 2nd Edition, Aldershot: Gower

Sheehan, K. (2001), "Email survey response rates: a review", *Journal of Computer Mediated Communication, Vol.* **6**, No. 2, available online at *http://www.ascusc.org/jcmc/vol6/issue2/ sheehan.html,* visited 25 February 2002

Sheth, J.N. (1977), *Multivariate Methods for Market Survey Research*, Chicago: American Marketing Association

Silverman, Franklin H. (1999), *Publishing for Tenure and Beyond*, Westport, CT: Praeger

Sloan, Alfred P. (1963), *My Years with General Motors*, New York: Doubleday

Smilowitz, M., Compton, D. C. and Flint, L. (1998), "The effects of computer mediated communication on an individuals judgement: a study based on the methods of Asch's social influence experiment", *Computers in Human Behaviour*, Vol. **4**, pp.311-321

Smith, C. B. (1997), "Casting the net: Surveying an Internet population", *Journal of Computer Mediated Communication*, Vol. **3**, No. 1, available online at *http://www.ascusc.org/jcmc/vol3/issue1/smith.html* downloaded 25 Feb 2002

Smith, D. M. (1972), *Interviewing in Market and Social Research*, London: Routledge and Kegan Paul

Smith, Wendell (1956), "Product differentiation and market segmentation as alternative marketing strategies", *Journal of Marketing*, July, pp.3-8

Sonquist, J.A. and Morgan, J.M. (1964), "The Detection of Interaction Effects", *Monograph*, Vol. **35**, University of Michigan, Survey Research Centre

Spears, M., Russell, L. and Lee, S. (1990), "De-individualisation and group polarisation in computer-mediated communication", *British Journal of Social Psychology*, Vol. **29**, pp.121-134

SSRC Working Party (1975)

Stake, R.E. (1994), "Case Studies", In: Denzin, N. K. and Lincoln, Y. S. (Eds.), *Handbook of Qualitative Research*, Thousand Oaks, CA: Sage Publications Inc.

Stocks, J.M.B. (1973), *Review Paper on Quota Sampling Methods*, Market Research Society Annual Conference Proceedings

Stone, S. (1984), *Centre for Research on User Studies (CRUS) Guide: No.6 Interviews*, Sheffield: Centre for Research on User Studies (CRUS)

Strunk, J.W. and White, E.B. (1972), *Elements of Style*, London: Collier Macmillan

Swoboda, S. J., Muehlberger, N., Weitkunat, R. and Scheeweis, S. (1997), "Internet Surveys by direct mailing: an innovative way of collecting data", *Social Science Computer Review*, Vol. **15**, No. 3, cited by Yun and Trumbo, *Comparative Response to a survey*

Taylor, Frederick W. (1911), *The Principles of Scientific Management*, New York: Harper and Row

Tull, D. S. and Albaum, G. S. (1973), *Survey Research: a decisional approach*, Aylesbury: International Textbook Co. Ltd

Tull, Donald S. and Hawkins, Del I. (1987), *Marketing Research*, 4th Edition, New York: Macmillan (6th edition 1993)

Ughanwa, D.O. and Baker, M.J. (1989), *The Role of Design in International*

Competitiveness, London: Routledge

Van Alstyne, M. and Brynjolffson, E. (1997), *Electronic Communities: Global Village or Cyberbalkans?",* *http://web.mit.edu/marshall/www/papers/ CyberBalkans.pdf,* cited in Ó Dochartaigh, *The Internet Research Handbook*

Varadarajan, P.R. (1996), "From the Editor: Reflections on Research and Publishing", *Journal of Marketing,* Vol. **60**, No. 4, pp.3-6

Wallace, P. (1999), *The Psychology of the Internet,* Cambridge: Cambridge University Press

Wancevich, J.M. and Matteson, M.T. (1978), "Longitudinal Organisational Research in Field Settings", *Journal of Business,* pp.181-291

Webb, John (2000), "Questionnaires and their Design", *The Marketing Review,* Vol. **1**, pp.197-218

Webb, John R. (2002), *Understanding and Designing Marketing Research,* 2nd Edition, London: Thomson Learning

Webster, Frederick E. (1992), "The changing role of Marketing in the Corporation," *Journal of Marketing,* Vol. **56**, No. 4, pp.1-17

Webster's Reference Library (2002), *Students" Companion,* New Lanark: Geddes and Grosset

Westburn Dictionary of Marketing (2002), *http://www.themarketingdictionary.com*

Whysall, Paul (2000), "Marketing Ethics – an overview", *The Marketing Review,* Vol. **1**, No. 2, Winter, pp.175-195

Wiggins, R. W. (2001), "The effects of September 11 on the Leading Search Engine", *First Monday,* Vol. **7**, No. 10, October, *http://www.firstmonday.org/ issues/issue6_10/wiggins/* downloaded 12 August 2002

Wilson, Alan (2003), *Marketing Research,* Harlow, FT: Prentice Hall

Wind, Y., Grashof, J.F. and Goldhar, J.D. (1978), "Market-Based Guidelines for Design of Industrial Products", *Journal of Marketing,* Vol. **42**, July, pp.27-37

Worcester, Robert M. and Downham, John (eds) (1988) Consumer Market Research Handbook, 3rd Edition London: McGraw-Hill

Wyden, Peter (1988), *The Unknown Iacocca,* New York: William Morrow and Company

Yates, F. (1953), *Sampling Methods for Census and Surveys,* London: Charles Griffin

Yin, R. (1981), "The Case Study Crisis: Some Answers," *Administrative Science Quarterly,* Vol. **26**, pp.58-65

Yin, R.K. (1994), "Case Study Research – Design and Methods", *Applied Social Research Methods Series,* Vol. **5**, 2nd Edition, Newbury Park, CA: Sage Publications Inc.

Yin, R.K. (1993), "Applications of Case Study Research", *Applied Social Research Methods Series,* Vol. **34**, Newbury Park, CA: Sage Publications Inc.

Young, S. (1973), "Pitfalls Down the Primrose Path of Attitude Segmentation",

European Research, November, pp.157-73

Yun, G. Woong and Trumbo, C. W. (2001), "Comparative response to a survey executed by post, e-mail and web form", *Journal of Computer Mediated Communication,* Vol. **6**, No. 1, available online at *http://www. ascusc.org/jcmc/vol6/issue1/yun.html* visited 25 February 2002

Index